*Exploring Texts:*
*The Role of Discussion and Writing*
*in the Teaching and Learning of Literature*

# EXPLORING TEXTS
## THE ROLE OF DISCUSSION AND WRITING IN THE TEACHING AND LEARNING OF LITERATURE

❧ ❧ ❧

*Edited by*

**George E. Newell**

*The Ohio State University*

*and*

**Russel K. Durst**

*The University of Cincinnati*

**Christopher-Gordon Publishers, Inc.**

Norwood, MA

Christopher-Gordon Publishers, Inc.
480 Washington Street
Norwood, MA 02062

Printed in the United States of America

10  9  8  7  6  5  4  3  2  1       98  97  96  95  94  93

ISBN 0-926842-24-2

# Contents

❧ ❧ ❧

*Dedication*

To our parents
Virginia and LaJoy Newell

*and*

the late Ruth and Bernie Durst

# *Foreword*

$ $ $

## *Arthur N. Applebee*

*National Research Center
on Literature Teaching and Learning*

T his is an interesting time in the teaching of literature, as the articles in this collection attest. The New Criticism, on which most of us were raised is beginning to lose its hegemony, as several decades of neglect, what we teach and how we teach it are receiving a careful reexamination by teachers and scholars. The most frequently proffered alternatives to New Critical perspectives usually emphasize one or another version of Reader Response theory. Reader-based approaches, however, are still poorly understood. Beyond the rhetoric of student-centeredness, what does it mean to teach and learn in a response-based classroom?

In a real sense, we do not know. Response-based approaches have been honored more in theory than in practice, and we have only a few good descriptions of what effective instruction looks like. The articles in this book are rich in their descriptions of what life in such classrooms can be like, but they also provide different visions of those classrooms for us to choose among as we tailor our instruction to the particular students with whom we work.

There are a number of misconceptions about response-based teaching that these articles should help dispel. One is the belief that in emphasizing student response, we give up all standards of quality and relevance — that, in fact, "anything goes." On the contrary, good response-based teaching requires, in Nystrand and Gormoran's words (Chapter 5) in a different context, "thoughtful and sustained examination of a given topic over a period of time." Students are forced to confront one another's differing perceptions of the texts they read, to return to the text for evidence for their claims, and

*xi*

to confront the differences in perspective that arise from variations in previous experiences and current preoccupations.

A second misconception about response-based teaching is that it deals only with second-rate, easily accessible literature — that even to begin, we must abandon standards of quality. But on the contrary, response-based teaching requires literature of depth and substance in order to work — "thoughtful and sustained examination" of the trivial and obvious is a sure recipe for disaster. At the same time, works of depth and substance can be drawn from many different genres, media, and traditions, opening up a broader field for literary studies that has been true in the past. This broader field is evident in the discussions presented here, but so is the high literary quality of the words discussed.

The final misconception about response-based teaching is that the teacher's role is greatly diminished as the focus shifts to what the students do and say. But again on the contrary, the role of the teacher is central to an effective response-based classroom. It is a more sophisticated role, however, than simply telling students what they must know; it requires modeling and guiding and shaping students' growing understandings as they learn how to read and write and think for themselves. The teacher remains the arbiter of what counts as knowing, drawing the boundaries of acceptable and unacceptable lines of argument, and introducing new concepts and more powerful strategies as they become appropriate within the developing classroom dialogue.

The chapters in this book are an important step along the way to sharpening our understanding of effective teaching and learning of literature, dispelling misconceptions while offering a wealth of practical approaches.

# *Preface*

— ❧ ❧ ❧ —

The teaching of literature has been and remains a staple of English instruction, but until recently the enterprise has languished amid seemingly more urgent needs, such as improving writing instruction and promoting "higher order thinking." However, teachers and researchers have now begun to redress (often collaboratively) the neglect of literary understanding and its role in secondary education. On the one hand, scholars are developing a well-articulated conception of the nature of literature and a well-constructed agenda to explore the implications of that conception for teaching. On the other hand, the National Writing Project and the Literature Projects are providing vehicles for teachers to share their knowledge and expertise. Within this compelling intellectual context we recognize the need for a serious reexamination of the contributions of literary education to schooling in general and to the teaching of English in particular.

The basic premise of the collection is that whatever contributions literary education might make to schooling, the development of students' understanding of themselves and the cultural communities in which they live must remain at its center. It is these understandings that must be challenged, refined, and enriched — through the process of reflection with activities that involve discussion and writing. Students' progress, then, is not marked primarily by their memorization of authors, literary periods, themes, or interpretations but by their learning to explore progressively more complex texts in the company of peers and with a more experienced reader, the teacher.

Even though students might read and discuss literature beyond the classroom, schooling offers a special and unique occasion for learning about and through literature. At the center of literature instruction are a teacher and students engaged in discussion and writing, coming together to exchange ideas and interpretations. What binds the chapters in this book together is a focus on the importance of students using language to make meaning, and an emphasis on an interactive notion of teaching and learning to foster this meaning making. How literature instruction might reconceptualize its mission using this language and learning perspective is a central theme of this collection.

We began this project with the idea of a book that would go beyond important but programmatic concerns such as decisions about the organization of instructional units, the selection of texts, or the teaching of literary genres. Instead, we sought to bring together recent scholarship that challenges reflective teachers to rethink the fundamental ingredients of their practice. We also wanted a book that had a specific theoretical orientation — language as a way of knowing — and a broad vision of the possibilities of literature instruction. Although we are aware of the vagaries of the individual reader, we envision "the reader" of this book to be experienced and beginning teachers, curriculum directors, and teacher educators. While teachers may read this book to enhance their own practice, the collection also provides compelling ideas to foster rich discussion in graduate courses. We believe this book represents challenges that are well-suited to recent attempts to make the work of literature teachers an intellectually strong and professionally fulfilling endeavor.

In the process of requesting, reviewing, and arranging the chapters for this collection, we have come to appreciate more fully the imaginative intellects of scholars and teachers involved in literature research and teaching. We were struck by a consensus of concern for a reader-based orientation grounded in the interplay of mind and text, and by the variety of ways of respecting and supporting the practical demands of teaching. Perhaps the single most important benefit of an edited work is its ability to focus on a single concern and to examine it from multiple perspectives and with many voices. Accordingly, we are particularly grateful to each contributor who allowed this project to intrude upon the already demanding daily grind.

We are also grateful to Sue Canavan and Hiram Howard, who sought us out, encouraged us, and taught us how to do a book. James Britton has been an important intellectual influence on our work, and anyone familiar with his writing will recognize our great debt to him. Thanks also to Mary Jo, George, Michael, and to Siusan, Alexander, and Jacob who willingly or not overheard our phone conversations and who granted us time away from them throughout the project. The teachers with whom we have worked encouraged us to face up to the realities of schooling and to keep firmly in mind the felt sense of working with students.

*G.E.N.*
*R.K.D.*
*October 1992*

# CHAPTER ONE

# Toward a Framework for Improving the Teaching of Literature

## Rethinking the Relationships among Students, Teachers, and Texts

— ❧ ❧ ❧ —

## George E. Newell and Russel K. Durst

T he second bell rings and a group of tenth graders of mixed abilities waits expectantly (if not quietly) for their English teacher to begin a lesson on "The Lottery," a short story by Shirley Jackson.

> Yesterday, at the end of class, we began talking about "The Lottery," and we agreed that since the story is set in a quiet village on a "sunny and clear day," the stoning of Tessie Hutchinson was quite a surprise. Today, to start off, I'd like you to write for about ten minutes to prepare for our discussion. I would like you to write about your reading of the story — how and when did you realize that things were not as they seemed at the beginning of the story, and that in the end, the lottery was not a pleasant matter? Consider the way the characters talked or acted that suggested a change in their mood. Don't worry about getting an answer; just let your writing do some thinking about that change.

After the sounds of paper shuffling and timid requests for "an extra pencil" subside, the room falls silent as students begin to write. Some write quickly, some furiously. Others sit and stare into space, make a note or two, hesitate, and then rush to finish just before the teacher requests: "Okay, now let's have a few of you read your responses." Within a space of about ten minutes, 30 tenth graders have begun to generate ideas and questions — why is Jackson's description of the village and its inhabitants so idyllic at the beginning of the story? What is the point of Tessie Hutchinson's death? How could seemingly normal people resort to such brutality?

In this scenario, we can begin to see what this book's contributors, as both teachers and researchers, have been spending a great deal of time trying to understand: what happens when a teacher, a text, and students come together to construct interpretations collectively by relying on the understandings of many individuals? From one perspective, this way of teaching a story may seem to be something of a waste of time — Why does the teacher begin with such uncertainty, with no real plan for what content to cover, and with just a glimmer of an idea (if he or she has experience) of what the students might write and then later discuss? No doubt beginning with students' understandings and puzzlements is inefficient if covering what more expert readers (teachers) or critics have said about "The Lottery" is the point of the lesson. But that is not the point at all. In this introduction we want to offer our thoughts on developing a new framework for the teaching of literature. To do so requires that we begin by reexamining our assumptions and rethinking what is often overly familiar about the way we lead discussions, the nature of the writing about literature we assign, and the validity of the assessments we employ.

## ASSUMPTIONS GUIDING THE TEACHING OF LITERATURE

Each era of literature teaching in high school and college has offered its own set of goals — memorization of authors and their works in the nineteenth century, solutions to life's problems in the progressive era of American education, the study of an academic subject shaped by the tenets of the New Criticism in the 1950s, a source of social and personal revolution in the 1960s, and a content for reading skills and for cultural literacy in the 1970s and 1980s.

Such a turbulent history, it can be argued, has left literature teaching without a central metaphor for instruction. Findings from Applebee's (1989; 1990) studies of literature instruction in American schools reflect this lack of a principled and directed approach to literary education. Though Applebee marshalled much evidence that teachers have a deepening sense that traditional text-centered models of literature teaching are no longer adequate, he also reported that, "The most widely used classroom approach involved a New Critical close reading of texts, and class discussion usually took the form of a dialogue leading students toward an accepted, teacher-sponsored interpretation. Reader response theory, to the extent it was acknowledged, was likely to be used as a motivating device on the way to close analysis of text, not as a legitimate approach in its own right" (Applebee, 1989, p. 37).

The sources of such practical compromises become obvious if we consider the rather contradictory assumptions currently driving the field. First, we have assumed that literature is a content area, like biology or history, that should concern itself primarily with specific facts and information about literature — literary themes, authors, characters and traditions. Such content clearly has a place in literary education, but as a primary goal this informational orientation seems to run counter to a consistent theme in discussions of literary understanding: the importance of both the reader and the text in the interpretive act. Second, we have assumed that since the professional critic's interpretation is the best informed, literary criticism is the most appropriate source of facts and information about literature. Yet, as a result, teachers' approaches to literature are often driven by canonized interpretations of specific works, a stance that often impedes efforts to foster students' deeper understanding of a text. Third, we have looked to traditional notions of literary study as the model for how to teach literature — typically a teacher leading a text-centered discussion that requires close, objective analysis. However, the English language arts profession has frequently criticized this model, especially after two decades of process-oriented writing instruction (Lloyd-Jones and Lunsford, 1989). Fourth, in selecting texts we have assumed that only the texts contained in the literary canon represent the best of the culture, and thus, it is those texts that must be taught in schools. These texts certainly have a place in the curriculum as valued representations of cultural wisdom, and yet we are aware that our school population is more ethnically, racially, and linguistically diverse than ever and that the literature of other, non-western cultures also possesses wisdom that can challenge and enrich the lives of all students.

By pointing out some of the paradoxes associated with literature instruction we do not mean to say that teachers, researchers, and theorists alike have not given these assumptions much thought. Much of the current pedagogical work in literature has shifted toward reader response theory with its concern for reader-based engagement and the development of interpretive communities. Several reader response critics and theorists, such as Rosenblatt (1976) and Bleich (1975), have published major pedagogical works, and others have become concerned with pedagogy (Fish, 1980; Scholes, 1985). Scholarly journals as well as practitioner-oriented journals contain an ample number of essays and research reports arguing for the importance of the thinking process in literary reading and understanding. However, we believe that to the extent that literature instruction is a field divided against itself, there is a void in conceptualizing new approaches to teaching literature.

## GOALS FOR THE BOOK

Accordingly, this book attempts to examine, within a language and learning framework, the ways discussion and writing shape literary understanding, an orientation that is not always apparent in the press of teaching. Rather than asking what we, as teachers, might say to students about a text, we might ask what role students play in formulating an understanding of a text. But where does language come into this? As a mode of representation, language allows students to make knowledge and their thinking available for reflection and revision. By speaking or writing what they know, they change it. Each chapter of the book presents theoretically principled and practical ways for English language arts teachers to use discussion and writing to guide students in the process of such understanding.

Recent developments in theories of reading, writing, and learning provide rich sources of new ideas, and this volume's contributors explore their uses in the teaching of literature. In general, we have attempted to articulate principled approaches and activities that teachers may employ in teaching literature to junior and senior high school students to enhance literary understanding.

In compiling this edited work, we hope to accomplish four goals:

1.  To explore ways of reconceptualizing the interrelationships of discussion, writing, and literary understanding by tapping new developments in the fields of reading and writing as well as in literary theory as the means by which we might construct reader-based activities. This seems a necessary first step toward developing general principles for literature instruction that will hold across various contexts.

2.  to establish the teacher's central role in creating environments for literature instruction, demonstrating the teacher's professionalism as reflected in the day-to-day decision making and planning is a key element in the reform of literature instruction.

3. To develop a new rationale for the role of literature in the secondary curriculum based on recent arguments for the value of literary ways of knowing as distinct and significant forms of reasoning. If higher order skills of interpretation and critical thinking are to be taught more effectively, the study of literature may be a particularly productive way of doing so.

4. to reexamine the roles of the teacher, the student, and the text within the framework of "social construction" — a view of the instructional process that bridges the complex and dynamic setting of the classroom and recent work in psychology and language learning.

We now turn to an exploration of the implications of each of these four goals.

## RETHINKING THE ROLE OF DISCUSSION AND WRITING IN LITERATURE INSTRUCTION

After two decades of efforts to reform the teaching of writing, English language arts teachers and researchers have again started asking questions about literature instruction. Although more than 25 years ago a great deal of time and energy was given to examining literature as a component of the English language arts curriculum (Commission on English, 1965; Squire and Applebee, 1968; Dixon, 1975), we are now looking with new eyes at literary understanding and at the efforts of instruction to support it. Considering what has occurred over that time, it is well we should.

In Applebee's (1989) study of "The Teaching of Literature in Programs with Reputations for Excellence in English" he reports two seemingly contradictory findings. On the one hand, he reports that the teaching of literature consumes about 50 percent of instructional time in the high school English classroom — a large portion of time when we consider that writing, an area that some would argue is a more urgent need, is taught about 28 percent of the time. On the other hand, Applebee also discovered that "The teachers in these schools lacked a vocabulary to talk about the process of literary understanding, or about the instructional techniques that might support such a process" (p. 37). Given the dearth of theoretically sound and practically useful new approaches to the most important component of the English curriculum, we believe that the time is right for a collection of essays that offers practitioners, teacher educators, and curriculum directors clearly articulated alternatives to the more traditional, text-centered approaches that now seem to dominate literature instruction.

One of the more persistent images of the literature classroom is of a teacher leading students to an interpretation of a literary text. Our view of literature instruction seeks to change, in several important ways, the traditional relationship among teacher, text, and student. Traditionally, teachers have considered students' oral and written responses to literature as tools for evaluation and testing. That is, when asking for discussion or writing about literature, teachers typically concern themselves with monitoring students' responses for a specific, perhaps teacher-sponsored, interpretation of the text. Using discussion and writing to evaluate literary understanding certainly has a place in the classroom, but we also believe that oral discussion and written responses can become tools for enhancing students' understanding of the text. This belief rests upon the assumption that language can become a means for acquiring knowledge, for reflecting on knowledge, and for reformulating knowledge in light of new insights whether they come from personal explorations or from participation in an interpretive community.

As we see it, adopting a language and learning approach to the teaching of literature represents one of the more significant changes we might make in literature teaching. Because oral and written language abound in literature classrooms, our perspective is based, not on a radical shift in what teachers do. However, it does require rethinking the significance of allowing students to discuss their literary responses (orally or in writing) with one another to arrive at their own interpretations of texts. Consider, for example, the experience of talking with a friend about a movie and discovering new insights into a character's motives or the significance of a dark and rainy final scene. School learning demands more public, less intimate forms of talk, but it is certainly possible to capture a similar spirit of inquiry and to provide contexts in which students can learn new ideas and skills in interaction with others.

However, efforts to reform the teaching of literature will require more than calls for increasing the amount of student talk and writing about literature. The teaching of literature now requires a major effort on three fronts: (1) a recognition of the central role of the professional teacher in the processes of teaching and learning and in the process of reform, (2) the development of a well conceptualized notion of the nature of literature and what it might contribute to schooling, and (3) the construction of a strong theory of literature instruction. Given that many teachers have not been exposed to recent developments in literary theory and that most of the work in theory has been oblivious to the pedagogical implications of the new approaches, this book explores how a language and learning framework as well as new theories of reading, writing, and literary understanding may contribute to reconceptualizing literature instruction.

## THE ROLE OF THE TEACHER IN REFORMING LITERATURE INSTRUCTION

Efforts to reform schooling have almost without exception ignored the teacher. Competency-based education, teacher-proof curricula, and state level programs of study are all examples of how the teacher has been overlooked. These represent attempts to reform schools from the top down rather than from the bottom up. Those of us who teach know that genuine change occurs when in the confines of our classrooms we interact with students and try to make our lessons work. This notion of curriculum as enacted in the process of teaching and learning has important implications for how we think about the teaching of literature.

In one sense, to include the practical knowledge of the teacher in reforming literature instruction requires that we define the curriculum as something that happens when teachers and students come together to study literature. A printed document may describe the scope and sequence of content to be imparted, but the literature curriculum becomes enacted when a teacher and students read, write, argue, share ideas, and interpret what they do and say.

Recent developments in English instruction such as the National Writing Project and the offshoot Literature Project have focused directly on the contributions of the teacher in the process of educational reform. The recurring theme that has emerged from these initiatives is that teaching is a profession that requires teachers to be regarded, and to act, as professionals who bear the responsibility of providing effective instruction for all students. Writing projects and literature projects contribute to this view of the profession by providing contexts in which professional teachers can share their practical knowledge with other successful and experienced colleagues.

Scholars have also begun to study the teacher as a professional whose instructional decisions are shaped by beliefs and knowledge. Shulman (1987) and Grossman (1990) have provided compelling evidence that effective teaching, including the teaching of literature, is best understood in terms of pedagogical content knowledge; that is, knowledge of how to transform the content knowledge of their field to enable students to learn. The primary assumption of their studies has been, "To reason one's way through an act of teaching is to think one's way from the subject matter as understood by the teacher into the minds and motivations of learners" (Shulman, 1987, p. 16).

The emphasis on teacher-as-professional with unique practical knowledge of teaching offers one of the most important forces in educational reform. This initiative provides a means for placing the teacher at the center of change and makes obvious the negative consequences of ignoring the role of teachers. However, such a movement requires that teachers take a key role in discussions about reform and serve as agents rather than as recipients of change. But how might teachers' knowledge about students, texts, and the contexts of schooling help broaden the vision of how to inform literature instruction? In other words, how might teachers' practical knowledge be integrated into discussions of change?

Because teachers make instructional decisions within the press of the moment, they are often guided more by narratives of their teaching than by abstract formulations based on a line of research or a theory. Marshall (1988a) reminds us that "teachers have come to encode their professional experience in narrative modes that capture the ambiguity and complexity of that experience (and) the knowledge embodied in those stories represents part of what teachers have learned from their experiences" (p. 7). Listening to those stories and understanding how teachers use them to shape their practices offers a much more complete vision of how to reform the field of literature instruction than does ignoring them.

Studies of the teaching of writing (e.g., Perl and Wilson, 1986) and the teaching of literature (e.g., Marshall, 1989; Zancanella, 1991) provide indirect yet compelling evidence for the value of understanding how teachers make sense out of the complexities of teaching by using narrative frames or, more simply, stories. These studies suggest that as teachers engage in reflective discussions of their practice, their notions of success (or failure) are based largely upon their students' reactions to the content and activities but more importantly upon the ebb and flow of the particular lesson. Rather than framing their accounts using abstract theory, they base them in terms of "what happened" and "what might happen next time" in their own classrooms with their own students; just as events in a successful story must have internal consistency, successful instructional episodes have a logic and coherence.

North (1987) points out that practical knowledge is driven by its own logic (pragmatic) and structure (experience-based). This focus on practical import suggests that new activities and the assumptions behind them will only be useful to the extent that teachers feel they can make them work for their own purposes, and, in turn, if they feel the ideas are consistent with their view of what is supposed to happen during instruction — with their students and under familiar circumstances. Accordingly, ideas that disrupt the flow of lessons or that are alien to what usually happens in the act of teaching may be disregarded as too theoretical or inappropriate for practice.

Considerations of how teachers describe, interpret, and reflect on their own practice have two important implications for the goals of this book. One is that regardless of how imaginative outside change agents are in their suggestions for reform, if teachers are not at the center of change or are not included in decisions about it, they will ignore external calls for change. The second is that if teachers make changes by considering how to introduce new materials and activities into the stream of their current practice, then modifications that require new criteria of success or a new set of assumptions about effective teaching will be difficult and complex to make. In this book various authors attempt to understand teachers' theories of practice and to describe the means by which teachers might reflect on the changes they deem appropriate. (See chapters by Langer, Newell and Johnson, Rogers and O'Neill, Klages, and Marshall.) Just as in the past the field has called for the centrality of the reader in literary understanding and student ownership over their writing, we must also focus on the teacher's central role and full participation in reforming literature instruction.

## RETHINKING THE ROLE OF LITERATURE IN THE SECONDARY CURRICULUM

Earlier when we reviewed assumptions currently driving literature instruction, we argued that canonized texts, canonized interpretations, and information about authors, themes, and literary history typically form the content of literature. However, current discussions of educational reform have focused on higher order thinking and reasoning as well as on mastery of content. This shift in focus raises the question of what kinds of thinking or knowing literature fosters. Put another way, if literature instruction is to play a role in reform we must consider the nature of the thinking that we are trying to promote as students read and study literature. Furthermore, it seems important to rethink the relationship between content and reasoning about literature and how we might continue to justify the study of literature in school contexts.

That literature instruction can be an ambiguous enterprise seems clear, but the reasons for uncertainty of purpose are often obscured by the rush of circumstance that surrounds the act of teaching — we teach literature because that is what English teachers do. Upon reflection we might consider some of our personal reasons why we studied literature and what some notable teachers and scholars have claimed for the role of literature in our culture and in our schools. On the other hand, schooling as an institution has its own purposes that cannot be ignored; testing, textbooks, and teaching loads often abet ways of teaching that run counter to reader-based approaches to literature. More often than not, the confusion over the purposes of literary education, as we argue here, is a result of conflict between its unique contributions and the demands of the more practical goals that schools have come to represent and value.

To list the more apparent (and historical) reasons for literature in the secondary school curriculum seems simple enough: (1) to ensure that students receive practice in understanding literary texts so that reading skills can be transferred to other kinds of texts — newspapers, magazines, textbooks, and the like; (2) to teach students about their cultural heritage by introducing them to canonical works; and (3) to prepare students for the rigors of academic work they will encounter in college. Though we would not deny the value of these purposes, we feel they do not adequately capture why many English teachers were originally drawn to and eventually hooked on reading literature. Even more, we feel such practical concerns do not speak to the unique contributions of literature to schooling.

Writing for the Dartmouth Conference in 1966, James Britton provides the essence of why children read literature as well as what teachers might try to foster in the study of literature:

> Literature is a construct in language, and language is of all the symbolic systems or modes of representation the most *explicit*, the best fitted, for example, to present a running commentary upon experience. It follows that much of the satisfaction in most literature comes from a contemplation of form given to events, a characteristic that distinguishes a work of literature from a sculpture or piece of music, where other forms are contemplated. A novel, in Suzanne Langer's terms, is "a virtual experience." The satisfaction in which a reader shares, therefore, must have something in common with the satisfaction he feels, not so much in having an experience as in looking back at an experience he has had; it is as though he were to look back at an experience he has not had. (p.3)

Here Britton offers, in part, an explanation for why we read literature — not in terms of reading skills, literary knowledge, or access to higher education, but in light of the satisfaction we obtain from seeing our own desires, concerns, and experiences taking shape in a poem, a play, or a story.

As Rosenblatt (1976) has explained, we do not merely have vicarious experiences with literature; we also come to a fuller understanding of our own experiences through literature as we reflect on what we value and why we live as we do.

This is the uniqueness of reading literature and discussing those readings with others, for literature provides a perspective on reality that allows for our subjective understanding. Even though other content areas in the curriculum may provide ways of reflecting on experience by means of rational and logical understanding, literature has the capacity to draw us into experiences so that we might make meaning from within and share our understanding of the world with others. Although we are arguing here for the special contributions of literature, we would be mistaken to argue that literary understanding is superior to other ways of knowing. Rather, we see literary experiences working in tandem with other, more objective ways of knowing that are part of the physical, biological, and social sciences that form the basis of the secondary curriculum.

In recent years, fields as diverse as psychology, law, and medicine have become aware of what Bruner (1986) calls paradigmatic (scientific) and narrative modes of thought. To possess a full understanding of the complexities of a problem or about how people live, the argument goes, we require both logic and objectivity as well as understanding of the ways humans construct their experiences. Whether working in the context of our academic or personal lives we need to call upon the contributions of the two modes.

As well argued and intriguing as these views of the role of literature in the lives of students seem, they have not had much play in schooling. One significant reason for this may be that as a field and as an area of the curriculum, literature instruction has separated the content of literature from the process of thinking and problem-solving. This brings us to a primary concern of this book: how we view the role of instruction and the understanding it nurtures will shape our decisions about what literature we teach, how we teach it, and how we measure our successes.

## SOCIAL CONSTRUCTION AS A NEW FRAMEWORK FOR LITERATURE INSTRUCTION

Over the past five years, the field of English language arts has begun to come to terms with the fact that the teaching of literature in American schools has stagnated. Instruction continues to focus on canonized texts and text-oriented approaches, assessment continues to be concerned with trivial aspects of literal comprehension, beyond the classroom students are reading less often, and new ways of thinking about students' learning have not penetrated the literature classroom. Accordingly, the efforts of teachers and scholars to rethink practice and to revitalize the enterprise of literature instruction require that we reconsider the learning and teaching of literature and work our way to a new theory of instruction.

Recent developments in literary theory and literacy research suggest a need to formulate a new theoretical framework based on the notion that the reader's experience with the text must remain at the center of our concerns. This perspective places awareness of the reader on at least equal ground with awareness of the text. That is, the act of reading must be considered as important as, if not more important than, gathering information about texts and authors. Perhaps the most significant role the teacher might play is one of guiding students in articulating their own responses for possible consideration and revision in light of what other readers — including the teacher, peers, and critics — say about literary texts.

A shift from text-based to reader-based approaches to literature is in our view a sign of progress, but it begs the more fundamental question of how to develop a theory of instruction that effectively guides the teacher in support of individual readers. Moreover, as we continue the shift toward reader-based approaches, the role of the teacher will need to be redefined as something other than purveyor of information about literature and translator of literary texts. This shift requires us to consider a new vision of literary understanding as constructed within the social dynamics of the classroom.

## *Literary Understanding as Socially Constructed*

Attempts to create a new vision for the role of literature in schooling lead directly to issues of learning and teaching and, more importantly, to the question of how literature instruction may be more effective. We believe that any reconceptualization of literature instruction must begin with the contributions of the teacher and students to instructional interactions around texts. Far too often our reform efforts have tended to shift focus to the process of how students learn or the curriculum to be taught without considering the interacting roles of the teacher and students.

Discussions of the process of literary understanding inevitably move in the direction of individual response that reflects the evolving skill of the individual reader (Squire, 1964; Rosenblatt, 1978; Langer, 1990). Instruction, on the other hand, is a social process based in the interactions of teachers and students. As students develop and as they engage in discussion and writing about literature, they use language to gain new knowledge and new skills. We believe that the split between concerns about the individual reader and the social environment of the classroom has divided both the practice and the theory of literature instruction; one focuses on mapping individual development, the other on describing the elements of effective instruction. Although both traditions are valuable, if literature instruction is to gain the necessary momentum for change, we need a more general understanding of what it means to "know" literature that connects individual development to the social processes that frame it. Put another way, we believe that literary understanding, though located in the individual who constructs it, is supported by social contexts that must foster, challenge, and shape it (Langer and Applebee, 1986; Bruner, 1986).

## The Role of the Teacher and the Role of the Students

To base a reconceptualization on a social constructivist view means two things for instruction: First, more attention must be paid to the social purposes to which reading and writing are put — students learn to read and to understand literature best when they do so in a way that is personally and socially meaningful; second, it means considering the order and sequence of activities that are used to support students' effort to complete tasks. This means providing students with specific instruction when they need support in attempting to do something new. Accordingly, students will have the opportunity to see how new skills and knowledge are necessary for helping them successfully complete assignments. For example, students might be asked to write double-entry logs (noting quotations, ideas, and images from the story on one side of the page, and reflective comments and questions about the information on the other side) while reading "The Lottery." The teacher can then intervene by asking students at what point the mood of the story begins to change. The concept of foreshadowing might then be introduced to enable students to understand how Jackson uses the reader's expectations to produce a shocking conclusion. As the students discuss and write about their growing realization of how the story works on them, a discussion of elements of foreshadowing may allow them to make sense of their reading of the story.

Within this social constructivist perspective there are three key questions for teachers to consider: Who is in control of the learning and why? What are the teacher's purposes for introducing activities? What are the contributions of the teacher and the students?

**Who Controls the Interaction?**   A key finding from studies of classroom discourse (Bellack et al., 1966; Marshall, 1989) has been that teachers generally initiate discussion, students respond, and the teacher evaluates their responses. For example:

*T:*    What device does Shirley Jackson use in the "The Lottery" to hint at the ending?

*S:*    Foreshadowing.

*T:*    Right.

Beyond the fact that the teacher, in this example, controls the focus of discussion, it is obvious that the students are merely required to slot-in a term. However, it is easy to misinterpret the question — who controls the interaction? — as a call for student-only control. Effective instruction provides for a range of interaction, including teacher regulated control. An important aspect of the craft of teaching is to recognize when students can direct a discussion and when the teacher must intervene to redirect and recast the flow of talk. Consideration of control also suggests how a teacher might evaluate whether students can independently interpret a text; strong teacher control throughout a literature lesson might suggest that the text is too complex or that the teacher's questions or activities are too difficult.

**What are the Teacher's Purposes?**   Though we understand the value of establishing goals for specific lessons, we believe a reader-based framework for literature instruction also provides for evolving goals and purposes. Within the course of discussion, teachers must encourage and motivate as well as challenge students to analyze and reflect upon their readings. In fact, in classrooms where the teacher is primarily concerned with student meaning-making, learning tasks get negotiated between teachers and students. As teachers, we have had the experience of beginning a discussion with a question that assumes a certain interpretation or familiarity with an author's intentions only to find that students have read the text in a different way. For example:

*Teacher:*    How does Updike (in "A&P") demonstrate that attempts at heroism can easily be misunderstood or even overlooked?

*Student:*    But I didn't see any heroes in the story.

This example illustrates that the teacher's role includes continuous assessment-in-action to judge if students need new skills and knowledge or simply more room to explore on their own.

**What are the Contributions of the Teacher and the Students?** When we consider whether or not an activity or sequence of activities works, the critical concern must be who is contributing what and how. As tempting as it is to assign activities and to ask questions based on the logic they seem to entail, students' own interpretations of texts must be at the center of the interaction. Sometimes students will need the teacher to present new information (the social and economic climate of the early 20th century south for a Richard Wright novel), to demonstrate how to perform a task (posing questions students might consider while reading a novel), to engage the class in problem-solving (using small group work to examine a character's motives), or to share interpretations in a whole-class discussion. Each of these strategies on their own may or may not be appropriate; any configuration of activities must take into account students' readings and their attempts to understand.

Developing a social constructivist perspective for literature instruction can only take us so far, for what is different about this framework in comparison to the more traditional models we discussed earlier is the new roles it demands of teachers and students. However, if our concerns are truly with students' own meaning making processes, it is a framework worth considering. To the extent that teachers are reflective practitioners and to the extent that teachers' professionalism matters, the possibilities of reform lie with them. The traditional view of literature instruction, with its emphasis on persistent evaluation to decide who has "learned" and who has "failed," has taken us to the point where we now recognize the superficiality of students' performances. The next step is to move beyond the limits of tradition and to provide students with opportunities to think more broadly and substantively about their literary understanding.

This book represents one effort in moving the field of literature instruction in that direction. We began with the intention of bringing together the most recent thinking of leading scholars in the field to examine the interrelationships of language, reasoning, and literary understanding; to offer strategies for using discussion and writing to support literary understanding; and to consider the implications of reader-response theory for developing a theory of practice. These explorations represent our vision of what a coherent approach to reconceptualizing the teaching of literature might include. As we studied the drafts and worked with the contributors, we realized that we had tapped a rich source of analytic and creative thinking focused on enriching the contexts for the teaching and learning of literature.

The book's title and organization suggest a compelling agenda that now seems critical as the field seeks to revitalize literature instruction. We sought to frame new approaches to literature with ways of exploring texts using writing and discussion — learning tools with which teachers are already quite familiar. Although we hope the chapters provide a way to rethink issues of literature instruction that remain central to the field, we also believe they will raise new issues and concerns to deepen teachers' professional commitment to improving the teaching of literature.

Even though the book does not include chapters written by secondary teachers about their practice, we believe the ideas of scholars who work closely and collaboratively with teachers in their professional endeavors will provide ways of fostering reflective practice. As you read through the chapters, it will become apparent that the contributors' own classroom experiences are still very much a part of their scholarship and that the issues they raise and the approaches they craft have evolved out of those experiences. Thus, to a large extent, the book represents and celebrates the excellent practice the contributors have witnessed in collaborating with teachers, an excellence they have sought in their own scholarship.

The reader will not find in this collection a particular section focusing on multicultural issues in the teaching and learning of literature. Issues such as the expansion of the canon (and the curriculum) to include works by minority writers that familiarize students with the cultures and sensibilities of various ethnic groups are not pigeonholed into specific chapters or a segment of the book. Rather, multicultural issues are considered throughout the collection. Wherever possible, contributors have used texts by minority writers in exemplifying the particular pedagogical issues under discussion.

The chapters are organized into four sections with each section attempting to enlarge the vision of the possibilities of change without overlooking the complexities that often accompany efforts to reform. The chapters comprising Part I address the ways reflective practitioners create environments for effective literature instruction and how researchers have attempted to understand how instruction fosters exploration, analysis, and revision of literary understanding. Those in Part II examine how discussion-based approaches both in large and small groups can be interesting and productive for students. The essays in Part III consider the pedagogical uses of writing as a means for initiating an exploration of texts and as a way of assessing the quality of students' understandings. The chapters in Part IV deal with the implications of adapting process-oriented, reader-based ways of teaching literature to the realities of schooling. Taken together, the four sections may allow us to see more clearly where we have been, what we now know, and what we need to do next.

## PART I:  LANGUAGE, LEARNING, AND LITERARY UNDERSTANDING IN THE CLASSROOM.

The chapters in this section are concerned with research that documents how teacher behavior facilitates learning and with research that draws upon the differing theoretical and practical knowledge that researchers and teachers offer. Judith Langer examines a series of instructional dialogues to illustrate principles underlying reader-based discussions of literature. Langer holds that effective discussions begin at the point where students have developed "initial impressions" generated from a first reading and that teachers' instructional support should build upon that tentative engagement. She suggests that this agenda ought to replace the teacher-centered, text-based agenda that currently drives literature instruction.

While Langer focuses on patterns of talk in two different kinds of instructional dialogues, George Newell and Judy Johnson explore the ways in which such differences shape general track students' writing and learning about literature. Newell and Johnson argue that general students should be challenged to read, discuss, and write about literature just as we do with academic track students. By tracing how class discussion becomes an extension of writing about a short story, they reveal the reading and writing abilities such students can demonstrate when provided teacher-guided support.

Although Theresa Rogers and Cecily O'Neill also concern themselves with discussion, they do so within the framework of improvised drama. In order to offer students a more compelling entry point into literature than the teacher-led discussion, they demonstrate how a literature teacher uses dramatic activities to build bridges for students as they traverse "multiple worlds."

Nystrand and Gamoran's large-scale study offers a portrait of the kinds of discussion that promote literary understanding. After examining student performances on a measure of literature achievement, they conclude that students' deeper and more substantive understanding occurred in classrooms described as "interpretive communities" — where the patterns of discussion become communal attempts to negotiate meaning.

## PART II: DISCUSSION AS INSTRUCTIONAL SCAFFOLDING

If the chapters concerned with classroom research in Part I describe what cooperative research between researchers and teachers can tell us about the value of discussion, the chapters in Part II offer a practiced feel for using reader-based discussion activities. Scholars such as Rosenblatt (1976) have argued that although literary understanding might begin in private, it can be enhanced through dialogue; that is, within a social context. Meanings are created through purposeful talk that provides each student with the means for rethinking his or her own opinions. Deborah Appleman and Susan Hynds, who argue that reading is both a private and social act, establish the range of possible ways of having "conversations" about literature, with each conversation requiring different roles for students, teachers, and texts.

Marjorie Roemer's chapter demonstrates the generative possibilities of recent reader-response themes for teaching. She takes us through a series of activities she has used in the college classroom to promote awareness of how we and other readers "see" a text. Rather than ignoring her students' initial readings, she builds upon them through a series of discussion activities that lead to a writing assignment asking students to reflect on how they have read a text.

Working within constructivist theories of reading that have established the significance of prior knowledge, Peter Smagorinsky presents a series of introductory activities for literature instruction. Smagorinsky's chapter suggests that although we may develop a whole panoply of activities, we must ask: Why am I doing this particular activity? and, How will it aid students in understanding complex texts?

Robert Tierney, Laurie Stowell, Laurie Desai, and Ron Keiffer take us into an English classroom in which a teacher orchestrates small group projects with the use of computers and hypermedia technology. The key to understanding the dynamics in this case lies not so much in the technology per se but in the teacher's use of the computers to support exploratory talk about literary and historical texts. Through the technology the teacher is able to facilitate dialogue for carrying out shared goals as students negotiate tasks and explore the possibilities of texts.

## PART III: USING WRITING TO SUPPORT AND TO ASSESS LITERARY UNDERSTANDING

Writing and literature, as taught in the English language arts classroom, have traditionally been joined in a "passionless marriage" (Marshall, 1988b). Although we might engage our students in reader-based discussions and project-oriented activities, when we assign writing about literature, we often do so to assess what they have already learned. The chapters in Part III argue that though writing is an important tool for assessment, it can be an even more powerful tool for promoting literary understanding.

Chris Anson and Richard Beach remind us that if discussion requires a social dynamic of give-and-take, students need time to reflect personally upon how they have read and understood a text. Rather than leaving the writer in isolation, the authors describe the uses of dialogue journals, in which "students and/or teachers exchange entries or letters containing their responses to texts, then respond to each other's ideas and/or continue to extend their own thought."

When considering alternative ways to assign writing about literature, we have usually considered how students might write about elements of the texts — character, plot, theme, and so forth. Such writing with its requisite thesis statement and argumentative stance often belies students' struggle to understand and to interpret a text. Michael Smith's chapter on autobiographical writing about literature offers another set of options that ask students to write about their transactions with texts. Smith develops a rationale for three different approaches: autobiographical writing *before*, *with*, and *against* the reading of literature, with each strategy directing students to differing relationships with texts. Any of these approaches may be appropriate to the extent they provide the teacher with a technique to support students' understanding.

How might we develop an assessment system in our classrooms that reflects our goals for literary education and marks students' success in achieving them? This is the question Anna Soter explores as she offers a full repertoire of evaluation strategies using writing as well as visual representation. Perhaps most importantly, Soter reminds us of the importance of informal, nonstandard assessments of literary understanding as well as the value of integrating evaluation into instruction. Such a view of assessment places the locus of control where it is most useful — in the hands of the teacher and learners.

## PART IV: READER-RESPONSE THEORY AND PRACTICE: NEW AGENDA FOR INSTRUCTION

In this final section, Steve Athanases, Mary Beth Hines, and James Marshall examine the complexities of adopting reader-based approaches to literature instruction. They also discuss some of the issues the field must concern itself with if such a shift is to occur. Athanases looks at the possibilities and problems of classroom discussion through the work of three reader-response theorists: Louise Rosenblatt, Stanley Fish, and David Bleich. Athanases reminds us that reader-response is not a monolithic theory, for each theorist assumes a different way of conceiving of texts and readers and of understanding the relationships between them. Perhaps most important are the questions Athanases raises regarding the teacher's role during discussion: How free can reading be? What, if anything, constrains literary interpretation, and who decides? If interpretation is reader-based, what function do the teacher's questions serve?

Hines also examines the relevance of reader-response theory to practice, but she does so by considering how the theory is enacted in a college literature classroom. Through the eyes of a teacher and a group of students, Klages demonstrates the texture and complexities of adopting a theory to guide instructional decisions and how one teacher transformed that conceptual framework into realistic and workable approaches to literature.

Attempts to reform literature instruction often call for teachers to revise their theoretical orientations toward literary understanding and then assume changes in classroom practice will follow suit. In the final chapter, Marshall examines continuing tensions in the field, such as the conflict between text-oriented and reader-oriented approaches to literature and how these tensions impose themselves on classroom life. Reform in the teaching of literature, Marshall concludes, must take full account of the logic and usefulness of the teachers' theoretical perspectives. Moreover, he suggests that we will need a "reflective discourse about practice." Our hope is that, in the spirit of Marshall's suggestion, this volume will contribute to that discourse by framing key issues, by suggesting principled teaching strategies, and by examining relationships between theory and practice. Through the process of reflection about our assumptions and about the practice of teaching literature, we might enhance the literary understanding of all students.

# REFERENCES

Applebee, A.N. (1989). *The teaching of literature in programs with reputations for excellence in English*. (Tech. Rep. No. 1.1). Albany, NY: Center for the Learning and Teaching of Literature.

Applebee, A.N. (1990). *Literature instruction in American schools*. (Tech. Rep. No. 1.4). Albany, NY: Center for the Learning and Teaching of Literature.

Bellack, A., Kleibard, H., Hyman, R., & Smith, F. (1966). *The language of the classroom*. New York: Teachers College Press.

Bleich, D. (1975). *Readings and feelings*. Urbana, IL: National Council of Teachers of English.

Britton, J. (1966). Response to literature. In J. R. Squire (Ed.). *Response to literature*. Champaign, IL: National Council of Teachers of English.

Bruner, J. (1986). *Actual minds, possible worlds*. Cambridge, MA: Harvard University Press.

Commission on English. (1965). *Freedom and discipline in English*. New York: College Entrance Examination Board.

Dixon, J. (1975). *Growth through English*. Reading, England: National Association for the Teaching of English.

Fish, S. (1980). *Is there a text in this class?* Cambridge, MA: Harvard University Press.

Grossman, P. (1990). *The making of a teacher*. New York: Teachers College Press.

Langer, J. (1990). The process of understanding: Reading for literary and informative purposes. *Research in the teaching of English*, 24, 229–260.

Langer, J., & Applebee, A. (1986). Reading and writing instruction: Toward a theory of teaching and learning. In E. Z. Roth Kothkopf (Ed.). *Review of Research in Education, Vol. 13*. Washington, D.C. : American Educational Research Association.

Lloyd-Jones, R. & Lundsford, A. (1989). *The English coalition conference: Democracy through language*. Urbana, IL: National Council of Teachers of English.

Marshall, J. (1988a). Two ways of knowing: Relations between research and practice in the teaching of writing. In J.S. Davis & J. D. Marshall (Eds.) *Ways of Knowing*. Iowa City, Iowa: Iowa Council of Teachers of English.

Marshall, J. (1988b). Classroom discourse and literary response. In B. F. Nelms (Ed.). *Literature in the classroom: Readers, texts, and contexts*. Urbana, IL: National Council of Teachers of English.

Marshall, J. D. (1989). *Patterns of discourse in classroom discussions of literature* (Report No. 2.9). Albany, NY: Center for the Learning and Teaching of Literature.

North, S. (1987). *The making of knowledge in composition*. Upper Montclair, NJ: Boynton/Cook Publishers.

Perl, S., & Wilson, N. (1986). *Through teachers' eyes*. Portsmouth, NH: Heinemann.

Rosenblatt, L. (1976). *Literature as exploration*. New York: Noble and Noble Publishers, Inc.

Rosenblatt, L. (1978). *The reader, the text, the poem*. Carbondale, IL: Southern Illinois University Press.

Scholes, R. (1985). *Textual power: Literary theory and the teaching of English*. New Haven, CT: Yale University Press.

Shulman, L. (1987). *Knowledge and teaching: Foundations of the new reform*. Harvard Educational Review, 57, 1–22.

Squire, J. (1964). *The responses of adolescents while reading four short stories*. (NCTE Research Report No. 2). Urbana, IL: National Council of Teachers of English.

Squire, J., & Applebee, R. (1968). *High school English instruction today*. New York: Appleton-Century-Crofts.

Zancanella, D. (1991). Teachers reading/readers teaching: Five teachers' personal approaches to literature and their teaching of literature. *Research in the Teaching of Literature*, 25, 5–32.

### PART ONE

# Language Learning, and Literary Understanding in the Classroom

❧ ❧ ❧

# CHAPTER TWO

# Discussion as Exploration

## Literature and the
## Horizon of Possibilities[1]

— ❧ ❧ ❧ —

## Judith A. Langer

The 1990s can be an exciting time for teachers of English, perhaps as exciting as the 1970s when dramatic changes began to take place in the teaching of writing. That reform was prompted by at least three agendas: First, business, industry, and the public-at-large were concerned about the writing abilities of high school graduates; second, research in reading, writing, and instruction was refuting product-oriented and hierarchical skills-associated views of teaching and learning, indicating that writing is a meaning-based process where the reader's and writer's ideas change and grow over time; and third, teachers were becoming aware that writing involves reasoning as well as reflection and that process-oriented instruction designed to support students through that process is more effective in helping them become better writers than the instructional focus on grammar and form that preceded it.

While the writing reform movement was a powerful one, leading to rethinking the teaching of writing in the English classroom as well as across the curriculum, it exacerbated the fragmentation of the various strands within the English curriculum. In general it focused more on students' ability to write about the content of other coursework than on the content of English coursework itself — literature. Thus, we have arrived at a new and needed pedagogical revolution, one that involves rethinking the teaching of literature. This change is prompted by widespread concern about students' academic performance and critical thinking abilities, by sociocognitive research indicating that students' approaches to reasoning are shaped in part by the context and interactions in which instruction occurs, and by English teachers' frustration with instruction based on a process approach to writing and on a traditional text-based approach to literature. It calls for rethinking instruction from the students' point of view, guided by approaches that validate students' own responses to what they read yet providing the support to help them question, probe, and reach more thoughtful understandings.

Until recently the teaching of literature has been guided primarily by New Critical theory (e.g., Brooks, 1947; Wellek and Warren, 1949), that calls for a close reading of the text, with particular emphasis on the narrator, the point of view, and the correct interpretation. Such an approach is text-based, placing the teacher in the role of knowledge holder and evaluator who leads the students to arrive at predetermined meanings and checks to see that these meanings are remembered and understood. It initiates students into the community of literary knowers who share the same approaches to, values about, and interpretations of the works they read. A body of reader response theorists (e.g., Bleich, 1978; Holland, 1975; Iser, 1978; Langer, 1990, 1991; Rosenblatt, 1938, 1978) offer an alternative to the New Criticism (Tompkins 1980). These theorists all see meaning as residing in the reader (although they differ in the degree of reader-text interaction), and regard readers as active constructors of meaning with personal knowledge, beliefs, and histories that affect their responses and interpretations, thus creating the potential for more than one correct interpretation. From such perspectives, instruction focuses on arriving at defensible meanings and refining them as well as considering the validity of other responses.

While reader-based theory has been espoused by English educators in recent years (Probst, 1988, 1992; Diaz, 1992; Diaz and Hayhoe, 1988; DeLawter, 1992; Hynds 1992), the New Critical approach still dominates the classroom (Applebee 1989, 1990), the instructional apparatus accompanying most literature anthologies (Applebee 1991), and literature assessment (Brody, DeMilo, & Purves, 1989). I think this is in large part due to the easy fit between New Critical pedagogy and traditional models of education where the roles of the teacher as knower and student as recipient have been well defined and internalized in teachers' minds. In contrast, the roles of the teacher and student in student-centered views of education have never been as clearly defined, and even the most well intended teacher of response-based instruction needs to develop his or her own models of routines for how discussions are carried out and when and how to help students go beyond their initial impressions.

## THE ROLE OF DISCUSSION IN READER-BASED INSTRUCTION

In recent years, my work has focused on redefining instructional theory related to teaching and learning processes in literature. My goal has been (1) to articulate principles underlying literature instruction that can be taught in methods courses and that can become the framework that teachers internalize and use to make daily decisions about their own teaching and their students' learning; (2) to develop a reader-based framework that can supplant the traditional text-based one that treats the teacher or text (rather than the student) as the center of knowledge and the place to focus instruction. Reader-based instruction values both critical and creative thought, but recognizes all meaning as initiated by and residing in the reader as a result of having transacted with the text. In this view, after having finished reading a work students are left with final envisionments or text worlds (see Langer, 1985; 1987; 1990) that represent their initial impressions, the ideas and images they come away with after the first reading. A focus on readers' final envisionments is the place to begin instruction, and the long range goal of literature education is to create a literacy of thoughtfulness (Brown, 1991) where students learn to go beyond these initial impressions as they develop deeper understandings, consider multiple interpretations, and take a critical/analytical stance toward both the content and the author's craft (see, for example, Langer, 1991; Petrosky, 1992).

While at first glance reader-based instructional goals seem easy to attain because they are at the heart of what most English teachers want their students to learn, in actuality they are very difficult to attain because English education pedagogy has not developed instructional approaches that lead to such endpoints. (Instead of beginning with the reader's initial impression and ending with the reader's own pondered and defensible interpretation and analysis, instruction generally begins with the text and ends with a predetermined, received interpretation.) Pedagogy has treated the comprehension of literature as additive, with the belief that explication of phrases and sentences along the way will lead to an understanding of the whole as opposed to the belief that discussion of the students' developed understanding (however incomplete or flawed) will lead to refinement of their understanding of the parts as well as the whole.

## *DISCUSSION AS EXPLORATION*

I have spent the past four years working on two related series of studies in an effort to provide English educators with principles that underlie reader-based discussion of literature and the ways in which instruction occurs during that discussion. The first set of studies (Langer, 1989, 1990 a, b) describe how readers make sense when engaging in a literary experience (when they make poems, in Rosenblatt's (1938, 1978) terms, as opposed to gaining information). This work indicates that when reading for literary purposes, readers explore a horizon of possibilities. In doing so, they juggle two sets of concerns — one dealing with the meaning of the work as a whole, the other dealing with their understanding of what they have read. They treat both sets of concerns as fluid, with a potential for ever-changing meaning. Because they expect their more global as well as momentary understandings to change as they make their way through a piece, they never take their new ideas as they find them but probe beyond; rounding our their understandings by exploring feelings, intentions, and actions. They investigate what those possibilities might imply for their understandings at the moment as well as where the piece might go. New understandings do not lead to endpoint, but instead reveal further areas for examination. In this way, an ongoing exploration of possibilities lies at the heart of a literary reading.

In the second set of studies, I have thus far worked collaboratively with some 21 middle and high school English teachers from city and suburban schools. Although our work has moved through many phases (see, for example, Close, 1990; Langer, 1990, 1992, in progress), in general the teachers' goals have been to create response-based classrooms where their students are encouraged to arrive at and ponder their own understandings and move beyond to form richer interpretations. My goal has been to study what works — and to identify the underlying principles of classrooms that help students to learn to study literature in increasingly more thoughtful ways. One of the earliest findings indicated that almost all productive instruction took place during discussion (both when the teacher was involved and when students worked in groups), and that the most productive literary reasoning students did during those discussions involved the exploration of possibilities. Elsewhere (Langer, 1991, 1992, in progress) I have discussed the principles underlying such discussions and the ways in which the teachers' use of instructional scaffolding supports students' growing ability to behave as literary thinkers. These articles explain ways in which the underlying culture of such classes calls for the active and thoughtful participation of all students, and teaches them how to engage in literary discussions as well as how to think in a literary manner. In the remainder of this chapter I will draw on two typical lessons to help us better understand ways in which teachers and students communicate with each other in discussions where students explore possibilities much of the time in contrast with situations in which this type of thinking seldom occurs.

## *THE GREAT GATSBY*

The following discussion takes place in Barbara Kray's 11th grade classroom in a suburban school district. The students ordinarily keep literature journals in this class, and are encouraged to jot down any questions they have as they read. Prior to this lesson, the students had read *The Great Gatsby* through chapter 3. This lesson, as many others, is spent discussing questions the students have raised. The teacher begins this lesson by focusing on the students' concerns about what they have read so far, and the students work together in addressing the issues raised. Rather than a right answer, Barbara encourages her students to explore possibilities. The discussion takes about 20 minutes, during which time they talk about seven topics. We can see that as the discussion moves along the students begin to develop possible interpretations, building upon their initial impressions, what others have said, and their own rethinking.

**Topic #1:** **Why Nick was invited.**

| | |
|---|---|
| *Teacher:* | . . . Christie, why don't you start us off? |
| *Christie:* | One thing I wrote down was I wasn't exactly sure why he was invited to Gatsby's party. Why was he invited? |
| *Teacher:* | Not why Gatsby, why Nick? |
| *Christie:* | Right. |
| *Teacher:* | Okay. Do you have any guesses? Any ideas at all? |
| *Audra:* | Just because he was a neighbor, and all the others were in- |

vited. Maybe . . . because he just lived so close, maybe Gatsby just needed someone he knows to be a true friend.

*Paul:* If he has a party and he has it for no reason . . .

*Jen:* They said that Miss Baker, she didn't know Gatsby, right? 'Cause it seemed weird that out of all that crowd, that Gatsby like took her aside and told her some secret. I didn't think she knew him at all, only knew who he was.

*Audra:* When he met her, and he met Miss Baker at Daisy's, I thought she said something about Gatsby, and he was curious because he didn't know anything about it but he never got a chance to ask her about.

*Jen:* So he did.

*Teacher:* She did. We don't know what the connection is, but she first mentioned Gatsby at Daisy's house. Has your question been answered Christie? Why (was Nick invited)? There are two possibilities. One is that everybody goes to the Gatsby mansion.

*Christie:* But he got invited by invitation.

*Teacher:* Aha. That's your question. Invitation. Okay, your suggestion is that he is a next door neighbor.

*Paul:* Yeah, and maybe that Gatsby just wanted another acquaintance, a different kind of acquaintance. Now all of a sudden he wants to tell him something.

*Christie:* It would seem like there was more, something more hiding.

*Teacher:* Your question is a good question. Ron?

*Ron:* Like a popular businessman.

*Teacher:* Who? Nick is a businessman of sorts. He's into stocks and bonds, or something like that.

*Ron:* Maybe he invited him there so he could heist something.

*Teacher:* It's a possibility. See, the thing is we don't know.

*Ron:* Maybe he wants a different opinion.

*Teacher:* Jen?

*Jen:* Like that scene when Nick was watching him by the water. Did Gatsby see him? It just seemed that there's a rumor going around the party that he supposedly killed some man, and maybe he's trying to wash that rumor away — like to get to know him before they make an opinion of him . . . .

The students begin this discussion tentatively, using their initial (and more superficial) impressions as a way to explore the piece in greater depth. Although Christie's initial question does not get answered, it serves to help Christie as well as the other students think about possible reasons why Nick was invited. In fact, when the teacher asks Christie if her question has been answered, she seems to go beyond her original question, this time opening exploration of possible covert intentions surrounding Gatsby's party list. This line of thinking leads the students to a brief and superficial discussion of rumors about Gatsby, in their early attempts to understand him better as a character.

**Topic 2:**     **Rumors about Gatsby.**

*Henry:*       Is he really German?

*Teacher:*     We don't know.

*Henry:*       Because we heard like at least people said he was German.

*Patrick:*     There's a lot of rumors.

*Teacher:*     There's a lot of rumors. What are some of the rumors?

*Patrick:*     That he killed a man. (Few students talking at once. Teacher hears someone say the word nephew.)

*Teacher:*     Who was he supposed to be a nephew of?

*Sala:*        Kaiser

*Teacher:*     Kaiser Wilhelm. Yes. And go ahead Jess.

Although the rumors about Gatsby only begin to be explored, the possibility of malevolence is introduced and left to ruminate and be picked up later.

**Topic 3:**     **Relationships — Gatsby and his guests.**

*Jess:*        I don't understand when he goes around to the party and he's asking people who Gatsby is, why everybody stares at him. Like, I don't understand that.

*Teacher:*     Who are you asking about?

*Jess:*        Nick, yeah.

*Teacher:*     Can you direct us to something?

*Jess:*        42, second paragraph, when he finally meets Gatsby, he said who's the host. Gatsby was just like amazed.

*Teacher:*     (reading) "Well, as soon as I arrived, I made an attempt to find my host, but the two or three people of whom I asked his whereabouts stared at me in such an amazed way, and denied so vehemently any knowledge of his movements that I slunk off in the direction of the cocktail table, the only place in the garden where a single man could (unt)." Okay, now what's your question?

*Jess:*    Why would he ask people? Why would they act that way? Why can't they tell him and say they don't know? They stare at him like, beastly.

*Teacher:*    Why? That's a good question. Why would they stare at him?

*Christie:*    Maybe the way he hosted this party. Different. Maybe he really didn't make any appearance at other parties. Didn't show up. I mean, he was there, but wasn't mingling with the guests. . . .

*Ron:*    Nobody knows who the real person is. The party is like a person gets adopted.

*Henry:*    Ron, now you got me confused. (laughter)

*Teacher:*    Christie, you made an observation?

For the sake of brevity, I have left out parts of the discussion about the party guests' relationship to Gatsby. However, in this part of the discussion, the students explore Gatsby's shadowy existence and lack of contact with his guests in contrast to their flamboyant behavior and unwillingness to confront their host or admit his distance. This leads to a brief discussion of Gatsby's other parties.

**Topic #4:    The parties.**

*Christie:*    I was gonna say maybe they were so amazed because he didn't, it was his first party that he had been to and he didn't know the style of the party that he threw (unt) 'cause it was more or less known to them and he didn't know it.

*Teacher:*    Yeah, we get the sense that these other folks are regulars. What is it that amazes you? This is a word I've heard come out of your mouths. What is it that amazes you? . . .

*Audra:*    It seems so elaborate that he goes, that these parties are regular parties, but they seem so elaborate and so huge, and so like things that you have to dress up for. People drunk and running all over the place, and people don't even know him.

*Teacher:*    Jess?

*Jess:*        In a way though, what Audrey said about everybody doing it. Because when he finally meets Gatsby and asks, Gatsby is like, "You don't know who I am." It was, you know, everybody should know who he was.

*Paul:*       They knew who he was, but they never really met him. . .

*Ron:*        Yeah, it seems like these people were in a fog.

Although the students discuss Gatsby's other parties, they seem to be doing so in order to understand him better, both as a character in his own right and in relation to the others. Thus, the discussion of other parties soon changes to a focus on Gatsby. At one point in this portion of the discussion, the teacher helps the students link what they are discussing with a rumor they discussed earlier, as a way to further explore the reasons for Gatsby's strange behavior.

## Topic #5:    Gatsby Himself

*Teacher:*    Yeah, Liz.

*Liz:*         I got the impression like he'd be the type that didn't want to have himself seen a lot, just like stay inside. And they say like he threw all these parties.

*Audra:*     I thought he was older.

*Teacher:*    So did I. Let's hear some more.

*Jen:*         I got the same impression. From someone who didn't seem very social, throwing these parties and that people came was so unusual. Didn't usually know them, but yet they're sitting around crying. Well, these people are crying.

*Teacher:*    Why were they crying? . . .

Since the students do not have much information about Gatsby except for his elusive behavior, they look for possible clues related to the rumors they have read about.

## Topic #6:    (Back to) Rumors

*Jess:*        It's like he's doing everything to get on people's good side. Like when that girl rips her dress. It wasn't his fault, but he insisted on it.

*Teacher:*    That's a good point. Now, why did he send her a new dress.

| | |
|---|---|
| *Voices:* | 'Cause it was his party. 'Cause it was his party and he felt responsible. He just didn't want any trouble. |
| *Teacher:* | Did he say that? |
| *Paul:* | She did, the girl did. |
| *Teacher:* | She said she thought he didn't want any trouble. That sort of goes along with the fact that he's a nephew of the Kaiser. That he's done some bad things. He killed somebody. |
| *Ron:* | He's trying to prove that the rumors that are going around about him were wrong. |
| *Teacher:* | Maybe. |
| *Ron:* | Like he's killed somebody. |
| *Audra:* | He cares what Nick thinks about the rumors. |

Since the students still don't have enough information to determine whether or not the rumors are true, they move back to Gatsby's reasons for having the parties in the first place as a means to further explore him as a character.

**Topic #7:    (Back to) The parties.**

| | |
|---|---|
| *Shelby:* | Why do these people go to his parties if he's supposed to be such a (unt)? . . . |
| *Teacher:* | Your guess is as good as mine. That's right, he is a party giver . . . . What's your thinking on the party? Shelby, tell us, what are your thoughts about the party? You've seen two parties, actually you've seen three. What's your thinking about those parties? |
| *Shelby:* | They're really weird. Like, he invites people he doesn't even know. |
| *Teacher:* | Okay. |
| *Paul:* | He's just trying to be nice. |
| *Teacher:* | Maybe. Ian, add something to that. What's your thinking about the parties? |
| *Ian:* | I don't think he's throwing them for himself. |
| *Teacher:* | Interesting observation. For what purposes, do you think? |
| *Ian:* | He's trying to make up for something. Feels obligated to. |

*Teacher:*    Well, maybe, Ian is suggesting he's throwing those parties 'cause he's trying to make up for something. He's done something and he's trying to atone for it or something. . . . (end of tape)

In this portion of the discussion, the teacher attempts to bring the remaining students into the discussion, continuing their exploration of Gatsby's motives. She closes the lesson by inviting all students to think about what they might expect to happen in the next chapter, and reminding them to jot down any thoughts or questions that they might have.

## FEATURES OF THE DISCUSSION

Altogether this is a fairly typical early discussion where students are encouraged to use their initial impressions as a way to explore possible meanings. The students haven't read enough or gotten deeply enough into the plot and characters to narrow in on preferred interpretations, argue for their own views, assume multiple perspectives, or engage in critical analyses. This occurs later, as the students' envisionments of possibilities build — with further reading, thinking, and discussion. However, even during this early-in-the-book discussion, we have seen ways in which students have been given the opportunity to go beyond their initial impressions in exploring Gatsby's character, and the story's plot, and to gain sensitivity for other points of view. Some of the topics of discussion were explored in greater depth than others, with the implicit understanding that these can be picked up later (during the same or subsequent discussions) as new thoughts connect with old issues, thereby moving the students' understandings along.

It is interesting to look a bit more closely at the kinds of thinking the students have exhibited during this discussion. Approximately 80 percent of the time the students explored possibilities (e.g., "I don't understand when he goes around the party and he's asking who Gatsby is, why everybody stares at him."; or "Maybe the way he hosted this party, differently.") This is the primary orientation readers take to literary experiences, particularly when they are entering into the world of the stories they read and living through the characters' experiences. In such cases, they treat their understandings as tentative, always subject to change. However, readers also enter into a less exploratory orientation some of the time, maintaining a more constant point of reference. This occurs when, for the moment, they wish to gain or share some very specific information, although it also occurs when they have purposely limited their reading to one particular kind of critical interpretation instead of following their own natural interpretive course. During this discussion, the students assumed this more informative orientation toward meaning 20 percent of the time.

If we consider the stances the students took towards the text, we learn that 54% of the time they were attempting to gain enough information to form an envisionment of the characters and events (e.g., "I wasn't exactly sure why he was invited to Gatsby's party."), 43% of the time they were extending their understandings by building and elaborating their envisionments (e.g., "Maybe he wants a different opinion.", or "They knew who he was, knew of him. But when they came face to face with him did not know."). Overall, the discussion of Gatsby was primarily a time for the students to step into and build a world of meaning and they did this where their readings left off, through a particular type of discussion — discussion as exploration. Let us compare this with another type of class discussion, one that more typically occurs in classrooms, one where recitation rather than exploration is the goal.

---

## TULARECITO

The following discussion took place in Margaret Steven's 11th grade classroom in a city school. Prior to this discussion the students had been given a photocopy of the short story "Tularecito" to read. This lesson, as many others in this class, focuses on text meanings and retracing the plot line of the story. The discussion takes almost 30 minutes, during which time they talk about 13 topics. Margaret focuses on the text and her students' comprehension, at a surface level. Instead of tapping the students' understandings and helping them question other possibilities, she has a right answer in mind for almost every question she asks, and we can see the students trying to fill in the information she seeks. When a student's response is what she is looking for she uses it; when it is different, she asks for other responses. Rather than helping her students learn to question and shape their own interpretations, she uses the students' responses as a way to shape their understandings to match her own.

**Topic #1:    Pastures of heaven**

*Teacher:*     What does the sentence itself mean? His origin? His past experience?

| | |
|---|---|
| *Terrence:* | His origin? |
| *Teacher:* | What is something that is cast obscure? |
| *John:* | Not clear. |
| *Teacher:* | Not clear, you see? What is the sentence saying? |
| *John:* | They're not clear where he came from. They're not clear where |
| *Teacher:* | They're not clear where he comes from. His origin. Okay, good. What or where is the pastures of heaven? What do you think it is? |
| *Tarek:* | A place in another world. |
| *Teacher:* | You think it's another world. Any guesses about that? "Pastures of heaven,: what does it sound like to you? What does it remind you of? Does it bring any ideas to mind? |
| *Tarek:* | Pasture or fields. |
| *Teacher:* | Pasture or fields. Okay, that's one thought. Any others? |
| *Ron:* | Church. |
| *Teacher:* | Church, okay. What else? All right, we'll come back to that and find out whether what you thought was correct or not, "the folks of the pastures of heaven." |

In this segment the teacher has selected a particular sentence, one she feels is important for her students to understand. Although her first question asks for the students' understanding of the entire sentence, she segments the text even further by asking them the meanings of particular phrases "cast obscure" and "pastures of heaven"). Thus, although the students have just completed reading the entire piece, they are drawn to focus not on the questions or understandings they have developed as a result of having read the story, but on particular ideas the teacher feels are related to the interpretation of the piece she wishes to lead them toward. Although the teacher's initial question about the meaning of the sentence is never completely answered nor its meaning fully discussed, she moves on to another question.

**Topic #2:    Do people believe the story of Tularecito?**

| | |
|---|---|
| *Teacher:* | What about the story about Tularecito? Do the people accept it? How do you know? |
| *August:* | (Reads) " . . . while his discovery is a myth which the folks of the pastures of heaven refuse to believe, just as they refuse to believe in ghosts." |

| | |
|---|---|
| *Teacher:* | All right, they're not likely to believe his story anymore than they are likely to believe in stories about ghosts. So they don't know where he came from. They don't believe the story that was given. |

In this segment, the teacher asks a question, and then provides the answer, along with her own interpretation. She then goes on to be certain the students know who the characters are.

**Topic #3:  Franklin Gomez**

| | |
|---|---|
| *Teacher:* | Who's Franklin Gomez? Ron, do you know who he is, Franklin Gomez? |
| *Ron:* | His employer. |
| *Teacher:* | An employer. Okay. That's good. |
| *Ron:* | Also, a worker. |
| *Teacher:* | He's an employer. I think that's a little closer. If you read the next line, that person in the second paragraph, you will figure out why we call him an employer. |
| *Matt:* | 'Cause he hired Pancho. |
| *Teacher:* | Yeah. |
| *Matt:* | He has to interview the ranch hand; he's the boss. . . . |

**Topic #4:  Pancho**

| | |
|---|---|
| *Teacher:* | Who's Pancho? |
| *Mario:* | The employee. |
| *Teacher:* | An employee, okay. Do you know anything else about Pancho? |
| *Mariloo:* | He's a Mexican Indian. |
| *Teacher:* | He's a Mexican Indian. |
| *Tarek:* | He's always sober. |
| *Teacher:* | What else? Is he always sober? |
| *Rock:* | When he's not in jail. |
| *Teacher:* | When he's not in jail, okay. |
| *Matt:* | He doesn't drive when drunk. |
| *Teacher* | All right. That's good. |

*John:*  When he arrives at work he's always sleepy.

*Teacher:*  Yeah, and that's important. Do you think he fools around? What gives you that impression? . . .

In this segment, once the students make it clear that they know who Pancho is, she turns the questions toward what he was like. Although the students provide some of their own responses, the teacher does not ask them to elaborate on them nor on what they mean in terms of his character. Instead, she leads them toward the particular trait she considers important, and then tries to get them to elaborate on this. Discussion continues in this manner:

*Lala:*  (referring to his drinking) . . . says once every three months.

*Teacher:*  Yeah. So, that isn't habitual, is it? Does he work? Is there any sentence in here that tells you he doesn't do his work? . . . . All right, what else do we find out about Pancho? Alberta, do you know anything more about him?

*Mariloo:*  He goes to confess his sins.

*Teacher:*  All right. He goes to confess his sins. So that tells you something about him. And then what does he do?

The entire lesson continues in this manner, with the teacher crafting her questions in a way that puts forward her interpretation of the story and the students providing short responses that may or may not get picked up. The plausibility of the students' responses is disregarded, with the teacher's focus on her desired response rather than on the students positing a plausible one. Further, the teacher's line of questioning leads to a building block approach to the story; the parts providing segments of meaning with the assumption that in some way, added together, they will lead to a full understanding. However, in this lesson, the bits remain fragmented, never woven back into a whole. We can see this in the last two segments of the lesson:

**Topic #12:  (Back to) the baby**

*Teacher:*  All right. Tularecito is a very different looking baby. Anything else about him?

*Edna:*  His head is bigger than the body.

*Teacher:*  Okay, his head is bigger than the body (writes on board).

*Lala:*         Deformedly broad shoulders

*Teacher:*      Okay. What does that mean? Are they normal like everyone elses? . . .

(On board at end of discussion:)

            Looks like:

            a little frog

            distorted

            no neck

            peculiar body

            loose legs

            head bigger than body

            deformedly broad shoulders

**Topic #13:  Gomez' attitude towards the baby**

*Teacher:*      All right, look at that statement again in the same paragraph that we just read. (Reads) "The baby's flat face together with his peculiar body caused it automatically to be named Tularecito, little frog. Although Franklin Gomez often called it coyote, for he said there is in this boy's face that ancient wisdom one finds in the face of a coyote." What attitude do you suspect just from reading this sentence?

*Edna:*         Doesn't care.

*Teacher:*      Okay, so he's not concerned about the baby's looks. What else might you figure out from that Carla? From that statement, "in this boy's face that ancient wisdom that one finds in the face of a coyote." Do you think he might be smart? Or have a special talent?

*Carla:*        Yes.

*Teacher:*      Okay, that's interesting. What I'd like to do right now is, does everyone have this question copied? I'll give them to you to-morrow in a more organized way. . . . . pass the stories forward, please, and those people who did not get a vocabulary sheet, would you come up and get them now?

Although the students' responses to the question "Anything else about him?" are correct (they are directly stated in the text), the teacher was hoping that one of the students would mention the baby's seemingly special abilities. However, when no students mention this, the teacher brings it up (in segment #13), and reads that section of the text aloud. She does not link the coyote-like attribution with anything the students had just listed nor does she try to connect to any of the previous parts of the story they have already discussed. Although the story will continue to be discussed the next day, the students are not directed to use their review of the text as the basis for a more comprehensive rereading of the piece, in order to formulate their own interpretations, to be discussed tomorrow. Instead, there is indication that the lesson will be much like this one, with the teacher's questions used as the focus of instruction.

## FEATURES OF RECITATION

Let us look a bit more closely at the kinds of thinking the students have exhibited in this lesson. Approximately 32 percent of the time the students were assuming a literary orientation by exploring possibilities in ways that brought them into the world of the story, and the rest of the time (68%) they took an information-gathering approach to understanding, searching for and providing information. If we consider the stances the students took toward the text, we learn that 87 percent of the time they were attempting to gain enough information to form an envisionment of the characters and events, and 13 percent of the time they were building and elaborating their understandings. This is largely due to the fact that their own final envisionments were not called upon; instead, the teacher's questions prompted them to build new envisionments — in line with the teacher's interpretations.

Although the teacher and students called this lesson a discussion, certain basic components of a discussion were missing. The participants (teacher and students or students and students) did not speak to each other; they did not respond to or build upon each other's ideas nor did the students elaborate on or refer back to their own ideas, although the teacher did. The role of the teacher and the role of the students followed a well-described pattern (Barnes, 1976; Mehan, 1979; Applebee, 1981; Langer, 1984) where the teacher is the holder of information and the students try to guess what the teacher knows and wants. This places the students in the role of guessers and the teacher in the role of evaluator. Thus, the students' thoughts focus on the teachers intentions rather than on their own understandings. Further, since the surface segments of the text seem to be held as the primary source of meaning (as opposed to the students' own growing envisionments of the story), there seems to be little motivation to step into the world of the text and live through the characters' experiences, emotions or actions.

## STUDENT-CENTERED AND TEXT-CENTERED LESSONS

We have seen two very different kinds of lessons, motivated by two very different views of literary knowing. From a student-centered perspective, the text is at best only a blueprint to be followed (more or less) by the powerful eyes and mind of a thoughtful and opinion-ridden reader — one who has lived a life full of experiences that will shade and shape the meanings he or she creates. This view assumes that there will be more than one defensible interpretation (and many indefensible ones) for each piece read. In contrast, from a text-based perspective, the meaning is locked within the text and a careful reading will reveal that meaning. This perspective moves toward one best interpretation of the piece, with others considered less defensible — flawed in some essential way. Let us look at the lessons once again to compare some of the ways each type of approach works itself out in the classroom discussion. In the discussion of *The Great Gatsby*, 14 percent of the topics were initiated and 14 percent were ended by the teacher; in other words, the students introduced and made final comments about the topics they discussed 86 percent of the time. This suggests that the students' concerns were presented for discussion, and they went on to another topic when the students were ready to do so. In contrast, in the discussion of "Tularecito," the teacher initiated 69 percent of the topics and ended 77 percent of them. The students opened and closed the discussion of the topics less than a quarter of the time. In this case, it was the teacher who maintained greatest control over what to talk about and when to move on. Similarly, of the total number of words spoken in the Gatsby discussion 58 percent were the students'. In contrast, 28 percent of the words were spoken by the students in the Tularecito discussion.

The Gatsby lesson, although a typical rather than exceptionally thought-provoking lesson, provides us with one example of how discussion can be used to move student thinking along. The students address their comments to each other as well as to their teacher, and the teacher guides them in the discussion — in ways to discuss as well as in ways to think about the content (see Langer, 1991). When she gives her opinion, the students accept it as such, understanding that there are multiple perspectives they can take and that the teacher's view, although valid, is not necessarily the one they must take, and certainly not out of hand, without more thought and exploration.

The Gatsby discussion is also an example of a typical, but not exceptional lesson, exploring a horizon of possibilities. However, it serves as an example of interaction and a pattern of thinking that takes place when the teacher invites the students to arrive at and move beyond their initial understandings through exploration. The discussion begins with the teacher inviting the students to bring up their concerns, and Christie begins with ". . . I wasn't exactly sure why he was invited. . . ." This is the sort of 'I don't understand' question most readers have at the end of a piece. This type of question doesn't signify that the students didn't know how to read, or didn't understand the piece very well, but that they have left their reading with a host of questions about motivations, feelings, and relationships — gaps that are left for the reader to ponder and construe. Because exploring the range of possibilities is at the heart of the literary experience, Christie's question is a good one. She has opened her understanding to another round of exploration — to move her understanding even farther along as she steps back into the story and tries to get to know Gatsby even better.

When class discussion is treated as exploration, students learn that as in real life, you get to know the characters and their behaviors best if you explore and imagine their intentions and actions and feelings from multiple perspectives. And, as in real life, you never really *know*; these interpretations are always tentative, to be reflected upon and further explored anew, with time and new ideas. They learn that the enjoyment of literature and the act of literary understanding, unlike reading in their other subjects, *involves* the exploration of an ever-changing horizon of possibilities. And it is this notion of discussion as exploring horizons of possibilities that I suggest needs to be at the center of the reform movement in literature.

## END NOTES

1.  Preparation of this chapter was supported under the Educational Research and Development Center Program (Grant No. R1176:0015) of the Office of Research and Improvement, U.S. Department of Education. I would like to thank Ester Helmar-Salasoo for having carried out the analyses of the discussions referred to herein.

# REFERENCES

Applebee, A.N. (1981). *Writing in the secondary school*. Urbana, IL: National Council of Teachers of English.

Applebee, A.N. (1989). *The teaching of literature in programs with reputations for excellence in English*. (Report Series 1.1). Albany, NY: Center for the Learning and Teaching of Literature, State University of New York at Albany.

Applebee, A.N. (1990). *Literature instruction in American schools*. (Report Series 1.4). Albany, NY: Center for the Learning and Teaching of Literature, State University of New York at Albany.

Applebee, A.N. (1991). *A study of high school literature anthologies*. (Report Series 1.5). Albany NY: Center for the Learning and Teaching of Literature, State University of New York at Albany.

Barnes, D. (1976). *From communication to curriculum*. Harmondsworth, England: Penguin Books.

Bleich, D. (1978). *Subjective criticism*. Baltimore: Johns Hopkins University Press.

Brown, R. (1991). *Schools of thought*. San Francisco: Jossey-Bass Publishers.

Brody, P., DeMilo, C., & Purves, A. (1989). *The current state of assessment in literature*. (Report Series 3.1). Albany, NY: Center for the Learning and Teaching of Literature, State University of New York at Albany.

Brooks, C. (1947). *The well wrought urn: Studies in the structure of poetry*. NY: Harcourt Brace.

Close, E. (1981). Seventh graders sharing literature: How did we get here? *Language Arts* 67, 8, 817–823.

DeLawter, J. (1992). Teaching literature: From clerk to explorer. In J. Langer (Ed.) *New directions in the teaching of literature: A focus on literary response*. Urbana, IL: National Council of Teachers of English.

Diaz, P. (1992). Literary reading and classroom constraints: Aligning practice with theory. In J. Langer (Ed.) *New directions in the teaching of literature: A focus on literary response*. Urbana, IL: National Council of Teachers of English.

Diaz, P. & Hayhoe, M. (1988). *Developing response to poetry*. Philadelphia: Open University Press.

Fitzgerald, F. S. (1925). *The Great Gatsby*. NY: Charles Scribner & Sons.

Holland, N. (1975). *Five readers reading*. NY: Oxford University Press.

Hynds, S. (1992). Challenging questions in the teaching of literature: A focus on literary response. in J. Langer (Ed.) *New directions in the teaching of literature: A focus on literary response*. Urbana, IL: National Council of Teachers of English.

Iser, W. (1978). *The act of reading*. Baltimore: Johns Hopkins University Press.

Langer, J.A. (1984). Literacy instruction in American schools. *American Journal of Education*. 93, 1, 107–131.

Langer, J.A. (1985). Levels of questioning: An alternative view. *Reading Research Quarterly*. 20, 586–602.

Langer, J.A. (1987). Envisionment: A reader-based view of comprehension. *The California Reader*. 28, 3, 4–7.

Langer, J.A. (1990a). The process of understanding: Reading for literary and informative purposes. *Research in the Teaching of English*, 24, 229–260.

Langer, J.A. (1990b). Understanding literature, *Language Arts, 67*, 812–816.

Langer, J.A. (1991). *Literary understanding and literature instruction*. (Report Series 2.11). Albany, NY: Center for the Learning and Teaching of Literature, State University of New York at Albany.

Langer, J.A. (1992). Rethinking literature instruction. In J. Langer (Ed.). *New directions in the teaching of literature: A focus on literary response*. Urbana, IL: National Council of Teachers of English.

Langer, J.A. (in progress). Reader-based literature instruction. In J. Flood and J. Langer (Eds.) *Literature instruction: Practice and policy*.

Mehan, H. (1976). *Learning lessons: Social organization in the classroom*. Cambridge, MA: Harvard University Press.

Petrosky, A. (1992). To teach (literature?). In J. Langer (Ed.) *New directions in literature instruction: A focus on literary response*. Urbana, IL: National Council of Teachers of English.

Probst, R. (1988). *Response and analysis: Teaching literature in the junior and senior high school*. Portsmouth NH: Boynton/Cook.

Probst, R. (1992). Five kinds of literary knowing. in J. Langer (Ed.) *New directions in the teaching of literature: A focus on literary response*. Urbana, IL: National Council of Teachers of English.

Rosenblatt, L. (1938). *Literature as exploration* (4th Edition). NY: Modern Language Association.

Rosenblatt, L. (1978). *The reader, the text, and the poem*. Cambridge, MA: Harvard University Press.

Steinbeck, J. (1984). Tularecito. *Literary Calvacade*. 28–35.

Tompkins, J. (Ed.) (1980). *Reader-response criticism: From formalism to post-structuralism*. Baltimore: Johns Hopkins University Press.

Wellek, R. & Warren, A. (1949). *Theory of literature*. NY: Harcourt Brace.

# CHAPTER THREE

# How Discussion Shapes General Track Students' Reasoning and Writing about Literature

❧ ❧ ❧

*George E. Newell and Judy Johnson*

In this chapter we explore a seemingly forgotten area of the English curriculum: literature instruction for general track students. These are the in-betweeners who do not qualify for the college bound track or for the remedial or non-college bound classes. Our experiences suggest that, for the most part, efforts to develop programs for general track students have been derived from two instructional legacies: one based on skills-oriented approaches and the other based on text-centered goals of college preparatory programs.

We do not deny the need to develop skills or to consider the exigencies of the text. On the other hand, we believe that effective instruction is defined by a creative balance of approaches that are employed according to the teacher's perceived needs of students; sometimes the teacher needs to provide students with opportunities to acquire new knowledge and skills, and sometimes students can work independently of the teacher. The teacher's role as decision-maker requires a reflective stance toward practice and the willingness to engage in experimentation with and observation of the content and process of learning and teaching. In this chapter, we discuss our efforts to explore how two approaches to discussing literature — one more teacher-dominated and the other more reader-based — shape students' writing and reasoning about literature.

## TEACHING LITERATURE TO GENERAL TRACK STUDENTS

Who are these students in general track English classes? What characterizes them as unique and as distinct from their noncollege bound or their academic tracked peers? What are some of these students' particular needs as they enter the English classroom? In his autobiographical examination of *Lives on the Boundary*, Mike Rose's (1989) description of his own academic life captures the experiences of many general track students:

> I developed further into a mediocre student and somnambulant problem solver, and that affected the subjects I did have the wherewithal to handle: I detested Shakespeare; I got bored with history. My attention flitted here and there. I fooled around in class and read my books indifferently — the intellectual equivalent of playing with your food. I did what I had to do to get by, and I did it with half a mind. (p.27)

This is the general track student who may plan to attend college or trade school or who may take a job for a while. Our experiences working with such students suggest that they often have a great deal in common with the noncollege bound students — they often slip between the cracks somewhere along the way. We are concerned that just as programs for non-college bound students' have been ignored, general track students' academic needs seldom receive our consideration during curriculum planning and curriculum revision.

Although we believe that programs for general students need imaginative restructuring and revitalization, our purposes here are somewhat less ambitious. In keeping with the major theme of this book, we want to focus on the range of possibilities that discussion and writing about literature hold as strategies for fostering reasoning and understanding in general students. Our experiences working with such students suggest that a great deal can be accomplished (and changed) in how we invite them into our conversations about literature. To a large extent, talking about text and teaching others how to write about text characterize how we define our work as English teachers. Since these activities reside at the center of what we do and who we are, it may be useful to consider how our interactions with general students shape what they might learn from the discussions we lead and from the writing about literature we assign.

Our experiences with general track students have taught us about the frustrations teachers experience. When George taught ninth grade English he kept a teaching journal in which he tried daily to come to terms with a range of issues and concerns. Many of the entries focused on frustrations that came with the realization of being ill-prepared for what English teachers were expected to do, including teaching literature to general students. Recently, as he prepared to write this chapter, he skimmed through a journal from his second year of teaching and found the following entry:

> Well, it's finally dawned on me: I have no idea what I am doing with my second period class. I have a sinking feeling that either they are not reading the short stories I have been assigning or, if they are, they can make little or no sense of them. Yesterday I found myself explaining the whole story to them . . . again. What's more, I'm as bored as they are. What I can't figure out is what matters the most — the students' own ideas or me telling them what they are supposed to know for tenth grade, for the test, or for who knows what.

This entry captures what we all know about the struggle with teaching literature in general tracked classes — the students can be brutally honest in their criticisms of the stories we admire and distressingly truthful in describing the confusion they experience during discussions. In one sense, their frankness may suggest that they are disconnected from the content; in another sense, they may simply have no way to understand the texts we assign. As English teachers, we know that general students test all of our assumptions about why we read literature and what we find personally and intellectually satisfying in talking about it.

Why teaching literature can be a difficult and demanding enterprise under the best conditions, seems clearer to us now than it did in our naive beginning years of teaching. We admit blaming the students for our frustrations. Then, it seemed ridiculous to question why general track students were expected to read and discuss the same literature and to write the same literary analysis essays that we assigned to our college preparatory classes.

## THE BIRTH OF A PROJECT

The project we developed to examine the relative effects of various approaches to discussion and writing on general track students' reasoning about literature has its origins in another joint endeavor. For a number of years, we worked together preparing student teachers to teach English.

Judy's classroom is a laboratory for new and unique approaches to working with all students, but especially the less successful ones. She takes her work with these students seriously, and her student teachers were amazed and, at times, befuddled by her success. For example, they found it difficult to explain what Judy did in her discussions with students that led to exciting discussions and engaging writing projects. In turn, we found it difficult to answer the student teachers' questions about how her strategies differed from more traditional approaches. Isn't the text important? Can we let students talk about anything? What are we supposed to look for in their writing if not for a particular interpretation?

As a teacher, Judy was concerned that to outsiders (including student teachers) her teaching often seemed like an idiosyncratic set of activities rather than a coherent and practical approach to teaching literature. She needed a clear rationale for the kinds of approaches she had developed. In our discussions, it became clear that she had been designing a more reader-based literature curriculum, but then a new set of problems emerged: If she wanted to base discussions and writing about literature on students' ideas and interpretations, how could she talk about learning and assessment? The scope and sequence charts and unit tests in Judy's 10th-grade literature curriculum mapped out in detail literary information (e.g., literary terms, authors, themes, etc.) that her students were supposed to know. However, because these materials represent outcomes rather than experiences that mediate learning, they were irrelevant to Judy's day-to-day planning: "My lessons and what the kids learn come out of what happens in class at least as often as they come from any formal planning." We realized that we wanted to construct a principled approach based on how students read and interpret texts, but to do so required that we also understand what works in a practical sense.

Our struggles to clarify what we feel matters the most in teaching literature to general track students led directly to the purpose of this chapter: to discern a set of underlying principles for using discussion and writing to teach literature. Together we explored how two approaches to literature instruction — a teacher-guided approach and a teacher-presented approach — shaped Judy's 10th grade general track students' writing and reasoning about a short story. The two approaches have great personal significance for each of us. They represent a great divide between teaching according to an institutionally sanctioned set of beliefs and teaching according to what we feel works. Moreover, they represent two different stances toward the teaching of literature; one assumes the need for the teacher to present a single, correct interpretation and the other assumes that teachers and students construct interpretations using exploratory talk (Barnes, 1976).

Following a discussion of our project and what we learned from our efforts, we will offer a set of guiding principles for using discussion and writing to teach literature. However, before moving into a description of what we learned from our collaborative study, we want to set it against the backdrop of literature instruction in American schools, especially in nonacademic tracked classrooms, and what recent studies have told us about the difficulties less successful students encounter when reading literature.

## LITERATURE INSTRUCTION AND LESS SUCCESSFUL STUDENTS

When we consider programs for students in general track and non-college bound classrooms, it becomes clear that as a field, literature instruction has not been concerned about the literary education of a considerable portion of the school population. Even in cases where individual teachers might devise an approach to teaching literature to such students, these teachers often find themselves working beyond the English department's concerns and priorities (Applebee, 1989). In general, there continue to be few attempts to plan curriculum and approaches that may foster an interest in and an understanding of literary discourse in nonacademic tracked classes. Moreover, when teaching nonacademic students to write about literature we have been particularly inconsistent.

In a recent nationwide study of literature instruction in American secondary schools, Applebee (1990) reported that by the time students reach the senior high grades, 80 percent of the writing they do is about literature. That literature and writing have a strong relationship seems obvious, but real inconsistencies continue to strain that relationship. In spite of the fact that teachers seem more aware of process-oriented approaches to literature than ever, their most typical writing assignment was clearly text-based essays rather than essays requiring students to write about their personal understandings. Nonacademic tracked students did somewhat less literature-related writing than students in college-preparatory classrooms, with the nonacademic tracked students assigned more exercise type tasks (e.g., answering study questions and writing summaries) and the college preparatory student assigned more formal essay writing about literature.

We can learn more about how discussion and writing might support literary understanding by considering how students make sense of literature as well as the difficulties less successful students encounter. These were Langer's (1990) central concerns when she examined the meaning-making processes of students as they read for literary purposes (reading short stories and poems). After examining the "envisionment-building processes" of seventh-grade students of varying academic abilities, Langer suggested four stances that readers rely on while reading literature: being out and stepping in, being in and moving through, being in and stepping out, and stepping out and objectifying the experience. Each stance represents an evolving understanding of the text, concluding with a final stance to reflect on that understanding.

Perhaps most significant for purposes of this chapter is that "Less as well as more proficient readers move through these stances when they read. However, in each stance the less proficient readers gather more superficial information than their better reading classmates do . . . " (Langer, 1990, p. 814). In many cases, these students were easily dislodged from their attempts to enter the text world as they encountered unfamiliar genres and literary language.

In a related study, Purcell-Gates (1991) examined how remedial readers read literary texts to give us a window on to the difficulties such readers have in trying to construct the meaning of short stories as a whole. Such information is important if we are to develop reader-based activities to support their reading, discussing, and reasoning about literary texts. Let's look closely, for example, at how one student (Melissa) attempts to make sense of a short story entitled "The House on the Hill" (Minturn, 1973). Near the end of the story, as Mark and his foster father (Sam) walk together, they notice that an abandoned house has been purchased. (Melissa's comments while thinking aloud as she reads are in italics.)

> "Well," said Sam, "someone finally bought this place. It's a good place."
> "You like it, too?" Mark asked. "I always have," Sam answered. "It just never had the right owners."
> *Maybe he wants to move in also.*
> Sam walked on slowly.
> *Probably so they could get closer and closer.*
> Mark stood there and thought of the things in the closet.
> *Probably there were ghosts.*
> The new owner would think the last people had left them.
> *Probably was his parents.*

The things weren't his any longer.

*Probably those who moved into the house.*

What is striking about this reading is that Melissa is working literally from sentence to sentence without any attempt to construct a coherent sense of the unfolding events in the story. Although we cannot be sure, this pattern may be an artifact of the kinds of exercises that dominate nonacademic track literature classrooms (Applebee, 1990) — answering study questions that may shift students' attention from one part of the story to another, short-circuiting a coherent, overall impression of a story's plot, characters, and central themes. Accordingly, we would argue that all students, especially nonacademic and general track students, must engage in more elaborated ways of exploring their understandings, and that discussing and writing about literature provide useful means of doing so.

That less proficient students have limited experience with discussing and writing about literature seems self-evident. What we do not know is what kinds of instructional activities might aid their understanding of literature and foster the development of strategies for making sense of a text. As one observer from Applebee's (1989) study commented, "Some teachers (of nonacademic students) simply do a watered-down version of what they do in college-prep classes, others avoid using extended writing activities, but there is a genuine sense of confusion about how to meet the needs of this group of students" (p. 35).

## READING, CLASSROOM DISCUSSION, AND LITERARY UNDERSTANDING

With recent developments in literary theory and discussion of their implications for teaching (Rosenblatt, 1978; Fish, 1980; Scholes, 1985), we have gained new perspectives on how instruction might support literary understanding. By extension, we have also begun to consider the pedagogical uses of discussion and writing as a way to foster students' exploration and construction of their literary understanding (Newell, 1990; Andrasick, 1990; Beach and Marshall, 1991). As we stated earlier, the field of literature instruction currently lacks a theory of instruction that might guide our approaches to curriculum and instruction in literature. However, teachers, researchers, and theorists have reached a consensus that reform in literature instruction must begin by looking at the interrelationship between teaching and learning and that classroom discourse plays a critical role in that relationship (Barnes, 1976). However, literature instruction is shaped by both tradition and current forces operating in the schools. We will be concerned with two approaches to instruction that represent conflicting views of teaching and learning: a teacher-centered model that we call "teacher-presented instruction" and a more collaborative model that we call "teacher-guided instruction."

In literature instruction, a fundamental tension often arises between the teacher's intentions and those of the students. While the teacher's goal may be to impart a complete and coherent interpretation of a text, students are often reading the text for the first time and may be unable to view the text as the teacher intends. When the discussion is fully regulated by the teacher in a way that ignores students' contributions, the result can be a teacher-centered presentation of a single interpretation — or, as George wrote in his teaching journal, "telling them what they are supposed to know." But students do have their own interpretations, and theories of reading comprehension and literary response suggest that if we ignore their interpretations we may be short-circuiting the fundamental goals of literary education.

In recent years, Langer and Applebee (1987) have argued that one way to lessen the underlying tensions between teaching and learning is to consider the differing roles of teachers and students in classroom reading and writing activities. Working out of the traditions of language learning studies (e.g., Vygotsky, 1962; Bruner 1978) that view language as a tool for understanding the world, Langer and Applebee (1987) argue that effective instruction is based on careful analysis of the instructional support or scaffolding that teachers may provide to help students successfully carry out tasks. They have proposed five components of effective instruction: ownership, appropriateness, support, collaboration, and internalization. Viewed in light of these criteria, reading and interpreting literature can be examined as opportunities for teachers and students to enter into a conversation about the content of a text. In the context of literature instruction, teacher-guided response activities provide carefully sequenced and structured opportunities for students to construct their understanding of a text in collaboration with their peers and the teacher. The teacher's responsibility in this model is not to put knowledge *into* students, nor to displace the skills and knowledge students already possess. In sum, Langer and Applebee's suggestions represent a model for considering how teachers can provide support to ensure successful student performance, and ownership opportunities to promote students' higher levels of reasoning and learning.

Accordingly, it seems that guided responses to literature represent one of the most viable alternatives to teacher-centered approaches to literature that now dominate high school literature instruction. With guided-response activities (e.g., Kahn, et al., 1984; Beach and Marshall, 1991), teachers are able to provide a way to facilitate student responses without overdirection or intrusion. The teacher's primary role is to assist students in elaborating upon and perhaps revising their initial interpretations without rejecting those interpretations as incorrect, a role not unlike that called for by process-oriented writing instruction. The practical implication of this approach is that familiar activities such as talking and writing about text may be viewed as tools for teachers to work in concert with students to construct interpretations. Thus, rather than using discussion and writing as ways to evaluate students' literary understanding, language activities may become ways of fostering it. Such uses of language are ways to broaden, not replace, the varieties of practices with which teachers are already familiar.

## EXAMINING THE NATURE OF SUPPORT IN TWO INSTRUCTIONAL UNITS

These were our concerns when we collaboratively planned two instructional units — one informed by a more traditional teacher-centered approach (teacher-presented) and the other informed by concerns for how students make sense of texts (teacher-guided). Each unit represents an approach with differing underlying assumptions about the teacher's role in supporting student discussion and writing about literature. Judy's two general track, tenth-grade classes — 45 students in all — participated in the project. Since we wanted to look directly at kinds of thinking and writing the two approaches engendered, we selected four students for case study work, two from each of the two classes. In order to tap into students' meaning-making processes during writing, we employed a special technique: As they composed their responses to a story, we interrupted them at specific points in their processes to ask them about their planning and revising strategies. We called the information we gathered "intervention protocols" to capture how we tapped into how and when they reasoned and wrote about the story.

As part of the two instructional units, the students in the two classes participated in discussion and wrote about a short story. The story, "Only Clowns Passing Through" (four pages in length) by Jeanne A. Taylor (1980), was selected by Judy because the story "challenges students to think about parents and their children who are struggling with different ethical choices." The story centers on the lives of a working-class black family and the inner conflict experienced by Amy when her teenage children and her husband demand that Amy place her live-in and eccentric mother in a rest home. As Amy tries to decide where her loyalties lie, her mother suddenly dies. Because the third person narrative leaves the question of why Amy uses all of her family's savings for her mother's funeral unanswered, the reader is left to examine her motives.

In order to tap the students' (in both classes) abilities to explore and elaborate upon their understandings of the story, we asked them to "Write a composition in which you explain why Amy decides to spend the family's savings and insurance money on Grandmother's funeral and for a monument at her grave site rather than a new home. Be sure to explain your ideas as to why Amy makes such a decision." Thus the writing task required the students to write analytically yet personally about and with a range of approaches to the story in order to interpret the main character's motives. More importantly, the assignment permitted us to examine how the instructional dialogue that developed during each of the two units affected what students took from the story.

## How We Organized the Two Instructional Units

The study took place over a period of four days for each instructional unit. The implementation of each unit followed the same pattern of one day for story reading, a day for oral discussion of the story, a day for prewriting instruction, with the students completing the writing assignment on the fourth day. At the end of the study, we talked about each of the instructional units, including which unit Judy preferred and why.

At the beginning of each class period, Judy briefly reviewed what the students would be doing and then distributed any materials they would be using during the session. For each day of the study, students had a full 50 minutes in which to work. During each class session, George observed and audiotaped the class and took field notes to understand how the discussion and writing differed across the two units and to assist us in later discussions of the project.

While their classmates were completing the essay writing assignment, the four case study students met with coinvestigators outside of class to complete the same assignment and answer questions for the intervention protocol. Like their classmates, the case study students had participated with their classmates in reading and discussing the story and engaging in prewriting activities prior to the essay writing. During the session, they were given a copy of the story and the assignment. They were asked questions about the task, about how they would begin writing, what they did as they wrote the essay, and their reaction to their complete essay. These sessions were audiotaped and transcribed for our analysis.

## The Two Instructional Units

**Teacher-Presented Response.** As we stated earlier, we entered this project with many shared concerns regarding the focus of the tenth-grade English curriculum in Judy's school. For example, teachers were expected to follow a set of guidelines that required students to define literary terms, to learn "appropriate" ways of analyzing literature, and to employ preset forms for writing essays about literature. To a large extent, our teacher-presented response unit was based on those guidelines as well as our own experiences with traditional approaches to literature instruction.

In this unit, Judy employed a text-centered approach by presenting an interpretation of the story and then posing questions to ensure that students followed that interpretation of the story. On the third day of this unit, she presented a ready-made structure (five-paragraph essay) that framed what her students could say about the story in essay form. As Judy presented an interpretation of the story (how the author reveals explicitly and implicitly the motives behind the central character's decision) the students were encouraged to record this information in notes to assist them in writing the essay. Accordingly, though the students were given support for understanding the story, they were encouraged to accept what Judy presented.

**Teacher-Guided Response.** In this unit Judy provided the necessary activities (e.g., a three-step, focused free-write activity examining the central character's motives) and assisted the students in writing their own response to the story based on what emerged from both small group and whole class discussions of the story. Thus, the students were given assistance in understanding the story while being encouraged to formulate their own interpretations. Moreover, Judy's approach to the essay response was more open-ended and encouraged students to use a flexible form for what they wanted to say about the story — a form that allowed students to include both textual knowledge and experiential knowledge they formulated from the small group and class discussions.

## Discussing the Short Story in the Two Approaches

In both units, Judy relied on process-oriented approaches, but she assumed a very different stance toward the students' own interpretation of the story. For example, in both cases she engaged her students in discussion, but as we will see the goals of each unit relied on a differing set of conventions or rules for participation.

During the teacher-guided unit, Judy had students work in small groups to characterize Amy's values. To do so, each group rank-ordered a list of values (loyalty, sincerity, pride, etc.) and then developed a rationale for their rankings (Kahn et al., 1984). Judy then asked each group to report their findings to the entire class for consideration and discussion:

*Judy:*      Greg, tell us why your group thought that love was something Amy values. Tell us why you thought it's love.

*Student 1:*  When she says . . . Well, she wanted a new life for her family. That was love.

*Student 2:*  She doesn't want . . . because she loves her mother, 'cause her mother took care of her for a long time, and now she feels she needs to take care of her mother because she is old and she can't take care of herself.

*Judy:*      Because she feels that somebody has done a lot of things for her, and she feels obligated to do things for her now.

*Student 3:*  She also loves her daughter. She loves everyone. But she loves her mother a lot. What it comes down to is that her mother raised her and she is going to die pretty soon. And she wants her to be happy.

*Judy:*      Does Amy just love her mother?

*Student 1:*  No. She loves her daughter, too. She loves everybody (laughter).

*Judy:*      How do you know that?

*Student 2:*  Because . . . she loves her daughter because she was going to choose her daughter over her mother. Here's where things got complicated.

*Judy:*      She was going to choose her daughter over her mother?

*Student 2:*  Well, it seemed like it to me. She loves her husband, but he wants her mother out of the house. Now Amy has to decide between people she loves and who love her, too.

*Judy:*      I think we have pretty good evidence that she was a loving person. What about loyalty? I think we talked about loyalty to her mother, too.

*Student 3:*  You see, that's the problem. Her loyalty to her mother makes it hard for her to be loyal to others in the family. That's where she has to decide what to do. She can love everyone . . . like that's a good idea, but she also realizes that loyalty has to count, too.

The tone and the direction of this discussion is established with Judy's request: "Greg, tell us why your group thought that love was something Amy values." Rather than basing the analysis of Amy's character exclusively on her own interpretations or with textual evidence, Judy begins with the interpretations the small group discussions had generated. Additionally, when Judy does offer new ideas about the story, she builds upon what the students have offered: After student 2 comments that "she needs to take care of her mother 'cause she can't take care of herself," Judy adds the notion of "obligation": "...and she feels obligated to do these things for her now." This new information is part of the communal process of constructing an interpretation of Amy's conflict between her role as a daughter and as a mother. Note that Judy then asks the student to explore Amy's dilemma: Should she be obligated to her mother or her daughter?

The teacher-presented unit fostered a somewhat different kind of instructional dialogue, as Judy dominated the discussion. In the following excerpt, she attempts to get the students to explain why Sissy, Amy's daughter, is proud.

*Judy:* If I say "proud," give me some details from the story that she is proud. What proof can you offer from the story?

*Student 1:* She doesn't want her Grandmother to be around her friends.

*Judy:* OK, She's embarrassed for her friends. What's something another character says about her that shows she's proud? What's something her mother says about her?

*Student 2:* I don't know.

*Judy:* Well, look. Remember Sissy goes to the mother and says . . .

*Student 1:* She says she won't stay . . . if Grandmother Delilah is there.

*Judy:* OK. Is that an example of being proud?

*Student 3:* Her pride is hurt 'cause she wants to sleep in her own bed.

*Judy:* OK. She is proud because she wants to sleep in her own bed. What else does her mother say about her? Doesn't someone call her uppity? Where is that in the story? Take a look at the story. Does the Father say it?

*Student 1:* No. Well . . . I thought it was the mother, Amy.

In this excerpt, Judy's questions require the students to attend to the details of story, but the teacher-centered nature of the questions seems to confuse them. Because Judy is pointing the students toward her interpretation rather than toward what they have taken from the story, the students struggle to discern a direction in the questions. From the students' perspective, the string of questions are not tied to a coherent line of thought, and consequently, the discussion does not provide a thoughtful exploration of Sissy's pride.

Later in our discussion of this part of the lesson, Judy commented that in working with nonacademic students teachers often try (1) to stay close to the literal elements of the text to avoid confusion (talking about personal experience and the text causes these students difficulty) and (2) to know in advance what answer you expect to check their comprehension of the text. In other words, the text-centeredness of literature instruction in nonacademic classrooms may be, in some cases, a result of the students' difficulties with reading literary texts rather than teachers' concerns for interpretive authority of the text itself. The discussions in each of the two units indicate how each unit presented students with different communication events. To get a rough idea of how much of each discussion was truly a conversation, we examined the transcripts from each unit by simply counting the number of communication units (identifiable remarks about a thought or behavior) in the transcripts.

Counting across the two days of the teacher-presented unit Judy had 76 percent of the communication units, while the students had 24 percent. In the teacher-guided response unit, the distribution of talk was somewhat more balanced, with Judy producing 58 percent of the communication units and students producing 42 percent. These patterns are indicative of the two different kinds of teacher control in the units. On the one hand, in the teacher-presented response unit much of the thinking and reasoning about the story and the essay assignment was in the teacher's control. On the other hand, in the teacher-guided response unit the pattern of talk indicated that while Judy still controlled the discussion she shared the floor more often with the students.

These patterns of discussion prior to writing about the story suggest that the interpretive agenda set by guiding students through the text allowed the writing task to become an opportunity for students to extend their own ideas about the story. On the other hand, the agenda set by presenting the students with a prepackaged interpretation provides a limited range of approaches to writing about the story. The effects of these patterns of discussion became evident in the ways the case study students composed their essays and in the quality of all the students' later responses to the story.

## Patterns of Reasoning while Writing

The most compelling finding from our qualitative analysis of the intervention protocols concerns the meaning-making processes and the approaches the four case study students used when writing about literature in the two instructional units. We want to use the students' remarks to argue that the students' planning and monitoring strategies were shaped by approaches employed in each instructional unit rather than simply by what they usually do when they write. Put another way, the students were just as capable of developing their own approaches to the story as they were capable of following Judy's interpretation and a preset form for reporting it. What ultimately made the difference in the students' choices was the nature of the instructional support provided by the discussions that developed in each unit. The comments that follow explore those differences as students conceptualized the demands of the task, planned the essay, evaluated their work-in-progress, and reflected on the quality of their essays.

**Conceptualizing Task Demands.** Curiously, when the case study students in the two units were asked "What is the assignment asking you to do?" they based their responses on the kind of support Judy provided. Michele, one of the students from the teacher-guided response unit, commented that, "Since we had to write about our ideas about Amy and then talk about that, I guess I can use my ideas from that. You know, we all have to have our own ideas." On the other hand, Pete, a student from the teacher-presented response unit, worried about using "the techniques for presenting characters and then spelling out what she [the teacher] said in class."

Thus, the pattern for responding to the writing task was set in the early stages of the writing, reminding us that in any writing condition specific strategies for attacking a specific task are what count the most rather than general prewriting skills often recommended by textbooks and employed in process approaches. Furthermore, when interpreting the writing tasks, all four students did so by relying on what the instructional units asked of them. In the teacher-guided unit this meant working through their own responses to the story; in the teacher-presented unit this meant giving the teacher what they believed she was demanding. These perceptions of the task led to rather distinctive approaches to planning what they might say in the essay.

**Planning the Essay.** When we asked the case study students "How are you going to get started with the essay?" we expected each unit to influence how they would choose their starting points. However, our review of the intervention protocols indicated that all four students, regardless of instructional unit, verbalized a kind of boiler plate notion of organization. "Well, I have to get down a thesis and then keep working on that to show why Amy made her decision." When we asked why they chose to begin with a thesis, the effect of their ninth-grade writing instruction was evident across all four students. "That's the way I learned last year . . . it's disorganized otherwise."

There was, however, a clear shift in thinking when we asked about their intention or purpose: "What do you want to say in the essay?" Here it became clear that the students who received support in the teacher-guided response approach did not see the task as unproblematic or routine. For example, Michele made it clear that Amy's decision to spend the family's money had no clear explanation and this led her to return to the prewriting she did the day before. "Well, it's not clear to me yet. When we discussed the story, we did answer three questions about Amy's decision. I want to begin with what I said there and see where I end up." Pete, a student from the teacher-presented response approach, seemed more sure of himself. "In a statement I'll say why Amy made her decision . . . three reasons why. I'll need a paragraph for each one." The differences in the students' planning suggest the influence of each unit. Michele saw the essay assignment as a way to share a response to the story; Pete believed his primary purpose was to demonstrate mastery of the material and control over what the story means.

**Evaluating Progress.** One of the concerns we had was how the students applied the knowledge they had about writing essays and the new knowledge they attained about the story from the two instructional units. We also wanted a more direct measure of how they used that knowledge while composing their essays. To do so we asked the students to pause after they had composed their first full paragraph to talk about "what you have written so far [summarize] and what you plan to do next [predict]."

Perhaps the most important difference that we saw in this segment of the intervention protocols was that the students in the teacher-guided response unit began to use the essay writing as a way to associate the experiences in the story with their own experiences. Specifically, they applied their knowledge of the conflicts that are part of family life to understanding the implications of Amy's decision to spend the family savings on her mother's funeral. The following remarks were made by Michele.

> I put that Amy had a terrible time deciding between her own physical comforts and her family's too and what she thought was right. This is the basic

point I tried to make. Then I also wrote about how I think love and loyalty have to count for a lot. That's the way I think about Amy. I think she was right in her decision. That's the way I'd decide.

When we asked Michele what she would do next with the essay, she explained how she would integrate narrative information from the text and her own feelings about the story. "OK, right now I'm still sorting out how I feel. I still have feelings to write about. I want to tell why Amy was right using the family's attitude and my own thoughts." Michele's consideration of her response to the story reflects her growing understanding of the story, an understanding guided by the integration of her experience and the experience narrated in the text.

On the other hand, the students in the teacher-presented unit saw their reading and understanding of the story as essentially over. Thus the purpose of the essay writing was to report that final reading. "In the first paragraph I wrote the name of the story, the family situation — poor and black — and dealing with the grandmother who was elderly. Then I told why Amy decided to spend her savings on the funeral. OK, then I get into three specifics that are going to be the body of the essay: She was unselfish, proud of her mother, and thoughtful."

**Reflecting on the Product.** At the conclusion of the essay writing, we were concerned about two things: (1) the students' evaluation of their essays, and (2) their perceptions of what they learned, if anything, from the essay writing.

The comments of two students in the teacher-guided response unit suggested that they were beginning to find what they wanted to say about the story, but their work was unfinished.

*Mary:* It's a good effort. I think I'm seeing what I think Amy was up to. You know, though I started to wonder (at the end) if Amy wasn't a bit selfish about the whole thing. Sure she was mad and all, but she should have talked it over better.

*George:* Do you think it's not a good effort or a poorly written piece?

*Mary:* Well, its okay for now, but I'd want to rethink a couple of things. And I think more writing would strengthen it. To tell you the truth, I am still writing this like a journal or something and that probably isn't good enough.

*George:* Do you see anything different about the story or about Amy now?

*Mary:*      No. It's not like that. I haven't really changed my mind. I am still thinking about all of it yet. That's what I mean. It's still not done. Like I am still trying to clarify it.

Pete, a student who participated in the teacher-presented unit, verbalized a different sense of what the essay was intended to accomplish. "When you do something like this you have to get to the point and then defend it, and that's what I did. This is like those times when you are under pressure and you rely on being clear about that point. That's what teachers look for, you know — 'OK, what's his point? And did he say it?'" These remarks about the completed essay suggest that Pete's primary concern is how to resolve a complex set of issues by forming a thesis statement or a generalization, a strategy that may not take him into the complexity of the story. In summary, the teacher-presented response unit that we constructed seems to have had effects on the students' writing not unlike what students are likely to experience when writing in test situations.

Because it is possible that the students we interviewed were unique in some way or they were simply guessing how we wanted them to respond, we also took time to read and to analyze systematically the content of all the students' essays. As we did so, it became apparent to us that the two instructional units led to written responses that were consistent with our hunches about the effects of the two approaches.

## The Students' Written Responses to the Short Story

If students' responses to literature are shaped by the purposes of classroom discussion, their written responses may even be more so, for writing is often graded while oral responses are usually not. Writing about literature in the two units required the students to adhere to a more closed (teacher-presented) or a more open (teacher-guided) set of guidelines.

In order to get a general idea of how the students in both units responded to the story, we divided their essays into T-units (independent clauses and their modifiers). We then coded each T-unit as descriptive of some element of the story (e.g., "The family was very close."), as a personal comment ("I thought that Sissy was a bit like my sister."), as an associative comment representing a connection between the story and the students' experiences ("That reminds me of a problem our family had once."), as an interpretive comment ("There's more to Amy's comment than I thought at first."), or as an evaluation of the story or a character's behavior ("That was not a kind thing to say.").

The distribution of various statements about the story in the essays indicates that the approaches engendered different thinking about the story. The essays written in the teacher-presented response unit allowed students a somewhat more limited range of response. About 43 percent of the statements were descriptive, which suggests a great deal of retelling of the story. Fifty-one percent of the responses were interpretive, with an emphasis on interpretation of content. Perhaps most revealing are the low percentages for personal statements (2.8 percent) and associative statements (0.7 percent). Given that throughout the teacher-presented unit the students were not asked to consider their own responses to the story, the low percentages for these two types of reader-based statements seem very reasonable.

The following segment of Jennifer's essay illustrates how she stays close to the text as she attempts to interpret the motives of the central character:

> In the story "Only Clowns Passing Through," Amy decides to use the money she had saved to buy a new house on her mother's funeral. She made this decision because she felt guilt, responsibility, and love.
>
> Amy felt guilty about her mother because her kids had not treated her right in the last few days of life. Her kids were embarrassed of the grandmother, and they didn't give her much love . . .

The essays written in teacher-guided response unit included more than three times the proportion of personal statements and more than four times the proportion of associative statements than the essays written in teacher-presented response unit. But more important, the essays written at the end of this unit included a greater distribution of literary response statements. If we assume that the essay writing activity at the end of the instructional units represents the students' attempts to synthesize what they took from their own readings of the story and the story discussion, this pattern suggests that in the teacher-guided unit students were able to rely on a greater range of approaches to understanding the story than in the teacher-presented unit.

Greg's essay is indicative of how students in the teacher-guided unit responded to the story with a full range of both experiential knowledge and textual knowledge:

> Amy had more love and loyalty for her mother rather than for her own children probably because she lived and was raised by her mother for such a long time. Amy felt the insurance money would best be spent by giving Grandmother Delilah a decent family burial instead of a burial by the state. Amy probably thought that through time, eventually, her family could

save and earn enough money to buy the house. This seems likely since the family seems resourceful and ambitious . . .

In my opinion, I think Amy would have been correct in doing such a thing. Amy's mother, or for that matter, anybody's mother does so much that spending all the savings on a decent grave site would hardly begin to repay your mother for all the hardships and troubles your mother endures for you.

## DISCERNING PRINCIPLES FOR EFFECTIVE DISCUSSIONS OF LITERATURE

Although the configuration of activities in the two units are valuable in their own right, our examination of the teacher-led discussions and their shaping influence on students' writing and reasoning led us to a set of more general principles. We developed these notions using two sources: (1) our own teaching experiences and practical knowledge, and (2) Langer and Applebee's (1987) model of "instructional scaffolding." To illustrate each component of the model, we will rely on the contrasting assumptions that shaped our two instructional units: the teacher-presented approach and the teacher-guided approach.

### Ownership.

Effective instructional tasks such as discussion and writing about literature must permit students to offer something of their own, including a personal interpretation of a text that leads to arguing (in writing) for that interpretation. In other words, for instructional approaches to be purposeful and coherent, they must be driven by a concern for supporting students' attempts to make sense out of their reading through discussion and writing.

In the teacher-presented unit Judy began with her interpretation of the story rather than with what the students had taken from the story. When she presented the students with a preset form for writing about the story, they were left with little room for reasoning about their interpretations or for using the writing to carry out their own purposes. While on the surface such strategies might appear to aid less successful students, the emphasis on the teacher's interpretation may actually impede the construction of their own understanding.

When Judy guided the students through a discussion of the characters' motivations, the discussion was more like conversation than recitation. Consequently, the writing task became a point of departure from rather than a reproduction of Judy's interpretation. Put another way, the writing assignment became a vehicle for students to rethink and revise their initial interpretations. Thus, by relying on the support Judy provided through the discussion, the students were able to clarify and then to take responsibility for their own ideas.

### Appropriateness.

Based on our experiences, we realize that finding the right level of difficulty and challenge in the tasks we assign to general students can be problematic. Judy commented during the project that "selecting activities for these students is often a matter of guessing, and trial and error." We realize that the formal curriculum, including scope and sequence charts or list of objectives, has been developed to aid such instructional decisions. On the other hand, these materials often ignore the fact that teachers often make moment-to-moment decisions based on their interactions with students. Accordingly, appropriateness means more than knowing the prescribed grade-level of materials and activities.

The teacher-presented unit looked a lot like traditional instruction that establishes in advance what students are to learn but fails to recognize or utilize the skills and knowledge students may contribute. This may be why students often perceive assignments as too difficult or too easy or why teachers and students seem to be working at cross-purposes. In developing the teacher-guided unit, we used open-ended tasks such as free writing and small group discussion to help students adjust to an appropriate level of challenge. As we have pointed out, as Judy raised the level of challenge by extending students' interpretations, the discussion became enriched and the writing more thoughtful. She provided the structure within which students could explain their interpretations. In brief, traditional teacher-centered instruction imposes interpretation, and student-centered instruction derives interpretation from what students bring to the discussion.

### Structured Process

Though "structure" and "process" may appear contradictory, "structured process" captures what we view as an effective configuration of tasks: Each task structures and contributes to the evolving process of understanding and learning. Both instructional units employed activities that are associated with process-oriented practice; for example, Judy used a discussion of the story as a prewriting activity in each unit. However, the distinguishing feature of the two units was not the specific activities but the sequence of activities in each unit. In the teacher-presented approach, the focus was on a specific interpretation and a specific organizational structure for the essay; it seems clear from our interviews with the students that these activities fostered nearly exclusive reliance on what the teacher wanted rather than the students' own choices. In contrast, the teacher-guided approach focused on teaching strategies for reasoning about the story; each activity contributed to an evolving understanding of the story leading to writing about that understanding. We assume that such approaches enable students to become more independent of the teacher and more likely to internalize new approaches and routines called for in analytic tasks.

### Collaboration.

If we are to create contexts in which less successful students are to read literature with purpose and meaning, we need to resist the temptation to evaluate student performance at every turn. While assisting students with the development of their own reasoning and writing about literature we need to delay evaluation to allow for the kind of explorations necessary for disciplined thinking. Such a shift in the teacher's role is not easy. For example, conventional wisdom often recommends that teachers "give a quiz to make sure students will do the reading." We are not suggesting that evaluation is always inappropriate; rather, we are suggesting that it be delayed until students have had the opportunity to come to terms with their own ideas.

We deliberately built a more collaborative approach into the teacher-guided unit. The discussion of the story is a good example. When Judy guided students into and through their own meaning making, there was a tentativeness in both the discussion and writing that we believe led to sophisticated and intelligent responses. On the other hand, when Judy attempted to impose an interpretation of the story on the students, the talk seemed more like recitation than conversation. Based on our analysis of the students' essays, the teacher-presented unit fostered more recall than analysis and more reproduction than reconstruction of ideas and interpretations.

### A BEGINNING

We began our project wondering if we could create a new set of guidelines and assumptions as well as a vocabulary for talking about teaching literature to general track students. Our discussion of "instructional scaffolding" and our references to "teacher-presented instruction" versus "teacher-guided instruction," "recitation" versus "conversation," and "text-centered" versus "student-centered" teaching offers some ways to map a new direction in rethinking literature instruction for all students, but especially for less successful students.

Discussions of literature programs for such students harken back to the 1960s when Squire and Applebee (1968) examined literature instruction in American schools. Obviously, we have not made much progress in improving the lot of disenfranchised and alienated students who inhabit our literature classrooms. As Jim Marshall and his colleagues have so aptly stated, "The challenge, then, is to recall that what we do with literature is but a small part of what we do in school, that school is only part of the larger culture, and that larger culture will always find a way to enter our classrooms . . ." (1990, p. 40). But though we must avoid naivete, we must also remain optimistic for we do have the knowledge and skill to bring about the needed change. The issue now is whether it matters to us and to what degree we want to commit ourselves to it.

Finally, we wondered how we became interested in teaching literature to general track students. Perhaps our own school memories of what it is like to be confused by a text or by a teacher's questions have inspired us; or perhaps our belief that schools should provide a place for all students to grow intellectually and imaginatively have engendered such concerns. Regardless of the source of our concerns, we believe it is time to attend to work where it is most urgently needed. Literary education offers one of the most important vehicles for personal and social change, for it is through our virtual experiences with literature that we can imagine far beyond the limits what is of immediate and practical value. This is what drew many of us to the English teaching profession to begin with, and it is what can draw all students to read and to fill their lives with the vast riches of human experience and cultural wisdom that literature offers.

## REFERENCES

Andrasick, K. D. (1990). *Opening texts: Using writing to teach literature*. Portsmouth, NH: Heinemann.

Applebee, A.N. (1989). *The teaching of literature in programs with reputations for excellence in English*. (Tech. Rep. No. 1.1). Albany, NY: Center for the Learning and Teaching of Literature.

Applebee, A.N. (1990). *Literature instruction in American schools*. (Tech. Rep. No. 1.4). Albany, NY: Center for the Learning and Teaching of Literature.

Barnes, D. (1976). *From communication to curriculum*. New York: Penguin Books.

Beach, R. & Marshall, J. (1990). *Teaching literature in the secondary school*. New York: Harcourt Brace Jovanovich.

Bruner, J. (1978). The role of dialogue in language acquisition. In A. Sinclair et al. (Eds.). *The child's conception of language*. (241-256). New York: Springer-Verlag.

Fish, S. (1980). *Is there a text in this class? The authority of interpretive communities*. Cambridge, MA: Harvard University Press.

Kahn, E., Calhoun, C. & Johannessen, L. (1984). *Writing about literature*. Urbana, IL: National Council of Teachers of English.

Langer, J. (1990). Understanding Literature. *Language Arts, 67*, 812-816.

Langer, J. & Applebee, A. (1987). *How writing shapes thinking: A Study of teaching and learning*. (Research Report no. 22). Urbana, IL: National Council of Teachers of English.

Marshall, J.D., Klages, M.B., & Fehlman, R. (1990). *Discussions of literature in lower-track classrooms*. (Tech. Report 2.10). Albany, NY: Center for the Learning and Teaching of Literature.

Minturn, S. (1973). The house on the hill. In K. Kleiman (Ed.), *Double Action* (pp. 64-71). New York: Scholastic.

Newell, G. (1990). Exploring the Relationships Between Writing and Literary Understanding: A Language and Learning Perspective. In A. Soter & G. Hawisher (Eds.), *Essays in the Teaching of Secondary English*. Albany, NY: State University of New York Press.

Purcell-Gates, V. (1991). On the outside looking in: A Study of remedial readers' meaning-making while reading literature. *Journal of Reading Behavior, 23*, (2), 235-253.

Rosenblatt, L. (1978). *The reader, the text, the poem*. Carbondale, IL: Southern Illinois University Press.

Scholes, R. (1985). *Textual power: Literary theory and the teaching of English*. New Haven, CT: Yale University Press.

Squire, J. & Applebee, R. (1968). *High school English instruction today*. New York: Appleton-Century-Crofts.

Taylor, J. (1981). Only clowns passing through. In O. S. Niles, J. Walker, & J.J. Tuinman. (Eds.). *Nova*. Glenview, IL: Scott and Co.

Vygotsky, L. (1962). *Thought and language*. Cambridge, MA: Harvard University Press.

# CHAPTER FOUR

# Creating Multiple Worlds

*Drama, Language, and Literary Response* [1]

— ♣ ♣ ♣ —

*Theresa Rogers and Cecily O'Neill*

## INTRODUCTION

Besides being an imaginative alternative to more typical literature activities in the English classroom, drama is a powerful instructional tool. Drama provides an opportunity to transform classroom interaction patterns so that student talk becomes richer and students' responses become the center of the literary interpretive process. With drama, the interpretive community of the classroom can be more inclusive of students' knowledge and voices, and classroom contexts can witness a "return of authority to students as readers and interpreters" of literature (Lindberg, 1986), in which students themselves become literary critics (Rogers, 1991).

The form of drama that we discuss in this chapter is a group improvisational process whose outcome is not any kind of presentation but the exploration of an improvised dramatic world for the opportunities, insights, and learning it offers. This kind of drama is not scripted or rehearsed; instead, it focuses on the dramatic process, using improvisational and teacher-in-role strategies to develop new dramatic contexts in the classroom. One of the best-known exponents of this method is the eminent British educator, Dorothy Heathcote (cf. Johnson and O'Neill, 1984).

This chapter has several parts. In addition to exploring the role of drama in the English classroom as a means of developing interpretive language and thought and to providing examples from our own work with one teacher and her English classroom, we suggest ways to incorporate drama strategies in any English classroom.

## CURRENT STATE OF CLASSROOM TALK

Talk is the invisible medium through which most classroom teaching and learning takes place; and, currently, there is a renewed interest in the way talk influences what people come to understand or learn both within and outside classrooms. This interest is evident in education (e.g., Cazden, 1988; Edwards and Furlong, 1978; Barnes, 1976; Green, 1983; Green and Harker, 1982; Hynds and Rubin, 1990; Wells, 1986) and related fields such as sociolinguistics and the ethnography of communication (e.g., Halliday, 1978, Sinclair and Coulthard, 1975; Saville-Troike, 1982; Mehan, 1979; Gumperz, 1981; 1986; Hymes, 1974; Erickson and Schultz, 1981). As Gumperz (1986) argues, teaching and learning are interactive processes, and what gets accomplished or learned depends on (1) what gets communicated through the curriculum and teaching strategies and on (2) students' perceptions of the norms of communication in the classroom (i.e., what they can say, when they can say it, to whom they can say it, under what conditions they can say it, and with what consequences).

What most classroom studies of secondary literature teaching tell us is that much of the classroom talk is teacher-directed, often comprised of questioning cycles that serve to recreate a teacher's interpretation of a literary work (e.g., Rogers, Green and Nussbaum, 1990; Rogers, 1991; Marshall, 1987; 1989).

An example will seem familiar to anyone who has been either a teacher or a student in a secondary literature class. In this example, the teacher and students are discussing part of the novel *When the Legends Die* (Borland, 1963), about a Ute Indian boy named Bear's Brother who is attending an agency school on a reservation. In this excerpt the teacher begins a discussion of the significance of the events in the story just prior to the boy being taken to the school.

*T:*     Now at the very beginning of this we said were were going to read the novel on several different levels. This [a scene where a mother bear is shot] seems like something very odd to put right in the middle of this scene with nature and the boy getting along with the bear. Why do you suppose the author includes those scenes right there at that point?

*St:*     Because that makes the bear cub alone, too, like Bear's Brother is.

*T:*     It points up the commonality between the two. Bear's Brother is alone and so is the bear itself alone. Good. Why else might he have included that?

*St:*     Like everything else is dying so like his dad his mom, now maybe the bear's gonna die.

*T:*     OK. Yeah. There's the comment about being surrounded by death here — for the boy.

*St:*     He wanted to give the boy a companion.

*St:*     Give him what?

*T:*     A companion or a friend. And that scene of the invasion of the white man into the peaceful — the peaceful terrain and nature. That is in sharp contrast with the way the boy has been living, isn't it? He's been singing songs and living with nature side by side. And then there's this miner who shoots the bear cub and the mother. And leaves the other cub alone to fend for himself. Then the boy comes along and, as you said, the two of them are getting together.

During this excerpt, the teacher signals in two ways that the students are to analyze or interpret the story: by reminding them of her statement about reading at different levels of meaning and by asking a question about the author's intention. A student responds with what appears to be an appropriate answer, but the teacher then signals that it is not the preferred answer by saying, "Why else might he have included that?" Another two students offer responses that are accepted by the teacher ("OK. Yeah"; "A companion or a friend"), yet it is the teacher who finally provides the complete preferred interpretation — the contrast of cultures of the white man and the Indian. In short, the teacher is doing the interpreting with some help from the students. Although she appeared to accept the interpretations of the students, she ends with her own, preferred interpretation.

In fact, the teacher herself was frustrated with this kind of literature discussion and it was, in part, because of this frustration that she was interested in working with us in incorporating drama into her literature curriculum. She felt there was a wall between herself and the students during classroom discussions of literature in which she realized that she was talking at, instead of with, the students; therefore, she wanted to try more creative techniques (cf. Cahill, 1989).

What this excerpt also illustrates is that while it is assumed that questions function in classrooms to build student knowledge, it is often the case that they actually can limit students' opportunities to analyze and interpret what they read or encounter (Rogers, Green and Nussbaum, 1990). In the excerpt above, as in many literature classrooms, student learning is compromised by teacher questioning, and there is little room for students to engage with the story personally, build their own arguments and responses, and explore their own interpretations.

These patterns of talk are not easy to change. In his introduction to a book on talk and learning, Rubin (1990) suggested that all the authors in the book call for more opportunities for students to talk in ways that allow them to express their own feelings and thoughts and to negotiate and build their own learning communities. Yet, the saying "Old ways die hard" is particularly true in classrooms. As teachers, we receive the bulk of our training by sitting through twelve or more years of our own schooling. What we learn there is "school talk," and that is what we tend to take with us back into our own classrooms.

In order to develop more student-centered interpretive communities in English classrooms, two things must be accomplished. First, we need to realize that classroom talk is more than idle chat or simply a form of reiteration of what one already knows; that talk is real classroom work, just as reading or writing are. We also need to realize that talk will be important in achieving success in classroom activities as well as being of enormous significance in the world outside school. Students often display differing degrees of ability to initiate and maintain conversations, and to take turns. They also exhibit differing competencies in being able to focus their attention, discriminate among ideas, and follow narrative or trains of argument while listening. These skills, essential for success in the world outside school, are seldom practiced, developed, or refined in classrooms where quiet, or mere reiteration, is the goal.

The second thing to be accomplished is to develop classroom contexts and frameworks to support the kind of talk that is purposeful and promotes exploration, interpretation, collaboration, and negotiation. Drama is an obvious, but too often neglected, way to promote, maintain, and structure this kind of talk.

## DRAMA AND CLASSROOM LANGUAGE

Language is at the heart of drama, whether on stage or improvised in the classroom. It is the means by which the drama is realized. The kind of talk that occurs in improvised drama is not school talk; nor is it merely social. It is precise and purposeful because it is generative. Dramatic worlds that arise through improvised drama are created, sustained, and developed through encounters and interactions, and particularly the verbal interactions of the participants. These interactions demand an alertness, a quality of listening, a verbal resourcefulness, and an active response. To engage in a form of behavior that demands an instant reading of and thoughtful response to a complex social situation requires a quality of engagement and concentration too rarely seen in the classroom. Both listening and talking skills of a high order are a necessary component of drama.

According to B.J.Wagner, the teacher's goal in improvisational drama is to set up a situation that allows for maximum student initiative. The role player must operate on at least a tacit understanding of the other person's world view.

> Through improvised drama, students can build social skills and become more sensitive listeners and more apt and mature conversationalists. They also grow in their capacity to send and receive increasingly complex and mature verbal messages effectively, independently, creatively, and symbolically. (Wagner, 1990)

Several studies have supported the claim that language use becomes broader and more complex and sophisticated during classroom drama activities (Felton, Little, Parsons and Schaffner, 1984; Booth, 1987; Carroll, 1980). For instance, Felton et al. (1984) found that drama provides opportunities for children to use language for a wider variety of purposes than is typical in classrooms. They found that during drama activities there was a higher incidence of interactional and expressive talk as compared to the high incidence of informational talk in classrooms normally. Informational talk, as they describe it, is chronological and concrete. Interactional talk focuses on people (rather than things), and expressive language is concerned with the feeling and thinking that are brought to bear on the drama problem.

The use of drama in literature classrooms also enables teachers and students to shed, at least momentarily, the practices associated with school talk in favor of the real talk that takes place outside classrooms. As Ken Byron (1986) observes, drama is a powerful tool for developing language because the classroom context is temporarily suspended in favor of new contexts, new roles, and new relationships:

> Those new contexts, roles, and relationships can make very different language demands on us from those of the real classroom, so new possibilities for language use and development are opened up . . . One of the important

features of the shift to an 'as if' context is that it has the potential to change quite significantly the patterns of communication and interaction in a classroom, and the teacher's part in those patterns. (Byron, 1986; pages 117–118)

This is due in part, Byron argues, to the fact that the issue or problem to be dealt with in drama becomes important in and of itself (rather than a problem set by the teacher for the students). When the issue or problem is encountered in the dramatic world, embodied in the roles and situations that arise, it acquires a personal significance for students. In the next section we will explore how these dramatic worlds arise in the classroom.

## CREATING POSSIBLE WORLDS THROUGH DRAMA

Patrice Pavis (1982) has usefully defined a dramatic text as that which lends itself to a fiction and is capable of being translated into a possible or "as if" world. The literary texts that students encounter in schools are fictions and are also capable of evoking possible worlds. However, in many English classrooms, students are required to respond to the fictional world of the text from a distance. Through using drama, this distance can be circumvented. Students are invited to enter, experience, and explore the imagined world. Their responses will no longer be entirely mediated by the teacher questioning but will be modified, extended, and enlarged by the group reaction to the fictional world of the text. Michael Benton (1979) has characterized the reader as not just an interpreter but also a performer, "who builds a mental stage and fills it with the people, scenes and events that the text offers him." When drama is one of the strategies offered in the classroom, readers are invited to transform the classroom into this "mental stage." They may appropriate the actual space of the classroom and transform it, as the playwright does the stage, into a new dramatic world, an alternate reality, but one that is constrained and circumscribed by the features of the literary text.

To create and enter this world does not necessarily require theater skills on the part of the teacher or students. Dramatic skills are based on students' natural ability to engage in make-believe, an ability that in younger children has a natural source in play but which in older students may have atrophied or been laid aside with other "childish" things. Such skills will need to be recalled and not just permitted but actively fostered through frequent and purposeful opportunities for their exercise. Play is characterized by a level of engagement, absorption, and concentration that many teachers would be glad to see in their students' work but which they rarely achieve. As the teacher in our study said:

> My students and I already had everything we needed to put this new method into effect — we had each other. The awesome ability to imagine, coupled with willingness to try something new, were probably the two key ingredients in putting drama activities to work in the classroom.

## *MULTIPLE WORLDS: DRAMA, LITERATURE, AND PERSONAL RESPONSE*

In encountering literary texts though drama, the result is a complex interpenetration of alternate worlds. First, the world of original text, which will exercise control over the dramatic worlds that grow from it. It operates as a "pre-text," whose existence is the reason or excuse for the drama and whose function is to set in motion the weaving of the new dramatic text, which will be generated in improvisation (O'Neill, 1991). Through the ages, playwrights from Aeschylus and Shakespeare to Arthur Miller and Tom Stoppard have used pre-texts as the basis for their work, finding them in myth, legend, history, and other playwrights' efforts. Many avant-garde ensembles base their performances on 'pre-texts' rather than on conventional play scripts. In the classroom, the novel, play, or poem that is the reason for using drama becomes the pre-text that will define the nature and limits of the world that arises from it and will help to frame the participants in appropriate roles in relation to the action. At the same time that it opens up certain expectations and possibilities, it excludes others.

The second world is the parallel drama world created in response to the literary text. It will share *some* significant features with the world of the text but may expand some and overlook others. The characters that inhabit this world may not appear in the original text, and the events and encounters that occur may have no exact parallel. But the drama world will illuminate the original and, above all, give students access to it. The keys that unlock the doors of this second world are buried in the original and can be discovered through a number of active and transferrable strategies.

The final world that infiltrates the classroom as a result of using drama is the personal world of the students, which emerges in the encounter of the literary and dramatic worlds and is validated by the exploratory and improvisational mode. Sometimes this personal world will be embedded in the dramatic world; sometimes it will surface consciously and be the focus of attention; sometimes it will appear in written responses. The active and creative nature of the drama world invites both a group and a personal response and validates these offerings.

As students enter first the world of the literary text and then the world of the drama, they are also able to bring, and indeed are encouraged to bring, their personal understandings. When students are able to keep some part of themselves in the interpretive process, they are more likely to participate in that process (Rogers, 1991). This process is akin to what Rosenblatt (1978) has described as the "lived through" experience of a literary transaction. It is from this transaction that a poem, and thus meaning, is created. The students are able to participate in an immediate and tangible experience of the drama "text." It is this tangible quality that makes these activities so available to students and so useful to the teacher and that can make a bridge between the abstraction of the written word and students' understandings.

In dramatic worlds, students construct and explore images, roles, ideas, and situations. They learn to manipulate language in order to bring into being people, places, and events that do not exist. They put their private understandings into a public form and give shape to ideas, feelings, and attitudes that might otherwise remain wholly private and unavailable. Students then reflect on these experiences to form their own interpretations (Edmiston, 1991). As Dorothy Heathcote has observed:

> reflective processes . . . in the end are what we are trying to develop in all our teaching. Without the development of the power of reflection we have very little. It is reflection that permits the storing of knowledge, the recalling of the power of feeling, and memory of past feelings. (Johnson and O'Neill, p. 97)

## CREATING MULTIPLE WORLDS IN THE CLASSROOM

The example of using drama to promote literary response and interpretation that follows is taken from our collaborative work with one teacher and her ninth-grade literature classes. As was mentioned above, the teacher was somewhat discouraged with typical classroom discussions of literature and was excited about using drama to promote literary understanding. At the time, she had been an English teacher for 15 years and was completing a master's degree. She is considered by colleagues and administrators to be an excellent teacher. We worked with all four of her English classes in a suburban high school near a large midwestern city. The classes were comprised of students with a range of abilities, the middle stream of students in their school. The teacher had planned three literature units based on the literature anthology selections: one unit on Edgar Allan Poe, another on *To Kill A Mockingbird* (Lee, 1965), and a third one on *When the Legends Die* (Borland, 1963).

Our purpose as researchers was to explore the use of dramatic activities as a means of encouraging students to participate in the literary interpretive process in more direct and engaging ways. We felt that drama would encourage students to become more involved with the literature to be studied and therefore be more likely to reflect on or interpret the works. We also hypothesized that this would affect the use of language — the quality of talk — in the classroom; that is, concomitant with a change of involvement comes a change of language structures and interactions. When students understand that texts are "representations of worlds waiting to be explored, challenged, and even improved upon" (Wells, 1991), they may be motivated to become active participants in the search for understanding that is implicit in the task of interpretation.

In doing drama with the ninth-grade students on *When the Legends Die*, the story discussed above, we found that the students' responses could be seen in terms of their exploration of three distinct but interpenetrating worlds: the world of the original text; the dramatic world that developed in relation to that text; and their own personal worlds, which remained a touchstone for the truth of their experience in the imagined worlds of text and drama.

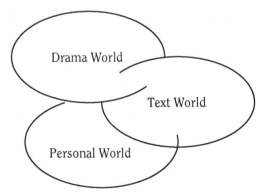

When we began, the teacher had some fears that the character of the Indian boy would present difficulties for the students:

> We read so many books that cast students in a different place and time, *To Kill A Mockingbird*, *Lord Of the Flies*, *When the Legends Die* — the story of an Indian who is living in a white man's world. Without the quality of empathy, I don't know how students can begin to understand the character. That's where the drama activities really, I think, made a big difference for my students, because it helped me to get in touch with the fact that in the course of a discussion I am talking *at* the students. They were not picking up on what the characters were feeling. I wanted to say, "Let's get in groups and do some drama to get in touch with what these characters are feeling, then we'll get back and talk about this question. But until you feel what they're feeling there is no sense in our trying to discuss the plot. How can I get to C if I haven't got to A and B?; and the A and B was getting in touch with what the characters are feeling."

The world that is evoked by the story of *When the Legends Die* is one of alienation and loss — the loss of parents, habitat, culture, and sense of identity — things that had previously been held dear. The challenge is to find a way of giving the students access to this apparently remote and unfamiliar world through a dramatic frame that is familiar to them — that of school.

In setting up dramatic activities for the students we were essentially reframing them in relation to the story. As Heathcote puts it:

> I take it as a general rule that people . . . become involved at a caring and urgently involved level if they are placed in a quite specific relationship with the action, because this brings with it inevitably the responsibility and, more particularly, the viewpoint which gets them into effective involvement. (Johnson & O'Neill, 1984, p.168)

Our objective in drama was to provide another way of looking at the character of Bear's Brother so that the students could come closer to a realization of the implications for the protagonist in adapting to a modern way of life. We wanted to move them from their student frame that is usually low status and relatively powerless in relation to the teacher's power in order to influence the classroom interactions. But we were also working from within the limitations of the students' limited knowledge of and response to the text.

We made the decision to find an oblique way of entering the world of the text — not as characters directly mentioned but as people who might encounter students of this kind. The drama world was introduced by one of us in role, as principal of a frontier school, welcoming potential teachers to the school.

*T:*       I'm very glad to welcome you here today to the frontier school board. I must say I'm very impressed to see so many young people coming into the teaching profession and especially young people like yourselves interested in working under the rather difficult conditions we face here . . . I have to warn you that if you want to work with these young people it will take a great deal of dedication, a great deal of hard work, and sometimes it's very frustrating. These young people coming here, they have no sense of civilization.

The drama world that is coming into being has much in common at this point with the world of the text. The students, as prospective teachers, began to question the principal.

*S:*       Why did you take these children in, I mean why did you . . . why do you want them to be more civilized . . . why don't you let them be like they want to?

*T:*       Oh, well, like they want to . . . I mean what would that be like? They would be living in shacks on the mountains. They would be unclean. They would be living like wild animals.

*S:*       That would be the way they want to live. That would be the way they were brought up to live.

*T:*       But for our purposes, the civilized ones . . . We are here to educate them. We are here to give them a proper religion.

*S:*       That's your education.

*T:*       They believe in spirits. They believe in all kinds of weird stuff.

*S:*       That's your education. They already have their type of education and type of religion.

*T:*       Yes, but it's not our type and we want them to be more like us.

*S:*       Why?

*T:*       Well, we want them to be citizens of the United States, for instance. We want them to be good citizens.

Here, the students are directly challenging the kind of authority represented by the principal. They are already seeing the principal's perspective as inimical to that of Bear's Brother. The world of the text is embodied in the role of the principal, and although the students are operating at a simple level of role at this point, their frame as visitors and potential teachers allows them to question, challenge, and contradict the teacher.

When the teacher-in-role stopped the dramatic interaction, there was an opportunity for the students to reflect as themselves on what had taken place. The teacher was careful to distance herself from the attitudes of the role she had been playing as principal.

*T:*   Let's stop the drama for a minute. What did you think of the person I was being?

*S:*   Very prejudiced. Very pushy. Not caring towards other people's feelings. Not very American.

*T:*   Not very American. OK. You (indicating a student and gesturing) went like that once. Did you feel like hitting me?

*S:*   Yeah.

*T:*   You did?

*S:*   Several times.

*T:*   Several times . . . . What was there about me that made you so angry?

*S:*   Like somebody coming up to me and telling me that ever since I've been alive I've done wrong and I'm doing wrong . . . I'd laugh in their face.

*T:*   I can see that you felt like that . . . Was the person I was pretending to be a believable character?

*S:*   Yes.

*T:*   Have you ever met anybody like that?

*Ss:*  Yes. Yes.

Here, the fact that the drama world is in a school setting, perhaps the social setting with which the students are most familiar at this point in their lives, allows the students to use their own knowledge and experience to make connections to the distant world of the text.

After this reflection outside the drama, students were invited to choose to be either the prospective teachers or one of the Native American students at the school. They talked quietly together, but it was noticeable that several of the students began to role-play as Indians with greater commitment. In role as principal once more, the teacher spoke to the prospective teachers.

*T:*   Now do you have any further questions for me, or would you like to tell me how you found the visit? Do speak freely.

S:      I understand their ways. I mean, I would be upset if someone came and took my ways away from me. So I understand where they're coming from.

S:      And you guys don't seem to treat them very well, either.

T:      Well, what do you mean? How would you change that?

S:      I don't know. You guys treat them like they're some different species. I mean different but —

S:      They seem unhappy.

T:      Unhappy? Did you all find that they were unhappy?

Ss:     Yeah. Yeah. Yeah.

T:      Of course, you can't always trust what they say.

S:      That's true.

S:      You can see it in their faces.

T:      You can see it in their faces? What do you mean by that exactly?

S:      Well, like when you're talking to them, communicating with them, you can tell whether they're telling the truth or if they're lying.

T:      Oh, I see. That's a very useful gift for a teacher, of course you know.

S:      They also said you teachers came and took them.

S:      Yeah, in the fields . . .

S:      Came and took them.

This session, where the students grew increasingly critical of the school's policy toward the Indian children, was interrupted by one boy, who had begun to role-play at a new level of engagement.

S:      You took our homes. You expect us to adapt to your ways, why don't you adapt to ours? Our homes. Our land. Tell us we have to change — to go your ways.

T:      Are you expecting me to go to your lodges? To your mountains?

S:      This is our land. You came here . . . stole it.

T:      Well, I'm afraid I don't quite agree with that . . . I mean . . .

S:      How are you going to . . .

T:      We made treaties with your people. All the time.

S:      And broke them. Broke them. You lied. White man lied.

*T:*      I don't pretend to be a politician, I'm just a teacher. I'm doing the best I can in difficult circumstances.

*S:*      It was our world first. You never owned it. You took it from us.

*S:*      We were here first.

What became apparent during this dramatic activity was an increase in the strength of role identification, which began to spread from one student to others in the group. A distinctive speech style began to emerge, as well as a tight and dramatic discourse structured by the dramatic encounter, the interpersonal dimension, and the need to try to solve the problem represented by the school administrator.

Both the structure and the interactions of the language changed during this dramatic activity. The students asked questions, challenged the teacher-in-role, and expressed their own feelings. The teacher often took the lead from the students as when the students insisted that the Indian students in the agency school were unhappy. In these examples, there is no longer a typical question, answer, evaluation cycle as was illustrated by the example presented at the beginning of the chapter; instead, the dialogue patterns are more like those found in conversations outside the classroom and even, at moments, come to resemble the language of the theater.

When the language structures and interaction patterns change, so does the content of what is being said. In both the discussion presented at the beginning of the chapter and in the dramatic activities, the same themes were being explored, yet in the drama activities there is personal engagement and commitment and a sense of urgency that is different from the detached tone of the first discussion. The students have been given a standpoint from which to view the text and the power to put their feelings into words. They have achieved one of the goals of literary work, which, according to Barthes (1975), is to make the reader no longer a consumer but a producer of text.

## BUILDING BRIDGES BETWEEN LITERATURE AND DRAMA

There are several basic strategies that can be readily employed in the classroom to make the students producers of text, and that can be transferred to different kinds of literature. They are all intended to provide opportunities to explore the text through the retelling, extension, elaboration, or enactment of events in the original text, as well as the exploration of individual characters' motives and behavior.

The first strategy is *teacher-in-role* as illustrated by the teacher taking on the role of principal in the example above. The teacher-in-role involves a "simple change in attitude to a stance that will generate the working through of the problem inherent in the selected task" (Heathcote and Herbert, 1985). In role, "the teacher can extend and challenge the students, make what is happening more significant, and elevate it to a higher plane" (O'Neill, Lambert, Linnell & Warr-Wood, 1976).

Gavin Bolton, whose analyses of drama in education have done much to clarify both its nature and purpose, claims that the practice of teacher-in-role challenges our very conception of teaching. He describes it both as a strategy for learning and a significant principle of teaching, which uniquely inverts the assumptions underlying the traditional pedagogical context:

> The teacher-in-role has power but it is not of the conventional kind. It carries within it its opposite: a potential for being rendered powerless . . . . The power relationship between pupils and teacher within the drama is tacitly perceived as negotiable. (Bolton, 1988)

This strategy, then, enables the teacher simultaneously to frame and facilitate the drama and to transfer power to the students.

The second strategy, *interviewing*, can be carried out with students working in pairs or small groups and requires commitment and interaction but no presentational skills. One of the students interviews the other but from a particular viewpoint, as the visiting teachers interviewed the native students in the frontier school. Other possibilities might be interviews with:

- Characters in the text, particularly minor characters;
- An invented person who might know a major character in the text and who might have a particular attitude to the events that take place;
- Invented characters not specifically described in the original text but whose presence may be deduced as in the example above.

It will be important for the interviewer to frame the interview with a particular attitude or relationship to the interviewee. A detective, an anthropologist, an historian, a social worker, a psychiatrist may all ask questions, but each will bring a particular professional concern to the task and an attitude to the subject of the interview.

A third useful strategy is that in which a still image, or *tableau*, is created by the students, working in small groups. In devising these images, the students use their own bodies to create a significant moment in the story, an abstract idea, or a mental state. This strategy requires the students to become involved physically, but does not demand any great theater skills. The images that are created may be naturalistic (for example, pictures for an illustrated edition of *When the Legends Die*) or more abstract (for example, an image of Bear's Brother torn between two worlds). In composing these images, students are using their knowledge and understanding of the text to engage in a highly selective, economical, and controlled form of expression that requires to be read and interpreted by the rest of the class. Tableaux can be used to discover and display what the students already know about a topic or theme; for example, they might create a series of tableaux to show what they understand of the religious beliefs of Native Americans, to develop a chronology of significant moments in the story, or to predict outcomes.

A fourth and particularly useful strategy, one that is essentially dramatic, is to set up an *inquiry* about events in the book. The question that can be asked about many texts is "Who's to blame?" In order to answer this question, it may be necessary to put a character or a community on trial, to establish a tribunal or a people's court, or, where any misdeeds have remained secret, to bring a character before the court of conscience. In the case of Bear's Brother, it might be necessary to arraign the United States government in front of some kind of international, supernatural, or cosmic court — perhaps the representatives of all the nations that were swept away by the white man — for the treatment that was meted out to Native Americans.

It may be possible to bring these strategies together by adopting a *media frame* as a context for the dramatic activities. Many texts have an explicit or implied public dimension that would lend itself to this approach. Both television and film use conventions and language with which young people are familiar and which they can easily reproduce. Television or radio news programs, documentaries, or talk shows can be set up, with interviews as a crucial element. Tableaux can be used to provide visual evidence or illustrate the issue that has been raised. A documentary on the treatment of Native Americans might focus on an inquiry into continuing discrimination; a television biography of Bear's Brother might include interviews with those who knew him at different stages of his life and could be illustrated by a number of tableaux. Each of these tasks requires a thorough knowledge of the text, and students would discover both what they knew and didn't know or understand.

One of the most significant outcomes of using drama approaches in the classroom is the effect such activities have on the students' writing. Frequently, students bring the same quality of interest and commitment and the same sense of style displayed in the drama activities to their writing. The following reports, written in appropriately professional language, were written by students in role as teachers in the school.

School Report

Student: Thomas Black Bear    Subject: Basketry

Thomas is a pleasure to have in class. He usually listens in class, although I frequently find him gazing out the window, as if he is looking for something. He sets himself apart from the other students and makes no attempts to have conversations with anyone in the class. However, his work in the class is unlike anything I have seen before. He won't use the materials I give him but uses willow stems instead. His fingers are extremely dexterous, and all his work is of very high quality. I'm not sure about any of his other classes, but Tom has a born-in skill for basketweaving. His ability is uncanny, and his work is superior to mine.

English Interim Report: Bear's Brother (Thomas)

Thomas is a very disruptive child. He rarely pays attention in class and spends all his time staring at a window. He insists the subjects taught here are of no use to him. He is also very reckless. He picks fights and interprets things the wrong way. He can't control his temper; he's like a savage who has no rules to live by. The school faculty has tried to discipline him, but, unfortunately, our attempts have ended in failure. I don't know what to do.

These students have taken a new attitude to the text. In the first example, not only has the student projected into the feelings of the young Indian boy but also into those of the teacher. In the second example, the student has carefully noted Bear's Brother's behaviors and imagined how a less sensitive teacher may have responded. These texts demonstrate the students' understanding of the original text and both extend and illuminate those understandings. Writing in role allows the students an accessible route to new linguistic registers, a grasp of genre, an increased awareness of audience, and a sense of themselves as writers as well as readers.

## CONCLUSION

By incorporating drama into the English curriculum, new worlds are created in the classroom that intersect to foster new knowledge and new understandings of literary works. In order to even participate in drama, students are encouraged to draw on their own experiences and their understanding of the literary texts to create and enter new worlds. It is this immediacy of experience that enables students to question, challenge, and reflect on issues, dilemmas, and events suggested by the literary pretext. As Ken Byron (1986) notes, "[A] paradox about drama . . . is that its strength resides both in its *concreteness* and in its *power to encourage abstraction*" (p. 127).

In the new worlds created by drama, meanings are negotiated rather than predetermined by the text or by the teacher so that the range of language use is broadened. The teacher in our study felt that the benefits of the drama activities spilled over into her literature discussions:

> Going into drama has given me a chance to know when I'm in a dead-end literature discussion, when I'm doing too much talking at the kids. I'm in tune to that now. And I realize the importance of getting kids engaged in their reading. I hadn't thought about that.

The teacher also felt that drama improved her relationship with the students:

> It wasn't until we had gotten into some of the dramatic activities that I felt as though they saw me as a person who was on their side. It really helped that way. I always felt cast in this role — teacher and students, here's the wall between us. I wasn't happy with it, and I don't think they were happy with it. But we didn't know how to get rid of the wall. And when we started doing the activities in drama, the wall started to come down a little bit.

Her comment is reminiscent of Dorothy Heathcote's observation that when you bring drama to a classroom, it's not what you know that is important but what you are.

The students also were very positive about their work with drama. As one student said, "I like the dramatic activities because all through school, books were explained pretty much by lecture. I like to think that I enjoyed the dramatic activities because they made literature walk and talk."

Drama, then, encourages an interactive and dynamic kind of classroom participation, where we can encounter the "dreams, desires, voices and utopian longings of our students" and where "a qualitatively better world can be both imagined and struggled for . . . " (McLaren, 1986). By incorporating drama into the English classroom, tired interaction patterns can be replaced with lively and engaging dialogues, and students can be empowered to question, challenge, and reflect on the themes of literary works.

## END NOTES

1. Funds for this project were provided by a grant from the National Council of Teachers of English Research Foundation, with additional support provided by The Ohio State University Small Grants program.

## REFERENCES

Barnes, D. (1976). *From communication to curriculum*. New York Penguin Books.

Barthes, R. (1975). *S/z: An essay*. New York: Hill and Wang.

Benton, M. (1979). Children's responses to stories. *Children's Literature in Education 10*(2) p. 68–86.

Bolton, G. (1988). Drama as Art. *Drama Broadsheet 5* (3).

Booth, D. (1987). *Drama words*, Toronto: Language Study Centre.

Borland, H. (1963). *When the legends die*. New York: Lippincott.

Byron, K. (1986). *Drama in the English classroom*. New York: Methuen.

Cahill, M. (1989). Using drama and role-play in a ninth-grade English class. *Literacy Matters, 1*(2), Spring, p. 3–8.

Carroll, S. (1980). *The treatment of Dr. Lister: A language approach to drama in education*. Bathurst, Australia: Mitchell College of Advanced Education.

Cazden, C. (1988). *Classroom discourse: The language of teaching and learning*, Portsmouth, NH: Heinemann.

Edmiston, B. (1991). What have you travelled? A teacher-researcher study of structuring drama for reflection and learning. Unpublished doctoral dissertation, The Ohio State University.

Edwards, A.D. & Furlong, V.J. (1978). *The language of teaching*. London: Heinemann.

Erickson, F. and Schultz (1981). When is a context? Some issues and methods in the analysis of social competence. In J.C. Green & C. Wallat (Eds.). *Ethnography and language in educational settings*, Norwood, NJ: Ablex, pp. 147–160.

Felton, M., Little, G., Parsons, B. & Schaffner, M. (1984). *Drama, language and learning*. NADIE Paper, No. 1, Australia: National Association for Drama in Education.

Green, J. (1983). Research on teaching as a linguistic process: A state of the art. In E. Gordon (Ed.), *Review of Research in Education* (10) Washington, D.C.: American Educational Research Assoc., 151–252.

Green, J. & Harker, J. (1982). Gaining access to learning: Conversational, social, and cognitive demands of group participation. In L.C. Wilkinson (Ed.), *Communicating in the classroom*. New York: Academic Press, p. 185–222.

Gumperz, J. (1986). Interactive sociolinguistics in the study of schooling. In J. Cook-Gumperz (Ed.), The social construction of literacy. Cambridge University Press, p. 45–68.

Gumperz, J. (1981). Conversational inference and classroom learning. In J.C. Green & C. Wallat (Eds.), *Ethnography and language in educational settings*, Norwood, NJ: Ablex, pp. 3–23.

Halliday, M. (1978). *Language as a social semiotic: The social interpretation of language and meaning*. Baltimore, MD: University Park Press.

Heathcote, D. & Herbert, P. (1985). A drama of learning: Mantle of the expert. *Theory into Practice*, 24 (3), pp. 173–180.

Hymes, D. (1974). *Foundations in sociolinguistics*. Philadelphia: University of Pennsylvania Press.

Hynds, S. & Rubin, D. (Eds.) (1990). *Perspectives on talk and learning*. Urbana, IL: National Council of Teachers of English.

Johnson, L. & O'Neill, C. (1984). *Dorothy Heathcote: Collected writings on education and drama*. London: Hutchinson.

Lee, H. (1960). *To kill a mockingbird*. Philadelphia: Lippincott.

Lindberg, (1986). Coming to words: Writing as a process and the reading of literature In Newkirk, T. (Ed.) *Only connect: Uniting reading and writing*. Portsmouth, NH: Heinemann.

Marshall, J.D. (1987). The effects of writing on students' understanding of literary texts. *Research in the Teaching of English, 21* (1), 30–63.

Marshall, J.D. (1989). *Patterns of discourse in classroom discussions of literature*. Report #29, Center for the Learning and Teaching of Literature, State University of New York at Albany.

McLaren, P. (1986). *Life in schools*. New York: Longman.

Mehan, H. (1979). "What time is it, Denise?": Asking known information questions in classroom discourse. *Theory into Practice, 28*, (4), p. 285–294.

O'Neill, C. (1991). Structure and spontaneity: Improvisation in theatre and education. Unpublished dissertation, Exeter University.

O'Neill, C. Lambert, A., Linnell, R. & Warr-Wood, J. (1976). *Drama guidelines*. London: Heinemann.

Pavis, P. (1982). *Languages of the stage: Essays in the semiology of the theater*. New York: Performing Arts Journal Publications.

Rogers, T. (1991). Students as literary critics: The interpretive experiences, beliefs and processes of ninth grade students, *Journal of Reading Behavior, (23)* 4, p. 391–424.

Rogers, T., Green, J.L. & Nussbaum, N. (1990). Asking questions about questions. In S. Hynds & D. Rubin, (Eds.) *Perspectives on talk and learning*. Urbana, IL: National Council of Teachers of English.

Rosenblatt, L. (1978). *The reader, the text, the poem*. Carbondale, IL: Southern Illinois University Press.

Rubin, D. (1990). Introduction. In Hynds, S., & Rubin, D. (Eds.), *Perspectives on Talk and Learning*. Urbana, IL: NCTE.

Saville-Troike, M. (1982). *The ethnography of communication*. Oxford: Basil Blackwell.

Sinclair, J. & Coulthard, R. (1975). *Towards an analysis of discourse: The English used by teachers and pupils*. London: Oxford University Press.

Wagner, B.J. (1990). Dramatic improvisation in the classroom. In D Rubin. and Hynds, S. (Eds.) *Perspectives on talk and learning*. Urbana, IL: National Council of Teachers of English.

Wells, G. (1986). *The meaning makers: Children learning language and using language to learn*. Portsmouth, NH: Heinemann.

Wells, G. (1991). Talk about text: Where literacy is learned and taught. In D. Booth and C. Thomley-Hall (Eds.). *The talk curriculum*. Portsmouth, NH: Heinemann.

# CHAPTER FIVE

# From Discourse Communities to Interpretive Communities

## A Study of Ninth-Grade Literature Instruction

♣ ♣ ♣

### Martin Nystrand and Adam Gamoran

## INTRODUCTION: THE CONTEXT OF LITERACY ACQUISITION

Literacy flourishes best in social contexts where literacy has cultural currency. In research on preschool (emergent) literacy, for example, many studies have documented the indirect effects of a rich home discourse environment on developing literacy skills. These studies have examined (1) the role of bedtime stories in the emergent literacy of young children (Heath, 1980); (2) the contexts in which preschoolers explore interests in writing and reading (e.g., Bissex, 1980; Gundlach, 1982; Scollon & Scollon, 1979; Teale & Sulzby, 1986); (3) the traditions and messages that parents transmit to their children about the uses of print (Heath, 1983); and (4) the game interactions of parents and children (Wertsch & Hickmann, 1987). These many studies affirm that, in order to track and understand the path of writing development in individual children, it is not enough to track the evolution of written forms, norms, and textual features. Beyond these, researchers must focus more comprehensively on students' interactions with others; which is to say, on the social context of their learning, which sanctions their reading and writing and consequently promotes values and expectations that are essential to literacy.

We believe that academic achievement and student learning work analogously and that the instructional ethos of individual classrooms plays a key role in students' learning by conditioning the kinds of interactions that occur between teachers and students and among peers. In our analysis, we view classrooms as *discourse communities*, examining the ways that instructional discourse affects student achievement in both eighth and ninth grade literature classes. We find that the oral and written interactions of teachers and students play an important role in both the constitution of the community itself and the negotiation of what students learn.

## CLASSROOMS AS DISCOURSE COMMUNITIES

Not all social groups are communities. Community involves membership and regular interaction concerning interests common to the members. This is why neighborhoods are more likely to be communities than large cities. Communities afford members the regular opportunity for self-expression; they take seriously each member's ideas.

We find that some classes we have studied are more community-like than others and that the extent to which they are so organized helps students to learn. We find, for example, that effective teachers of literature skillfully elicit sustained language from their students — in both talk and writing. In sharp contrast to teachers who rely on lecture, worksheets, and recitation, these teachers involve their students in discussions and have them write regularly and extensively. They ask them to write about what they have read, and they discuss what they have read as well as what they have written. In responding to student writing, they read and respond not just as examiners but also as trusted adults (cf. Britton et al., 1975).

Students in these classes quickly learn that what they think and say matters. Literature is not, for example, just one more domain of information to master and remember in these classes; these teachers skillfully help their students relate their readings to their own experience. In talking about literature, moreover, these teachers ask many questions without first prespecifying the answers (we call such questions *authentic*); they do not ask just *test questions*, which are characteristic of recitation. An important effect of these authentic questions is to promote ownership by opening the floor to student ideas. The teachers also show students that they take them seriously by following up on many of their answers, something linguists call *uptake* (i.e., the incorporation of a previous student answer into a subsequent question [Collins, 1982]). Authentic questions and uptake are two discourse features we discovered that seem to transform classes into communities. The purpose of our study was to examine the effect of such a transformation on student achievement.

## STUDY DESIGN

To examine the role of discourse in constituting classroom communities and to investigate their effects on student learning, we studied eighth and ninth grade English instruction in eight Midwestern communities. Six were public school districts: Three were in small-town or rural areas, with one junior high and one high school apiece; one was suburban, with three middle schools and one high school; and two were urban, adding five middle and three high schools to our sample. The other two communities contained Catholic high schools that drew students from a number of urban and suburban K–8 feeder schools. Sixteen middle schools, which fed into nine high schools, participated in the study. We visited the eighth grade classes during 1987–88 and the ninth grade classes during 1988–89. In both the eighth and ninth grade studies, more than 1,100 students completed tests and questionnaires in both fall and spring, and the teachers responded to questionnaires and interviews about classroom activities. Also in both studies, each class was visited four times by a trained observer, twice during fall semester and twice during spring semester. On these occasions, the observer noted the time spent in different kinds of activities — such as lecture, seatwork, discussion, and so on — and recorded and coded all teacher and student questions for a variety of items noted below. In the ninth grade study, we observed 224 sessions of 52 different classes and coded 11,043 questions. Further details on data collection, as well as results of the eighth grade study, summarized above, are provided elsewhere (Nystrand and Gamoran, 1991b).

## KEY FEATURES OF INSTRUCTIONAL DISCOURSE

As Mehan (1979) notes, most classroom discourse takes the form of recitation in which the teacher asks a question, a student responds, and the teacher evaluates the answer. Typically teachers employ recitation to review previously learned material, such as homework, and to test informally the extent of their mastery of it. Hence, most teacher questions during recitations seek to elicit student reports (recitals) of essential information. The following transcript, in which a ninth grade English teacher leads his class in a review of homework and study questions concerning Book I of *The Iliad*, is typical:

*Teacher:*    According to the poet, what is the subject of *The Iliad*?

*Student:*    Achilles' anger.

*Teacher:*    Where does the action of the first part of 'Book 1' take place when we enter the story?

*Student:*    On the Achean ship?

*Teacher:*    Well, they're not on their ships. Let's see if we can give you a little diagram . . .

*Student:*    Was it on the shore?

*Teacher:*    Yes, it's on the shore. Let's see if we can kind of visualize where everything is here. [proceeds to draw on the board] . . . Remember that Troy is on the coast of Turkey — at the time called Asia Minor — so let's see if we can — okay, this is the scene, and all of the ships are anchored — a thousand ships are anchored here. . . . So the war has been going on now for how long?

*Student:*    Ten years.

*Teacher:*    "Ten years." You have to understand — the battle takes place only during the day time . . . [draws some more on the board] So this is approximately what it looked like. . . . Now the city is immense, much larger probably than what we consider the [our own city]; it could be as large as all of [our own] county.

*Student:*    There was a wall all the way around it?

*Teacher:*    Oh, at least. Consider some of the walled cities of ancient times. . . .

*Student:*    Didn't they put a wall up in Ireland?

*Teacher:*    In Ireland? I'm not familiar with that. . . . So, let's take a look at some of the other questions. . . . What's the story behind the quarrel . . . it deals with Achilles and Briseis and Agamemnon and Chryses and Chryses' daughter, Chryseis, and how Agamemnon takes Briseis away from Achilles to replace the prize, Chryseis, who has gone back to her father. What is the result of the quarrel between Agamemnon and Achilles?

*Student:* He's not going to participate in the battle anymore.

*Teacher:* "He's not going to participate in the battle anymore." What's the common custom of Greek warfare and prizes?

*Student:* That the prizes that they get . . . .

[Recitation continues]

In this excerpt, the teacher rehearses student knowledge, checking to make sure students have understood all the main points. There are right and wrong answers, and if students don't know the correct answers, they guess. One gets the impression here that the teacher has asked these questions before and will ask them again, basically in the same order year after year; the students' responses have little if any effect on this exchange. Information in this lesson goes only one way: from teacher to students.

Now consider a teacher-student exchange from a ninth grade English class studying *The Odyssey*:

Teacher: What does Odysseus do to the guys who eat the [lotus] flower?

*Student:* Drags them back by "main force" and ties them.

*Teacher:* What do they discover?

*Student:* Don't they land on another island — is that the one?

*Teacher:* Actually, they go to two places in this chapter: the Land of the Lotus Eaters and the Cyclops. What does Odysseus want to do [there]?

*Student:* Make friends and get food, provisions. . . .

*Teacher:* Why make friends?

*Student:* What if they can't give it [provisions] to you?

*Teacher:* That's an important point — if they can't or won't; let's wait a minute on that. What does [Odysseus] want to do?

*Student:* He's curious — wants to find out about the Cyclops, but the Cyclops goes against Zeus' laws.

*Teacher:* What would have happened if [Cyclops] had not violated Zeus' hospitality laws?

*Student:* Odysseus' men wouldn't have been killed and Odysseus captured.

*Teacher:* Odysseus is so wise — why didn't he know?

| | |
|---|---|
| *Student:* | When they're going away, how come [Cyclops] is praying to the gods? |
| *Student:* | I thought all the Cyclops didn't believe in the gods. |
| *Teacher:* | They don't, but Odysseus does. He still has to use his own wits — his wisdom — to get himself out of these scrapes, and, in the cave . . . it's interesting why a nonbeliever would pray. Where do we see Odysseus' cleverness in the cave? |

[Discussion continues]

Compared to students in the first transcript, students in this excerpt contribute more of their own ideas to the class, no doubt because their teacher follows up on their contributions by incorporating their answers into her subsequent questions (i.e., uptake), thus expressing expectations not merely for covering the main points of the text but also for interpreting the text coherently. Hence, when a student explains that Odysseus visits the Land of the Lotus Eaters to "make friends and get food, provisions," the teacher asks, "Why make friends?" And when a student notes that "the Cyclops goes against Zeus' laws," the teacher responds by asking, "What would have happened if [Cyclops] had not violated Zeus' hospitality laws?"[1] If the teacher in the first transcript seems to follow a script of preset questions closely — checking off as he goes the points as *he* covers them — the teacher in the second excerpt approaches instruction much as one might engage in conversation (cf. Nystrand and Gamoran, 1991a) and focuses on the points *students* make. This distinction explains why the second transcript is less choppy and more coherent than the first: In the second excerpt, questions are much more prompted by previous responses since the teacher actually interacts with the students. We say that discourse characterized by such interrelatedness shows coherence. Uptake is an example of discourse coherence; so, too, are class sessions that involve discussion of reading assignments and writing assignments that require students to deal with their readings.

More than the first, the course of the second lesson depends on what students say as much as what the teacher has planned. Clearly, what students say counts in this class, and it is consequently no surprise that these students actually say much more than those in the first: The average length of student responses in the first class is about five words whereas the average length of student responses in the second transcript is about nine, almost twice as long. Whereas the first transcript is characterized by short answers and tentative guesses, the second transcript depicts students who are trying out their own ideas and who respond to each other as well as to the teacher. The quality of instructional discourse is consequently higher in this class than in the first.

An example of even higher quality classroom discourse comes from a ninth grade class discussion of *Roll of Thunder, Hear My Cry*. Just prior to this exchange, a student (we shall call him John) has just read his plot summary of Chapter 4 aloud to the class, and the teacher has attempted to write his key points on the board.

| | |
|---|---|
| *Teacher* | [to the class as a whole]: Wow! What do you think about that [referring to John's plot summary]? |
| *Student:* | It was very thorough. |
| *Teacher:* | Yeah, pretty thorough. I had a lot of trouble getting everything down [on the board], and I think I missed the part about trying to boycott. [Reads from the board] " . . . and tries to organize a boycott." Did I get everything down, John, that you said? |
| *John:* | What about the guy who didn't really think these kids were a pest? |
| *Teacher:* | Yeah, okay. What's his name? Do you remember? |
| *John:* | [indicates he can't remember] |
| *Another student:* | Wasn't it Turner? |
| *Teacher:* | Was it Turner? |
| *Students:* | Yes. |
| *Teacher:* | Okay, so Mr. Turner resisted white help. Why? Why would he want to keep shopping at that terrible store? |
| *John:* | There was only one store to buy from because all the other ones were white. |
| *Teacher:* | Well, the Wall Store was white, too. |
| *Another student* | [addressed to John]: Is it Mr. Hollings' store? Is that it? |
| *John:* | No. Here's the reason. They don't get paid till the cotton comes in. But throughout the year they still have to buy stuff — food, clothes, seed, and stuff like that. So the owner of the plantation will sign for what they buy at the store so that throughout the year they can still buy stuff on credit. |

*Teacher*     [writing on board]:  So "he has to have credit in order to buy things, and this store is the only one that will give it to him."

*John:*     [continues to explain]

*Teacher:*     [continues to write on board]

*Another student:*     I was just going to say, 'It was the closest store.'

*Teacher*     [writing on board]: Okay — it's the closest store; it seems to be in the middle of the area; a lot of sharecroppers who don't get paid cash — they get credit at that store — and it's very hard to get credit at other stores. So it's going to be very hard for her to organize that boycott; she needs to exist on credit. Yeah? [nods to another student]

[Discussion continues]

Perhaps the most striking feature of this class is the extent to which John gets the floor. This segment of class discussion closely examines his ideas, and the teacher's role — almost the complete opposite of the teacher in the first transcript — is to take notes and probe his thinking. Rather than evaluating John's responses as right or wrong and then going on to the next question, she warrants their importance by writing his ideas on the board and inviting him to elaborate fully. Virtually all the teacher's questions, moreover, are authentic: She is not looking for particular answers to her questions but rather seeks to be informed, in this case on one student's thinking. Hence, when she asks John, "Why would he want to keep shopping at that terrible store?", she is not simply testing his knowledge but rather drawing out his own thinking. This excerpt displays extensive discourse coherence; the class *discusses* students' *written summaries* of what they have *read*; discourse is piled upon discourse upon discourse.

Compared to the first transcript, the latter two transcripts — and especially the third — illustrate many engaging qualities of high-quality instructional discourse, characterized by extensive interaction between teachers and students and among peers. During question-answer exchanges, for example, the teacher fosters this interaction through uptake and authentic teacher questions, as noted above. These are substantively engaging because they demonstrate to students that their teacher is seriously interested in the development of their own thinking and not just whether they can accurately report information from other sources.

Uptake and authentic teacher questions also contribute to the coherence of instruction by sustaining the examination of topics of inquiry.

Rather than choppily jumping from topic to topic, as in the first excerpt, high-quality classroom discourse promotes reflectiveness because teachers follow up on student responses.

Discussion, the thoughtful and sustained examination of a given topic over a period of time involving substantial contributions and reflections by both teacher and students, is potentially the highest form of classroom discourse. Technically, we define discussion as turntaking among students and teachers that departs from the normal structure of classroom discourse [consisting of (a) a teacher question followed by (b) a student response followed by (c) the teacher's evaluation] by not obligating students to wait for the teacher's evaluation before responding themselves to another student's response, and where their teacher, rather than evaluating a student response, joins in and becomes a conversant. Discussions typically include relatively few questions; most often these questions clarify ideas and information ("By that do you mean?") and are consequently authentic since, rather than quizzing each other, conversants exchange only that information they actually need to know. In addition, discussion displays regular uptake so long as the conversants listen and respond appropriately to each other. Typically discussion comes about during question-answer when a student volunteers an observation (not a question) that substitutes for teacher evaluation. When discussion occurs in the midst of question-and-answer, it transforms recitation into conversation (cf. Nystrand and Gamoran, 1991a) and is, therefore, particularly valuable for promoting reflection.

Teachers can extend such reflection beyond the time constraints of individual lessons, moreover, by asking students to write regularly and extensively on the topics of their studies and discussion. In a study of eighth grade English instruction, Nystrand (1991a) found that effective teachers of literature regularly assign extended pieces of exposition. He also found that frequently completing short-answer exercises degraded overall recall and depth of understanding. This result is consistent with Applebee's (1984) contention that, because writing tends to promote recall of what it focuses on, such "narrow-banded" activities as short-answer exercises are likely to hinder total recall, in other words, helping students to remember trees at the expense of understanding the overall shape of the forest. In addition, it seems likely that, because they elicit cryptic, fragmented discourse, short-answer exercises promote superficial involvement with literature; in so doing, they trivialize students' experiences with literature. All in all, students learn literature best in classroom discourse communities that encourage substantial student response to literature in both classroom interaction and writing.

These various types of teacher-student interaction help explain key features of classrooms as discourse communities. To begin, these three class-rooms illustrate different norms for instructional discourse and for discussing literature. For example, by stressing coverage of main points over depth of interpretation and student thoughtfulness, the first teacher mainly promotes the procedural engagement of students — paying attention in class, regularly completing assignments, and so forth — whereas the other two teachers foster a more substantive engagement with literature. Procedural engagement is a necessary but not sufficient condition for learning.

The teacher in the third class, in particular, recognizes that reading literature, as opposed to exposition, requires the reader to "appropriate" the text (cf. Applebee, 1974; Rosenblatt, 1938) by relating the narrative to her own values and experience. A literary text is fundamentally different from a news report, involving more than information of the sort that is covered adequately through recitation and short-answer study questions concerning who, what, when, where, and why. Because of this, effective literature instruction does more than teach knowledge about literature. More to the point, effective instruction teaches a particular way of reading (Purves, 1991). When we read such nonfictional texts as newspaper and magazine articles, we read for the main point. By contrast, we read novels and short stories aesthetically by "living through" the narrative, savoring "the qualities of the structure ideas, situations, scenes, personalities, emotions, called forth, participating in the tensions, conflicts, and resolutions as they unfold" (Rosenblatt, 1988, p. 5).[2] For these reasons, learning how to read and fully experience literature involves personal response, and it just this process that ample authentic teacher questions tend to promote.

The three teachers promote fundamentally different ways of reading literature. The first teacher emphasizes recall, while the second teacher teaches more indepth understanding. It is the third teacher, however, who enables her students to "live through" the narrative and read aesthetically. If the second class is a discourse community, the third class represents a specialized discourse community — what Stanley Fish (1980) calls an *interpretive community*. The first teacher (and to some extent the second) deals with fiction much as one might nonfiction, as an exercise in processing information and finding the main idea, whereas the third teacher encourages a qualitatively different kind of reading involving personal response. As Purves notes, "a major function of literature education is the development of what one might call preferences, which is to say habits of mind in reading and writing. One must learn to read aesthetically and to switch lenses when one moves from social studies to poetry. . . . [Texts] become literary when a reader chooses to read them as aesthetic objects rather than as documents" (Purves, 1991). The third teacher, more than the second and far more than the first, helps students make this distinction.

The character of these classroom communities is revealed, moreover, by the social roles and interactions the teachers sanction for their students. In the first lesson, the discourse of recitation defines students' roles as passive witnesses to the teacher's performance. By contrast, the discourse features of the latter two classes, including discussion as well as authentic teacher questions and uptake, enable students to become active partners in an unfolding dialogue. Consequently, in each of these classes, student engagement mirrors the extent to which student voices and ideas are allowed and encouraged to contribute to the discourse of the classroom community. Engagement does not occur in a vacuum but rather in classrooms characterized by extensive reciprocity and social interaction approaching conversation between teachers and their students about the subject.

---

## RESULTS FOR ACHIEVEMENT IN NINTH GRADE LITERATURE

Our research has sought to understand the characteristics of classroom discourse communities that foster indepth understanding and suggests that the more instruction is characterized by substantively engaging, high-quality discourse, the higher students' achievement is likely to be and they are thereby more likely to learn how to read literature well. We reason that when the quality of discourse is high, students are not merely following classroom procedures but are also contributing to the substantive content of instruction. In other words, completing homework is necessary but not sufficient to high levels of achievement.

Our eighth grade study supported these predictions (see Nystrand and Gamoran, 1991b). Students who were behaviorally disengaged — for example, those who spent little time on homework and who failed to turn in writing assignments consistently — scored lower on a test of literature achievement. At the same time, classes characterized by more authentic questions, more uptake, more discussion, and more coherence showed evidence of higher achievement.

## Variables and Methods

To assess our perspective at the high school level, we collected survey and observational data from the ninth grade classes described earlier. Students provided key information on participation by estimating the amount of time they spent on homework in English and the proportion of their reading and writing assignments they completed. Measures of instruction came from classroom observations and teacher questionnaires. Observational variables were created by coding the questions asked during class sessions according to the concepts described above. These included (a) *authenticity*, the proportion of teacher questions that were authentic computed as the proportion of the teacher's questions that were authentic, plus half the proportion of quasi-authentic question[3]; (b) *uptake*, the proportion of questions that followed up on a previous response; (c) *discussion time*, the average number of minutes per class period spent in discussion.[4] An essential variable we obtained from teacher questionnaires was (d) *discourse coherence*, the frequency with which teachers reported discussing readings, writing about readings, relating readings to other readings, and discussing writing assignments in class.[5]

To see how participation and discourse quality affects achievement, we attempted to design a test that was suitable for all 52 English classes yet was sensitive to the curriculum covered in each class. Each teacher kept a weekly log of texts used and pages covered. From these logs, we constructed lists of all the short stories, novels, and plays read in each class, and from the lists we selected five readings that were representative of each class's selections. For the test, we asked a series of questions about the selected readings. The questions ranged from simple recall (e.g., "Who were the main characters in *To Kill a Mockingbird*?) to ones requiring in-depth understanding ("Relate the ending of *To Kill a Mockingbird* to the main conflict and to the ending"). Thus, the same questions were asked of each class, but the stories they concerned varied, depending on what students had actually read during the year.[6]

## RESULTS

Most of our results are consistent with earlier findings. The more often students completed their reading and writing assignments, the higher their literature achievement. Classes with fewer students off task produced higher achievement as well. Increased discussion time failed to raise achievement, but uptake and discourse coherence significantly affected student learning. For example, achievement was about 1.7 points higher in classes whose lessons were typically well connected, compared to classes in which activities were fragmented.[7] Although this is a modest impact,[8] it is one among several aspects of classroom discourse that might be improved. The full regression results are displayed in Table 5-2..

Initially, it appeared that authentic questions had no effect or even a negative effect on achievement. Reexamining our data, we discovered that many class sessions with high proportions of authentic questions had nothing to do with literature. Some, for example, concerned test-taking skills and attitudes ("How do most of you feel about tests?"; "What would your parents say if you got an A on next week's test?"), some had to do with brainstorming ("What things would you associate with lying in the sun?"), and some even had to do with grammar ("Did you ever wonder why we have helping verbs?"). It appeared that in classes defined as "low-ability" (e.g., remedial and basic English classes), only 25 percent of the authentic questions concerned the texts they were reading. By contrast, in honors and accelerated classes, about 68 percent of the authentic questions asked had to do with literature texts. With this pattern in mind, we hypothesized that authentic questions would have different effects in different kinds of classes. We found, indeed, gains from authenticity in honors classes, losses in remedial classes, and no effects in the regular classes.

To illustrate these results, let us compare five "effective" classes with five "ineffective" classes. By effective and ineffective, we mean classes with the highest and lowest achievement scores at the end of the year, after taking account of students' demographic backgrounds and writing and literature skills at the beginning of the year. (By controlling for demographic and initial achievement differences, we are not simply comparing high- and low-ability classes, although ability grouping may be related to the categorization: Indeed, one of the least effective was an honors class.

Our findings are presented in Table 5-1, which provides one way of characterizing the discourse community in effective and ineffective classrooms. Clearly, students' participation was more substantial in the effective classes: They spent about 45 percent more time on homework and were about 10 percent more likely to complete their reading and writing assignments. The effective classes also stand out in uptake. Although teachers in the ineffective classes asked a higher proportion of authentic questions overall — 31.1 percent versus 23.8 percent — teachers in the effective classes posed a

**Table 5-1    Comparison of the five highest- and lowest-achieving classes.**

| *Variable* | *Data Source* | *Top 5 Classes* | *Bottom 5 Classes* |
|---|---|---|---|
| **Participation** | | | |
| Homework time (hrs:min per week) | Student questionnaire | 1:41 | 0:56 |
| Percentage of writing completed | Student questionnaire | 91.9% | 80.0% |
| Percentage of reading completed | Student questionnaire | 84.3% | 76.7% |
| **Discourse** | | | |
| Coherence (instances per week; see text) | Teacher questionnaire | 11.0 | 10.1 |
| Percentage of questions showing uptake | Observed | 35.5% | 19.3% |
| Percentage of teacher questions that were authentic | Observed | 23.8% | 31.1% |
| Percentage of authentic teacher questions about literature | Observed | 35.1% | 70.2% |
| Total amount of time spent in discussion for all classes during all 4 observations (minutes:seconds) | Observed | 2:20 | 5.27 |
| Average amount of time spent in discussion per observation (seconds) | Observed | 7 | 17.1 |
| Total amount of time spent discussing literature for all classes during all 4 observations (min:sec) | Observed | 0 | 1:24 |

Note: Categorization based on analysis of residuals from regression of literature achievement on sex, race/ethnicity, socioeconomic status, fall reading skills, and fall writing skills.

Table 5-2    Effects of instructional discourse on ninth-grade literature achievement. Dependent variable: Spring literature achievement (mean = 21.82, s.d. = 7.66). N = 971 students, R2 for regression = .52. (*p<.05, **p<.01.)

| Variable | Mean | Standard Deviation | Regression Coefficent | Standard Error |
|---|---|---|---|---|
| **Background variables** | | | | |
| Sex (female=1) | .51 | .50 | 1.47** | .37 |
| Race (black=1) | .07 | .26 | −.47 | .71 |
| Ethnicity (Hisp=1) | .09 | .28 | −1.56* | .65 |
| SES | −.02 | .80 | .44 | .25 |
| Fall reading | 31.88 | 5.34 | .40** | .04 |
| Fall writing | 5.71 | 1.28 | .90** | .15 |
| **Ability groups** | | | | |
| Honors/accelerated | .24 | .43 | .25 | .96 |
| Basic/remedial | .10 | .30 | −1.11 | 1.12 |
| Othera | .09 | .29 | .57 | 1.16 |
| **Behavioral engagement** | | | | |
| Writing completed | 87.88% | 19.68 | .03** | .01 |
| Reading completed | 83.04% | 24.62 | .03** | .01 |
| Homework time (hrs/wk) | 1.27 | 1.27 | .18 | .15 |
| Offtask in class | 3.22% | 3.27 | −.12* | .06 |
| **Instructional discourse** | | | | |
| Authentic questions: | | | | |
| In honors classes | 24.30% | 11.41 | .10** | .03 |
| In regular classes | 28.13% | 18.81 | −.02 | .01 |
| In remedial classes | 27.40% | 18.86 | −.09** | .03 |
| In other classes | 36.90% | 26.03 | −.20** | .03 |
| Uptake | 25.90% | 11.26 | .09** | .02 |
| Discussion | .24 | .48 | −.02 | .04 |
| Coherenceb | 13.01 | 7.07 | .12** | .03 |

a Other classes include two classes in a school-within-a-school program, and two classes in a heterogeneously-grouped school.

b Coherence measure based on teacher responses to the following questions, coded on a weekly scale:

About how often do students in your class write about (or in response to) things they have read?

About how often do you discuss writing topics with your students before asking them to write?

About how often do you and your class discuss the readings you assign?

When you ask students about their reading assignments in class, how frequently do you attempt to do each of the following: Ask them to relate what they have read to their other readings.

About how often does your class relate its discussion to previous discussions you have had?

much higher proportion of authentic questions about literature than did teachers in the ineffective classes (70.2% vs. 35.1%); the latter teachers tended to ask authentic questions about other topics.

There was little discussion in either group of classes. During all four observations of each class, we observed only a little more than two minutes of discussion in the weak classes (an average of about four seconds per class) and less than six minutes of discussion in the strong classes (or about 17 seconds per class). In the weak classes, none of this discussion concerned literature; in the strong classes, only 84 seconds did. Given these findings, it is not surprising that discussion had no effect on achievement.

## *DISCUSSION*

For the most part, our results support the conceptual formulation and descriptive analyses presented earlier. Classes characterized by higher levels of student participation and higher-quality instructional discourse tended to produce higher achievement in literature. One reason the "effective" classes outperformed the "ineffective" classes is that they offered a discourse community conducive to the study of literature. Such an environment substantively engages students because they become significantly involved in the flow of discourse: What they say matters.

The results also raised an important caveat for our claims about the impact of classroom discourse on achievement. In emphasizing the importance of what kinds of questions teachers were asking, how students were responding, and how these responses were evaluated, we probably paid too little attention to what the teachers and students were talking *about*. Hence, we were surprised to find a negative effect of authenticity on literature achievement until we learned that many of the highly authentic lessons occurred when no literature was being addressed. Future work in this area must give more weight to the *content* of classroom discourse in addition to examining the form it takes.

## CONCLUSION

We find, then, that students learn literature best in classes characterized by substantial experience with and response to literature; that is, when their teachers successfully transform their classes into interpretive communities. As a minimum, effective teachers of literature frequently and regularly assign novels, dramas, and short stories; and as a minimum, the students regularly complete their assignments. Students' completion of their assignments is especially important because coherence of discourse depends on it: If students are to discuss and write about their readings, they must first obviously complete their readings and, then, their writing. In effective classes, the teachers treat the works as aesthetic objects, encouraging students to relate to the narratives, plots, themes, characters, and images in terms of their own experience. Authentic teacher questions help students to make just such relationships. As a result, students do more than learn about literature in these classes (though they surely do that); in classes organized as interpretive communities, they learn how to read aesthetically. Teachers, of course, are the key to this instruction and instruct the students partly by the attitudes they bring to their teaching but especially by the questions they ask that instructively highlight particular parts of the text and, especially, draw out students' responses to the text. It is largely through these questions that teachers turn their classes into interpretive communities since it is such questions that instruct students what to pay attention to, what to ignore, and just how to pay attention.

## ACKNOWLEDGEMENTS

The authors appreciate the suggestions of Stuart Greene, Fred Newmann, David Schaafsma, and Michael Smith on an earlier draft, as well as the guidance of Courtney Cazden for the intellectual direction of the project. The authors also appreciate help for the following: (a) collecting classroom data; Mark Berends, John Knapp, and Jim Ladwig; (b) reading and evaluating student tests; Stephen Fox, Carol Franko, Elaine Klein, Susan Koenig, Mary Morzinski, Marcia Reddick, Mark Scarborough, and Lorna Wiedemann; (c) proofing classroom data: Mary Jo Parks, and Marcia Reddick; (d) assisting with programming: Craig Weinhold. Special thanks go to Mary Jo Heck for listening to tapes of all ninth-grade classes and verifying computer transcripts of the observation, as well as managing the entire dataset of class-room discourse. The authors also are indebted for the contributions of the teachers and students who participated in the study reported in this paper. This paper was prepared at the National Center on Effective Secondary Schools, Wisconsin Center for Education Research, School of Education, University of Wisconsin-Madison, which is supported by a grant from the Office of Educational Research and Improvement (Grant No. G-008690007-89), Any opinions, findings, and conclusions or recommendations expressed in this publication are those of the authors and do not necessarily reflect the views of this agency or the U.S. Department of Education.

## *ENDNOTES*

1. With uptake the teacher must do more than simply repeat some word or phrase that a student has used; the teacher must actually base a question on it. Uptake occurs only when a student response actually affects the course of discussion. In the first transcript, for example, when a student asks, "On the Achean ship?" and the teacher replies, "Well, they're not on their ships," this is not uptake.

2. As Rosenblatt (1978, 1988) explains, learning to read literature requires learn-ing to distinguish between *efferent* and *aesthetic* readings: hence, we read newspaper reports, for example, "efferently," carrying away with us "the bot-tom line" or what psychologists call the gist of the text. By contrast, reading "aesthetically" requires "living through" and experiencing vicariously the "story world."

3. A quasi-authentic question is one that has no *single* prespecified answer but a definite set of answers. For example, "In your opinion, why did Huck Finn help Jim escape?" would be coded authentic, but "According to your lecture notes, what was one of the reasons for Huck's helping Jim escape?" would be coded quasi-authentic.

4. In our study, discussion is narrowly defined as occurring when the discourse transcends the usual question-response-evaluation mode to comments offered by more than one student, often without interruption by the teacher. Thus, ordinary recitation or question-answer sessions are not coded as discussion.

5. The following questions in the teacher questionnaire were coded on a weekly scale and summed to indicate contiguity:

   "About how often do students in your class write about (or in response to) things they have read?"

"About how often do you discuss writing topics with your students before asking them to write?"

"About how often do you and your class discuss the readings you assign?

"When you ask students about their reading assignments in class, how frequently do you ask them to relate what they have read to their other readings"

"About how often does your class relate its discussion to previous discussions you have had?"

"About how often do you and your class discuss things students have written about?"

6. The tests were scored holistically on a variety of dimensions, such as recall, depth of understanding, understanding of characters motivations, and so forth. Each test was scored by two readers and the marks were averaged. Interrated reliability was computed as a correlation of .82.

7. The contrast between coherent and fragmented classes is computed as the difference between one standard deviation below the mean on coherence, and one standard deviation above the mean (a gap of about 14), times the regression coefficient for coherence (.12): $14 \times .12 = 1.68$ points.

## REFERENCES

Applebee, A. N. (1974). *Tradition and reform in the teaching of English: A history.* Urbana: The National Council of Teachers of English.

Applebee, A. N. (1984). Writing and reasoning. *Review of Educational Research, 54,* 577–596.

Bissex, G. (1980). *Gnys at wrk: A child learns to write and read.* Cambridge, MA: Harvard University Press.

Britton, J., Burgess, T., Martin, N., McLeod, A., & Rosen, H. (1975). *The development of writing abilities: 11–18.* London: Macmillan.

Brookover, W. B., Beady, C., Flood, P., Schweitzer, J., & Wisenbaker, J. (1979). *School social systems and student achievement; Schools can make a difference.* New York: Prager.

Collins, J. (1982). Discourse style, classroom interaction and differential treatment. *Journal of Reading Behavior, 14,* 429–437.

Fish, S. *(1980). Is there a text in this class?* Cambridge, MA: Harvard University Press.

Gundlach, R. (1982). Children as writers. In M. Nystrand (Ed.), *What writers know: The language, process, and structure of written discourse* (pp. 129–147). New York: Academic Press.

Heath, S. B. (1980, November). *What no bedtime story means: Narrative skills at home and school*. Paper prepared for the Terman Conference, Stanford University, Stanford, CA.

Heath, S. B. (1983). *Ways with words: Language, life, and work in communities and classrooms*. New York: Cambridge University Press.

McLaren, P. (1985). *Schooling as a ritual performance*. London: Routledge and Kegan Paul.

Mehan, H. (1979). *Learning lessons.* Cambridge, MA: Harvard University Press.

Nystrand, M. (1991a). Making it hard: Curriculum and instruction as factors in the difficulty of literature. In A. Purves (Ed.), *The idea of difficulty in literature and literature learning: Joining theory and practice*. 141–156. Albany: State University of New York at Albany Press.

Nystrand, M. (1991b). On the negotiation of understanding between students and teachers: Towards a social-interactionist model of school learning. Paper presented at the 1991 Convention of the American Educational Research Association. Madison: The Center on School Organization and Restructuring.

Nystrand, M. & Gamoran, A. (1988). *A study of instruction as discourse.* Paper presented at the 1988 Convention of the American Educational Research Association. Madison: The National Center on Effective Secondary Schools.

Nystrand, M. & Gamoran, A. (1991a). Student engagement: When recitation becomes conversation. In H. Waxman and H. Walberg (Eds.), *Contemporary research on teaching.* 257–276. Berkeley: McCutchan.

Nystrand, M. & Gamoran, A. (1991b). Instructional discourse, student engagement, and literature achievement. *Research in the Teaching of English, 25*, 261–290.

Polanyi, M. (1958). *Personal knowledge.* London: Routledge & Kegan Paul.

Purves, A. (1991). Indeterminate texts, responsive readers, and the idea of difficulty in literature. In A. Purves (Ed.), *The idea of difficulty in literature and literature learning: Joining theory and practice*, 157–170. Albany, NY: SUNY Press.

Rosenblatt, L. (1938). *Literature as exploration.* New York: Appleton-Century.

Rosenblatt, L. (1978). *The reader, the text, the poem: A transactional theory of the literary work.* Carbondale, IL: Southern Illinois University Press.

Rosenblatt, L. (1988). *Writing and reading: The transactional theory.* Technical report no. 13. Berkeley: The Center for the Study of Writing.

Teale, W. & Sultzby, E. (Eds.). (1986). *Emergent literacy: Writing and reading*. Norwood, NJ: Ablex Publishing Corp.

Wertsch, J. & Hickmann, M. (1987). Problem solving in social interaction: A microgenetic analysis. In M. Hickmann (Ed.), *Social and functional approaches to language and thought* (pp. 251–266). New York: Academic Press.

### PART TWO

# Discussion as Instructional Scaffolding

♣ ♣ ♣

# CHAPTER SIX

# Worlds of Words

## Dialogic Perspectives on Reading and Response

❧ ❧ ❧

## Deborah Appleman and Susan Hynds

Sometimes, when young, you have a dream of something you have not yet experienced and on waking feel set ahead, as though the player controlling your life had moved you several spaces on the board. You have a strong feeling of having been advanced in experience. That was my feeling on encountering *Hamlet*. Knowing him, I felt more worldly, advanced a space or two. Like millions before me, the more I looked, the more I found, and forty years later, the more I look, the more I still find [.] (MacNeil, p. 130)

In describing his discovery of Shakespeare's *Hamlet* as a high school student, Robert MacNeil exclaimed, "Never before had there been such an instant connection between something I felt and a set of words to describe it — giving me both distance from my feelings and better understanding of them" (p. 127). Shakespeare's prose, in MacNeil's words, "released me a little from the prison of my self-absorption, and hooked me into a wider, grander scheme of things. They made me larger, freer" (p. 127).

In this chapter we argue that reading is both a private and a social act. In a sense, we carry on private conversations with ourselves every time we encounter a book. These imaginary monologues are not entirely private, however. They arise out of conversations we may have had with the people in our own lives, out of conversations with fellow readers about books, out of imaginary conversations with authors and the characters they create.

These dialogic relationships ultimately release us from our narrow selves and into the "grander scheme of things" that MacNeil describes. In the process, they make us essentially "larger" and "freer," both as readers and as human beings.

The theories of Lev Vygotsky (1978) and Mikhail Bakhtin (1973) have been the impetus for theories of pedagogy built on the notion that meanings are created through purposeful social encounters or dialogues. This social view of reading is not new. Even Louise Rosenblatt (1983), who extols the virtue of private aesthetic experience, has remarked: "Just as the personality and concerns of the reader are largely socially patterned, so the literary work, like language itself, is a social product. The genesis of literary techniques occurs in a social matrix" (p. 28). Several explanations have been offered for the kinds of dialogic relationships that exist within the literary reading process.

Readers often enter into a dialogic relationship with authors and texts (Vipond, Hunt, Jewett, & Reither, 1990). When reading is approached dialogically, the text is envisioned as a "conversational partner" (p. 130), and meaning-making is "a collaborative process" (Vipond, et al., 1990. p. 113). Reading dialogically in this sense means becoming aware of authors' possible intentions and how those intentions evoke readers' responses.

Readers also engage in self-dialogues. Deanne Bogdan (1990) defines "dialectic" in the reading process as a shifting between engagement and detachment. At times, Bogdan argues, the reading process can be described as "stasis," or an "intensely personal and private experience" (p. 119) that renders readers incapable of a critical or distanced response. "Dialectic," on the other hand, occurs when the reader participates in the "complex and subtle juxtapositionings between the world of the imagination and the 'real' world, between the ideology of the text and that of the reader's sense of self" (p. 134). She argues that readers constantly shuttle between their private, "pre-critical" experiences and their more outward, critical understandings.

Readers also engage in real or imagined dialogues with teachers and other readers in the classroom literary community. Drawing upon the work of Bakhtin (1973), Hanssen, Harste, and Short (1990) argue that the "seemingly private" act of reading actually depends upon an elaborate network of prior social interactions that influence the current reading experience. Their model of learning and teaching as a dialogic process "points to the need for students to engage continually in the exchange of ideas, to be involved in dialogues of different kinds" (p. 261). They argue that such dialogues "are not simply motivational or reinforcing, they provide the foundation of learning" (p. 261), as students create their ideas.

Not all of these reading dialogues are in the form of spoken words. Class discussions, group work, and reading conferences with teachers and peers are only a few of the possibilities. As Peter Elbow (1985) has pointed out, writing can have "speech-like qualities" (p. 290). He argues that "speech is usually social and communal, writing solitary. But we can make writing communal too by having people write together and to each other in ways that are worth spelling out in more detail" (p. 290).

In addition, Elbow (1986) argues for the importance of dialectic in learning: "We do not just GET concepts and ideas, we MAKE them" (p. 87). Elbow stresses the importance of a dialectic of opposing viewpoints and perspectives. As students embrace contradictions and contraries, they deepen their understanding of literary texts. Within the literature class-room, there are many ways to mine the dialogic potential in students' writing, reading, talking, and listening. Our intent in this chapter is to bring these conversations out of the realm of possibility and into the words of students and teachers.

## CONVERSATIONS BETWEEN READER AND TEXT

Although many accounts of the literary response process are built around some version of the "reader-text" relationship, the text is more, as Rosenblatt suggests, than "inkspots on the page." The text becomes a medium through which readers carry on a host of imaginative dialogues. Within the process of literary reading, readers envision texts as authorized creations, aesthetic objects, purveyors of information, cultural artifacts, and elements of a larger intertextual framework.

### Text as Authorized Creation

There is usually a point where readers begin to look beyond the words of a text and see the author behind them. When this happens, they adopt a "point-driven" orientation and begin to see reading as an imaginary dialogue between the author and themselves (Vipond, Hunt, Jewett, & Reither, 1990). "Dialogic" reading, as Vipond and his colleagues term it, makes readers more aware of how texts affect them.

As readers allow themselves to become, in a sense, more vulnerable to texts, their growing awareness of authors' intentions makes the literary work more vulnerable to them. Often they are able imaginatively to "rewrite" the original text as they consider how it was created and how they responded to it. Paradoxically, readers must open themselves to authors' manipulations to understand them. Critical distance demands an awareness of self as well as an awareness of the author's craft.

Thus, becoming aware that texts are authorized invites readers into a process of self-analysis as well as the more distanced understanding of authors' motives. Readers ask questions like: "What is the point of this narrative?" "How does this text do what it does?" "What can I learn about myself through my response to this text?" "What can I take away as a writer through the experience?"

These questions can be explored by encouraging readers to keep track of their own response processes in reading logs, as a way of understanding both themselves and the text. For instance, teachers may ask them to keep track of not only what they are reading but also how they read each text during the course of a semester or year. These "process accounts" can be placed in a reading journal and discussed during conference time as a way of understanding which texts are difficult to read, which are compelling or provocative, or which create vivid mental pictures. Wherever possible, published writers can be invited to talk about their own writing processes. In conversations with teachers and fellow writers, students can learn a great deal about how texts are created and how they evoke responses from readers.

In this excerpt, Jessica, an eleventh grade student, converses with an adult about her private experience of reading James Baldwin's *The Fire Next Time*:

*I:*      What hit you the hardest? What do you think was the one book that you closed and went "Oh my God."

*J:*      I think that *The Fire Next Time* hit me very, very strongly. It's not something that I would particularly choose to read again but not because it was bad. Because it got the point across the first time. I don't know if I'd want to be confronted with it again. Also, it's more of something that forces you to look at what's going on. You can't really absorb yourself into it as much as a fictional story or a fictional narrative. Because you're dealing with what's going on in your life and your society and your beliefs and your everything and not someone else's. I finished reading it and I felt a lot of different things. . . . I've never seen that point of view. I've never even thought about that point of view before. I've never been confronted with it. . . . I was really angry and also felt guilty and I also felt generally irritated. And I figured that was a good sign because that means it did what it's supposed to do.

*I:*     Maybe that is what literature is supposed to do.

Thus, in recounting her personal response to James Baldwin's work, Jessica becomes aware of his artistic choices.

## *Text as Aesthetic Object*

Sometimes we simply get lost in books. They become engaging experiences that demand nothing except our total, rapt attention. Here, our inner dialogues are wordless and private. The reading experience is not a means to an end but creates its own significance in our lives. It does not stop with the reading moment but is extended through time and changes us as we approach other readings. We are never the same after reading "The Love Song of J. Alfred Prufrock" or *Catcher in the Rye*. In aesthetic reading, we are caught up in living imaginary life of the text, not reflecting upon it. Literature is not only informing and enlightening, but transforming as well.

As we carry on these private, preverbal conversations, we are enlarged and engaged. The experience is both selfless and selfish. We lose ourselves through immersion. Yet, ultimately, we find ourselves through the insights and experiences we gain.

This engagement creates positive habits and attitudes that render us lifetime readers. We learn about ourselves as readers through discovering what engages us; we develop preferences for authors as we try, over and over again, to recreate the aesthetic pleasure of living within the world of the text. We may even learn techniques that we can bring to our own writing. But, by definition, these dialogues are always invisible. As teachers, we see evidence of them only in what our students do before or beyond the reading. We may not see evidence of them at all.

Since aesthetic dialogues are always invisible, many opportunities should be provided for readers to choose their own texts and respond only when they feel the need to emerge from the privacy of their own experience. Teachers can model reading for pleasure; they can set up reading corners where students can become lost in books. They can encourage and support aesthetic absorption by conferencing frequently with students about what books have been most compelling. However, if our goal is aesthetic reading, students should never be held accountable for their inner dialogues. Even within a classroom setting, these pleasure readings should be kept "irresponsible."

Instead of attending classes during her senior year of high school, Kendall Hailey embarked on a year of independent reading. In her book, *The Day I Became an Autodidact*, she records her responses to a variety of texts from Euripides to the Romantics. Her journal responses allow us to overhear her private conversations with texts. For example:

> Dickens said, "I have a favorite child and his name is David Copperfield." I think he may turn out to be mine too. Dickens is said to create such larger-than-life characters, but I have never read about ones that seem more real. They live on even after you have finished the novel, when so many great characters seem to fade away as you turn the last page. Proust spent so much time with Swann, but I confess I wouldn't know him if I met him on the street, whereas I pray every day I'll run into the Aged One from *Great Expectations*.
>
> Aristophanes has cheered me up considerably. I've read *Lysistrata*, *The Birds*, *The Clouds*. I am ashamed to say he was the Greek I dreaded reading (because I thought he'd be silly — I hate a silly ancient).
>
> What he is is lyrical. Reading *Clouds*, I felt as if I were floating in them. I can't believe that the happiness these ancient works give has been here for twenty-five hundred years and still remains so fresh.
>
> I am falling in love with every Greek I meet. (p. 91)

Through immersing herself in reading and then reflecting on the process afterward, Kendall Hailey learned to approach the text as an aesthetic artifact. There was no teacher directing the process or choosing the texts. Her reading was privately chosen and privately experienced. From these moments of aesthetic absorption, she discovered a great deal about herself as reader, critic, and human being.

## Text as Purveyor of Information

At very basic levels, texts are sources of meaning. These meanings can come in the form of information, personal awareness, textual understandings. Readers are not passive recipients but are co-creators of these meanings. Although "information-driven" reading (Hunt & Vipond, 1985) is perhaps more associated with non-literary texts, peripheral learning goes on in literary reading as well. Readers inevitably build stores of knowledge about the world, about culture, and about historical events through the reading of literature.

Interestingly, these learnings from literature are not directly acquired through classroom activities but indirectly experienced as readers try to make sense of the stories they read. They ask themselves questions about social norms, about historical facts, or about the meanings of words in particular ages and eras. Because literary reading is usually private, readers are free to be naive, to risk ignorance, to consult other sources, as they build a private store of knowledge for other readings.

Sometimes, however, the complexity of literary reading causes readers to become mired in the process of understanding and comprehending. When this happens, it's all too easy to begin breaking the reading process down into manageable parts, teaching literary texts as exercises in reading comprehension. Direct teaching of historical, biographical, and factual information before every reading experience can focus readers on textual trivia. Such techniques can silence the imaginary conversations between reader and text. There is no question that a great many literary texts are difficult. Some are historically or culturally unfamiliar; others are written in strange dialects; still others have so many ambiguities and interpretive gaps that readers are unable to make sense of them.

One of our biggest challenges as teachers of literature should be helping our students to see reading as a playful act of meaning-building. Readers should be encouraged to keep track of their questions as they read. These questions can be the springboard for opportunities to learn about culture, about history, and about language. They can be shared in small groups and kept on a chart in front of the room for everyone to discuss. They should arise out of readers' natural curiosities and not from the study guides at the back of the anthology. As readers learn to derive real questions from their reading, they learn to speculate and hypothesize, to use literature as a springboard for inquiries about the world.

In these dialogues, readers ask questions like: "What does this text mean to me?" "How does it reflect, oppose, or challenge my personal experience?" "What knowledge can I take away to keep or use in other readings?" Beyond these private issues, readers also ask questions like: "What might this text mean to others?" "How does my interpretation fall within or outside other interpretations?" "What can I learn about my own attitudes and beliefs through conversations with others?"

Many times, when literary readings generate an interest in particular historical or cultural periods, teachers can pair literary and nonliterary texts within the same reading unit. Readers can compare fictional narratives with magazine or newspaper accounts of the times. In journals, students can keep track of their ongoing hypotheses, questions, and hunches. These questions and hypotheses can be used each day to generate conversations about the historical or cultural background of literary texts.

## *Text as Cultural Artifact*

The reading of literature brings readers into contact with a host of cultural and social experiences. Readers can learn to see the literary text as both cultural mirror and social catalyst. This approach to reading goes beyond the traditional period or historical-biographical treatments. Dialogues about culture can emerge as readers become critical commentators on their own writing, in the context of other writings. Readers can begin to understand how their own writing reflects their social and cultural assumptions. These questions become enriched and elaborated as readers encounter published texts that further challenge their cultural assumptions. Readers can be encouraged to correspond with published authors, asking them about the cultural and social influences that surrounded their work.

When texts are viewed as cultural artifacts, readers act like anthropologists, looking backward from the text at hand to the cultural beliefs and events within which it is embedded. At other times, readers become historians, as they move outward from their literary readings into factual readings about historical events. In these dialogues, readers pose critical questions about how texts reflect, represent, or challenge society. As they begin to realize the impact that writing has on social attitudes and beliefs, they become students of cultural change.

Literary texts also open a window on interpersonal relationships. Readers learn to examine assumptions about social roles, motives, values, and beliefs. Through reading, they participate vicariously in other relationships, other families, other worlds. In the safety of this otherness they experiment with cultural and social alternatives and can develop tolerance. The spectatorship of literary reading (Britton, 1984) provides a psychological space within which to experiment imaginatively with friendships, love relationships, alliances, and oppositions. Through these textual relationships, readers develop new understandings of real world relationships.

Texts can be juxtaposed with other texts as an invitation to talk about social assumptions and beliefs (for example, pairing a Judy Blume text with a feminist novel). Readers can dramatically recreate interpersonal relationships through role playing or imaginatively represent characters' viewpoints through readers theater, chamber theater, or choral reading.

Teachers do not have to be experts in drama or speech to design meaningful oral experiences for students. Often the students themselves can select scripts and assign parts for readers theater and choral reading. The conversations that surround this process can be as enlightening as the final performances. Students learn to ask questions such as: "Who seems to be 'speaking' in this part of the text?" "Does the narrator seem to be taking very different stances from one part of the text to another?" "Could we assign two narrators?" "Are there different voices throughout this text?" "What seems to be going on in the mind of the narrator or of particular characters?" Reading texts in this way opens a window on a whole host of social, cultural, and interpersonal understandings.

### Text And Intertext

Texts also operate within a web of other texts. "Intertextual" dialogues may begin with questions about how texts are like or not like other texts. In these imaginary conversations, readers learn to speculate not only about literary techniques but also about their own interpretive strategies as they become aware of other readings in their experience.

In these intertextual conversations, readers explore questions like: "How does this text compare with other texts that I have read?" "What other readings do I bring to this one?" "How has my response to this text been shaped by my previous reading encounters?"

Intertextual conversations go beyond traditional literary essays, in which readers compare and contrast classroom readings. Teachers must create classroom conversations that have real human purposes and outcomes. Students, for instance, can write critical essays to be shared with other students on a regular basis or kept in class files for use by other students who are "shopping" for books. In reading logs, they can speculate on how books, characters, or situations evoke memories of other readings.

Thus, the literary text acts as a catalyst to imaginary and real dialogues. Through their encounters with texts, readers speculate on authors' motives, become immersed in aesthetic experience, learn about the world, and become more aware of social, interpersonal, and intertextual relationships. Surrounding this more private aspect of reading are the conversations that occur in the world of the classroom. In the next section, we will explore the kinds of dialogues that can happen between readers and their teachers.

### CONVERSATIONS BETWEEN READER AND TEACHER

In the introduction to her book, *In the Middle*, clearly one of the most influential works on literature instruction in the past decade, Nancie Atwell recounts her evolution as a teacher from a creationist who "set in motion, managed and maintained" a yearlong curriculum from behind a big teacher's desk to a learner in a classroom that continually changes. By changing her position in the classroom both physically and pedagogically, Atwell changed the course of the conversations about literature that took place in that classroom, from teacher-dominated discussions often bordering on monologue to a wide range of dialogues between teacher and students. In this section we will examine the range of dialogic possibilities that are possible when teachers and students consciously choose their position in the classroom conversation.

## *Teacher as Literary Expert: Monologic Instruction*

In many literature classrooms, the teacher remains the primary explicator of the text. Probst claims that most literature programs "continue to treat literature as something to be received" (p. 36). The interpretive responsibility rests largely on the teacher, and students are often silent observers to the teacher's own exercise in meaning-making. Transcripts of such classes reveal that teacher talk often outweighs student talk by three-to-one (Marshall, 1988). In such discussions, students' participation, when it does occur, is often "minimal, consisting of brief answers to relatively straightforward questions" (p.47). This kind of fill-in-the-blank response is more likely to occur in discussions that "are meant to arrive somewhere, usually at an interpretation that the teacher has had in mind all along" (p. 48). As Marshall rightly points out, students' oral responses to literature may be constrained when a single interpretive agenda, usually that of the teachers', is the shaping force of the discussion. The danger of such an approach seems clear. Either students are limited to factual oral responses, offer nongenuine teacher-pleasing responses, or, realizing the lack of opportunity for spontaneous discourse, become silent.

This linguistic paralysis or silence may be traced in part to many teachers' instructor-centered orientation to teaching literature. When the teacher remains behind the big desk and conducts "conversation" with predetermined ends, there is little opportunity for constructive, student-generated dialogue in which private literary understanding can be shared and transformed in a social context.

## *Teacher as Facilitator: Dialogic Instruction*

According to Mallioux (1990), the goal of reader-response criticism is to talk more about readers than about authors or texts. A shift toward response-centered instruction significantly affects both reader talk and the classroom conversational turns. Probst (1988) describes the role of teachers in a reader-response classroom:

> They have taught their students to respond gently and humanely to one another; they've encouraged tentative, probing, uncertain statements; they've broken the class into smaller, safer, more intimate groups, they've avoided debate as the model for classroom talk. (p.33)

He further points out that in order to achieve this kind of atmosphere, the literature classroom:

> [M]ust be a comfortable, non-combative place, where half-formed ideas may be explored, where personal, even private, matters might occasionally creep to the surface to be addressed with delicacy and kindness. It must not, above all, have winners and losers. It must not value correctness above investigation, conformity above exploration, answers above questions." (p.33)

In such a classroom, dialogic learning can begin to take root.

The teacher can promote dialogue about literature in a variety of ways. Circle discussions, Japanese style, where each student speaks and no one speaks twice until all have spoken at least once may at first blush seem somewhat contradictory to our notion of a natural conversation, but it can discourage dialogue dominators and encourage those who tend to remain silent. Journal entries can serve as conversation openings. By beginning with a written response to a literary text, we "provide time and opportunity for an initial crystallization of a personal sense of the work" (Probst, p.33).

All of these strategies can move the classroom conversation from a teacher-dominated monologue, sprinkled with perfunctory student responses, to a lively and spontaneous dialogue where students talk genuinely with the teacher and with each other about literary texts.

## Teacher as Fellow Reader

Another dialogic possibility occurs when the teacher is situated not as a literary expert but as a fellow reader. Too often, teachers concern themselves primarily with producing polished or old responses to a text. Even in a more response-oriented classroom, teachers may find themselves managing or facilitating student responses rather than offering their own perspective.

One way to promote fresh dialogue is to change frequently our choice of literary texts. When we tirelessly (or perhaps tiredly) teach the same texts,

texts that are new to students but are no longer surprising to us, we run the risk of producing stale dialogue in which the teacher is not a genuine participant but a reader of a practiced pedagogical script. Probst endorses the idea of reading new books along with students in order to:

> model the tentative, questioning exploration of a text. Teachers who do this have joined the class as another reader, and that change in roles seems to increase the significance, in the students' minds, of their own readings. (p.33)

When teachers become fellow readers, they also change the nature and form of classroom discourse. By writing dialogue journals with students about their self-selected reading, Atwell (1987) and her students engage in a different kind of literary talk. As Atwell discovers, literary talk in dialogue journals that begins as "gossip" quickly spills into other textual considerations, such as literary style, biographical information, genre, literary merit, and the response process itself.

The tone of the teacher's conversation in such dialogue journals is critically important. Taking the stance of a co-respondent rather than a red-penned evaluator encourages the open exploration and freewheeling literary talk that reflectively engages students not only with literary texts but with their own roles as readers as well.

The role of teacher as fellow reader can also affect whole-class dialogue. By modeling the struggles and pleasures of readers when they first encounter texts, by not having a predetermined end point for the discussion, the teacher can facilitate classroom talk in which interpretive responsibility is shared equally by teachers and students. Negotiating meaning becomes a genuine exploration rather than a rehearsed catechism in which the responses of students are shaped by the teacher's already established interpretation of the text.

Classroom conversations in which the teacher positions herself as a reader rather than as a literary expert look very different from the kinds of discussions that are teacher-dominated. For example, this group of eighth grade readers is responding to "Growing Up," a poem by Harry Behn (1975). The teacher has just asked them to share their private images as they listened to the poem:

S:   I see a man remembering when he used to go on picnics with his family and how he played with his imagination, pretending there was tigers and stuff like that. He had rocks and he just played in the forest and pretended that they were jungles or something like that.

*T:* And then what happens? What about the second part?

*S:* Then he grows up.

*S:* Then he grows up and he realizes that was just his imagination and everything's gotten — just his imagination.

*T:* When you feel yourself growing up, is that a good feeling or a sad feeling?

*S:* Sad.

*T:* Like give me examples for each.

*S:* Like, when you're younger, you can't wait till (you) grow up, can't wait till I grow up and then when you get older you look when you were younger you see all the good times that you've had and things get harder and you wish that you were younger.

*T:* Can you think of something specific that you have been through, that you looked back and said I wish I was five or I wish I was two or I wish I was a baby again.

*Students Together:* Yes, Yes, a baby.

*S:* When we were like, when I was real little at Disney World, we were walking through EPCOT and like I saw all these kids in strollers and I was like, oh man, I wish I was in one of those.

*S:* I would like to be a baby again because, like if you did something wrong, it wasn't your fault, because you are too young to know anything and you couldn't get in trouble for it.

*T:* Josh, how about you? How do you feel about growing up? Is it sad, happy, both?

*S:* I want to get old enough to drink in five years.

*S:* Yeah, until 21 and then stop growing. They should lower the drinking age (laughs).

*S:* Sixteen is real good.

*S:* Yeah, I wouldn't mind being sixteen.

*T:* I can remember one time I was in the doctor's office . . . and this little girl was sitting next to her mother. And all of a sudden, she started crying for like, no reason, and she just crawled up into her mother's lap, and her mother just put her arms around her. And I remember just having this experience. Like, yeah, I'm too old to crawl up into my parent's lap, or anybody else's lap. But I don't think we are ever too old for the need to be comforted and cared for.

By positioning herself as a fellow reader, this teacher introduces her private reader-text dialogue into the public arena of classroom discourse, thus encouraging students to do the same. The interplay of private dialogues with the public dialogue of class discussion is consonant with Rosenblatt's (1985) claim that literature provides a "living through," not simply knowledge about. Thus, the literary talk that ensues is not about literature as content but literature as experience.

## Teacher as Dialogic Partner

The structure of most classrooms, with 20 or 30 students and a single teacher, restricts the possibilities of extended literary talk with individual students. We struggle with how to conduct more than a dozen conversations simultaneously or how to conduct private conversations in public. Although dialogue journals enable students and teachers to engage in private written conversations, opportunities for face-to-face literary talks with individual students are equally important.

Lengthy conversations with students allow a variety of discourse possibilities that are more difficult, if not impossible, in the context of the whole classroom. Students can more fully explore and reflect upon their own reading processes by reflecting on past readings or by engaging in think alouds. Intertextual responses are also more likely to occur as students and teachers broaden their discussion from a single work to several literary texts. One-to-one conversations that allow students to focus vertically on their reading histories and memories can foster those links more effectively.

In this conversation, Mary, a twelfth grade student, discusses some of her current readings:

*Mary:* I really liked Baldwin. I was really impressed with what he had to say. Especially with *The Fire Next Time*, because it was the only piece of work that we read that was not fiction . . . I guess it felt more up-to-date than anything else. We read so much of English, Jane Austen, and Charles Dickens, that I couldn't relate to it as well.

*Interviewer:* In what way are Charles Dickens and James Baldwin trying to do the same thing?

*Mary:* They're trying to change the society that they live in. But I think that it was more effective with Baldwin because he didn't fictionalize it. And that does trivialize it. At least I thought that *Hard Times* was. It became a sort of a soap opera. . . . The main message is sort of blurred. Whereas what Baldwin is trying to say is right on the table, he lays it on the line and you just accept it or you refuse it. . . .

*Interviewer:* Would you like to read more social criticism, like "A Modest Proposal?"

*Mary:* I remember reading Virginia Woolf's *A Room of One's Own* and I remember because I read that and then I read, about a month or two later, *The Fire Next Time*, and I could see so many parallels. I related much better, because I was a woman, than to *The Fire Next Time*.

*Interviewer:* In fact, you might want to think about Jane Austen in terms of Virginia Woolf too.

*Mary:* When I read *A Room of One's Own*, I felt so guilty about hating Jane Austen.

In this section we have presented a variety of contexts in which conversations between teachers and students can arise. The dialogic quality of literary understanding suggests that the private conversations that emerge in a reader's transaction with a text can be fruitfully brought to play in both oral and written discourse.

By recognizing the full range of dialogic possibilities and by refusing to dominate the classroom discourse, the teacher may open up a kaleidoscopic array of conversations about texts, where the shifting roles of speakers, listeners, students, teachers, and texts can lead to the social construction of a shared literary understanding.

## CONVERSATIONS AMONG READERS

Everyone else in the house has been asleep for hours. I sit here stretched out on the carpet in front of the fire in the lounge, my third cup of tea beside me, absorbed in the world of "The Scarecrow" (Westfall, 1981). . . . Nothing — not even the thought of the irresistible lethargy that will, I know, descend on me around mid-day tomorrow in my classroom — nothing has the power to wrench me from the world which I inhabit for this moment until the last page has been read and the covers can be closed, their contents escaped and jostling, in a myriad of images . . . I shall think more about this book. I shall also sleep now, for I am satisfied that I have it; it is mine, stored away for reordering, reconsideration, remade by me alone in this free, comfortable silence, to be remade again when I talk about it to a friend or try to get a student to read it, though I wouldn't want to do that just at this moment. Tomorrow, the classroom, where reading can never be quite like all this. To begin with, there are thirty other people present, and all thirty-one of us, even if we're reading "silently," are aware of those other human presences, in subtle, if not overtly disturbing, ways. (Brown, 1987, p. 93)"

In this passage, Lola Brown eloquently describes the differences between public and private reading. In the world of the classroom, the essentially private and individual act of reading literature becomes a shared, collective experience. In the presence of other readers, the purposes of response expand from the personal and privately aesthetic to social and communicative ones. The response mode necessarily moves from the monologic quality of a reader's inner speech to a dialogue where one's responses will be shared, examined, argued, questioned, and perhaps misunderstood. In this section, we explore the dialogic structure of reader-to-reader responses and suggest ways in which "those other human presences" can contribute to, rather than inhibit, an individual reader's responses to literature.

The classroom is a community of readers, whose range of individual responses can color, enhance, and enrich the response process. Responding conversationally requires students not only to formulate a response to a literary text but also to understand the social conventions that guide public discourse (Cooper, 1990, p. 73).

As every classroom teacher knows, adolescents are constantly in conversation with one another — about music, athletic events, dances, world events, and, especially, each other. The challenge for the teacher of literature is to turn the natural tide of adolescent discourse to literary texts. In this section, we will explore some ways to do that.

### Reader as Co-respondent

Small groups provide a way to match students' social agenda (to talk with peers) with the classroom agenda (to talk about texts). Students can engage in small group discussions about literature, focusing on a common text or on individual readings. Small groups can increase the likelihood that more reluctant speakers will offer their responses and can prevent teacher domination of class discussion. Many teachers have had the rewarding experience of floating from group to group, overhearing snippets of literary discourse that are perceptive and original. As Thompson (1987) has argued:

> It is in the security of the nonjudgemental small group that students are most likely to use the expressive, exploratory, thinking-aloud kind of informal language so productive of learning. They will use it for expressing honest feeling, for making connections between their real and fictional worlds, and for the consideration of other people's viewpoints that might expand their individual perspectives. (Thompson, 1987, p. 267)

In addition to small discussion groups, readers theater provides a novel way for readers to share their responses to literary text. Readers theater presentations are often more significant for the process they generate than for the dramatic literary interpretations that result. Readers negotiate private meanings as they struggle toward a common goal: a dramatic interpretation of a literary text. Students confer about appropriate textual passages, discuss the relative significance of plot development, argue over the nuances of character, and compare their visual images of both character and setting. As they create their dramatic interpretation, they also create a new collective meaning of a text. The public presentation of their performance enhances the students' feeling of ownership in their shared interpretation.

Dialogue journals also cast the reader as co-respondent. In addition to promoting reader-teacher conversations, dialogue journals may also be used to facilitate student exchanges. Students are fascinated by the interior peek into their peers that sharing journals can provide. Conversing for a variety of purposes enables students to view journals as a real communicative tool rather than as an artificial diary designed only for the teacher's evaluative eyes. Students can also sustain longer, more fully elaborated responses to texts in journal form than they can in fleeting oral dialogue. Here, too, the physical absence of the teacher can also facilitate genuine reader discourse.

In the following journal response to Judith Guest's novel *Ordinary People,* Judy and Lisa exchange views on everything from parental roles to literary merit:

Judy begins:

> Some of the things I remember most about the book are when Con had those nightmares of his suicide attempt and when he was in the hospital getting shock treatment. It was a very realistic story and I think Judith

knows how to make people get a real good idea of what she is talking about. I was grossed out by the parts, but they were very real.

I think Cal was a really good father. He had no father and he just picked up on fatherhood like that. He treated Con with respect and showed how much he loved his son. He doubted himself a lot but I think that's normal. Many people doubt themselves. Anyway, it shows in the end that Cal knows what he's doing. Beth doesn't know the first thing about being a mother. She didn't give a damn about Con. She cared about Cal, but not Con.

I guess some women are not cut out to be mothers — like Beth. I'm glad she left at the end. But, I do think she should have said good-bye to Conrad. After all, he is her own son. She could've tried to make Con see that she was still his mother. A simple good-bye would've been fine. They're a family. You're stuck with your family through good and bad.

Conrad really progressed. He showed the biggest improvement in the book. At first, he was nervous and scared about every little step he took. Then he got stronger and could deal with his feelings, problems, etc.

Lisa responds:

I really didn't pick up on the nightmares and flashbacks from the hospital. I thought they were really gross, but I didn't understand a few of them. I thought it was kind of confusing.

I also think Cal was a good father, but I hadn't really thought about it. He didn't even have a father to know what one was about but he did a great job anyways. He was always worried about him and was always checking to see how he was doing. I really liked the fact that they could just talk together, especially in the end when Beth had left. I also agree with you that Beth was a lousy mother. I thought she was very selfish in that everything that happened, happened to her. When she said that Con only cut his wrists to get at her, and to make her feel bad is really selfish. Wouldn't a normal mother wonder if Con had some problems instead of doing it out of spite. I thought it was good that she left but I got the feeling that she would be back.

I also thought that Conrad progressed. He was scared at first, but then he grew stronger. I really liked his character and cheered him along the whole way.

In their written conversation, Judy and Lisa acknowledge and enlarge upon each other's responses. Lisa, for example, admits that she "had never really thought of" Cal's abilities as a father or Conrad's nightmares before reading Lisa's response. She agrees with Judy's interpretation of Beth's character but adds her own unusual prediction that Beth may return. Thus, student responses are not simply shared through dialogue journals; they are enriched.

### Reader as Teacher, Bookpeddler, and Critic

"If we want our adolescent students to grow to appreciate literature, another first step is allowing them to exert ownership and choose the literature they will read." (Atwell, p.161)

Book talks provide one way of promoting reader-reader dialogue. At first blush they may seem similar in content and form to the age-old oral book report. Book talks, however, can promote a more spontaneous and less superficial mode of response if students are not limited to brief plot summaries and character sketches. In book talks, individual readers share their enthusiasm for a book they read on their own and share elements of their private responses with the class. Students are positioned as experts (not even the teacher may have read the book they selected) and can field a variety of queries from the class. Students can present the talk as a character from the book, can present the plot as a storyboard or can share a creative written response, perhaps a poem or a journal entry that the book inspired. Most importantly, book talks provide a way for a single reader's response to a text to be spotlighted and privileged within a classroom context.

Groups of students can collaborate on oral presentations about texts. Presentations can revolve around formal textual analysis, discussion of theme, different critical interpretations of text, or simply a sharing of individual readers responses to a text. Like readers theater, the conversations generated by the process are as valuable as the final presentation. Again, group presentations remove the teacher from the position of authority and cast student-readers in the role of experts who have a good deal to say about a literary text.

For two weeks, a class of twelfth grade students had been working in groups to present a novel through several critical perspectives. They had studied several critical theories as a class — feminism, Marxism, reader-response, and structuralism — and had to apply at least two of those theories to a novel they would read with three to four other students. Class time was divided between reading, discussion, and organizing the presentations. What follows is an excerpt from their teacher's journal:

Kids were remarkable in handling this independence. The first day a couple of groups came to me to ask for advice — someone in the group was not keeping up with the reading — what to do! After a few days a couple of kids reading *The Hobbit* came in with a surprising and alarming report — they were ahead.

My role in all of this was to keep my mitts out of it. I roamed from group to group, helped where needed, but pretty much listened to some great discussions from the students.

The presentations were thoughtfully done. Each group followed the directions and addressed all components. The final writing on this unit was a two part journal entry — one on the book and one on the process . . . The reaction to the process was awesome. Overwhelmingly kids responded about the success of working together, of each person working hard, not letting just a couple of kids do the work. Kids talked about the profound discussions about literature they had late into the night — and without a teacher!! Some kids observed that they didn't think they could figure out symbols, etc. without a teacher, and they found out they could.

## CONCLUSION

In further describing his response to *Hamlet*, this time aided by Olivier's delivery, Robert MacNeil writes:

> The words . . . lifted me to a not quite earthly plane, transported me for long moments into another realm of time and being; a poetic world, in which the flow of words controlled the weather and the climate, the cast and light of the day, and the mood of the people . . . The sounds of words put a precious mist over reality and I was inside the mist. (pp. 127–128)

Far from being exclusively a silent and solitary activity, reading invites dialogue. In this chapter we have argued that the private and social nature of reading give rise to a wide array of private and public conversations — dialogues seeded in literary texts. We have described a variety of such conversations between reader and text, between teachers and readers, and between readers themselves. In each of these situations, texts, teachers, and readers are cast and recast into different conversational roles. We have also described several ways that teachers can encourage the private stirrings and questionings that arise as responses to literature are spoken, shared, and transformed.

The dialogic approaches discussed in this chapter provide ways for readers to describe their responses to the worlds created by words, as MacNeil has. Such literary conversations enable a classroom of readers to respond together "inside the mist" of literary worlds, making those worlds more palpable, more knowable, more real.

## *REFERENCES*

Atwell, N. (1987). *In the middle: Writing, reading, and learning with adolescents*. Upper Montclair, NJ: Boynton/Cook.

Bakhtin, M. (1973). *Marxism and the philosophy of language*. New York: Seminar Press.

Bogdan, D. (1990). In and out of love with literature: Response and the aesthetics of total form. In D. Bogdan & S. Straw (Eds.) *Beyond communication: Reading comprehension and criticism*, pp. 109–137. Portsmouth, N.H.: Boynton/Cook.

Britton, J. (1984). Viewpoints: The distinction between participant and spectator role language in research and practice. *Research in the Teaching of English, 18*, 320–331.

Brown, L. (1987). Rendering literature accessible. In Corcoran, B. & Evans, E. (Eds.), Readers, texts, teachers (pp. 93 118). Upper Montclair, NJ: Boynton/Cook Publishers, Inc.

Elbow, P. (1985). The shifting relationship between speech and writing. *College Composition and Communication, 36*, 283–303.

Elbow, P. (1986). *Embracing contraries*. New York: Oxford University Press.

Hailey, K. (1988). *The day I became an autodidact*. New York: Delta.

Hanssen, E., Harste, J.C. & Short, K.G. (1990). In conversation: theory and instruction. In D. Bogdan & S. Straw (Eds.) *Beyond communication: Reading comprehension and criticism*, (pp. 259–281). Portsmouth, N.H.: Boynton/Cook.

Hunt, R., & Vipond, D. (1985). Crash-testing a transactional model of literary learning. *Reader, 14*, 23–39.

Mailloux, S. (1990). The turns of reader-response criticism. In C. Moran and E.F. Penfield (Eds.), *Conversations: Contemporary critical theory and the teaching of literature*, (pp. 38–54). Urbana, IL: National Council of Teachers of English.

MacNeil, R. (1989). *Wordstruck*. New York: Penguin Books.

Marshall, J. (1988). Classroom discourse and literary response. In B.F. Nelms (Ed.), *Literature in the classroom: Readers, texts, and contexts*, (pp. 45–58). Urbana, IL: National Council of Teachers of English.

Probst, R.E. (1988). Readers and literary texts. In B.F. Nelms (Ed.), *Literature in the classroom: Readers, texts, and contexts*, (pp. 19–30). Urbana, IL: National Council of Teachers of English.

Rosenblatt, L. (1983). *Literature as exploration*. New York: Modern Language Association.

Thomson, J. (1987). *Understanding teenagers' reading: Reading processes and the teaching of literature*. New York: Nicols Publishing Company.

Vipond, D., Hunt, R., Jewett, J., & Reither, J., (1990). Making sense of reading. In (R. Beach & S. Hynds (Eds.) *Developing Discourse Practices in Adolescence and Adulthood,* pp 110–135. Norwood, N.J.: Ablex.

Vygotsky, L. (1978). *Mind and Society*. Cambridge, MA: Harvard University Press.

# CHAPTER SEVEN

# Reading As a Person

### ♣ ♣ ♣

## Marjorie Roemer

I had observed a pretty lackluster class. After my visit, I tried to think with the teacher about questions that might have elicited more animated and more engaged response from her students. The teacher, a graduate teaching assistant, said, "I really don't know what sort of questions to ask them about literary texts." I: "Well, have you studied any literary theory? Do you know anything about reader-response?" She: "Yes, of course, but I can't teach theory to college freshmen."

## A PROBLEM

I savor this story because it so well represents what I take to be a central problem: the idea that theory exists in and for itself and that its meaning is unrelated to its applicability in practice. And the corollary position: that we can have good practice that is blind to the theory it articulates. Nothing would be more untenable than trying to explain Derrida's *Of Grammatology* to college freshmen (except, perhaps, trying to explain it to high school students or junior high schoolers). Yet, I will argue in this essay that the insights of poststructural theory are usable and liberating for classroom teachers teaching literature to students of any age. The language of contemporary theory is complex and sometimes off-putting, but the possibilities that contemporary theory opens are freeing and exhilarating, for both teachers and their students. For the beginning teacher whom I spoke of earlier, as for many others with whom I have worked, what we do in the classroom has no connection with theory or philosophy; it has no connection with what one counts as knowledge, how one thinks meaning is communicated, and certainly nothing to do with any question one might ask (or neglect to ask or be afraid to ask) about the larger purposes of education, specifically the purposes of studying texts as we do in literature classes. Yet, without a sense of purpose or program, the exercises we perform in the classroom are arbitrary and arid. We can ask our students what year the author was born or how they can tell if the poem is a sonnet or who the speaker of the poem is, but if we have no coherent sense ourselves about where all this is going and why it matters it is hard for us to communicate to students the urgency or the power of these questions or their answers.

Nine times out of ten when I observe a class I ask myself the unspoken question that hangs so heavily in the air: "Why are we doing this?" For the most part, I don't think teachers know. It is in the syllabus, on the test, at the back of the chapter, on the scope and sequence chart, but what is its meaning in the world?

For those of us teaching English in this part of the century, this question about the meaning of texts and their uses in the world is the hot topic. The best, most highly sophisticated minds in our field are waging battles about what constitutes a text, what constitutes literature, what "a reading" is, who authorizes it, and on what grounds. These are also the questions that arise in the most unsophisticated classes. The least socialized students will ask why your reading is preferable to theirs, how anyone is supposed to know that water is a symbol for rebirth, and why they should take your word for it. Most, except for the few who will grow up to be writers or English teachers themselves, leave our classes with these questions unanswered (although with the sense that these questions were clearly "rude" or out of bounds). Also, most leave thinking that English teachers are some weird tribe dedicated to picky, unrealistic notions of correctness and willing to go into transports at some language that merely sounds flowery or remote to them. Their experiences in our classes certainly don't suggest to them that those rude questions are the essential ones or that the manipulation and appropriation of texts are not some marginal mark of middleclass refinement but are, in fact, what constitutes power and autonomy in an information society like our own. So, our discussions and our concerns often remain quaint aesthetic hobbies or repressive exercises in the drill and the mindlessness that authority can compel rather than life or death issues about how students will constitute themselves and their lives in the world.

More recently, I sat in on a class where the teacher had written on the board a quotation attributed to George Bernard Shaw: "Reasonable men accept the world as it is; unreasonable men try to change it; therefore, all progress depends on the unreasonable men." Asked to discuss this, the class shuffled around these phrases and decided that Shaw had gotten it backwards, that he must have meant to say it the other way around. But the discussion was finally ended by a young woman who said, with the considerable disdain that an 18-year-old can summon, "These are just words." So the issue crystallizes, to look at the power of "just words" and to try to fathom how we can help this young woman to see the relationship between words and actions, between verbal formulations and the parameters of our possibilities.

These relations between power and language have been the subject of much contemporary study. As so many others have remarked, reading in the classroom is fundamentally about reading and writing the world, how words shape us and how we can shape them.[1] To abdicate language is to abdicate authority. That overlapping meaning that includes both the act of writing your own text and the exercise of power is a crucial overlap, the place where our subject becomes of critical importance to lives lived, not just to aesthetic sophistication.

## A THEORETICAL MOVE

The title of this chapter is an allusion to the piece by Jonathan Culler called "Reading As A Woman" (in *On Deconstruction*, 1982). I choose this reference because in this piece Culler is talking about a development in feminist critical practice that moves through a series of different positions in relation to reader-response theory and I think the progression is illuminating for any description of critical reading. As Culler tells it, the first moment of feminist criticism involves readings or reinterpretations built on the ground of "women's experience," taking for granted that experience and its difference. (This is a kind of early reader-response development.) In the second moment, or mode, feminist practice tries to theorize what women's experience is and how it is constructed (another move in reader-response theory that sees the self as constructed in much the same way that the readings of texts are constructed). In the third version, feminist criticism becomes a way of critiquing dominant, patriarchal modes of production and exchange (a position to which reader-response theorists move as they begin to align themselves with work in cultural studies).

I make this reference here, not to introduce Jonathan Culler's work directly to high school freshmen or even to college freshmen but to consider the implications of this work for the way we introduce our students to reading literary texts. In applying Culler's formulation, I wish to extend it, then, to include not only issues of gender but issues of class, race, and all the other marks of difference among us as well.. In simple form the idea is something like this: I want my students first to notice and to reflect on the fact that we do read differently from one another, to explore and to try to account for those differences. This is, perhaps, Culler's first moment, to invoke our own experience as a given and a determinant. Then, I want us to begin to look at how we have learned to read the way we do; how much of reading is programmed, resting on prior reference and assumption; and how much patterning and shaping have gone into the construction of our natural responses — something like that second moment. Then it is my hope that in this experience of reading together, seeing difference, and seeing the construction of difference (and also the construction of consensus) we might be able to reread ourselves as well as the texts we encounter, not only the texts studied in class but all the texts that shape who we are, that shape both our lives and our fantasies.

In this way, I would hope that the process of reading in the classroom is not represented as based on arbitrary strategies delineated in textbooks, the province of teachers and scholars only, abstracted from daily practices in the world, but that reading (literary texts as well as one another) is seen as the way we survive in the world, the way we become persons. As all English teachers know, the real payoff is in rereading. Rereading ourselves may be the ultimate goal; it is surely a way of making ourselves active agents in the construction of who we will become.

## A PRACTICAL MOVE

One of the difficulties in our work, it seems to me, is the paucity of conversation that crosses back and forth from theory to practice. One either theorizes or practices; one does not systematically theorize practice or consciously shape practice to theory. Here I would like to make a small step in that direction by describing in some detail an opening exercise I do with students in an introduction to literature class. (I have done it most often with college freshmen, but I have shared it with teachers at all levels who tell me that it has broad applications for use with much younger students.) This account is a hands-on description of practice, but it is practice that is theoretically grounded as I shall try to elaborate.

The first, or second, day of class, before we have begun to study literary texts together, I share a group of photographs with the class. These (and the exercise to follow) come from a remarkable and richly evocative book, *Another Way of Telling* by John Berger and Jean Mohr (1982). The section of the book that I am using here includes five photographs and is called "What Did I See?" I usually work with only two or three of these photographs. These can be reproduced in slides, transparencies, or prints. The exercise involves showing a photograph and asking students to write explanations of it. The question is "What Do You See?" Students write for as much as ten minutes, no less than five minutes, in response to this prompt. Then the class divides into groups, fours or fives. Each student shares with the group what he or she has written. Students are asked to discuss frankly and fully the differences in their responses and interpretations and to try to track what has sparked their particular response and how it diverges from some others. Do they all see the same thing, or do they see different things? Where do the differences arise? Do they interpret a cue differently, or do they notice a different cue altogether? Are there personal associations or private sources of knowledge that change or shape their particular response in its difference from another's?

This could be done with any group of photographs (and teachers have been using photography in this way for years). For our purposes, photographs work better than art prints because they suggest much more immediate access to the actual. The value of these particular photographs is that they are in themselves interestingly provocative and ambiguous and also that the book offers an account of other people's responses to them. So, after the set of five photos in Berger and Mohr's text there are nine people interviewed who express their responses to each, and these are followed by an account of "What was happening."

I will describe here the use of two of the photographs. One is of a young man with longish hair, frowning slightly, somewhat hidden by a flowering shrub. The second is of a group of intense looking, dark-skinned men. They are all fairly young; all are seated, wearing white shirts and some skirt-like garments. They stare toward the camera. When students write and get into groups they begin to share their responses. These may be all over the map. One will think about who is taking the photograph, what is the situation. That person may extrapolate from other picture-taking experiences. ("Does he know he's being photographed?" "Are they facing the camera, or someone else?" "He's frowning because he's facing into the sun. My husband always complains when I take his picture that way.") Others will tune in on very different levels. "Compositionally, the picture of the men is very strong." "Is that a cherry tree? Perhaps it's Washington, D.C." "Is the man urinating behind a bush?"

Some students will produce a story to account for the details they notice. Others will just describe details. Others will make speculations about surrounding circumstances. One will notice that the young man appears to have a camera himself; others will not have picked up that detail. Some will place the geographic location of the photo of the group; others will either not notice the clues to this or not have the experience to interpret them so precisely. Students sometimes ask, "What should we be noticing?" or, "This makes me think of something else, but that's beside the point, isn't it?" For our purposes, the photographs work well to elicit exactly this wide range of disparate and relatively unselfconscious response. Because our course is an English class, not a photography class, less is at stake in being "wrong" about a photograph than in being wrong about a literary text so we get a muddle of response. Also, there has for the most part been less antecedent training in how to talk about photographs so students are not able to anticipate what the teacher wants. This is not, then, an exercise in getting the right answer; it is a genuine muddle. The process is relatively free and unconstrained by previous teaching or expectation. There is also something about photographs themselves that feels less mediated than about literary works. These pictures are, of course, not absolutely unmediated, but we proceed to read them as though they were. These documents come to us as "facts," seemingly incontrovertible, and we exercise on them our everyday deductive powers, not some special set of school-learned skills.

In this exercise we have a relatively neutral field on which to begin our discussions. For the getting-to-know-you activities of the first days of a class this is particularly useful; it is also useful, as we shall see, as the ground on which to raise our communal ideas of critical practice. After the groups have engaged in fairly spirited exchanges about the different interpretive possibilities that the pictures raise for them, we open the floor to full-group discussion, asking particularly that students highlight the differences in interpretation that developed in their earlier discussions. What emerged as observation or response in their conversations?

After a few moments to explore these questions, we turn to the responses that our text elicited from the nine people interviewed. They are identified as "a market-gardener, a clergyman, a schoolgirl, a banker, an actress, a dance-teacher, a psychiatrist, a hairdresser, and a factory worker." The range in their responses is very interesting. Of the young man behind the flowering shrub, the clergyman says: "Tomorrow belongs to the young! An image of hope. His face and his shirt are touching. I have to stop myself saying: 'Spring!'" The schoolgirl responds to the same photo: "A bloke in a tree which is in flower. He's hiding and playing. And he wants to show to somebody that he's hiding" (50). If several of the photographs and responses are shown, it is interesting to look at the patterns of response that emerge for each viewer, what Norman Holland might name "identity themes."[2] We can linger for a few minutes on comparisons between the responses of these subjects and our own, the kinds of alternatives that such a range of responses suggests for interpretive activity. Then we reveal, perhaps the most interesting piece of the material, "What was happening." In the case of this first photo the answer is "Washington 1971. A demonstration against the war in Vietnam. 400,000 demonstrators in front of the White House. The young man had climbed the tree so as to see better and to take his photographs" (51).

The final part of the exercise (perhaps the ending of a long class period or a set of classes) involves some more writing, a reflection on the experience we have had. What does our previous series of discussions tell us about interpretation or reading in this broad sense? Students are asked to write for up to ten minutes on this question: What have we learned here about the processes of interpretation: our own, other individual's, and the group's? Again, in a very long session we might hold some group discussion after the writing. In a shorter session we might begin the next class with this discussion.

## EVOLVING THEORY FROM PRACTICE

What emerges? At the least we can easily ascertain the following: (1) Different details are noticed by different people. (2) The same details are often differently interpreted by different people. (3) People make associations that shape their responses. (4) People generalize in different ways from the same concrete details. (5) People's assumptions about the world and about human behavior shape what they observe. (6) In responding to a photograph one may make up a narrative to account for the circumstance and identify with particular characters, thereby providing emotional motivation for the moments pictured; one may make aesthetic observations; one may use the picture as a historical puzzle and try to elicit factual data from it about place, time, and situation; one may use the photograph primarily as a springboard to other associations and memories; one may thematize the material to shape a symbolic reading; and, of course, one may shift roles constantly, using one mode of response at one moment and another the next. There are many ways to read photographs.

Where does this get us? Well, for one thing we've had at least a day, or several days, of fairly spirited and engaged exchange. People have gotten to know one another. (We have learned, from Jack's extraordinary prescience, that he has a sharp eye for detail and that he has been to Sri Lanka, the setting for the second photograph. We've heard some funny stories about Mary and her experiences taking pictures of the family on a recent trip to Yosemite.) This is no small thing to accomplish in the very first week of class, but we have established several other important things that will shape everything else to follow in this course.

We have decentered authority in the class so that the work of exploration has been done by many voices. (No matter what school you visit, any walk down the halls will remind you of the indefatigable obduracy of teachers' voices talking into the void.) We have insisted that what students bring with them (in the way of experience, perceptions, knowledge, and canniness) is the starting ground for our work. Rather than insisting, over and over again as so much of our education does, that students arrive empty, to be filled, created, shaped only by what this course teaches, we have made a link between the work of everyday life and the work of the classroom. In insisting that our students are already experienced readers, we are validating not only that their knowledge in and of the world is related to our work with texts but also their entrance into our classroom in their own wholeness. They, as people with affiliations and histories, will be readers. Nothing that they are, or think, will be irrelevant to their own experiences of reading in this course, and we hope that nothing that we read will be seen to be irrelevant to who they are. Concomitant with this, we are validating the usefulness, the necessity even, of an exchange of different perspectives in our work together. In so many classes in which texts are used to produce single, authoritative interpretations there is no particular purpose for group instruction. Nothing substantially changes because we have 25 people reading together rather than a single reader alone in a room. In this course those 25 different readers will help to shape one another's experience because one of the things we will have observed in these first days is that other people's observations and experiences may modify our own. When Sarah noticed that the dark shadow at the young man's chest was probably a camera, that led us all to look again and to take advantage of her sharp eyesight. When Bill remarked that all the men in the second photo were of similar age, we pondered a fact that seemed relevant once he said it, even if we had not ourselves noted it at first. When we read the banker's response to that second picture quoted in the text: "This image immediately brings to mind the stirring of the Asian masses. As racial types, they have fine features, and their expression suggests that they are questioning the why of their existence, which is probably very precarious" (50–1), we couldn't help but reflect on how much one's own preconceptions and one's own position in the world shape what one sees. The picture of a culture obviously different from our own stirred a chain of alienated, sometimes patronizing, sometimes fearful responses that we could observe here as textual response became our subject.

Additionally, we have validated the use of writing as a tool to help us have access to our own responses, for the writing is crucial here. These moments of mandated reflection and rumination make the exercise work. Informal writing for personal discovery is part of our affirmation of each person's voice.[3]

Before leaving this analysis of the exercise it might be well to study just a little bit more carefully the list of differences that we elaborated as a result of this short reading experience together:

1. The difference in details noticed. As we said, Sarah noticed the camera; many of us did not. It's hard to say why a detail registers for one person and not for another, but it is certainly true that a detail originally unnoticed can become of great significance in building an interpretation once it is pointed out. (Here it is Sarah, an amateur photographer, who can supply the clue, not the teacher with her specialized knowledge of prosody or literary allusion.)

2. The same detail conveys different meanings. For the people interviewed in the book, the tree in flower has immediate meanings — spring, nature, sexuality, hope — so they translate what was, in fact (at least as stated here), a political event into an amorous one.

3. Associations shape our responses. An example of this follows from the previous set of responses; the actress says the flowering tree makes her think of spring and sexuality and then she says, "It reminds me of the moment in Fellini's *Amarcord* when the man exclaims, 'I want a woman!'" (51). Here, a prior experience becomes linked with the present one and shapes it in a particular direction.

4. People generalize differently from the same evidence. The group of men suggest a mass and a mass of a different culture from these viewers. They each respond to this "fact" with different attitudes. The factory worker says, "From their faces and their eyes, you can see that they don't eat every day." But the clergyman says, "I see in it [this photograph] all the problems of our Christianity." And the actress: "A group of men like choral music."

5.  The alternative strategies that one employs in responding to a text include the psychological identification with others and the projection of one's own themes into the work. They also include experience of the aesthetic, historical, and symbolic relations suggested by the work. Probably we have already indicated enough about the range of possibilities here and the extent to which they are inextricably interwoven, one mode rapidly alternating with another, one kind of response grafted onto another. It will be the business of our course to explore these more methodically as we proceed; it is enough for now to have named some of the possibilities and not to have foreclosed any.

In opening our class in this way we have shifted the subject of study from text to response to text. We have named our subject as interpretive practice without even introducing the literary. In decentering authority we have also foregrounded the question of authority on many counts. We have said, implicitly at least, that the teacher's voice will not be the only one in the *room*, and perhaps not the deciding one; that difference will be not only accommodated but explored as the means by which we all grow and learn. We have also raised a series of questions about authority with regard to texts. Perhaps the most interesting of these is the relation between "What was happening" and what we, as individuals and as a group, have seen in the photos. What is the status of the actresses' observations about *Amarcord* in light of the fact that what was actually happening was a particular political rally at which this young man was ostensibly a demonstrator? For my purposes here, it is not necessary to enter into a long harangue on this subject, but it would seem to me that raising the question is very useful. It is, of course, the central question posed by reader-response theory: Should (or can) authorial intention and historic circumstance absolutely constrain readings or should (or must inevitably) reader desire play a role in shaping the experience of texts? In the photographs we have a clear, palpable example of the relation between actual events, authorial viewpoint (the photographer's role in selection of just this moment at just that angle with just this degree of light), the text itself (as the trace of this moment in this event), and our own readings or responses. This experience will be the base for us to consider these questions in the somewhat murkier realm of literary productions: the relation of the author's intentions, the actual historical circumstances, and the responses that students themselves have to these works, shaped as these responses are by both cultural and personal histories.

## ELABORATING THEORY

In turning back, then, to Culler and his analysis, we can reformulate what it is we have begun to set in motion through this particular experience of beginning exercises. We have established in the opening moments of this course a reader-response direction for study; part of what we will examine in this class will be the effect of texts on people: We are looking at *how* we read as much as *what* we read. There are, of course, arguments all over the place about the appropriateness of this move, and for the purposes of this paper I have more or less taken it as a given that attention to response is a good thing. Rather than recapitulating the tortured terrain of the discussion around this issue, let me just assert that for engaging beginning students' attention I can think of no surer approach than that of reader-response.[4] Students are automatically interested in both their own responses and in those of their peers. Without affective investment it is difficult to get any but the most highly motivated students involved; when the subject is affective investments, the path is smoothed toward interest both in the process and in the products that prompt such a process. Attention to text follows naturally from attention to response to text.

So, in this reader-response pedagogy, we have paid some attention to the experience of readers, their natural response to text (so far the texts have been pictures, but they will next be literary works); that is, we have followed Culler's first stage. In being attentive to individual responses, we have immediately observed the differences from individual to individual. Here we begin to approach Culler's second moment. We begin to notice how readings (and readers) are constructed. In the Berger text it is clear that situation or circumstance and training shape readers. While we are all facing the same text, we are each performing separate kinds of readings, and there is some consistency to the kinds of readings we are each performing. One of us is an unfaltering moralizer; another is a down-to-earth, tell-it-like-it-is reporter; another identifies with the males in a photograph, someone else with the unseen females. In this first exercise we have not gone very far toward Culler's third moment, but we have made an opening that will make that move possible. We have, for one thing, problematized some of what would ordinarily be taken for granted in such a class. We have in a variety of ways raised the question of authority. We have, as we said, decentered our own and the text's. We have fostered enough exchange of different perspectives in the class to make the issue of perspective itself problematic, and we have unmistakably raised crucial questions about what constitutes a text and how.

## APPLICATIONS: MAKING THE LEAP FROM PICTURES TO WORDS

I will not here elaborate in such detail the next step — the move from this exercise with photographs to what will ultimately concern us in this course, the interpretation of literary texts — but I will suggest some of the contours of that modulation. As we confront readings together, we try to build on the activities, the insights, and the trust we have already communally established. We might begin, for instance, with the familiar Robert Frost poem "Stopping By Woods." Students reading that poem might be asked to record their own initial responses. These can be sequenced in a variety of ways. One approach is to ask for three separate independent readings and to ask students to mark their copy of the poem in different colors for each reading, making marks around words, phrases, connections, and ideas that seem important or interesting to them on that reading (see Newkirk, 1984). Or we might offer a series of questions for students to consider: What emotions did you feel as you read the work? What was your very first response? What did you see happening? What memory does the work call to mind? What idea or thought was suggested by the work? What is the most important word in the work? What sort of person do you imagine the author to be? Does this work remind you of any other literary work (or film or text of any kind)? (See Probst, 1988.) Probably we would not inundate our students with all those questions at once, but we'd try out a few to get them responding uninhibitedly, and we'd work out ways to get these responses shared, in pairs, in fours, in the entire class. Each time we would be looking, not for immediate consensus and agreement on the *one* right reading but for a diversity of response, and we would be talking about that diversity. We would be noticing again why it was that Wayne immediately understood this to be a poem about death, while Arthur couldn't imagine what would lead him to that conclusion. We would be responding, honestly, to the effect of those rhymes and that rhythm upon us. Do they trivialize the poem for some; heighten its impact for others? Does the situation seem absurd to one person; deeply moving to another? Not being constrained to worship the text and being free to reject it on any number of grounds, students can more easily be open to persuasion to observe and experience things that their initial readings did not promote.

As we move toward more sustained work, we try to keep the same sense of fluidity and experimentation; the same regard for the complex, exploratory, shifting nature of responses. Rather than force students into paper topics that encourage them to solidify and defend single readings, we urge them toward forms that, initially at least, stimulate them to look at the contradictory nature of their own responses and the complexity that other people's differing responses urge upon them. A paper topic that has worked well for me (and that owes much to the essay by Newkirk already cited) is an assignment that asks students to tell the story of their reading of a particular work, how they responded in one way and then subsequently changed or extended their reading in light of some new perception.

I will quote here the work of one such student. This is Judy Ann Lopez (1987) wrestling with the Frost poem. Here's the second paragraph of her essay:

> I may have had an easier time making sense out of this work had the first line in the beginning stanza not read: "Whose woods these are I think I know." This opening line influenced my interpretation of everything that followed, distorting the entire poem's meaning. From my very first reading onward, I attempted (and I must say quite persistently) to attach the concept of God to "woods." This association was the result of my preconceived notion that grandiose scenery signifies God's omnipresence. Each time I read the poem, I continued to look for references to God.

Here is a later paragraph:

> My next moment of revelation was equally distressing. I had discovered a line in the first stanza, critical to the poem's meaning, that I had previously skipped over: "He will not see me stopping here." I began to understand that, perhaps, it was not God the poem referred to; His all-encompassing vision would not have missed this hesitation. My problem, however, was that denying this religious aspect threatened to shatter everything I had worked so hard to understand.

Here we have a student looking and looking again, examining her own processes of making meaning and learning how to revise and reconsider them. I would argue that this kind of engagement with texts promotes the kind of intellectual development that should be most precious to us — students responding, considering and reconsidering, gathering the data of their own responses and sifting through the contradictions posed by text and response. In this student paper we have an example of that process as carried out by one individual; in a class discussion we have the opportunity to model that process as it is enacted by many individuals together.

## WHY ARE WE DOING THIS?

But have we answered our own heavy question: Why are we doing this?

There are two kinds of answers, I think. One, the global response, is that texts are places where we can see complex human forces in contest; we understand human agency, psychological motivation, political exigency, the force of tradition and the enabling constraints of forms through the texts that we inherit and through our ways of studying them. To learn to read texts richly, as scenes wherein authors grapple with the divergent claims that being human in the world puts upon us, is to instruct ourselves in the lessons of lives lived. So, every culture passes on its texts, its stories about what it takes to live in the world. In our over-specialized, academized and instrumentalized schools, however, too often these purposes get blunted or submerged so that all that remains is a series of classic texts to be mastered in some fashion as a mark of entry into a level of literacy that demarks social privilege and mobility. Therefore, for our more specific and immediate purposes, we want to rescue the study of texts as relevant and enabling for our students, not in some trendy, of-the-moment way, but through work that makes them see the human meanings of reading and writing in all their multidimensionality. Texts become interesting when the process of both their writing and their reading becomes situated in terms of human struggle. As teachers know, the story of "the dark lady" and Shakespeare's sonnets begins to add new drama to poems that might at first seem merely "academic." The story of the reclusive life of Emily Dickinson or the persecution of Galileo begin to sketch out the human contours of their acts of composition. The story of the circulation and the use of texts can be similarly absorbing. The ways in which texts have been appropriated and have changed the contours of a world are in themselves significant studies, whether it is in the reading experiences of Richard Wright, or Malcolm X, or of Scott Momaday. One of our first aims, then, must be to restore texts to a position where their relation to a real world is reinscribed. Rather than continuing to hold up books at arms' length as sacred, unapproachable talismen, it is our first business to promote free and even irreverent access to them. Demystifying the relations of text, circumstance, author, and reader, humanizing them back into reality, is a useful beginning.

So, our first move has been to provide immediate access to texts and to throw open for inquiry the questions about these important relations between created works and our ways of making approaches to them. It will be instructive to quote Jim Merod here (1987). In discussing the training that it takes to help students to become critical readers, he says, "It requires us to show that texts are strategies, that they carry values that exert a force in the social world. . . . Seldom are students trained in college classrooms to read texts as if they related to the world of human choice and decision, to the interpretive dynamics of every rhetorical mode and moment" (pp. 11–12).

With poststructuralist theory has come an impulse to historicize both texts and readings of texts, to place each of them back into historical circumstance rather than to imagine a transcendent sphere in which inspired writings and inspired readings combine to reveal the human condition freed from any biasing human commitments. It is this historicizing impulse that has led to talk about "situated" texts and readers. This has been the burden of our opening classes, and it leads us, naturally, not to an all-homogenizing vision of an undifferentiated humanity, but rather to the perception of particularities, differences, ranges of response, and responses that in themselves are contradictory and multilayered.[5] So, situatedness and difference claim an important part of our attention when we define our work as the study of reading practices or of interpretive acts of any kind. This emphasis, itself, has meaning and significance for us and is in direct opposition to the approach (still dominant in many classrooms) that universalizes texts to make them into static monuments for veneration. It is, of course, Allan Bloom and E.D. Hirsch who are the most recent and most widely visible advocates for such dehistoricized study. I would like to rely on the words of Stanley Aronowitz and Henry Giroux (1991) to name more emphatically this difference between the pedagogy that turns texts into icons to be uncritically limned by later generations and the pedagogy that frees critical intelligence to make creative and changing uses of the past we inherit. In these remarks they cite Allan Bloom and E.D. Hirsch as the most conspicuous proponents of a a view of textual study at odds with the one I espouse here:

> Read against the recent legacy of a critical educational tradition, the perspectives advanced by both Bloom and Hirsch reflect those of the critic who fears the indeterminacy of the future and who, in an attempt to escape the messy web of everyday life, purges the past of its contradictions, its paradoxes, and ultimately, of its injustices. Hirsch and Bloom side step the disquieting, disrupting, interrupting problems of sexism, racism, class exploitation, and other social issues that bear down so heavily on the present. This is a form of textual authority and discourse produced by pedagogues who are afraid of the future, who are strangled by the past, and who refuse to address the complexity, terror, and possibilities of the present. Most important, it is a public philosophy informed by a crippling

ethnocentrism and a contempt for the language and social relations fundamental to the ideals of a democratic society. It is, in the end, a desperate move by thinkers who would rather cling to a tradition forged by myth than work toward a collective future built on democratic possibilities. (52)

I would not undercut the power of these remarks; let me end by saying that they affirm for me the essential ideological significance of *what* we do in the classroom and *how* we do it. They also serve to remind us that theory and practice are inextricable.

## NOTES

1. There are any number of books that might be cited that make clear the relations between the study of texts and the cultural issues that shape the world we live in and the world from which those texts arise. This is a quick survey of some disparate examples of such works: Atkins and Johnson (1985), Freire (1985), Giroux (1983), Scholes (1985), Spivak (1987).

2. Norman N. Holland (1975) elaborates this idea in relation to the reading of texts. The term derives from Heinz Lichtenstein's use of it in clinical practice and is explained in some detail by Holland.

3. On the question of writing as a means of discovery Peter Elbow (1981) is one of the major spokespersons. On the question of writing-to-learn, or the writing-across-the-curriculum movement, see Fulwiler (1979, 1983).

4. Two of the best introductions to this discussion are to be found in Tompkins (1980) and Moran and Penfield (1990).

5. Jonathan Culler (1982) offers a good introduction to this question of what he calls "the curious divided structure of 'experience.'"

## REFERENCES

Aronowitz, S., & Giroux, H. (1991). *Postmodern education*. Minneapolis: University of Minnesota Press.

Atkins, G. D., & Johnson, M., (Eds.). (1985). *Writing and reading differently*. Lawrence, Kansas: University of Kansas Press.

Berger, J., & Mohr, J. (1982). *Another way of telling*. New York: Pantheon.

Culler, J. (1982). *On deconstruction*. Ithaca: Cornell University Press.

Derrida, J. (1974). *Of grammatology*. Baltimore: Johns Hopkins University Press.

Elbow, P. (1981). *Writing with power*. New York: Oxford University Press.

Freire, P. (1985). *The politics of education*. MA: Bergin and Garvey.

Fulwiler, T. (1979). Journal-writing across the curriculum. In *Classroom Practices in Teaching English*. 1979–1980. Urbana IL: National Council of Teachers of English.

_____. (1983). Why we teach writing in the first place.(1983). In Patricia L. Stock (Ed.), *Fforum: Essays on theory and practice in the teaching of writing*. Portsmouth, NH: Boynton/Cook.

Giroux, H. (1983). *Theory and resistance in education: A pedagogy for the opposition*. South Hadley, MA: Bergin and Garvey.

Holland, N. (1975). *5 readers reading*. New Haven: Yale University Press.

Lopez, J. A. (1987). A revelation that almost never came. Paper submitted for English 2B at the University of California, Santa Barbara.

Merod, J. (1987). *The political responsibility of the critic*. Ithaca: Cornell University Press.

Moran, C., & Penfield, E. (1990). *Conversations*. Urbana IL: National Council of Teachers of English.

Newkirk, T. (1984). Looking for trouble: A way to unmask our readings. *College English, 46* (8), 756–66.

Probst, R. (1988). *Response and analysis: Teaching literature in junior and senior high school*. Portsmouth, NH: Boynton/Cook and Heinemann.

Scholes, R. (1985). *Textual power*. New Haven: Yale University Press.

Spivak, G. (1987) *In other worlds*. New York: Methuen.

Tompkins, J. (Ed.). (1980). *Reader-response criticism*. Baltimore: Johns Hopkins University Press.

# CHAPTER EIGHT

# Preparing Students for Enriched Reading

## Creating a Scaffold for Literary Understanding

❧ ❧ ❧

### Peter Smagorinsky

From a little after two o'clock until almost sundown of the long still hot weary dead September afternoon they sat in what Miss Coldfield still called the office because her father had called it that — a dim hot airless room with the blinds all closed and fastened for forty-three summers because when she was a girl someone had believed that light and moving air carried heat and that dark was always cooler, and which (as the sun shone fuller and fuller on that side of the house) became latticed with yellow slashes full of dust motes which Quentin thought of as being flecks of the dead old dried paint itself blown inward from the scaling blinds as wind might have blown them. There was a wisteria vine blooming for the second time that summer on a wooden trellis before one window, into which sparrows came now and then in random gusts, making a dry vivid dusty sound before going away: and opposite Quentin, Miss Coldfield in the eternal black which she had worn for forty-three years now, whether for sister, father, or nothusband none knew, sitting so bolt upright in the straight hard chair that was so tall for her that her legs hung straight and rigid as if she had iron shinbones and ankles, clear of the floor with that air of impotent and static rage like children's feet, and talking in that grim haggard amazed voice until at last listening would renege and hearing-sense self-confound and the long-dead object of her impotent yet indomitable frustration would appear, as though by outraged recapitulation evoked, quiet inattentive and harmless, out of the biding and dreamy and victorious dust.

With these two sentences William Faulkner opens *Absalom, Absalom!*, easily one of the most challenging, perplexing and brilliant contributions to American letters. Perhaps you experienced some anxiety in reading this passage. Perhaps you stumbled over the stacks of adjectives, became lost in the tangles of modifiers, found yourself in a straightjacket of syntax, or were paralyzed by the arcane language. Perhaps you found the character so bewildering that, while the images enabled you to envision her, you found her as impenetrable as Faulkner's prose.

If you've had any of these disconcerting responses, then you're like most of us: *Absalom, Absalom!* is a notoriously difficult read, proceeding from this barely fathomable beginning and spiraling into uncharted realms of complexity. I've read the novel several times and feel that I've barely begun to grasp its full meaning. If you found the opening paragraph labyrinthine, you've got a lot of company.

You've also shared the same feeling that a lot of your students have when reading challenging literature. Often our own maturity, fluency and familiarity with the texts we assign cause us to forget how stupefying it is for many students to read quality literature. Yet their difficulty in taking simple content quizzes, their reliance on Cliffs Notes and their struggles in class discussions should tell us that their interactions with literature are often fraught with a sense of confusion and forbidding, much like our own when we read texts that challenge us.

If we have ever experienced frustration in understanding any kind of text, from Faulkner to appliance manuals, then we can empathize with our students in their attempts to comprehend literature. Reading is one area in which what you don't know most certainly *will* hurt you. If your vocabulary is short on words such as "indomitable" and "recapitulation," then Faulkner won't make much sense to you. If you can't follow sentence structure then Faulkner will leave you hopelessly befuddled. If you are unaware of the significance of wearing black in our society, then Rosa Coldfield's attire will not imply to you the grimness of her existence. If you do not know that a cold field will remain barren, or that Faulkner at times uses names (such as Flem and Mink Snopes) to suggest the nature of his characters, then the plight of the opening paragraph's central character will not be fully clear to you.

In the business world you've got to have money to make money. In the literary world you've got to have knowledge to gain knowledge. An important job for teachers, then, is to help provide an appropriate context of useful knowledge to prepare students for their reading. We can already hear E.D. Hirsch shouting in our ear: "Cultural knowledge is what students should know! Cultural literacy is the key!" Undoubtedly, factual knowledge — in some cases particular to a culture — affects comprehension. Without knowledge of the Old Testament, for instance, we cannot fully understand Faulkner; consider, for instance, the title *Absalom, Absalom!* Researchers, however, have identified many other kinds of knowledge that go into successful reading. At the heart of theories related to prior knowledge and reading is the idea that we benefit from having a *cognitive map* to facilitate comprehension; that is, some sort of framework that helps the reader anticipate the meaning of the text (Beck, Omanson & McKeown, 1982). Psychologists have found such girding to be of utmost importance in comprehending new information, even more critical than additional time studying the material itself (Bransford & Johnson, 1971).

Our cognitive maps come in the form of knowledge. Sometimes it is a simple factual base: In order to understand the manual that accompanies our new computer we have to have prior knowledge of the monitor, the keyboard, and so on; neophytes often become frustrated when the language, concepts and components become increasingly obscure. At other times our knowledge comes in the form of textual structure: When reading an appliance manual we know what to expect because we have read many other similar manuals that more or less follow the same organization. This knowledge of the structure of the text is known as *schematic knowledge* and is helpful in understanding new, similarly structured texts that we come across.

Several researchers (i.e., Clark, 1990; Hillocks, 1986) have argued that the knowledge we use in understanding new information comes in four general areas: both declarative and procedural knowledge related to content, and declarative and procedural knowledge related to form. I will use this organization to present ways in which teachers can design instruction that helps provide students with procedures for establishing an appropriate knowledge framework for interpreting literature.

I have divided the remainder of this chapter into two sections. In the first section I discuss content knowledge and how it affects comprehension and then provide several kinds of classroom activities that teachers can design to help students consider appropriate content knowledge prior to reading so that their experience will be richer. In the second section I will discuss knowledge of literary *form* and how it affects comprehension, and again provide examples of classroom activities that teachers can use to facilitate student understanding.

The theory that motivates the instructional approach I'm taking is more psychological than literary, although the approach is compatible with much literary theory. In general I'm suggesting that students need a prior framework for understanding the texts they read. That framework may come in many quite different ways and often in many ways at the same time. One important prior framework is the knowledge of a "story script" that we have developed through our personal experiences. For instance, in my own experiences I may have felt a great emptiness, a feeling of loss so profound that my world was cracking and crumbling around me. I might use my understanding of the pattern of my experience — my story script, or my schematic knowledge — to relate personally to Rosa Coldfield and understand her story better. Or I may use my understanding of the Old Testament to interpret the title *Absalom, Absalom!* to anticipate that the story will serve as an allegory for a son's failed rebellion against his father and then use my knowledge of Civil War history to interpret the story as representing the South's failed rebellion against the North. Or I may use my knowledge of Faulkner's reliance on a spiral narrative form — that is, his method of retelling the same story over and over from different perspectives, each time adding new information to deepen our understanding of the action — to help my interpretation of the novel. The list could go on and on, and I would probably use all of these interpretive frameworks together to arrive at a coherent understanding of the novel as a whole.

The activities I'll describe are predicated on the idea that students often have appropriate knowledge (although probably not as sophisticated as that needed to read *Absalom, Absalom!*) prior to reading that could inform and enrich their reading, but that they do not spontaneously draw on it; and that an important part of a teacher's role is to design classroom activities that enable students to tap their prior knowledge for greater understanding. This cognitive theory may overlap with other theories for understanding literature: It is compatible with Hirsch's theory of the importance of cultural knowledge, with Rosenblatt's theory on the importance of personal knowledge, and so on, although it is incompatible with the idea that any of these theories by itself is sufficient.

I will elaborate this argument throughout the following sections. For now let us proceed to the importance of content knowledge and how teachers can help students to use it to inform their reading.

## CONTENT KNOWLEDGE

Declarative knowledge related to content refers to the facts a person knows. Hirsch (1987) and Ravitch and Finn (1987) have argued that students lack this knowledge base, thus accounting for any number of educational and societal failings. Proponents of "basic" education believe that factual knowledge is the cornerstone of education without which no further learning is possible. Their reform agenda calls for a heavy emphasis on factual knowledge that they claim is absent in our schools, the evidence being students' inability to recite it on demand.

Yet other research belies the claim that our schools no longer teach the facts. Goodlad's (1984) extensive study of schools and schooling (Ravitch and Finn base their claim on test scores, rather than on observations of actual classrooms) reveals an educational system that could well be the world of Gradgrind and McChoakumchild, as described here by Charles Dickens in *Hard Times* in the chapter "Murdering the Innocents":

> "You are to be in all things regulated and governed," said the gentleman, "by fact. We hope to have, before long, a board of fact, composed of commissioners of fact, who will force the people to be a people of fact, and of nothing but fact. You must discard the word Fancy altogether. You have nothing to do with it. You are not to have, in any object of use or ornament, what would be a contradiction in fact. . . . You must see," said the gentleman, "for all these purposes, combinations and modifications (in primary colours) of mathematical figures which are susceptible of proof and demonstration. This is the new discovery. This is fact. This is taste."

Goodlad's report is phrased in the terms of a modern scholar rather than in the literary style of Dickens, but what he found was roughly the same, although the classrooms he observed were more boring than harsh. The problem, it seems, is not that teachers do not teach facts; Goodlad's report indicates that the facts dominate our schools now as much as they ever have. The problem appears to be instead that students are not remembering the facts well. From our own experiences we know that we tend to remember information that we find interesting or useful, which suggests that the facts students are taught are either inherently meaningless — which is not very likely — or are taught in a way that does not stress how students can use them in important ways. Perkins and Salomon (1988) have suggested four reasons why students do not retain knowledge or apply it to new situations:

1.  They don't learn it well initially.
2.  They learn the knowledge well enough but do not learn when to use it.
3.  The knowledge is presented as static and disembodied when students should learn it with a sense of discovery and imagination.
4.  They have trouble transferring the knowledge from the situation in which they learn it to other contexts (including testing situations).

The first of these reasons is a problem that, depending on whom you talk to, is due to the student or the instruction. Often teachers blame students for not remembering material studied, asserting that they don't care, are unmotivated to study, are lazy, watch too much television, are diverted by other interests, and so on. Undoubtedly these factors can contribute to a lack of retention of school-related knowledge, but teachers can help students remember what they study in school. Studying material in a meaningful context, for instance, helps students to regard knowledge as a tool that they may use subsequently in similarly structured tasks (The Cognition and Technology Group at Vanderbilt, 1990). We might contrast this with the memorization of disembodied facts, such as the items on E.D. Hirsch's list. Among the items on his list, for instance, are Puritan, witch-hunt, Nathaniel Hawthorne, *The Scarlet Letter*, Senator Joe McCarthy and Mc-Carthyism (but not, interestingly enough, Arthur Miller or *The Crucible*). The imaginative teacher sees immediately the potential for combining these thematically-related concepts into a unit of instruction that enables students to learn important cultural knowledge in the context of potentially meaningful activities such as reflecting on personal ethics, reinterpreting incidents of mass hysteria and ostracism that they have witnessed, and finding modern analogies to the situation.

Hirsch, on the other hand, argues that knowledge needed for effective communication is "vague and superficial" and based on "an initial stereotype" (p. 16); studying the facts he has assembled would "ensure that [our children share] a minimal core of background information," the knowledge of which we could assess with general knowledge tests "for diagnosing areas of a student's knowledge and ignorance" (p. 141). The consensus from psychological research, however, tells us that memorization of discrete facts is a poor way to retain information, with 50 percent of memorized information forgotten within one year and 80 percent forgotten with two (Tyler, 1949, p. 39). Hirsch is probably on track when arguing that cultural knowledge is important in understanding and communicating within one's own culture. His shallow notion of knowledge, however, seems more compatible with the ineffective approaches to schooling that he purports to be reforming than with effective teaching and learning as described by psychology researchers.

The other three reasons for the poor transfer of knowledge identified by Perkins and Salomon address the problem of "inert" or "passive" knowledge; that is, knowledge people have learned but fail to draw on in solving new problems (Whitehead, 1929). A person might, for instance, learn how to settle disputes at work but not use those strategies for settling disputes at home. Thoughtful instruction can help students connect their inert knowledge to school subjects and thus use their prior understandings to create a context for comprehending new material. Unfortunately, schools tend to present information as facts instead of as tools.

My intent with the activities that follow is to illustrate ways that teachers can help students transfer appropriate, previously learned content knowledge to their English classes in order to improve literary understanding. The general instructional approach emanates from a view of literary understanding developed by George Hillocks, Jr. and extended by his students: Curry (1987), Gevinson, Hillocks, Littell, Rehage and Smith (1984), Johannessen (1990), Johannessen, Kahn and Walter (1984), Kahn, Walter and Johannessen (1984a, 1984b), Kern (1983), Smagorinsky (1989, 1990, 1991), Smagorinsky and Gevinson (1989), and Smagorinsky, McCann and Kern (1987).

The thrust of the activities issues from an assumption about the purposes of literature study at the secondary level, an assumption at odds with the premises behind much secondary schooling. One educational tradition assumes that literary study and literary scholarship are one and the same; that the movement toward "relevance" (finding personal connection between the reader and the text) is frivolous and takes students away from a higher understanding of literature. My assumption in suggesting these activities is that high school students have different purposes in their reading than college students do. High school students are not being initiated into a discipline and in most cases are not engaging in scholarship; in other words, they are not mini-professors or mini-graduate students but are kids who have an opportunity to read for pleasure and understanding and yet who have often found their school-assigned reading to be of little interest or value to them. The activities are designed to help them draw on their prior knowledge — often from personal experiences that are embedded in their cultures — to enable them to see connections between their own lives and those of literary characters. Once this empathic bond takes place students are more likely to engage the text and find their reading worthwhile and educational.

To help students connect appropriate prior content knowledge to literary issues, I will suggest five kinds of activities: opinionnaire/survey, scenarios/case study, simulation/role playing, personal experience writing, and writing about related problems. In order to promote the connection of prior knowledge to literature, I would suggest explicit attention to the connection between the ideas discussed during the engagement in these activities and the problems that come up in subsequently studied literature. I would also recommend the persistent and systematic use of activities to introduce literature in order "to saturate the context of education with attention to transfer" (Perkins & Salomon, p. 29). If the classroom is organized to encourage students to connect their own prior knowledge to school problems and to use school problems as tools to help them solve personal problems, then students will be more likely to find their education to be personally worthwhile and engaging. They will thus be more likely to retain the knowledge that is integral in their lessons.

The activities follow the general principles of instructional "scaffolding," an instructional approach that provides students with strong initial support and gradually turns the responsibility for learning over to them. Applebee and Langer (1983) describe the essential features of the method:

> Teachers approaching instruction from this perspective must (a) determine the difficulties that a new task is likely to pose for particular students, (b) select strategies that can be used to overcome the specific difficulties anticipated, and (c) structure the activity as a whole to make those strategies explicit (through questioning and modeling) at appropriate places in the task sequence. (p.169)

Introductory activities can provide initial scaffolding that supports students' efforts to establish a prereading framework that helps them anticipate problems in comprehending literature.

## INTRODUCTORY ACTIVITIES TO SUMMON APPROPRIATE CONTENT KNOWLEDGE

### Opinionnaire/Survey

An opinionnaire or survey is a set of controversial statements designed to solicit students' opinions about issues that are central to the consideration of a literary concept. A teacher needs to understand two important factors prior to designing an effective opinionnaire or survey: the concepts in the literature, and the concerns and experiences of the students. The activity helps to create a bridge between the two to help students anticipate the problems in the literature.

Let's say, for instance, that students are going to read a series of short stories in which characters must battle hostile forces in order to survive, such as Jack London's "To Build a Fire," Daphne du Maurier's "The Birds," Steven Vincent Benet's "By the Waters of Babylon," Barbara Kimenye's "The

Winner," J. Nutuko Nzioki's "Not Meant for Young Ears," and a longer work such as Claude Brown's *Manchild in the Promised Land* or Willa Cather's *O Pioneers!*. Teachers designing opinionnaires or surveys should:

1.  *Understand the concepts in the literature* in order to determine the issues that students would profit from considering prior to reading.
2.  *Enter the world of the students* to discover the level at which students will connect with these issues.
3.  *Develop controversial statements* that will spark a lively discussion related to the problems in the literature.

Here is an opinionnaire designed to get students talking about problems that will come up in reading literature about survival:

*Each of the following statements expresses an opinion. At the end of each statement, put an "A" if you agree or a "D" if you disagree.*

1.  If robbers break into your house while you're at home, the best thing to do is to let them take what they want and hope that they don't hurt you.
2.  Might makes right.
3.  Only the strongest survive. There's no place for weaklings in this world.
4.  Anyone from anywhere in my town can go anywhere else in town and feel perfectly safe, welcome and unthreatened.
5.  If you're outnumbered, it's OK to fight dirty.
6.  I agree with Teddy Roosevelt, who said, "Speak softly and carry a big stick; you will go far."
7.  Nature is a force of good in the world; only people are capable of doing wrong.
8.  War doesn't prove who's right, it only proves who's left.
9.  When two countries go to war, it's usually for a good reason.
10. I admire people who put themselves in dangerous situations and then work themselves out of them.

Students should respond to the opinionnaire individually and then compare and discuss their answers. The teacher's role should be to moderate the discussion rather than to express a personal opinion.

The design of a survey is much the same as the design of an opinionnaire, the difference being that instead of giving their own opinions students interview ten people or so from outside the class and record their opinions. The responses then serve as the basis for an all-class discussion.

## Scenarios/Case Studies

Scenarios and case studies describe problematic examples of people who find themselves in thorny situations that parallel the circumstances of the literary characters. Scenarios tend to be briefer and intended for small group discussion followed by a whole class comparison of the small group decisions; case studies tend to be more detailed and complex and used for more extensive study, such as when small groups lead the whole class in an analysis of a single case. The basic structure and design process of the two is similar, however. The teacher should:

1.  *Identify problematic aspects of the literature* that could form the basis for a series of scenarios or cases (five is a good number).
2.  *Enter the world of the students* to represent the problems in terms they can understand.
3.  *Develop scenarios or cases* that depict the problem in students' terms.

The following set of scenarios could prepare students for a reading of literature concerned with conflicts with authority figures, such as "The Golden Calf" from Exodus, James Baldwin's "The Man Child," Bordon Deal's "Anteaus," Mary Lavin's "The Story of the Widow's Son," Louisa May Alcott's *Little Women* and Paddy Chayevsky's "The Mother."

*Each of the following scenarios involves an individual coming in conflict with an authority figure. In a small group of four students, read each one carefully. Then, as a group, rank the characters according to how much you admire them, putting #1 by the scenario in which you admire the character's behavior the most, #2 by the scenario in which you admire the character the second most, and so on. You must rank all five of the scenarios; no ties.*

1.  Justin Time was on his high school football team. He didn't start but was a reserve linebacker who often played when the team went into special defenses. After a tough loss, the coach mistakenly thought he heard Justin laugh at something as the team was walking back to the locker room. Enraged that a player was not taking defeat seriously enough, the coach ordered Justin to crawl across the parking lot on his elbows in front of the whole team and a few hundred spectators, yelling at him at the top of his lungs the entire time. Justin thought that a good

team player always does what the coach says so although he initially denied that he had been the one who'd laughed, he ended up following his coach's orders without arguing.

2. Sybil Rights was a bright young woman, although her grades didn't always reflect it because she didn't always do what her teachers wanted her to do. One time her history teacher gave the class an assignment in which they were to outline the entire chapter from the textbook that dealt with the American government's decision to drop the atomic bomb on Japan. Although every other student in the class did the assignment, Sybil refused, saying that it was just "busy work" and that she would not do assignments that she thought were a waste of her time. She decided that she could spend her time better by actually learning something about this incident, so she wrote an essay on the morality of the bombing that she intended to enter in the school's annual essay competition. She ended up getting a zero on the assignment, which lowered her grade for the marking period from a B to a C.

3. Mo Skeeto was a young American soldier stationed in France in World War II. His troop was one of many battling the enemy in a hilly region of Europe. They had the enemy outnumbered, but the enemy was well positioned at the top of a hill and the Americans couldn't seem to gain any ground in spite of their superior numbers.

   Finally, an order came down from the commanding officer that Mo's troop should charge the hill. It occurred to him that his troop was being sacrificed to create a diversion so that other troops could rush up and make a sneak attack from behind while the enemy was fighting his troop off. Mo thought that this was a stupid plan that was doomed to failure and that his life was going to be sacrificed needlessly. Yet, he followed his orders, charged the hill, and like everyone else in his troop, was killed. Sure enough, the master plan failed. After Mo's troop was wiped out, the sneak attack from behind was successfully rebuffed and the enemy still held the hill.

4. Robin DeBanks had a job working at the local hardware store after school. Usually, she did whatever was necessary, such as unpack boxes, work the cash register, or put price tags on merchandise. She almost always had something to keep her busy.

   One day, however, a heavy rainfall kept business down. At one point there were no customers in the store and she had taken care of all the little jobs, so she was standing around doing nothing. Her boss hated to pay her for nothing and so told her to scrub the linoleum floor of the store with an abrasive cleaner, a job that Robin reckoned hadn't been done in years. She thought that this task was utterly ridiculous and a waste of her time, but she didn't want to risk losing her job, so she got a bucket, a brush, and some cleanser and went to work.

5. Frazier Nerves stayed out too late with his girl friend one night, and his parents reacted by grounding him, confining him to his room every night for a month. He thought that this was excessively harsh but knew that arguing would only make matters worse. Still, he had a great desire to see his girl friend; not only was he madly in love with her, but he also knew of other boys who found her attractive and he thought that if they were not to date for a month he might lose her to someone else. Desperate to maintain his relationship with her but fearful of parental repercussions, he started sneaking out through his window every night after his parents had gone to bed for a late evening rendezvous with his girlfriend. He made it through the month without getting caught and with his relationship still intact.

Students rank the characters in small groups and then compare their responses in an all-class discussion. The scenarios should be problematic enough that students do not reach an easy consensus. The discussions, then, should force students to examine closely their attitudes toward authority figures and consider carefully the kinds of dilemmas the literary characters will face.

## *Simulation/Role Playing*

Most classes include a few students who are theatrical, or at least hams. These students can engage in simulations of circumstances that parallel those of the literary characters. For instance, students reading about cultural conflicts (i.e., Chinua Achebe's "A Man of the People," Pearl Buck's "The Frill," Abiosch Nicol's "The Devil at Yolahun Bridge," Nadine Gordimer's *Livingstone's Companions*, and George Orwell's *Burmese Days*) could role play situations in which characters from different cultures come in contact with each other (being careful not to stereotype or demean the characters they play). A teacher would need to:

1. *Identify important literary issues* that students will need to confront to understand the material.

2. *Enter the world of the students* to create circumstances into which they can easily project themselves.

3. *Develop circumstances and roles* for students to play.

Possible simulations for literature concerning cultural conflicts would be a teenager from Wyoming moving to New York City, a multiethnic student council planning the prom, a foreign exchange teacher on the first day in an American classroom, a student transferring from an all-girls Catholic school to a multiethnic public school, and so on. Followup discussions could focus on the dynamics of cross-cultural interactions, how majorities can impose their values on minorities, how newcomers must acclimate themselves to new expectations, how right behavior in one culture is regarded as wrong in another, and which factors enable one culture to prevail over another.

## *Writing about Personal Experiences*

Students can write informally — perhaps in journals or reading logs — about experiences that are similar to those of the characters they will study. The act of writing can promote reflection about important experiences that will help students relate to the problems confronted by the characters. In having students produce appropriate personal experience writing, a teacher might:

1. *Understand the problems in the literature*. Often the literature centers on a theme, such as friendship (as found in John Galworthy's "The Apple Tree," Somerset Maugham's "The Letter," Miguel de Cervante's *Don Quixote*, Herman Hesse's *Narcissus and Goldmund*, and Joyce Carol Oates' *Solstice*). The range of problems displayed in the literature, however, may be quite broad. The teacher then needs to identify the kinds of problems that students will need to consider in understanding different aspects of the general theme.

2. *Enter the world of the students* to determine which of these issues they will be most likely to grasp and reflect upon fruitfully.

3. *Develop a range of suggestions* for topics for students to write on.

Students preparing to read literature concerning friendship might be given a choice of the following prompts:

1. Describe an experience you've had in which someone you thought was your friend turned out not to be.

2. Describe an experience you've had in which a strong friendship almost fell apart but survived.

3. Describe an experience you've had that illustrates why your best friend is your best friend, and describe a second experience concerning someone who seemed to be a friend but turned out not to be. How are they different?

One option with personal experience writing is to have students interview a significant person in their lives, perhaps a parent, and then prepare a narrative of that other person's experience. When students interview their parents about literary topics it brings the parents in closer contact with what their children are doing in school and helps create some intimacy between parents and children due to the sharing of their personal lives.

As a follow-up activity to either the personal experience narrative or the interview narrative, students can get in groups, select one narrative, and dramatize it for the class. Students thus see a variety of examples of possible behavior to prepare them for the problems experienced by the literary characters.

## *Writing about Related Problems*

Tom McCann (Smagorinsky et al., 1987, p. 18, 43) has developed a procedure for creating a problematic situation parallel to that in a work of literature and having students write an argument in favor of a solution to the problem. For instance, in Steinbeck's *Of Mice and Men*, two related situations occur: A man has a strong attachment to an old dog whose geriatric miseries and unspeakable stench become so intolerable that other characters suggest he put it to death; and George must decide whether or not to kill Lennie. McCann developed an advice column format to introduce these problems, presenting a letter from a young boy who has an old dog that has grown decrepit and pathetic. The boy's family is pressuring him to put the dog to sleep, a horrible decision since the dog is the boy's oldest and dearest companion. The students' task is to play the role of advice columnist and write an argument in favor of a solution to the problem. In doing so, they must express an understanding of the complexities of the dilemma and look at the problem from several perspectives. Teachers who wish to design such an activity should:

1. *Identify the problems in the literature* that are important for students to recognize and contemplate.
2. *Enter the world of the students* to create a set of circumstances within their radius.

**3.** *Design a problem and format,* perhaps using McCann's advice column medium as a means of eliciting a response.

The following is a possible way to introduce *The Scarlet Letter* to students:

*Pretend that you are a famous newspaper columnist who gives advice to people who write letters to you. Often their problems concern crucial moments in their love life that they need advice about. What kind of advice would you give to the following person? Make sure that when you write your responses that you are supportive of the person's problems and give a thoughtful answer. Make sure too that whatever your advice is, you give several reasons why the person should follow it.*

Dear Answerline,

I am a teenage girl who lives in a small town out in the middle of nowhere. It's the kind of town where everybody knows everyone else and everybody sort of minds everybody else's business whenever they can. It's also the kind of town where everybody is pretty much the same: We all come from the same kinds of backgrounds, we all go to the same church — you know, that sort of thing. People in my town don't care much for strangers or people who are different.

Well here's my problem. It's a very big problem, one I can't figure out by myself. I'm not even sure how to explain it, because you see I've gotten myself in a bit of trouble, and as a result I've got a very big problem, the kind of problem that might cause me to go on a vacation out of town for about nine months or so, if you get what I mean. Except I can't even do that since all of my relatives live right here in town. I mean, people in my town just don't do that sort of thing. And now I've got this very big problem that I don't know what to do about it. Because if my problem ever came right out in the open, if you get my drift, no one would ever talk to me. I'd be a real outcast, my parents would disown me, the school board would probably kick me out of school, all of my friends would turn their backs on me, I'd be all alone in the world (well except for this one little companion, if you follow me). So this is a very bad situation.

But that's not my only problem. As you can imagine I had some help getting into this situation, and my helper is a *very* well respected person in town from a *very* well respected family (*both* of his parents are deacons in the church, and he himself wants to go into the ministry) and he says that he'll help me all he can when all is said and done but that if word ever got out about his, uh, involvement in my situation then he would be so ashamed that he and his whole family would have to leave town for good and that he'd suffer in torment for all eternity for disgracing the church and ruining his family including all of his ancestors and descendants (including one that you might say I have a particular interest in). I respect him and I love him so I don't want to drag him into this, at least not publicly, but I really need to do something because my problem isn't getting any smaller, if you get what I mean. Please don't suggest any extremely drastic situations, by the way — you know, the kind that would involve doctors and would make me feel sad and horrible and regretful for the test of my life. So tell me, what should I do?

Desperately,

Bulbous in Butterfield

Students can discuss possible solutions in small groups and then either produce a group composition or disband and write their solutions individually.

---

## KNOWLEDGE OF FORM

Often knowledge of the form of a literary work can help a reader comprehend the work's meaning. Gevinson et al. (1984), Smagorinsky and Gevinson (1989) and Smith and Hillocks (1988) have identified two general types of literature for which form-related knowledge can inform understanding: works sharing particular characteristics of *rhetoric* or *style* and works sharing format *generic* properties. Frequently instruction based on form-related knowledge is not beneficial for students for two reasons: (1) it focuses on *declarative* rather than *procedural* knowledge, and (2) it is based on a misguided sense of genre.

Form-related instruction, like content-related instruction, is ineffective when it concentrates on the skills of labeling and recall rather than stressing the importance of how to use the knowledge. When instruction in form focuses solely on labeling the parts of a work, all it teaches students to do is to label parts; it does not provide procedures for making meaning of the work based on an understanding of the formal elements. An example of this is the study of a genre such as the sonnet: Students are instructed in the conventions of the form such as the rhyme scheme and then tested on their ability to label the parts they have been taught. Such instruction does not give students procedures for using generic knowledge to interpret the poem's meaning.

Many secondary curricula are also built around an ill-considered notion of genre. Following the organizations of literature offered by anthologies, these curricula group works according to categories such as short story, novel, nonfiction prose, poetry, and drama. The assumption behind this organization is that reading one poem will help students understand the next; that the works of Ogden Nash and Ezra Pound share important properties because they are both written in verse; or that "an understanding of plot and character in Thurber's short story 'The Secret Life of Walter Mitty' enables a reader to understand . . . the problems in Hemingway's 'The Short Happy Life of Francis Macomber'" (Smagorinsky and Gevinson, p. 29). The plot of "The Secret Life of Walter Mitty" does not follow the conventional linear form but jumps about considerably. Studying the plot of this story, therefore, is not helpful in reading and understanding stories that have a spiral narrative form, that begin in *medias res*, that jump back and forth in time, and so on.

I subscribe more to Aristotle's notion of genre — works such as satire, tragedy, epic and so on that share formal properties — that provides instead a means of organization that enables readers to make inferences about meaning due to the implications of shared elements. Students reading a series of Westerns, for instance, can develop a cognitive map based on certain formal properties: white settlers attempting to tame the West, often by means of agriculture or ranching, and overcoming obstacles such as natural elements, desperadoes, wild animals, and Native Americans, often relying on particular characteristics to overcome them. Variations on these elements often concern the morality of Western expansion and the settlers' attitudes toward the obstacles they face: In some Westerns the Native Americans are depicted as savages; in others, as noble victims. An awareness of the story structure helps students anticipate and adjust to variations in the form.

Following are ways in which to introduce students to formal elements and help them learn procedures for interpreting literature based on formal knowledge.

## INTRODUCTORY ACTIVITIES FOR KNOWLEDGE OF LITERARY FORM

### Rhetoric/Style

An understanding of rhetorical techniques and particular styles can help students make inferences about a literary work's meaning. Typically, however, literature anthologies treat rhetorical and stylistic issues superficially, by providing students with definitions and illustrations of such complex devices as irony and symbolism and then expecting students to interpret literature that uses them; or by treating point of view as a matter of identifying a perspective such as first person omniscient narration and then expecting students to understand a narrator's reliability.

Students require procedural knowledge for such sophisticated feats of literary understanding. Smith has identified a meticulous series of procedures for comprehension of works involving irony (1989) and narrator reliability (1991) following from a task analysis of the problems involved in understanding literature requiring such knowledge. The design process of the task analysis and design of activities includes the following considerations:

1. *Identifying the knowledge required to understand the literature.* In the case of irony, this means recognizing such clues as a conflict of facts within the work, as in Shelley's "Ozymandias" when the king declares himself "king of kings," yet his statue lies in a "colossal wreck." Smith, basing his work on a theory originally forwarded by Wayne Booth (1975), identified a total of five clues that students could use to identify a potentially ironic situation in literature: a straightforward warning in the author's own voice, an obvious error in the text, a conflict of facts within the work, a conflict between the author's style and the narrator's, and a conflict between the author's beliefs and the narrator's.

2. *Developing procedures for understanding literature.* Smith identified three steps that students could use to detect and interpret ironic literature: (1) use a recognition clue to detect possible irony, (2) reject the surface meaning of the poem, and (3) reconstruct the real meaning.

3. *Designing activities to teach students these procedures.* Students need practice in using the procedures on material that is accessible to them. In introducing students to the procedure for recognizing a conflict of facts within a work, a teacher could use a humorous cartoon such as those by Gary Larson in "The Far Side." One, for instance, depicts a brutal torturer whose victim is stretched out on a rack in order to extract information from him, with the caption reading, "Still won't talk, huh?...Okay, no more Mr. Nice Guy." Students can see the conflict easily in a user-friendly medium, one that they enjoy a great deal. In introducing a sophisticated concept teachers can often find material that students latch on to quickly and then gradually move them through more sophisticated examples. The Bloom County (now Outland) and

Mr. Boffo comic strips provide good introductory material for teaching irony, enabling students to move to more complex — yet still accessible and entertaining — material such as columns by Dave Barry and Art Buchwald, and finally into literature, often using poetic popular songs as a bridge between ironic entertainment and literature.

The comprehension of ironic literature, then, is not well facilitated by an issuance of the definition of a term and an example but requires the thoughtful and careful planning of instruction in both declarative and procedural knowledge. Teachers planning instruction in rhetorical or stylistic techniques such as connotation, imagery, metaphor, symbolism, propaganda, parody, and author characteristics need to understand the nature of the comprehension problems presented to students and to plan instruction that teaches them *how* to go about their reading, using simple, accessible materials as introductions.

## *Genre*

Knowledge of generic elements can help students prepare for reading literature of similar structure. Once again, however, students need more than just labeling skills; they need to know how the elements contribute to meaning. Teachers can use a general approach to designing instruction that parallels that outlined for planning lessons for rhetorical/stylistic knowledge:

1. Identify the knowledge required to understand the literature. A teacher can do this either through consulting reference works or making decisions based on personal observation. Let's take a genre such as *satire*, which students are often familiar with though even they lack formal knowledge. Satiric literature aspires to ridicule and expose the follies and vices of humanity, using such techniques as exaggeration, understatement, diatribe, and irony. Students need to be able to identify the target of the satire, understand the author's motives in ridiculing the target, broaden the satire beyond the scope of the particular work under study, and identify the satirical techniques used by the author (Hillocks, McCabe & McCampbell, 1971, p. 259).

2. *Develop procedures for understanding literature.* Often when studying a genre students already have some scriptal knowledge based on previous experience with the genre. In sophisticated genres such as satire a teacher might need to point out to students satires they have read or seen and extract the elements from their knowledge of the material.

Most students, for instance, have seen satirical television shows such as "Saturday Night Live," read satirical comics such as "Doonesbury," and seen satirical films such as "One Flew Over the Cuckoo's Nest." Teachers can draw on students' prior knowledge of the genre to teach procedures for recognizing and interpreting satire through these accessible materials.

3. *Design activities to teach students these procedures*. Familiar materials can provide a good introduction to an understanding of satiric techniques. Most students have seen teen-oriented films that satirize the adult world, from *Ferris Buehler's Day Off* to *A Nightmare on Elm Street* (any volume will do). Students can get in small groups to discuss the depiction of adults in movies of this kind, considering how the adults are characterized, how the filmmaker makes these characteristics seem foolish, and what the effect of the satire is. Through this accessible medium, students can practice the procedures they will need to use in interpreting more complex and unfamiliar works of literature.

The introductory activities discussed here are effective in two important ways. Cognitively, they provide a prereading framework for understanding literature. They also make students and their knowledge important sources of knowledge. As Nystrand (1991) has argued,

> Why should authentic discourse promote depth of understanding? First, the character and tone of classroom discourse set important expectations for learning. When teachers ask genuine questions about what students are thinking (and not just to see if they have done their homework), they promote fundamental expectations for learning by treating students seriously as thinkers — that is, by indicating that what students think is interesting and indeed worth examining. In effect, they treat each student as a *primary source of information*, thereby giving them all an opportunity to deal with things in their own frames of reference. Authentic questions prominently underscore the character of instruction where students are "major players" in the forum of the classroom, where communication is not a one-way affair, and consequently where the terms of reciprocity between teachers and their students are upheld not merely in procedures but in substance as well.

The research of Goodlad tells us that students tend to be spectators (and bored spectators at that) rather than major players. The instructional activities outlined here can help bring them into the game and make the outcome dependent on their contributions.

# REFERENCES

Applebee, A. & Langer, J. (1983). Instructional scaffolding: Reading and writing as natural language activities. *Language Arts, 60*(2), 168–175.

Beck, I., Omanson, R.C., & McKeown, M.G. (1982). An instructional redesign of reading lessons: Effects on comprehension. *Reading Research Quarterly, 17,* 462–481.

Booth, W. (1975). *A rhetoric of irony.* Chicago: University of Chicago Press.

Bransford, J.D. & Johnson, M.K. (1972). Contextual prerequisites for understanding: Some investigations of comprehension and recall. *Journal of Verbal Learning and Verbal Behavior, 11,* 717–726.

Clark, R.E. (1990). A cognitive theory of instructional method. Paper presented at the annual meeting of the American Educational Research Association, Boston.

The Cognition and Technology Group at Vanderbilt (1990). Anchored instruction and its relationship to situated cognition. *Educational Researcher, 19*(6), 2–10.

Curry, J. (1987). Improving secondary school students' inferential responses to literature. Unpublished doctoral dissertation, The University of Chicago.

Gevinson, S., Hillocks, G., Littell, S., Rehage, L., & Smith, M.W. (1984). [Prospectus for a literature anthology series: Grades seven through twelve.] Unpublished manuscript.

Goodlad, J. (1984). *A place called school: Prospects for the future.* NY: McGraw-Hill.

Hillocks, G. (1986). The writer's knowledge: Theory, research, and implications for practice. In A.R. Petrosky & D. Bartholomae (Eds.), *The teaching of writing.* (pp. 71–94). Chicago: The University of Chicago Press and The National Society for the Study of Education.

Hillocks, G., McCabe, B. & McCampbell, J. (1971). *The dynamics of English instruction.* New York: Random House.

Hirsch, E.D. (1987). *Cultural literacy: What every American needs to know.* Boston: Houghton Mifflin.

Johannessen, L. (1990). Teaching the Vietnam war: Two short stories. *Notes Plus,* September, 12–15.

Johannessen, L., Kahn, E. and Walter, C. (1984). The art of introducing literature. The Clearing House, 57, 263–266.

Kahn, E., Walter, C. & Johannessen, L. (1984a). *Writing about literature.* Urbana, IL: ERIC and National Council of Teachers of English.

Kahn, E., Walter, C. & Johannessen, L. (1984b). Making small groups work: Controversy is the key. *English Journal, 73,* 63–65.

Kern, S. (1983). The effects of introductory activities upon reading comprehension: An exploratory pilot study. Unpublished master's thesis, The University of Chicago.

Nystrand, M. (1991). Making it hard: Curriculum and instruction factors in difficulty of literature. In A. Purves, (Ed.), *The idea of difficulty in literature and literature instruction: Joining theory and practice.*, Albany, NY: SUNY Press.

Perkins, D.N., & Salomon, G. (1988). Teaching for transfer. *Educational Leadership*, September, 22–32.

Ravitch, D. & Finn, C. (1987). *What do our 17 year olds know?* New York: Harper & Row.

Smagorinsky, P. (1989). Small groups: A new dimension in learning. *English Journal, 78*(2), 67–70.

Smagorinsky, P. (1990). Developing the social conscience through literature. In P. Phelan (Ed.), *Classroom practices in the teaching of English: Vol. 25. Literature and life: Making connections*. Urbana, IL: National Council of Teachers of English.

Smagorinsky, P. (1991). *Expressions: Multiple intelligences in the English class*. Urbana, IL: National Council of Teachers of English.

Smagorinsky, P., & Gevinson, S. (1989). *Fostering the reader's response: Rethinking the literature curriculum, grades 7–12*. Palo Alto, CA: Dale Seymour Publications.

Smagorinsky, P., McCann, T. & Kern, S. (1987). *Explorations: Introductory activities for literature and composition, grades 7–12*. Urbana, IL: National Council of Teachers of English.

Smith, M.W. (1989). Teaching the interpretation of irony in poetry. *Research in the Teaching of English, 23*, 254–272.

Smith, M.W. (1991). *Understanding unreliable narrators: Reading between the lines in the literature classroom*. Urbana, IL: National Council of Teachers of English.

Smith, M.W. & Hillocks, G. (1988). Sensible sequencing: Developing knowledge about literature text by text. *English Journal*, 77(6), 44–49.

Tyler, R. (1949). *Basic principles of curriculum and instruction*. Chicago: The University of Chicago Press.

Whitehead, A.M. (1929). *The aims of education*. New York: MacMillan.

# CHAPTER NINE

# New Possibilities for Literature Teaching and Technology

— ❧ ❧ ❧ —

## Robert J. Tierney, Laurie Stowell, Laurie Desai, Ron Keiffer

Woody Allen in his book of short stories entitled *Side Effects* included a tale in which a professor in search of a discreet affair was introduced to an inventor who had created a machine with very special effects. The machine allowed readers to choose a book and a scene within the book that they cared to enter. For example, the professor chose to enter the book *Madame Bovary* and found himself transported into her boudoir. Such fantastic possibilities seem more farfetched than they really are.

It seems equally impossible to imagine students in the literature classroom involved in similar experiences. However, we would suggest that as technology grows, develops, and changes that such possibilities are far more a part of reality than they are of fantasy. In fact, given the capabilities of today's computers to provide access to a wide range of information and to display textual, visual and aural images, the precursors to such experiences are currently available to our students.

As we begin to consider the experience of the professor in Woody Allen's tale and the future possibilities afforded by technology, as a transition we might also consider traditional language-rich classrooms where students are surrounded by different and varying forms of media. In these classrooms the teacher encourages students to go beyond the content of the text to explore multiple texts and to represent their learning in an oral as well as a visual manner. Reports are not merely rewritten pieces taken from the encyclopedia or book reports detailing the main character and theme; instead they are a rich source of information displayed with a variety of media. For instance, students in one high school classroom have begun the exploration of fantasy and are reading a wide variety of texts — George Orwell's *Animal Farm*, Ray Bradbury's *Farenheit 451*, and Ursula K. LeGuin's *The Wizard of Earthsea*. While each of these texts are quite different, they share common characteristics of the fantasy novel and allow the students to explore the range of texts found in this genre. The students are encouraged to extend their reading of these texts in many ways, such as through class discussions or the writing and illustrating of their own fantasy pieces. Some students have gone beyond the text and have created pictures and sculptures of alternate worlds. Their art work has become the focal point of many class discussions and has helped other students visualize worlds beyond our own. Students interested in design have created figures representing specific characters and have created costumes they believe to be appropriate for the text.

Classrooms such as these that involve learners in thematic exploration of learning have always had multiple resources available to them. In the past such multimedia classrooms have involved students with paints, crayons, clay, film strips, and a rich assortment of texts, With the advent of television and video tape, teachers began to include film and interactive educational television into the learning process. Computers have added still more interactive potential to the classroom. Today teachers can find prepackaged, interactive multimedia kits, can pull together their own projects, or can encourage their students to develop their own multimedia presentations. Computers allow for the retrieval of vast amounts of information and for the richness of multiple images and sound. Students can develop new ways of exploring and communicating ideas. They can examine simulations, crisscross in countless ways different texts, cross-reference video portrayals, or animate their own work and so on.

## A CLOSER LOOK AT A CLASSROOM AND INTEGRATED COMPUTER USAGE

To consider some of the possibilities that technology might afford teachers, let's visit a classroom using technology in an integrated fashion.

In conjunction with engaging her students in the reading and discussion of selected works, Ms. Carlin, a high school English teacher, has been preparing to teach a unit on civil rights for several weeks. There are a few texts that Ms. Carlin would like all students to experience in some way that especially illuminate this theme, such as Thoreau's *Civil Disobedience,* Shakespeare's *Julius Caesar,* Gandhi's autobiography, and the writings of Martin Luther King, Jr. With the help of the school media specialist, she has gathered materials and resources that she will suggest her students explore in the study of this topic. The collected materials include poems, short stories, magazine articles, videotapes, speeches, letters, and novels on this topic. Ms. Carlin feels that the text of a novel is only a place to begin in literature study. Emanating from the literature she intends to have the students explore the issues of civil disobedience, to consider how these issues relate to their lives, to compare different occurrences of civil disobedience, and to relate their consideration to various texts tied to such issues. She wants her students to be able to make connections to related literature; to understand how the context in which any text is written, and the author's own views, affect the writing, and how different texts by the same author compare.

To these ends she decides to have the students engage in some whole class activities as well as small group explorations of subtopics. To do this she has set up some software that all the students will view at the opening of the unit — a hypercard stack that will enable students to view the array of options open to them to study as well as relevant background information and related texts. The students simply choose the topic in which they are interested and direct the computer to present the information that is available. The computer can reference and locate details on various topics including graphics, still photos, and video. The students will then proceed to explore the issues in which they are interested and will eventually be expected to pull together their exploration of issues for their classmates.

The following day, Ms. Carlin brings this software to class and sets it up on a network fileserver so that each student can view it on one of the computers in the room. She thinks of herself as a sort of museum guide. She discusses with the students what they would like to explore and guides them to the rooms of this mini-museum, or rather the various texts, video, and/or software they might explore. She has asked the students to explore a variety of texts related to this theme and find a way to share what they learn with the rest of the class. Her students view a screen that looks like this:

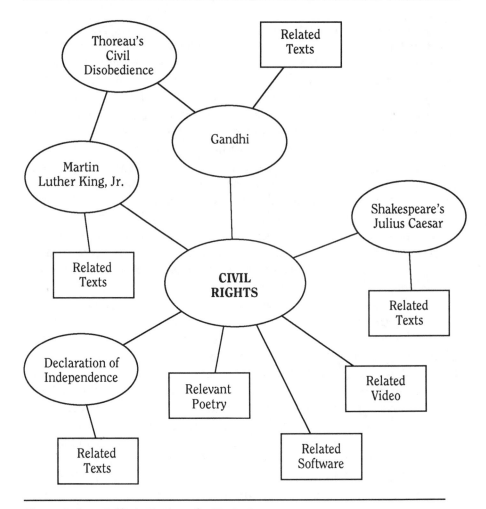

**Figure 9-1:**   **Carlin's Options for Project**

After the students have selected their topics of study, a visitor to this classroom might see students engaged in various projects.

The class begins with a discussion of the issue of civil disobedience, and the teacher selects portions of some of the books that the students are reading to share with the class. The teacher uses these brief readings as a basis for discussion of the issues of civil disobedience that they are exploring through their projects. One particularly noteworthy discussion focuses on the relationship of Julius Caesar to civil disobedience. Several groups suggest that there are interesting parallels between some of the issues portrayed in the play and the experiences of Gandhi as well as of King. The teacher explores with the class the kind of progress made by the different groups and invites the class to offer suggestions to one another. The students then move to working in groups; the class is quickly abuzz with conversation.

At one work station comprised of a computer with video disk hookup, two students are investigating the texts of Martin Luther King, Jr. The students already had some background material that they knew about King. In an attempt to keep track of the events in his life, they added information about King's life that they acquired from various books and other sources. Then they organized a time line and reorganized their notes. They are now at the point where they are delving into his speeches as they think about planning a presentation about the specific issues addressed by King in his oratory and actions. Apart from coming to grips with his message, they want to create a powerful and lively educational experience for their class. Ideally, they want to raise the class consciousness to the issues and, at the same time, to try to get the class thinking about how his message and actions might be applied. At the moment they are exploring relevant material and deciding how best to compile it. Jason has found a video disk that contains news clips of the civil rights marches of the 1960s led by Dr. King that they are viewing on the computer screen. On another video disk they have found Dr. King's "I have a dream" speech. Rachael has discovered an audio tape of Rosa Parks speaking about her memories of the day she refused to give up her seat on the bus, which led to her arrest and the subsequent bus boycott in Montgomery. Ms. Carlin points out the texts of relevant court cases on civil rights from a CD ROM that they might use. She chats with the students for a few minutes about what they see as the key issues and the kinds of things that they are learning from the different sources. She asks them to think about ways they might engage their classmates in these same issues. Then she moves on to the next work station.

Here a group of three young men — Sadi, David, and Sam — have decided to investigate Gandhi's contribution to civil rights. They have already decided to read his autobiography. They have just returned from the library, where they discovered a wealth of material on his writings and speeches from printed texts, software, and various sources on a CD ROM. As Ms. Carlin approaches they are discussing how the material on the video disk relates to the material in the book. To deal with the complexities and amount of different types of information they are dealing with they decide to create a hypercard stack. They will have to sort through the massive amounts of information, decide how best to organize it, and set up "pathways of knowledge" that will connect the ideas. The hypercard is a convenient tool for doing so. It allows stacks of cards composed of notes or illustrations to be tied together in various ways. Each of the three boys selects the subtopics of interest to him, and these will be the different pathways they will pursue. Their opening screen for this project appears like this:

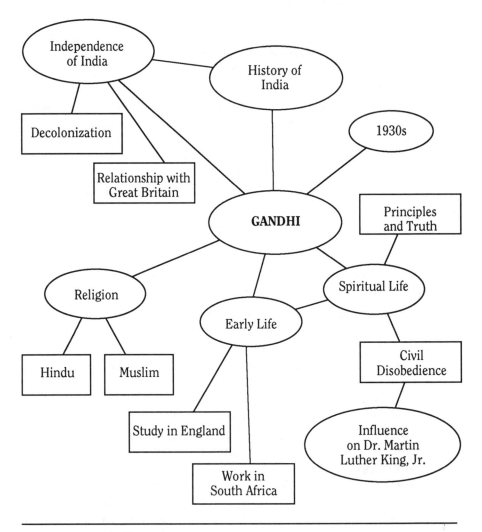

**Figure 9-2:   Gandhi Project**

They envision that one of the advantages of their hypercard stack will be the access it will afford their classmates. Any one of these paths could be pursued to the degree of depth determined by the reader. Learners move at their own pace and in pathways that appeal to their own logic. Sadi, David, and Sam decide to start with something manageable. Since David is somewhat of an expert in using this technology they will depend upon him to troubleshoot difficulties they have. He is interested in the possibilities this technology affords him in going beyond a simple text to one that is less static and more dynamic and interactive. David encourages the group to consider exploring the film footage from the movie "Gandhi" as a resource that they might examine and incorporate into their project.

Jason and Rachael have read about Gandhi's influence on Martin Luther King, Jr.'s thinking. They engage in discussion with Sadi, David, and Sam about ways that they could connect their two projects, by sharing information that they gather and perhaps connecting the presentations in some manner.

The group at the next work station originally began working with Sadi, David, and Sam, but broke away when they decided their interests were more specific. They have decided to explore the issue of civil disobedience and Thoreau's work regarding it. They have decided to simulate Thoreau's trial, in which the reader can take the position of either the prosecutor or the defense. They are currently gathering the materials the "attorneys" for each side would find necessary for Thoreau's defense or prosecution. They have decided to set up hypercard stacks for each position. Each attorney will have the information at his or her disposal, and will decide how best to use it when the time for the mock trial arrives.

Prepackaged software are also available for student and teacher use so that students can draw on the existing rich resources and incorporate them in their studies. Certain news services have taken the video clips from the evening news that had previously gone into storage and began publishing video disks for the education market. Using HyperCard as a navigational tool, the interactive video disk enables users to draw upon the recorded video information

Keiko and Chris, also interested in the work of Martin Luther King, Jr., are sitting in front of two computer screens, side by side, engaged in using a piece of prepackaged software that is coaching them to write their own piece about civil rights from Martin Luther King, Jr.'s perspective. This software contains a wide variety of sources of his spoken and written texts. It invites the reader to comment on the texts he or she is reading and then write a text of his or her own. It poses questions and prompts to the reader, who then decides whether to incorporate them into the piece or not. Keiko has begun by accessing all the references that focus on civil rights. The computer quickly searches and compiles a list. As the students read through the documents, questions and comments appear in a sidebar about the ideas contained within the text. As Keiko and Chris read through a document, they jot down notes about their responses on the adjoining computer. After they have read through the documents, they will access another piece of software that will coach them through a piece of writing. Questions and comments will appear on the screen that will enable them to organize their ideas and present them in an effective manner.

As Ms. Carlin moves around the room to investigate other projects, she visits a group interested in Julius Caesar. The students have chosen to work on the cast, costumes, and stage design for their interpretation of a scene from *Julius Caesar* and then make an animated movie or record of their work. They are working with the Director's Notebook component of the software, by which they can browse through an archive of hundreds of costumed actors and props on video disk and make selections that suit their interpretations. All these elements are placed on a staging space, and the students can work out the scene by moving characters across the stage to create blocking patterns which are recorded. After these students have made these decisions they will then work with the storyboard group.

Another subgroup of this larger group is utilizing another piece of software that enables them to design a storyboard on the computer screen for the scenes they will perform and videotape for the class. They have decided only to perform the key scenes in the play that are illustrative of civil rights. The storyboard enables them to block out the scenes they will film, much like filmmakers and advertisers do. After the storyboard has been finalized, it will be printed and handed over to the videotaping group so that they can make decisions regarding the filming of these scenes. Ms. Carlin takes a look at their storyboard, asks their reasons for the scenes they have chosen, and makes a few suggestions.

Next, she strolls over to a group of young ladies who have decided to explore the Declaration of Independence. They have accumulated a large stack of materials in conjunction with delving into its origins, history of the times, the writing and the writers, as well as the correspondence between John and Abigail Adams during this time and a Declaration for Women written some years later by Elizabeth Cady Stanton. As a way of organizing their thoughts and engaging their classmates in the activity they are planning to lay out the material on the various aspects that they are exploring. Tonya, Seyla, Jamie, and Julie have also added an interactive element; in conjunction with the material that they have laid out they want to engage others in pursuing certain issues. To this end they plan to develop an elaborate display in the room together with a computer file which uses HyperCard to present the information and engage the reader. Their display and stack invite the reader to make comments and answer questions during the reading of the stack. Ms. Carlin also notes that they have begun a declaration of rights for students and are soliciting input from the class so that they will have a collaborative document declaring the rights of high school students. Ms. Carlin has suggested that the group speak with their social studies teacher for suggestions of other documents of this nature that they could include. They respond that they are especially eager to include a text representing the views of Native Americans. Ms. Carlin suggests that they look at the text of the speech by Chief Seattle.

Ms. Carlin then returns to her own work station, where she is working out the details for her own final project. She is attempting to orchestrate a kind of first hand experience with some of the individuals that the students are addressing in their projects. To this end, she has been preparing an experience akin to what was depicted in "Bill and Ted's Excellent Adventure" or what has come to be referred to as a "virtual reality." While virtual reality technology is currently unavailable to the classroom, she thinks she can simulate a version of it with her students. Her goal is to unify the various aspects of the unit by inviting both fictional and nonfictional people to a dinner party: a kind of meeting of the minds. Utilizing the knowledge and insights they have gained from their own studies, individual students will portray Martin Luther King, Jr., Coretta Scott King, Gandhi, Indira Gandhi, Thoreau, Julius Caesar, Brutus, Thomas Jefferson, Elizabeth Cady Stanton, and the like. The rest of the class will attend the dinner party and will have an opportunity to interview and discuss the issues of civil rights with the honored guests. Ms. Carlin will serve as host. Although the exchanges will need to be rehearsed to some degree, there will be an element of spontaneity at the dinner party. Students will be in costume, and food will be served that reflects the origins of the various guests.

Eventually virtual reality technology will enable students to enter the worlds of these individuals and talk with them, much as they would at Ms. Carlin's dinner party. Sadi, David and Sam could enter Gandhi's era and experience the sights, sounds, and smells of India. Jason and Rachael could march alongside Martin Luther King, Jr. in Montgomery, Alabama. Tonya, Seyla, Jamie, and Julie could sit down with Thomas Jefferson and offer suggestions in the writing of the Declaration of Independence. Ms. Carlin's students will be able to manipulate these virtual realities in order to gain new insights, understand different perspectives, or create new and better worlds.

During the last ten minutes of the class period, Ms. Carlin brings the class together to discuss some of the issues with which they have been wrestling, some of the breakthroughs that they have made, or issues that they have found exciting as well as others that they find irrelevant. In addition, she has the students share sections of text (verbal or graphic) that were especially meaningful, pithy, or eerie.

The example of Ms. Carlin's class may not match how you might approach the treatment of literature or the particular set of books and writings included in her class. Our intent was to offer an example to illustrate the use of technology. The orientation that we adopted stresses the integrative use of technology in the literature classroom as an aid to learning and student engagement. We admit that we have left undeveloped issues such as hardware demands, costs, technical support needs, and other matters that can occur. Our goal was to bring to the fore some possibilities. In particular, we hoped that the following attributes and issues would be foregrounded.

## ATTRIBUTES AND ISSUES RELATED TO TECHNOLOGY-BASED LITERACY

### Access to Information

While technology does not control access to information, it can expedite access and expand upon the possibilities that might be within easy reach. In Ms. Carlin's class the students were given ready access to a broad range of topics. Indeed, technology puts a range of treatments of different topics at the students' fingertips. Obviously, the quality and depth of treatment may vary, and there are no assurances that students will find what they need or, once accessed, build the kinds of bridges that make such ideas usable. Still, technology can provide students and teachers background information that may be important and may not be readily available or accessible otherwise. As a result we suspect that in Ms. Carlin's class both teacher and students are apt to want to take advantage of the possibilities at the same time as they realize this may suggest a shift in teaching and classroom activities so that they work to the students' and teacher's advantage. At Brown University, a number of classes have been given opportunities to access information in contexts similar to Ms. Carlin's class, and they have noted that a new relationship among students, teachers, and texts evolves. For example, George Landow in his article entitled "Hypertext in Literary Education, Criticism, and Scholarship" offered the following illumination:

It is 8 p.m., and after having helped put the children to bed, Professor Jones settles into her favorite chair and reaches for her copy of Milton's *Paradise Lost* in order to prepare for tomorrow's class. A scholar who specializes in the poetry of Milton's time, she returns to the poem as one returns to meet an old friend. Reading the poem's opening pages, she once again encounters allusions to the Old Testament, and because she knows how seventeenth-century Christians commonly read these passages, she automatically catches these allusions. Furthermore, her previous acquaintance with Milton allows her to recall other passages later in *Paradise Lost* that refer to this and related scriptural texts. At the same time, she recognizes that the poem's opening lines pay homage to Homer, Virgil, Dante, and Spenser and yet simultaneously issue them a challenge. Meanwhile, John H. Smith, one of the most conscientious students in Professor Jones's survey of English literature, begins to prepare for class. What kind of poem, what kind of text, does he encounter? Surely the *Paradise Lost* he reads must be the same one read by his instructor — or is it? Whereas Professor Jones experiences the great seventeenth-century epic situated within a field of relations and connections, her student encounters a far barer, less connected, reduced poem, most of whose allusions go unrecognized and almost all of whose challenges pass by unperceived. An unusually mature student, he pauses in his reading to check the footnotes for the meaning of unfamiliar words and allusions, a few of which he finds. Suppose one could find a way to allow Mr. Smith, the student, to experience some of the connections obvious to Professor Jones. Suppose that he could touch the opening lines of *Paradise Lost*, for instance, and the relevant passages from Homer, Virgil, and the Bible would appear, or that he could touch another line and immediately receive a choice of other mentions of the same idea or image later in the poem or elsewhere in Milton's other writings or, for that matter, interpretations and critical judgments made since the poem's first publication.

Hypertext, electronically linked text, enables students to do all these things. Unlike books, which contain physically isolated texts, hypertext emphasizes connections and relations, and in so doing, it changes the way texts exist and the way we read them. It also changes the roles of author and reader, teacher and student.

## Ways to Interconnect and Pursue Intra- and Intertextual Connections

The notion of intertextuality or connectivity is central to understanding the possibilities of technology and what is occurring in Ms. Carlin's classrooms. As students are addressing one topic they are apt to access some background information. As they read on, they access other ideas and so on. These connections to various ideas represent other texts that extend, refine, or represent a variation on a topic or issue related to the focus of their assignment. They might be spurred by a momentary interest in the author's background (e.g., Did Shakespeare ever visit Rome?) or a question about links across topics (e.g., Martin Luther King's relationship to Gandhi). But just as a student may find himself or herself having difficulty pulling together ideas from a stack of books or various sources, so students can become overwhelmed or limited in their abilities to take advantage of the sources they can access through technology. Sometimes the focus of a particular literature experience can become bogged down in material intended to supplement and extend. At other times the students may need various amounts and kinds of support to take advantage of the connections. Essentially, technology offers students a workbench which can draw from several texts simultaneously and stacked on top of one another. Sometimes it may help keep track of the stacks. Mostly it requires the students to avoid getting lost or overwhelmed or unfocused. It is as if some of the major advantages of computers can be their unmaking.

## Cross-referencing, Reorganizing, and Indexing

Tied to these notions of intertextuality, computers afford powerful ways to cross-reference, index, and locate information. Students can rapidly check on material that is indexed whether they are interested in revisiting an event or conversation or interested in the possibility of foreshadowing by an author. In Ms. Carlin's class the students might choose to access film clips via the video disk or simply locate references that they might track down in a library. They can develop their own cross-referencing tools, keep tabs on their own files and thoughts — that is, pursue the equivalent of verbal spread sheets and data gathering files by which they might keep their thoughts organized or pursue a different take on a topic.

## Ways for Meeting Individual Needs
## Opportunistically and in a Menu-like Fashion

Computers afford the possibility of help, support, or shifts in approach customized or tailored to meet individual pursuits. There are two terms for describing this tailoring that we find useful — *menu-like* and *opportunistic*. The technology offers the equivalent of a menu of possibilities and support systems that students can choose from and they can avail themselves of the opportunity to do so at almost any time. These menu-like and opportunistic capabilities are usually not available to students without technology unless they are working under close supervision, such as in a one-to-one tutoring situation. There are limitations, but these are understandable. Just as the menu at certain restaurants may or may not meet your needs so the menus may or may not be as thoughtfully developed as they need to be. Furthermore, just as the service you are afforded at different restaurants may be more or less efficient and congenial, so too using the menus may be time-consuming, cumbersome, and unfriendly.

## A Wide Range of Computer Software Exists

In Ms. Carlin's classroom students were accessing what might be referred to as productive software, which allows them to generate their own texts and stacks of material. This kind of software might be viewed as being at one end of the continuum — that is, so that students can be engaged in creating their own personal platform. An example of this was the Gandhi project. Toward the middle of the continuum there exist platforms that support the students developing their own material and slotting it via the use of prearranged structural configurations of information. For example, some software makes available to students the resources (e.g., graphics, sound bytes that students can choose from and edit) as well as possible frameworks they might adjust or modify. The Shakespeare project is representative of this kind of stack. At the other end of the continuum there are various self-contained stacks that involve students in accessing and navigating their way through somebody else's compilation of information and resources. Examples of pre-packaged programs of this nature are those put together by ABC News.

## A Shift to Less Verbocentric Approaches to Idea as Well as Access to Multimedia

A key feature of technology is the access to graphics, sound, animation, images, and video. Whereas the integration of graphics and images in the traditional classroom demanded an array of cumbersome equipment (slide projectors, opaque projectors, VCRs, TV monitor, overhead projector, tape recorder) and usually special time put aside to use this equipment, now technology puts these possibilities into the hands of the individual students as a resource for exploring topics as well as a composition tool for integrating images and sound with the written word in a manner that is dynamic, multilayered, multidirectional, and graphic. Such a possibility may not seem significant on an initial consideration, but, if you will, contemplate the ramifications of placing at a student's fingertips the ability to interface with the written word various images, as well as to capture, edit, paraphrase, and restructure video images as one might using a word processor. Indeed, some theorists suggest that these developments foreshadow a breakthrough as major as the printing press; we would suggest a major shift away from solely verbocentric ways of knowing.

In his essay, "As We May Learn," Weyer writes about issues related to: multimedia, learning, and hypermedia systems. Weyer calls for hypermedia systems to be developed that will allow fundamentally new organizing principles for knowledge and new navigational and manipulation tools for the learner (Weyer, 1988). Multimedia may be a natural bridge between the multisensory learning we experience in life and the kind of learning that takes place in the classroom. Life in general and learning in particular are multimedia, multimodal experiences; perception and experience are highly dynamic and personal, not well portrayed by static text. A multimedia perspective not only changes the manner in which we represent content, but it also changes the way that we present and organize content. Multimedia makes it possible to represent phenomena in a variety of ways. Those multiple representations aid the learner by providing unique and complementary information about the object being studied. Multimedia tools can provide highly motivating incentives for learning. The reader can be involved in multimedia design, a composing rather than only reading or browsing. The static and animated graphics of hypermedia bring aspects of visual design and composition into the authoring process that are not present in print texts.

## Ways to Create Experiences That are Virtually Akin to Being There

With the advent of virtual reality, or technology that can simulate images and situations which heretofore existed only in our thoughts and imaginations, developers have already created three-dimensional worlds in which readers or writers can engage with their environment. With the use of helmets and goggles to create audiovisual environments and gloves with multiple sensors attached, users find themselves not only inside these virtual televised worlds, but also able to manipulate objects as they move in and transact with their simulated environment. Currently, these environments are offering prospective pilots the opportunity to practice air flight; architects, to design and examine alternative spaces; and doctors, to model and practice surgical techniques. In future years they will afford readers opportunities to enter the world of text and to meet and interview characters, authors, and other readers. Virtual reality moves multimedia experiences several steps beyond that provided by the aural and visual elements and multiple layers of hypertext environments. These environments give the user a feeling of immersion in a situation via video images and touch sensation and allow the possibility of interaction within the environment (e.g., walking around, lifting, and so on).

While the quality of the images and the sensory feedback is only an approximation, these environments serve as useful facsimiles for judging designs, modelling structures and operations, and practicing procedures. In terms of reading and writing, they have the potential to afford readers an experience with literature that might not be realized otherwise, except to an extent in one's mind's eye. In an interview with Gene Bylinsky, David Zeltzer, director of the computer graphics and animation group at MIT's Media Lab, recently offered an account of one possibility. As he stated,

> If we provided you with a digitized version of Moby Dick, there's no reason why you couldn't have your own cabin on the Pequod. You could talk to Starbuck as he went after the White Whale. There's enough room in the narrative for you to be involved, without changing the plot . . . You may feel a little like Jimmy Stewart in "It's a Wonderful Life", like a ghost walking around in that world . . .

## Technology is not a Panacea

Technology can be used as an excuse for engaging students in rote-like learning activities, the extensive use of worksheets (electronic), and limited renditions of good books through text and film. Indeed, we are sensitive to the hype that is given to software packages that do little more than occupy student time. Regardless of the nature and quality of the software, students need to be supported in their learning to maximize the possibilities that the students can achieve. It is important to realize that the computer is first and foremost a tool. The level and nature of the investment of the students; the systems they enlist to negotiate tasks, make meanings, and explore possibilities; the focus and attitudes of students to their task and their view of their role — all are essential concerns in the teaching and learning process, whatever the context.

## SOME CLOSING REMARKS

So how do you currently view the use of computers in the teaching of literature? Do computers serve as the vehicle for allowing students to explore, engage with, maneuver, and manipulate ideas? Has the emergence of computers expanded the students' exploration, engagement with, and discussion of the sound, image, and multilayered nature of the texts that they read? Have these emerging technologies introduced into your classrooms this new genre of text that these multimedia platforms afford? Or are you skeptical about technology and its role in the teaching of reading and writing? Do you feel consoled by the suggestion that technology is expensive? We would suggest that such skepticism may be unwarranted and such complacency ill-founded. What we have described are not dreams of the future, but components of the present, and we ask you to consider how you may involve your students in appropriating them in dynamic and creative ways in today's classrooms for their world of tomorrow.

Coming to technology from a background in literature and literacy, we are cautious lest technology compromise the literature. In the hands of sensitive teachers we do not see this happening. Instead, we see technology as serving to complement and aid the teaching of literature at the same time as it offers the possibilities of new genres of text — that is, dynamic and multilayered texts interfaced with image, sound, and other sensations. These new genres have a potential to afford our students new vehicles for exploring and sharing ideas in ways our rather linear, print-based, and bound books have not.

Finally, do not think that the authors of this chapter have little regard for the integrity of literature and the sanctuary as well as inspiration that occurs between the pages of literature. We would suggest that the opposite is the case. We are all lovers of literature as well as concerned educators.

## REFERENCES

Allen, W. (1975). *Side effects*. New York: Random House.

Bylinsky, G. (1991) The marvels of 'virtual reality'. *Fortune*, June 3, 1991.

Landow, G (1989). Changing texts, changing readers: Hypertext in literary education, criticism and scholarship in reorientations. In T Morgan & B. Henricken (Eds.), *Literary theory, pedagogy and scholarship,* (pp. 114–129). Urbana, IL.: University of Illinois Press.

Stefanc, S. & Weiman, L. (April, 1990). Multimedia: Is it real? *MacWorld* (pp. 116–124).

Weyer, S. (1988). As we may learn. In S. Ambron & K. Hooper (Eds.), *Interactive multimedia* (pp. 87–103). Redmond, WA: Microsoft Press.

### PART THREE

# *Using Writing to Support and Assess Literary Understanding*

❧ ❧ ❧

# CHAPTER TEN

# *Using Peer-Dialogue Journals To Foster Response*

——— ❧ ❧ ❧ ———

## *Richard Beach and Chris M. Anson*

## CHARACTERISTICS OF PEER-DIALOGUE JOURNALS

This volume suggests a number of different ways of using writing and speaking to enhance the quality of literary response. To these suggestions we add the use of peer-dialogue journals. In using peer-dialogue journals, students periodically exchange their entries that consist of their informal, spontaneous responses to literature. As we will argue, rather than simply responding for themselves as in a solo journal, in exchanging entries with each other, students have a social purpose and motivation to explore and extend their responses.

As illustrated below, peer-dialogue journals represent a hybrid form that combines the characteristics of formal written essays, oral conversation, solo journals, and teacher-student dialogue journals.

formal written essay

solo journal

peer-dialogue journal

teacher/student dialogue-journal

oral conversation

This hybrid form combines the positive characteristics of these forms while transcending each of their limitations. To understand the value of the dialogue journal as a hybrid form, we will compare and contrast some of their characteristics.

In responding in formal written essays, students' thinking is often driven by a logical thesis/support text structure. For example, in writing about a topic such as "Why is Willy Loman a tragic hero?" students formulate a hypothesis about Willy Loman as tragic hero and then cite reasons from the play supporting that hypothesis. Typically, students are evaluated on the basis of the amount and quality of their supporting evidence. Given these criteria, students assume that they need to adopt a pose of definitiveness or feigned authority. To cite the metaphors of standard composition textbooks, they must "win over their audience" by "proving" themselves as authorities on the topic. They may also assume that revealing any doubts about the validity of their position undermines this projected sense of authority. Since many students have difficulty writing literary critical analysis, achieving this pose of knowledgeable authority creates considerable anxiety.

In contrast, students experience considerably less anxiety in engaging in oral conversation or in writing a journal because they can explore their responses in a more informal, tentative, and exploratory manner. For example, in responding in a small group to John Updike's story, "A & P," one student, Mike, says the following to Susan:

> I really like the way Updike described Sammy's perceptions of the customers in the store. And I liked his descriptions of the girls. It's all very realistic; it's just the way I'd picture it — the little old ladies pushing around their carts and then these girls in bikinis strolling into the store. If I was bored, something like that would just blow me away. I don't know though, the way Sammy describes those girls — it's pretty sexist. What do you think?

To which Susan responds:

> Well, yeah Mike. It's *very* sexist. Sammy's just ogling the girls. He focuses just on their bodies. And his friend, he's making a lot of lewd comments that just goads Sammy on. But, Mike, you said you liked his descriptions of the girls. I know that you think he maybe sexist, but doesn't that bother you — that fact that you liked the descriptions?

Such talk has an honest, informal, exploratory flavor. Both Mike and Susan are exploring their responses without the formal constraints of written essays. Mike isn't trying to prove his points in order to win over Susan. He's actually willing to admit that he's not sure about his feelings (something rarely found in formal essays) when, in addressing Susan, he says, "I don't know though, the way Sammy describes those girls — it's pretty sexist." Mike is therefore seeking some verification of a momentary hunch or hypothesis — the idea that Sammy is sexist.

Susan not only acknowledges Mike's hypothesis but she also throws it back on him as being somewhat disingenuous — the fact that even though he perceives Sammy to be sexist, he still likes the descriptions. So Susan's reaction both verifies and challenges Mike, possibly encouraging him to reflect on his own attitudes and beliefs.

This exchange illustrates a number of differences between the forms noted above, differences that point to the value of peer-dialogue journal writing as a hybrid form. For many students, the reciprocal exchange in dialogue journals is "closer to talk written down than any other school writing" (Shuy, 1988, p. 81). This conversational exchange, according to Michael Halliday (1979), tends to focus on unfolding processes, while written language tends to focus on products. As Halliday notes, "writing creates a world of things; talking creates a world of happening" (p. 93). Thus, a dialogic exchange in writing involves unfolding, tentative responses, responses that encourage students to express opinions and challenge each other's perspective.

In writing their own essay or solo-journal response to a text, students usually generate their own ideas without the assistance of others. By contrast, in oral or written conversation, participants follow the Grician maxim of relevancy — they attempt to stick to an emerging point or idea around which the conversation revolves. They are therefore mutually constructing a point or idea through their social transaction (Vipond, Hunt, Jewett, & Reither, 1990). The very fact that, in a conversational exchange, students consistently return to a key topic (for example, the question of Sammy's or Mike's own sexist perspective) serves to highlight the need to explore that idea as a key point or idea.

Participants in oral or written conversation also anticipate their audience's reactions by posing questions to be answered by their audience. Had Mike written his responses in an essay or solo journal, he may not have attempted to seek out another's verification by asking Susan, "What do you think?" Their social transaction created an ongoing support system for exploring responses. As research on teacher/student dialogue journals indicates (Peyton & Seyoum, 1989; Schatzberg-Smith, 1988; Staton, Shuy, Peyton, & Reed, 1989; de la Luz Reyes, 1991), teachers model strategies for extending their thinking, ongoing feedback that may not occur with essay writing. For example, de la Luz Reyes compared writing in literature logs written by ten Hispanic middle school students with their writing in teacher-student dialogue journals. In the literature logs, students were asked to respond to specific questions summarizing perceptions of the text. She found that the students wrote more and had more positive feelings toward the dialogue journals than was the case with the literature logs, particularly when they were writing about their own families or culturally relevant matters instead of school-related topics. She also found that, in some cases, despite the teachers' best efforts in responding to the dialogue-journals, the students still had difficulty exploring their thoughts.

These results point to one of the social limitations of the teacher/student dialogue journal. It may be that students are unwilling to perceive themselves as equal authorities with their teachers. Thus, for example, in one study of 38 college students engaged with dialogue journals with their teachers, only 12 students posed questions, and they only posed 18 questions (Schatzburg-Smith, 1988). In contrast to the teacher-student dialogue journal, students engaged in peer-dialogues create their own social support network. While younger students may need more guidance from a teacher than older students, older students may be less reluctant to share some of their feelings with a peer than with their teacher, whom they may perceive as both a partner and an evaluator.

While it lacks the immediacy of oral conversation, the peer-dialogue journal also has advantages over oral conversation. Participating in face-to-face nonverbal conversation can be intimidating for some students, particularly those that are reluctant to assert themselves. The anonymity inherent in written exchanges may reduce students' fear of asserting themselves in conversation. For example, Mabrito (1991) compared high and low apprehensive college writers' exchanges on electronic mail and in face-to-face groups. The high apprehensive writers offered more directions for revisions in the electronic mail exchanges than in the face-to-face groups. Mabrito argues that the electronic mail served as an equalizing force for the high-apprehensive writers, who might be intimidated by the face-to-face interaction. The reduction of nonverbal intimidation particularly benefits females, who, in face-to-face interactions, talk less than males. Mulac (1989) showed that male college students talk more than females in mixed-gender groups because the males are perceived to convey an appearance of power. Had Susan been intimidated by Mike's assertiveness in a group discussion, she may have been reluctant to challenge him.

Mabrito also found that the high apprehensive writers were more apt to use the suggested electronic-mail comments than the comments from the oral exchange because they retained more of the information from reading than from listening. This points to another advantage of written versus oral dialogue: In reading over each others' entries, students may be more likely to reflect on each other's responses than is the case with oral conversation. Moreover, the dialogue-journal exchange between partners over an extended period of time encourages reflection for a purpose — to formulate a reply or response. Had Mike received Susan's response in writing, and knowing that he was going to write a response to her, he may have reflected on the meaning of her challenge to a greater degree than in a conversation. Thus, the peer-dialogue journal builds on a social interaction that serves to stimulate further exploration of responses than is often the case with written essays or oral conversation.

## STRATEGIES FOR EMPLOYING PEER-DIALOGUE JOURNALS

Given these advantages for the peer-dialogue journal, we now suggest a number of strategies for using this method to foster response in the classroom.

### Establishing Social Relationships

From our own experience, perhaps the most important benefit of peer-dialogue journals is to help students establish positive social relationships. Without positive social relationships, students are reluctant to share their responses. Because students often do not know each other personally, they need to use their entries to build their relationship. Rather than maintain an impersonal pose, partners need to disclose personal experience or share their own opinions. The very fact that students are willing to self-disclose or share opinions implies that they are willing to share their more personal, private selves with others. In some cases, our students described their own autobiographical experiences associated with the topic under discussion, taking courses, or writing journals. The other students often reciprocated, citing their own related experiences.

Based on interviews with her sixth graders about her journal comments, Judith Boyce (1987) found that the students most preferred those comments that created a personal dialogue with the student, "in which I was just another human being rather than the teacher" (p. 133). Similarly, Nancie Atwell (1986) found that in exchanging letters with her eighth graders, the most interesting letters from her students occurred when she "responded as a curious human being . . . when I leveled with readers about my own experiences, tastes, and opinions, sharing freely and frankly" (p. 276).

In our own research (Anson & Beach, 1989), we found that students' initial exchanges were crucial to establishing a social relationship. By initially revealing their own personal interests or concerns — disclosing themselves and addressing each other by name — the partners set the stage for a collaborative relationship.

## Sharing Difficulties

Students in our study also established a bond with each other by sharing difficulties with course assignments or texts. When one partner admitted having difficulty understanding a text or concept, their partner frequently responded, sharing similar difficulties or attempting to help their partner cope with the difficulty. For example, in their responses to the story, "The Stone Boy," Mike noted to Mary that he had difficulty understanding why, after he had accidentally shot and killed his brother, Arnold went out and picked peas rather than report the death. Mary responded by noting that she, too, was puzzled by Arnold's actions. She then noted that she believed Arnold simply does not know how to cope with the reality of his brother's death so he continues to do something familiar to him, like picking peas. In a subsequent entry, Mike, having read Mary's hypothesis, proffers his own explanation — that Arnold may have been reluctant to report the accident because he feared that he would be presumed guilty. By acknowledging difficulties and sharing possible solutions to understanding these difficulties, partners are modeling problem-solving processes for each other. Teachers could help students define difficulties by asking them to use their entries to specify ways in which they do not understand a text (Kirby, Nist & Simpson, 1986). Sharing their difficulties and solutions serves to bolster their partners' relationship.

## Barriers to Building Relationships

At the same time, our research also showed that there were barriers to building social bonds. In some cases, students considered the instructor, not their partner, as their primarily audience. They described their partner in the third person, as in "like myself, Melanie was also perplexed by the assignment." Other students had difficulty accepting the differences between themselves and their partners in their attitudes, interests, knowledge, and learning styles. For example, while one student used her entries to carefully summarize the class discussions or text, the other student would use the entry to explore ideas evoked by the text. Another partner in a pair would assume a dominant stance, creating an unproductive competitive relationship. Edgar Schon describes this as a win/lose game which is driven by "a model of unilateral control, win/lose strategies of mystery and mastery, withholding of negative feelings, and surface rationality" (p. 135). As a result, each partner "strives to impose his or her way of seeing on the other rather than enter the other's world" (p. 136).

In some cases, the propensity to assume authoritative roles is related to gender. In a study of the nature and length of exchanges occurring in a peer conference on a computer network, Selfe and May (1991) found that males, particularly high-profile males, sent more messages, raised more new topics, and expressed more disagreements than females. Even when participants employed pseudonyms, the males still dominated. This suggests that it may be difficult for students with competitive personalities to engage in a productive dialogue.

Students can overcome these barriers only if they are commited to mutually constructing knowledge in a noncompetitive manner. If they are concerned with pleasing the instructor as primary audience, then they may perceive their partner as a competitor rather than as an equal. As Friere and others have pointed out, engaging in an authentic dialogue requires an equal status in roles and a sense of a collaborative, mutual exploration of knowledge. This means that teachers need to create an environment in which students perceive each others as equals, despite their inevitable individual differences.

### *Fostering Informality*

In our research, we also found that some students have difficulty with more informal writing. They often assume that their entries need to be coherent, logically organized mini-essays. Rather than using their writing to spontaneously explore responses, they believe that they need to formulate a thesis which is then supported with evidence. One reason for the lack of spontaneity is that students have difficulty making explicit their own unfolding, free-associative thinking.

To encourage the process of making explicit free association, we employ a think-aloud activity, using a poem or short excerpt from a story (Lytle, 1982). Students pair up, with one student as the reader and the other as the audience. The reader makes explicit their thoughts as they read specific lines or stanzas; a useful metaphor for describing this process is that of a sports commentator describing their thinking process as a game. The audience provides nonverbal feedback that encourages the reader to keep pursuing their thinking. Learning to reveal one's spontaneous thoughts in think-alouds should ideally transfer to the journal writing.

We also demonstrate a more informal mode by giving students sample entries from previous courses that contain examples of informal writing — expressing self-doubts, raising questions, doodling, complaining about the course, sharing incidents, and so forth. In recording their thoughts spontaneously in their journals, students are not concerned about making definitive pronouncements. They are often testing out or experimenting with ideas in the form of tentative hypotheses (Dasenbrook, 1990). In sharing these tentative hypotheses in a collaborative spirit, they are seeking some reaction from their partner that serves to verify, refute, challenge, corroborate, extend, or contradict their ideas.

In more informal entries, students also make explicit an inner dialogue between alternative voices — themselves as "student," "teacher," "employee," "partner," "narrator," "character," and so forth. For example, in an initial entry involving a response to "A & P," Donna adopts a range of different roles in writing to her partner, Terry:

> Let's see, the teacher wants us to share our responses — "try to make explicit your thoughts" [TEACHER] — Terry, I don't know if I can make explicit ALL of my thoughts. You said that you felt uneasy about doing that, especially when someone else's reading [PARTNER]. Hey, as my mother said, you can always talk to me [MOTHER]. Not that I always did. About the check-out boy in "A & P," he think's that he's hot stuff. He imagines somehow that if quits in front of them — he says, "hoping they'll stop and watch me" [NARRATOR] that they will be impressed. Typical male attitude — "I'm the hero and you're the damsel in distress" [CRITIC] — what a bunch of B.S.

In this entry, Donna is adopting a variety of different roles and voices — that of a teacher, partner, mother, story narrator, and a critic. In doing so, she is modeling for Terry a relatively informal mode which Donna may or may not reciprocate in her own entries, experimenting with a similar inner dialogue. And, in her entry, Donna is openly expressing her opinions about "A & P." Terry is more likely to respond to these opinions than if Donna had simply summarized the story.

Also, one partner's entries serve to prompt or trigger the other partner's responses. In reading over Sue's angry critique of a story, Eric writes his own critique. The more provocative an entry, the more likely it is to set off the other's reactions. An outrageous opinion or a moving autobiographical experience evoked by a text is more likely to prompt the other to respond than a dry summary. The same phenomenon occurs with prompts for writing solo journals. In a study of the effects of prompts for journal writing on fourth graders' responses, Kelly and Farnan (1991) compared the effects of text-based journal-writing prompts that entailed summaries of books ("Tell me about your book") versus more reader-based prompts, for example, "What character was your favorite? Why?" "If you could be any character in the story, who would you be?" They then analyzed the students' responses according to the level of students' ability to generalize or criticize their reading. As expected, they found that, in responding to the summary prompts, the students were more likely to summarize without analysis. In contrast, in responding to the reader-based prompts, the students were more likely to analyze or criticize their reading. Similarly, in responding to provocative entries, students may be more likely to engage in higher level thinking.

### *Reacting to Each Other's Entries*

It is also useful to provide students with examples of optional ways to respond to each other's entries. If a student receives little or no reaction, they may feel ignored or snubbed, undermining any evolving sense of collaboration. At the same time, if students do react, it is important that they respond in a nonjudgmental manner, employing what Elbow (1981) defines as reader-based descriptive comments. In giving reader-based responses, a partner, using an I-statement, describes the fact that or the way in which they were engaged, intrigued, baffled, confused, overwhelmed, and so on by specific statements in their partner's entry. For example, in talking about Celie in *The Color Purple*, Terry notes that "Celie really starts to assert her own rights as a woman. She's starting to realize that she has her own set of beliefs, her own voice." In responding to this statement, Donna notes that, "I was really intrigued by your idea of Celie developing her own sense of voice. At the same time, I was wondering about whether her own "voice" was her own, or something she gets from the other more "liberated" women around her." Donna's response gives Terry some sense of acknowledgement and verification regarding the idea of Celie's voice. Donna is also challenging Terry's conception of voice as a unique, individual matter, a challenge that provokes Terry to cite her own reader-based response: "Donna, I was a little confused about the idea of getting one's voice from others. That seems to me to be a contradiction." In her response, Donna describes her own confusion in a nonjudgmental manner, inviting Terry to clarify her idea in a subsequent entry.

As in oral conversation, students may also be intrigued by which idea from many different ones  in an entry their partner may pick up on. By noting that Donna picked up on the idea of voice, Terry recognizes that she has formulated an idea worthy of her partner's notice.

All of this requires a high degree of tolerance for others' ideas, however tentative or tenuous. Students who sense that their partner will be overly judgmental or intolerant of their ideas will simply clam up, undercutting their willingness to acknowledge the worth of each other's ideas.

### Sharing Related Experiences and Texts.

Given the informal nature of journals, students may also share common autobiographical experiences or recollections of responses to other texts. As in oral conversation, one student's anecdote may trigger their partner's memory of similar or related events. A story about an embarrassing moment will evoke recollection of other embarrassing moments. In responding to "A & P," Terry recalls an experience of working in a grocery store:

> Just like Sammy, I was working at the check out counter at one of these all-night 7–11 type stores. One night I was working pretty late, when in comes this guy who looked like he'd had one too many drinks. I was the only one in the store, so I was really nervous. Well, this guy starts weaving down some of the isles. Then, all of a sudden, he knocks over this pile of peaches. And the peaches start rolling all over the place. And then he steps on one, which made a mess, so he gets really angry and starts yelling. But then I started to feel angry, so I yell at him that he'd better leave the store, so he starts towards me, and I pick up the phone and start to dial 911. I guess that he saw me pick up the phone so he heads for the door. It's like I had some control over the situation, some kind of power that Sammy didn't have.

Having read Terry's account, Donna then recalls her own experience of working in a department store and witnessing a customer shoplifting. Picking up on the idea of control, she recalls that she had no control over the situation, and finds herself empathizing with what she perceives as Sammy's lack of control. In both cases, by elaborating on their recollections, students begin to reflect on the meaning of their experience (Beach, 1990; Smith, this volume). The very fact that partners are sharing their narratives encourages such elaboration. In order to make that narrative tellable to a partner, students add details, comments, and asides that drama- tize the unusual nature of an event (Labov, 1972). As illustrated below, hav- ing reflected on the meaning of that event, they then compare and contrast their own experience with their perceptions of current text.

For example, by describing her own feelings of nervousness and anger, Terry is able to reflect on her own sense of control over the situation. This allows her to contrast her sense of control with that of Sammy's. She was also modeling for Donna the process of linking her experience to "A & P."

The same process occurs with recalling related texts. In another entry, Donna is responding to *The Color Purple*. In describing Celie, she is re- minded of Maya Angelou's autobiography, *I Know Why the Caged Bird Sings*. By elaborating on her perceptions of both characters, she notes that both are coping with patriarchal authority figures. Terry picks up on Donna's intertextual links by citing another related text's character, Edna Pontellier in *The Awakening*. Thus, each evoked, related text triggers recol- lections of other texts, setting up a chain reaction of intertextual links that continues through their exchange of entries.

In our research, we found that, in mixed-gender pairs, males tend to have more difficulty sharing related experiences than females. As Bleich (1988), Flynn (1983), Fox (1990), and others have found, some males in our study adopted an analytic, detached stance. They may therefore perceive

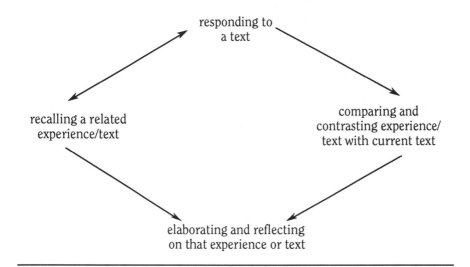

**Figure 10-1 Processes of Defining and Elaborating on Relationships between Current Texts and Past Experiences/Texts**

shared autobiographical responses as irrelevant to the need to focus on the text. And, as Deborah Tannen (1990) has found, women use conversation primarily to create and sustain relationships, while males use conversation to conduct the business of the world. Because they perceive the dialogue exchange as "rapport talk" (Tannen, p. 89), females may perceive the exchange primarily in terms of giving and receiving help. In contrast, males value talk as a means of preserving their status through demonstrating their knowledge and skills. They may therefore perceive the exchange as "report talk" (p. 89) — as primarily an exchange of information and knowledge. As Tannen notes, males are more comfortable in larger groups in which they use talk to claim attention through public display of their knowledge and skills. The more private context of journal writing may reduce males' need for public display, encouraging them to develop their potential for "rapport talk." For example, given their perceptions of talk as conveying an image of "he who knows," males may have difficulty admitting that they do not understand something or need help in responding to a text. By talking openly about how these gender differences may influence their exchanges, males may begin to recognize that they no longer have to assume authority roles in their relationship with their partner.

### Adopting Alternative Roles

These gender differences point to the value of learning to adopt alternative roles or social identities in the journal. In responding to texts, students are constructing a host of different roles constituted by different perspectives and versions of reality. To experiment with a range of different perspectives, students could also switch roles, each adopting the other's perspective, responding as if they were the partner. They could then reflect on their experience, noting how differences in their responses reveal differences in their knowledge, attitudes, beliefs, and interests. Partners could also adopt the roles of different characters, writing to each other as if they were extending the dialogue of the text. For example, in responding to *Ordinary People*, one student could assume the role of the suicidal son, Conrad, while the other could adopt the role of the father. Each student could then describe his or her reaction to events in the novel from his or her respective character's perspective. The son could react to his father's strained attempts to help him and the father could describe his desperation in not being able to help his son. They could then stand back and reflect on their feelings about adopting these roles.

Students could also use their journals to participate in what we describe as "writing role play." Rather than conducting a role play with oral exchanges, students exchange entries as memos or letters to other students in a group. Teachers create a role play situation based on scenes from a text or on issues/dilemmas associated with a text. In our own research (Beach & Anson, 1988), we studied high school and university students' exchange of memos as they participated in a mock hearing about a school policy issue. They adopted a range of different roles — principal, students, teachers, parents, and others — and exchanged memos designed to influence each other. We found that the older students were more adept at employing different discursive and rhetorical strategies than the high school students. The older students were more likely to begin their memos with an attempt to establish a social relationship with their audience through openers such as, "As your good friend and neighbor, I am writing you concerning a matter that concerns both of us." This suggests that, in keeping dialogue-journals, older students may be more socially adept in their written communication than younger students.

### *Reflecting on Their Own and Their Partner's Responses*

As part of their exchange, students may also stand back and reflect on their own or their partner's response. This encourages them to go beyond simply describing their responses to reflecting on the larger meaning of those responses. The format of the dual entry journal in which students put their perceptions/reactions on one side of the page, and their reflections about those perceptions/reactions on the other side serves to foster such reflection.

In reflecting on their own or their partner's responses, students may consider the larger social or cultural meanings of their responses. For example, in their responses to *The Color Purple*, both Terry and Donna are reflecting on their responses to Celie's development of voice in terms of their beliefs about women's development.

Students could also reflect on differences and similarities in their own responses. In reading Mary's responses to "A & P," Mike notes that Mary is consistently concerned with characters' power relationships. In a subsequent entry, Mike then asks Mary if her concern with power reflects her own need to transfer expectations and needs for power or control onto others. Mary responds that her interest in power stems from her own sense of powerlessness in her job. She cites some examples of power struggles at her job, relating those struggles back to the text. In reflecting on her descriptions of power struggles, Mike then replies by describing some of his own similar work-related experiences, something that Mary then reflects on for Mike. Each reflection triggers a further reflection, leading to a mutual exploration of the nature of power and work.

At the same time, Mary and Mike may also reflect on the differences in their beliefs and attitudes. Mike notes that "Sammy was heroic — he was trying to save these women from humiliation." In her reply, Mary notes that Mike's response is "driven by a typically male fantasy 'knight-in-shining-armor' scenario." Mike then reflects back over his responses to the story and possibly realizes that his conception of "being heroic" represented his "male fantasy" attitude. It is unlikely that he would have pursued this critical self-scrutiny without Mary's questioning him, questioning that creates some disequilibrium.

In the process of reflecting on each others' responses, students may therefore challenge what Bakhtin defines as "monologic" positions characterized as fixed, unified perspectives. For example, in responding to a number of different texts, Donna states that "all men are, by nature, downright oppressive." Terry then responds with examples of instances in which men are both oppressive and not oppressive. In order to examine the problematic, ambiguous nature of such generalizations, students use their entries to "keep talking to themselves and to one another, discovering their affinities without resting in them and clarifying their differences without resolving them" (Bialostosky, p. 224).

Students can also reflect on the quality of the exchange itself. Each partner describes their perceptions of the relationship and steps that could be taken to improve that relationship. In assessing the relationship, it is important that students describe their own perceptions of what is happening in the exchange or their own feelings about the relationship with "I am feeling that . . . " statements, as opposed to judging or blaming their partner. For example, a student believes that her partner is not attending to her own responses. Rather than judging the partner as inattentive or self-centered, judgments that will only undermine the relationship, the student may note that "because I haven't received many comments from you about my responses, I feel left out of our exchange."

## EXPANDING THE EXCHANGE: THE CLASS "DIALOGUE BULLETIN BOARD"

Another, expanded form of the dialogue journal is the class "dialogue bulletin board." In this method, students write out their responses to texts on three-by-five cards and put them on a bulletin board. Then, other students read these responses and react by adding other three-by-five cards or Post-it Notes adjacent to the original cards. Alternatively, using a word processing program with shared discs, or a computer lab network, or a Hypercard program, a teacher can create a computer bulletin board in which students respond and react to each others' responses. For example, in a Hypercard program, students would be presented with a card listing a number of different texts they have been reading. Students could then select a text and, after reading over all of the other students' responses to that text, then add their own responses. These responses may be further organized by a visual map according to the student to whom the response was made, the nature of that response ("agree" versus "disagree," etc.), and invitations to other students to respond. By studying the map, students can then determine the direction of the conversation in order to decide on a point to enter that conversation.

This form of the dialogue journal differs considerably from the partner exchange in that students are responding to multiple audiences in a less intimate public forum. Students may therefore not have the opportunity to focus on building and improving specific relationships. On the other hand, students are exposed to a wide range of divergent responses, at least some of which may be provocative enough to trigger some reactions. Students may also sense that each of their own individual contributed responses are serving to build a sense of the classroom as a community.

---

## THE COLLABORATIVE, DIALOGIC ESSAY

As we previously argued, the traditional literary analysis paper often encourages a definitive, monologic stance that may preclude exploration of optional, dialogic perspectives. Thus, while students are encouraged to collaboratively and dialogically explore competing perspectives in their journals, when it comes time to write their essays, they must shift their rhetorical stance to adopt what may be a more confining mode.

However, if the dialogue journal is used as prewriting to develop material for a collaborative, dialogic essay, and if students are collaboratively writing their essays, they may be more likely to adopt a dialogic orientation. In a dialogic essay, partners, drawing on their journal writing, develop, in a more formal, systematic way, two or more divergent perspectives on the same text within the same essay. Using word processing to place each perspective side-by-side on the page, partners develop their responses. Thus, if Mike and Mary wrote a paper on "A & P" based on their dialogue journal exchange, they would each present their own perspective juxtaposed next to each other on the page.

At various points during their essay or at the end, students can, as they did in their journals, reflect on the differences in their languages, perspectives, attitudes, beliefs, purposes, and roles as readers. For example, both Mike and Mary could discuss how their gender roles and attitudes shaped their responses. In this way, the more formal essay writing serves as a natural extension of the dialogue journal writing.

## TEACHER RESPONSE TO AND EVALUATION OF DIALOGUE JOURNALS

Ideally, if the partner is perceived as the actual audience, peer-dialogue journals serve to shift the focus away from a concern with teacher as audience/evaluator. However, students may be so obsessed with pleasing the teacher that they simply ignore their partner, even to the point, as we found, of addressing their partner in the third person.

In order to minimize that concern with evaluation, teachers could adopt the role of coach, who responds to the journals as an observer/participant as opposed to an evaluator (Geisler, 1991). In their role as coach, teachers provide descriptive, nonjudgmental feedback to students about the nature of the students' interaction.

Teachers can respond by sharing their own ideas, becoming third-party participants. In their analysis of exchanges between a teacher and sixth grade students with limited English proficiency, Peyton and Seyoum (1989) found that students wrote longer entries and t-units when the teacher responded to the students' topics or expressed opinions than when the teacher introduced topics or asked questions. Similarly, college students responded with shorter entries when their teacher did not respond or responded primarily with questions (Schatzberg-Smith, 1988). In an experimental study examining the effects of different types of teacher reactions to journals, Gordon (1991) randomly assigned elementary education majors to three different groups — one group that received sharing comments, the second questioning reactions, and the third, no reactions. By comparing changes in entries over time, she found that the students receiving the sharing comments were significantly more likely to increase the degree of elaboration, conceptualization, expression of voice, use of metacognitive stance, and entry length than were students in either the questioning or no reaction groups. Interviews with the students indicated that the students in the sharing group developed a sense of their own professional status and responsibility through their exchanges. As one student noted, "She wrote to me like I was already a teacher. I even started seeing myself more and more like that. I got to really know her because of the journal" (Gordon, 1991, p. 145).

In our own classes, we give oral reactions to students on cassette tapes. We find that, in giving oral as opposed to written comments, we are more likely to engage in dialogic, conversational responses than when we provide written comments. We react by citing our own responses to the texts under study and to the students' entries. We also *describe* our perceptions of the students' interaction, providing them with positive comments about the ways in which the partners are interacting with each other. For example, we may describe the fact that the partners are acknowledging each other's ideas, asking each other questions, sharing their own personal experience, or reflecting on their own and the other's responses. We hope that our descriptive comments provides students with a vocabulary to assess what they learned from using the dialogue journals during a course.

Students may then incorporate their entries into a portfolio assessment. By reviewing their entries and exchanges at the end of a course, partners can collaboratively reflect on their long-term growth in not only their responses but also the quality of their interaction. (see Tierney, Carter, & Desai, 1991; Belanoff & Dickson, 1991, for a discussion of portfolio assessment). The partners would also highlight and caption their entries to illustrate the different kinds of learning that occurred. This may include such things as learning to:

- socially interact in a productive manner
- respect each other's ideas, attitudes, and beliefs
- elaborate on their responses
- understand the nature or types of responses employed
- use each others' entries to trigger subsequent entries
- define and mutually examine difficulties in responding
- develop their autobiographical experiences as related to the text
- prepare for discussion or, as prewriting, for papers
- pose questions that precipitate subsequent responses

Once students document changes that did or did not occur from the beginning to the end of a course in their entries, they could then cite reasons for changes or the lack of changes. In our own research on changes in dialogue-journal writing during a ten week undergraduate linguistics course, we found that, as a group, the students changed in some areas, but not others. To determine those changes, we analyzed the initial journal entry, and then two entries from the beginning, the middle, and the end of the course.

The students' entries were categorized in terms of whether or not they were summarizing material, employing narratives, or reflecting on the material. There was no consistent pattern of change in the extent to which the students summarized material, employed narratives, or reflected on the material. The students were more likely to use their journals to reflect on (75%) than summarize (25%) the course material.

We also categorized whether the entries were formal versus informal and unfolding versus preplanned. There were consistent shifts in the percentage of students employing these features. In the beginning of the course, 72 percent of the journals were categorized as formal, as compared to 28 percent informal. By the end of the course, the percentages were about even. There was a slight increase in the percentage of students whose entries were categorized as unfolding as opposed to preplanned, from 76 percent to 81 percent. This means that, over time, the students shifted somewhat to employing a more informal, exploratory approach.

The entries were also categorized in terms of whether the students were inviting their partner to respond or responding to their partner (the two were not necessarily linked). If, during an entry, the students issued even one invitation or made one response to their partner, that entry was categorized as a "yes" in terms of inviting or making a response. In the beginning of the course, only 17 percent of the students were inviting their partner to respond. By the middle of the course, approximately 30 percent of the students were inviting their partners to respond. And, while only 10 percent of the students in the beginning of the course were responding to their partners, by the middle of the course, 30 percent were responding. This still means that the majority of the students were neither inviting their partners nor responding to their partners. We attribute some of this not only to the nature of the course but also to a lack of ongoing instruction in how to respond to each others' journals. All of this suggests that students need some guidance in how to make the most productive use of dialogue journals. As we found in other classes, providing students with illustrative examples of exchanges from previous classes serves to model strategies for conducting productive exchanges.

In summary, we believe that, as a hybrid form that meshes both oral and written forms, dialogue journals can help students learn to not only articulate their responses, but also to explore and extend their responses in collaboration with others. At the same time, we believe that students need some encouraging teacher response and some instruction. All of this serves to shift the burden of learning to explore responses to the students as collaborative learners.

## *REFERENCES*

Anson, C. M., & Beach, R. (November 1989). Characteristics of effective versus less effective dialogue journals. Paper presented at the Annual Conference of the National Council of Teachers of English, Baltimore.

Atwell, N. (1987). *In the middle*. Portsmouth, NH: Heinemann.

Beach, R. (1990). The creative development of meaning: Using autobiographical experiences to interpret literature. In D. Bogdan & S. Straw (Eds.), *Beyond communication* (pp. 211–236). Portsmouth, NH: Heinemann.

Beach, R., & Anson, C. M. (1988). The pragmatics of memo writing: Developmental differences in the use of rhetorical strategies. *Written Communication, 5*, 157–183.

Belanoff, P., & Dickson, M. (Eds.). (1991). *Portfolios: Process and product*. Portsmouth, NH: Heinemann.

Bialostosky, D. (1989). Dialogic criticism. In. G. D. Atkins & L. Morrow (Eds.), *Contemporary literary theory* (pp. 214–228). Amherst, MA: University of Massachusetts.

Bleich, D. (1988). *The double perspective: Language, literacy, and social relations*. New York: Oxford University Press.

Boyce. J (1987). Visions of communication: The use of commonplace books in the English class. In G. Bissex & R. Bullock (Eds.), *Seeing for ourselves: Case study research by teachers of writing* (pp. 127–128). Portsmouth, NH: Heinemann.

Dasenbrock, R. (1991). Do we write the text we read? *College English, 53*, 7–18.

de la Luz Reyes, Maria. (1991). A process approach to literacy using dialogue journals and literature logs with second language learners. *Research in the Teaching of English, 25*, 291–313.

Elbow, P. (1981). *Writing with power*. New York: Oxford University Press.

Flynn, E. (1983). Gender and reading. *College English, 45*, 236–53.

Fox, T. (1990). *The social uses of writing*. Norwood, NJ: Ablex.

Geisler, C. (1991). Reader, parent, coach: Defining the profession by our practice of response. *Reader, 25*, 17–33.

Gordon, C. (1991). *The effects of teacher response on students' dialogue journals*. Unpublished doctoral dissertation, University of Minnesota.

Halliday, M. (1979). *Language as a social semiotic*. London: Edward Arnold.

Kelly, P., & Farnan, N. (1991). Promoting critical thinking through response logs: A reader-response approach with fourth graders. In J. Zutell & S. McCormick (Eds), *Learner factors/teacher factors: Issues in literacy research and instruction* (pp. 277–284). Chicago: National Reading Conference.

Kirby, K., Nist, S., & Simpson, M. (1986). The reading journal: A bridge between reading and writing. *Forum for Reading, 18*, 13–19.

Labov, W. (1972). *Language in the inner city*. Philadelphia: University of Pennsylvania Press.

Lytle, S. (1982). *Exploring comprehension style: A study of twelfth-grade readers' transactions with text*. Unpublished doctoral dissertation, University of Pennsylvania.

Mabrito, M. (1991). Electronic mail as a vehicle for peer response. *Written Communication, 8*, 509–532.

Mulac, A. (1989). Men's and women's talk in same-gender and mixed-gender dyads: Power or polemic? *Journal of language and social psychology, 8*, 249–270.

Peyton, J., & Seyoum, M. (1989). The effect of teacher strategies on students' interactive writing: The case of dialogue journals. *Research in the Teaching of English, 23*, 310–334.

Schatzberg-Smith, K. (1988). *Dialogue journal writing and the study habits and attitudes of underprepared college students*. (Unpublished doctoral dissertation, Hofstra University).

Schon, D. (1990). *Educating the reflective practitioner*. San Fransico: Jossey-Bass.

Selfe, C., & Meyer, P. (1991). Testing claims for on-line conferences. *Written Communication, 8*, 163–192.

Shuy, R. (1988). TITLE In Stanton, J., Shuy, R., Peyton, J., & Reed, L. (Eds), Dialogue journal communication (pp. ). Norwood, NJ: Ablex.

Smith, M. (1993). Autobiographical writings in the study of literature. In G. Newell & R. Durst (Eds.), *Exploring Texts: The role of discussion in the teaching and learning of literature*. (pp. 211–230). Norwood, MA: Christopher-Gordon.

Staton, J., Shuy, R., Peyton, J., & Reed, L. (1988). *Dialogue journal communication*. Norwood, NJ: Ablex.

Tannen, D. (1990). *You just don't understand me*. New York: Ballantine.

Tierney, R., Carter, M., & Desai, L. (1991). *Portfolio assessment in the reading-writing classroom*. Norwood, MA: Christopher-Gordon.

Vipond, D., Hunt, R.A., Jewett, J., & Reither, J.A. (1990). Making sense or reading. In R. Beach & S. Hynds (Eds.), *Developing discourse practice in adolescence and adulthood* (pp. 110–135). Norwood, NJ: Ablex.

# CHAPTER ELEVEN

# Autobiographical Writing in the Study of Literature

— ♣ ♣ ♣ —

## Michael W. Smith

In John Updike's "Tomorrow and Tomorrow and So Forth" Mark Prosser is trying to lead a discussion of Macbeth's "Tomorrow, and tomorrow, and tomorrow" soliloquy without much success. As Updike describes it, "He perched on the edge of the desk and leaned forward beseechingly. 'Now, honestly. Don't any of you have some personal feelings about the lines that you would like to share with the class and me?'" One timid girl offers a sentence that is greeted by laughter from the class. Another explains, "It seems so *stupid*." Updike continues,

> Mark winced, pierced by the awful clarity with which his students saw him. Through their eyes, how queer he looked, with his long hands and his horn-rimmed glasses, and his hair never slicked down, all wrapped up in "literature," where, when things get rough, the king mumbles a poem nobody understands. The delight Mr. Prosser took in such crazy junk made not only his good sense but his masculinity a matter of doubt.

Every teacher of literature can empathize with Mark Prosser's discomfort. Current theory and research are making it increasingly clear that readers must relate their lives to literature if they are to have meaningful transactions with texts. As Nystrand (1991) explains, teachers who want to promote depth of understanding "[should] take care to help students see relations between the narrative worlds of the works they read and their own individual experiences." But how can teachers encourage students to see these relations? A number of researchers and theorists have suggested incorporating autobiographical writing before reading into a study of literature as a way to do just that.

Unfortunately, the connections between writing and reading in general are, in Greene's (1992) words, "underspecified," a state of affairs even more acute for autobiographical writing in the study of literature. All of the advocates of autobiographical writing in the study of literature share the belief that doing such writing necessarily changes the politics of the classroom by authorizing students' voices. However, there are important differences in the specific suggestions that theorists make. Indeed, I have identified three distinct kinds of autobiographical writing about literature: autobiographical writing *before* reading, autobiographical writing *with* reading, and autobiographical writing *against* reading. Exploring the similarities and differences among these kinds of writing is important for teachers, for in choosing one over another, teachers commit themselves to different instructional procedures; they make statements both on their beliefs about their students' abilities and attitudes and on the nature of literature; and they work to achieve different goals.

## AUTOBIOGRAPHICAL WRITING BEFORE READING

### The Nature of the Instruction

To use autobiographical writing before reading, teachers identify an issue that is central to a text and ask students to write about personal experiences they have had that relate to that issue before they read. For example, consider the thinking one might do in preparing to teach Morley Callaghan's "All the Years of Her Life" to a class of eighth-graders. In the story Alfred, a young man who has recently left school, is caught stealing by Mr. Carr, the druggist who employs him. After Mr. Carr calls Alfred's mother, Alfred waits uncomfortably for he is afraid of the scene that she will cause. But Alfred is surprised; his mother instead demonstrates a "kind of patient dignity." He realizes that Mr. Carr has become aware that his mother is "really a fine woman." The story closes in Alfred's house. After replaying the evening's events, Alfred decides that he'd "like to tell her she sounded swell." He moves to the kitchen where his mother is fixing herself some tea. As he enters, he sees his mother drinking, her lips "groping loosely as though they would never reach the cup." And with this vision "his youth seemed to be over; he knew all the years of her life by the way her hand trembled as she raised the cup to her lips."

On the surface this seems like an excellent story to teach to eighth-graders. Certainly they are in a time of their lives when they are making discoveries about themselves and the people close to them. However, Squire (1964), in his seminal study of adolescents' responding as they read four stories, found that many students neglected this aspect of the story and instead seized on the conflict between Alfred and his mother. They relied, in Squire's terms, on the stock response that when adults and adolescents are in conflict, the adults are almost always wrong. To help a very diverse group of eighth grade students recognize and respond to the theme of discovery, some colleagues and I (Schultz, Hamann, and Smith, 1990; Hamann, Schultz, Smith, & White, 1991) asked them to write on the following prompt before they read the story:

> We're going to be talking about a story in which a character learns some-thing about someone he thought he knew. To prepare you to read and discuss that story, think back to a time when someone's behavior sur-prised you — when something someone did made you realize that maybe you didn't know that person as well as you thought you did. Please explain your experience in writing. As you write, you should think about what you learned about the person, what happened to help you learn it, what had prevented you from understanding it in the first place, and what effects learning it had on you. We'll be sharing these in small groups.

The key to writing effective prompts is to identify issues with which students will have had some experiences but ones that might not be readily evoked by the text. Effective prompts should be open-ended, cuing neither an appropriate written response nor an interpretation of the story. For example, one eighth-grader responded to the prompt with the follow-ing:

> This girl that I knew I thought she was my best friend until one day she met my boyfriend. She was always flirting with him and he was always flirting with her. I got really mad at both of them so I broke up with him and my friend said she was really sorry and she also said that she would never go out with him because she could never do that to me. So I said O.K. And so we stayed friends. About a week later my x-boyfriend asked her out and she said yes and my friend knew damn well that I still liked him. I couldn't under-stand why she lied to me. I never thought that she could be so mean and so I learned that she wasn't a very good friend in the first place.

The personal experience that the student recalled in writing prior to reading was not directly related to motherhood or to shoplifting. However, she certainly retrieved from memory a situation in which she learned something that had surprised and changed her, a memory that helped her have a meaningful transaction with the story. (See Hamann, Schultz, Smith, & White, 1991, for a discussion of how autobiograhical writing before reading affected this student's response.)

In this method of instruction, once students have written and shared their writing they should move on to the reading and discussion of the text under consideration. The autobiographical writing provides background for the discussion of the text, and although it may become the object of classroom discussion, the text remains the primary focus.

## Underlying Assumptions

Like any instruction in literature, autobiographical writing before reading implies certain beliefs about, among other things, where meaning resides, the purposes for teaching literature, and the abilities and attitudes of students. In the first place, using autobiographical writing before reading implies a belief that meaning resides in the transaction between the reader and the text, a belief perhaps most clearly articulated by Rosenblatt. As she explains in *Literature as Exploration* (1976), "[t]he benefits of literature can emerge only from creative activity on the part of the reader himself" (p. 278). To explain the reader's involvement, Rosenblatt (1985) introduces the idea of the evocation, "the aesthetic transaction with the text . . . in which the reader selects out ideas, sensations, feelings, and images drawn from his past linguistic, literary, and life experience, and synthesizes them into a new experience . . . " ( p. 40). Iser (1978) makes a similar argument: "Apprehension of a literary work comes about through the interaction between the reader's presence in the text and his habitual experiences. . . . As such it is not a passive process of acceptance, but a productive response" (p. 133).

Autobiographical writing before reading is informed by the belief in the importance of the activity of the reader. However, in this approach to instruction, the autobiographical writing is used to help students enter the world of the text, a goal that derives from the belief that texts constrain the universe of meaning available to the reader. This, too, is a belief that Rosenblatt and Iser expound. Rosenblatt (1978) explains it this way:

> First, the text is a stimulus, activating elements of the reader's past experience — his experience both with literature and with life. Second, the text

serves as a blueprint, a guide for the selecting, rejecting, and ordering of what is being called forth; the text regulates what should be held in the forefront of the reader's attention. ( p. 11)

Iser (1978) also notes that texts constrain meaning: "The text mobilizes the subjective knowledge present in all kinds of readers and directs it to one particular end. However varied this knowledge may be, the readers' subjective contribution is controlled by the given framework" (p. 145).

Autobiographical writing before reading, then, presumes both that readers must make connections between their lives and the literature they read and that some connections are better than others. Indeed, Brian White and I argue (in press) that some personal connection may actually disengage readers from the text.

We found that readers who adopt what we have called an association-driven orientation to reading enhance neither their response to literature nor their understanding of their lives (Smith 1991; Smith, 1992).

Our results jibe with those of Squire (1964), who contends that

> . . . association of the elements in the story with the personal experiences of the reader is dangerous to interpretation only when uncontrolled. In most cases readers seem to perceive far too few of these relationships. Occasionally, however, a reader appears to give such free reign to every haphazard memory which recurs to him while reading that he is completely distracted from the narrative at hand. (p. 45)

Our arguments presume that something is lost when students are completely distracted from the narrative at hand. Because autobiographical writing before reading has as its ultimate goal increased engagement in and understanding of a world of another's making, teachers who use it likely will share a belief about the power of literature eloquently articulated by Booth (1983):

> . . . nothing I can hope to invent myself should be allowed to replace the exercises in the the imagination that attending to great imaginative works provides. These works can provide what George Santayana called "imaginative rehearsals for living," what Kenneth Burke calls "equipment for living" — but they can do so only if we make them at least equal partners in the dance. (p. 212)

Because autobiographical writing before reading helps students recall and elaborate relevant experience before they read, it is designed to promote the kind of attention that will allow students to have the experience that Booth describes.

Using autobiographical writing before reading also implies beliefs about students' attitudes and abilities. It presumes that at least some students will not make autobiographical connections between their lives and the literature they read in school. This presumption has its foundation in a variety of possible causes. Some students, for example, may view literature as something completely separate from their lives. Marshall (1989b) found that this attitude is prevalent among urban students. He illustrates this point with the example of a student who was asked to write about how "Raymond's Run" made the student feel. The student's response that "It didn't make me feel like nothing" is especially telling as the story was likely chosen because the teacher thought it was relevant to the lives of urban students. Other students might not make connections between their lives and literature because of an actual cultural gap between their lives and those depicted in the stories they read. However, even those students who perceive connections might not make them, perhaps because adolescent readers do not feel they have the authority to apply their life experience. I have found, for example, that readers who have not had success in school are less likely to apply personal experience to a text than are students who have been successful readers (Smith 1991). This is understandable. Many students have been told in many different ways that they are poor readers. As a consequence they may devote all of their mental energy trying to do well what they have been criticized for failing to do: understanding the meaning of words and remembering literal information.

But even successful readers might not apply their lives to the literature they read. They may remain submissive to texts, thinking it is the text's job to make any connections that need to be made (Smith, 1992). They may simply not know that applying life to literature is something that readers do, especially if their view of the reader's role is conditioned by classroom discussions of literature, for as Marshall (1989a) found, teachers seldom ask students to make these kinds of connections. Autobiographical writing before reading is designed to overcome all of these potential problems. The prompts are designed to direct students' attention to parallels between their lives and the situations about which they read, which should minimize the feeling of separation and the cultural gaps that may exist. Simply asking students to write about their lives as preparation for reading vests them with an authority they may otherwise not feel and demonstrates to them a teacher's belief in the importance of students' connecting their lives to the literature they read.

Autobiographical writing before reading also is based on an understanding of the difficulty readers have in reconstructing a text's meaning when they approach it without an appropriate frame of reference. Classic studies by Bartlett (1932) and Bransford and Johnson (1972) strongly suggest the difficulty of establishing that frame of reference after reading has been completed. Because the frame of reference with which readers approach a text significantly affects what they attend to, understand, and remember, we argue that only the most able readers will be able to reconstruct connections between their lives and the literature after they have read.

## The Effects of Autobiographical Writing before Reading

Autobiographical writing before reading appears to have positive effects on both students' understanding of and attitude toward literature. White's (1990) study strongly suggests that autobiographical writing before reading can enhance younger adolescents' understanding of literary characters by helping them to move beyond surface descriptions and to focus more on abstract character traits.

White also found that the students in his study who had written about relevant autobiographical experiences before they read appeared to be more engaged in the reading and discussion of stories than were students who had done no writing. White supports this conclusion by noting that students who had written about relevant autobiographical experiences before they read were significantly less likely to make off-task or contentless (for example, "I forgot") remarks in classroom discussions. If students are genuinely engaged in a story, there should be few such remarks.

In a follow-up study in a more diverse classroom, we (Smith and White, in press) also found that autobiographical writing before reading appeared to have a positive effect on students' attitudes. When we compared the results of attitude surveys students completed after they had read stories and then again after they had discussed them in large or small groups, we made an interesting discovery. We found that the students who had engaged in autobiographical writing before reading tended to like stories better than those who did no writing, but that the difference between the groups was not significant. However, when we compared the responses that individual students made immediately after reading the stories to those they made after discussing the story in large or small groups, we found that while there was no significant difference between prediscussion and post-discussion attitudes of the students who engaged in autobiographical writing before reading, students who had not engaged in autobiographical writing before reading liked the stories significantly less after discussion. We argue that such writing may mitigate the potentially alienating effects of classroom discussions.

Another measure of interest is personal investment, the willingness to become personally involved while interacting with subject matter and class-mates. While the students who had not written before reading engaged in comparatively empty and boring discussions, the students who had written before reading engaged in more fast-paced, thoughtful give-and-take (Hamann, Schultz, Smith, and White, 1991; Smith and White, in press). In sum, when students in our studies had first written before reading, they made more abstract inferences, offered significantly fewer off-task and content-less remarks, and seemed to be more personally and substantively engaged both in the texts and in class discussions of those texts.

## AUTOBIOGRAPHICAL WRITING WITH READING

### The Nature of the Instruction

By autobiographical writing with reading I mean using journals to help students articulate their developing understandings of both their life experience and the texts they are reading. According to Beach (1990), five processes are involved when readers relate texts and experiences. First, readers are reminded of related experiences. Second, they elaborate their experiences in writing. This elaboration helps them engage in the third process, using their experiences to reflect on the text. As they develop their understanding of the text, they can use the point of the text to help them reflect back on their experience, which is the fourth process. Finally, readers reflect on the relationship between their experiences, including their experience of reading, and those of the characters about whom they were reading, exploring the similarities and differences and what accounts for them.

Beach (1990) provides an example of a student's writing that demonstrates these five processes (the student who was responding to John Updike's "A & P," a story in which Sammy, the teenage check-out clerk who narrates the story, quits his job as a gesture to protest the way his manager treated three bikini-clad girls who enter the store):

> There have been times I could have murdered my bosses for a stupid move or decision they have made. For example, I have worked under a manager

who would play favorites with his female employees. I was miserable when he played favorites between us. I though of quitting but instead I talked to him about the way we felt about his favoritism game. Although from that day on I was never his "favorite" again, he never expected me to brown nose because he knew how I felt and why I felt that way.

I'm glad I was honest. I maintained both a job and the respect I deserved by thinking before acting.

Sammy's heroic gesture seems silly because of what he risks — loss of his college money. It isn't worth making a point to his boss and impressing some girls in a swimming suit. If Sammy had such a problem with his manager, he could have talked to his manager or even talked to the girls about his feelings, but to quit was irrational and immature.

I realize what he stands for as a character. Sammy is something I am not — the heroic romantic worker. He puts himself into his job and stands for what he believes.(p. 224).

Although Beach notes that some students may not need specific prompting to do the sort of reflecting that will enhance their ability to make meaningful connections to texts, others may need a systematic series of prompts. He suggests that teachers ask questions to encourage students to use each of the five processes that he identified. For example, to evoke related experiences, Beach suggests that teachers might ask, "What are some of the characters' feeling? Have you had any similar feelings? Do those feelings remind you of any experiences?" or other similar questions (p. 233). To help students use their experience to reflect on the text, he suggests that teachers ask questions like these: "What did you learn about life from your experience? What does the point of your own experience suggest about the point of the text" (p. 234)?

Unlike autobiographical writing before reading, autobiographical writing with reading is designed to do more than establish a frame of reference for the story. Beach suggests that students could share their responses in small groups, which could trigger subsequent narratives or provide a springboard for the discussion of the differing perspectives students bring to literature. Beach also notes that teachers could use students' autobiographical responses to literature as prewriting for longer "phase-autobiographical" essays. (See Beach 1977 for more discussion of phase autobiography.) He also suggests that students could use their journals to explore the relationship between their "portrayed self" and the characters in a text or to relate their experience of one text to their experience of others.

## *Underlying Assumptions*

Although there are important differences between autobiographical writing before reading and autobiographical writing with reading, these two approaches do share some important assumptions about literature. Obviously both approaches presume the importance of readers' making connections between their lives and the literature they read. Both share Rosenblatt's and Iser's vision of an active reader engaging in a transaction with a text. In addition, both also share the view that literature has some communicative purpose. Beach explains how his work with autobiography is informed by a belief in the value of adopting a reflective orientation. He uses the work of Britton (1984) and Vipond and Hunt (1984; Hunt and Vipond, 1985, 1986, 1987) to explain the importance of students' reflecting on the value or significance of both their own experiences and the experiences about which they read. This argument presumes that something exists to reflect on, what Vipond and Hunt call a "point." Beach argues that students who develop their autobiographical responses as narratives "define their social beliefs," or in some cases "discover the point of their story." What is true of the student writers, of course, must also be true of the authors they read. Although Beach does not argue that literary texts have a single reproducible meaning, he does encourage teachers to help their students understand texts, to interpret the point(s) an author makes. Like autobiographical writing before reading, then, autobiographical writing with reading presumes that readers are rewarded when they make efforts to understand an author's creation.

Despite sharing these important assumptions, autobiographical writing before reading and autobiographical writing with reading also imply a number of conflicting beliefs. Perhaps most significantly, each suggests a different attitude toward schema theory. In brief, schema theory suggests that we can only understand experience on the basis of what we know. The categories into which we organize our knowledge are called schemata. Autobiographical writing before reading adopts the belief that readers approach texts with schemata in place that in large measure control their understanding of texts. Beach, however, cites Beers (1987) and Whitney (1987) to argue that such a view is too restrictive; that reading involves the creation and application of new schemata, not just the application of existing ones. It is from this view that Beach develops his recursive model. He explains that his research suggests that readers develop new schemata as they read, which in turn affect their understanding of the text, which then creates still more new schemata and so on.

Another important difference in the theoretical underpinnings of the two approaches is that autobiographical writing with reading places greater emphasis on the importance of the goal of helping students understand themselves. Although Beach argues that narratives provide a way of knowing both the world and oneself, he emphasizes the latter kind of knowledge. Indeed he argues that readers read in large measure to "define or reconceive their own attitudes, beliefs, or social roles" (p. 218). In contrast, autobiographical writing before reading emphasizes enabling students to understand an author's creation. In autobiographical writing with reading, students' experiences may well be the focus of discussion whereas in autobiographical writing before reading the aim is to use students' experiences to enliven and inform their discussion of the text.

The two approaches also differ about students' ability and inclination to make connections between their lives and the literature they read. As I explain above, autobiographical writing before reading presumes that students may not make those connections for a variety of reasons: because they regard literature as something completely separate from their lives, because of a real gap between their lives and the literature they read, because they lack the confidence to assume the role of an active reader, or because they simply do not know that it is a reader's role to make these sorts of connections. Autobiographical writing before reading is designed to overcome these barriers by raising students' attention to possible connections before they read. Autobiographical writing with reading, on the other hand, presumes that literature will naturally evoke related experiences for readers.

Although these two approaches make different presumptions about students' ability and inclination to relate their life experience to literature, they share the belief that students will benefit from the reflection upon and the articulation of their experience that writing requires. As Beach (1977) explains:

> Many students often have little opportunity to stand back and reflect on experience in a formal manner. They are daily bombarded with entertainment and information, by media which require little reflective thinking beyond immediate superficial experience. (p. 3)

Using either approach requires students to invest time, giving reflective attention to their lives in ways they may not do on their own.

### The Effects of Autobiographical Writing with Reading

Beach's (1990) study of autobiographical writing with reading was primarily designed to explore the kind of writing students actually did. In his analysis of 49 students in two literature methods courses, he examined the response strategies students used, the relationships between the strategies, the level of interpretation, and the kinds of links used. His most notable findings are that the degree of engagement with a text was related to the degree to which students described the text and cited related experiences, that the degree to which they cited related experiences was related to the degree of interpretation, and that the extent to which students elaborated their experience was related to what he calls the "point-drivenness" of the experience. Taken together, these analyses strongly suggest that students who most fully develop their experiences will benefit from them the most. Perhaps more illuminating than these correlations, however, was his analysis of the features that characterized readers' successful use of their autobiographical writing. He found that students who were successful in using their previous experience to reflect on a text conceived of their past experiences in terms of violating norms, a conception that Beach argues gives rise to a thematic understanding of experience; empathized with the characters' perspectives; employed narrative strategies in relating their experience; and adopted a reflective orientation. Although Beach does not attempt to measure the effectiveness of autobiographical writing with reading in comparison to doing no writing, the examples that he gleans from his data suggest that students who do these things improve their understanding of their lives and of the literature they read.

## *AUTOBIOGRAPHICAL WRITING* AGAINST *READING*

By autobiographical writing against reading I mean the writing of response statements as advocated by Bleich (1975, 1978, 1988). He defines response statements as follows: "A response statement aims to record the perception of a reading experience and its natural, spontaneous consequences, among which are feelings, or affects, and peremptory memories and thoughts, or free associations" (1978, p. 147).

Response statements are autobiographical in two regards. In the first place, they provide a record of the reader's experience of reading. Secondly, they are autobiographical because they require readers to elaborate associations. Bleich (1985) offers his own response statement on Kafka's "A Country Doctor" to illustrate how teachers can use response statements. What follows is an excerpt from the second paragraph of Bleich's response statement:

I am greatly attracted by the seemingly violent and arbitrary motions at the beginning — the snowstorm and the helplessness of the doctor. The bad weather and the cold reminds me of evenings when I used to return home with my father from visiting his parent in winter — it was cold and I comforted myself with the though of my cozy bed at home. But also, I remember thinking that my father was not as well able to stand the cold as I was, and this was one of a series of thoughts about his physical frailty, which I never mentioned to him or to my mother or took any action about. (p. 257)

Bleich argues that affect and association are the basic components that comprise any person's emotional response to anything. Drawing on the example of psychoanalysis, he argues that the authenticity of associative analogies can be determined by noting the importance of the relationship used to demonstrate the feeling under consideration. As a consequence, response statements are filled with stories about parents, siblings, friends, and lovers. I am terming such writing autobiographical writing *against* reading (besides the obvious demands of parallelism) because such writing is similar in important ways to criticism, one of the modes of textualization that Scholes (1985) delineates. For Scholes, criticism, which he defines as the production of text against text, depends on differentiating the subjectivity of the reader from that of the author (see p. 40). I use the term because Bleich's ideas are rooted even more strongly than are Scholes's in a belief in the importance of readers' exercising and understanding their own subjectivities.

Whereas autobiographical writing before reading and autobiographical writing with reading are techniques that teachers could incorporate into their classes, perhaps even using them only on occasion, autobiographical writing against reading requires a different kind of commitment. Rather than incorporating autobiographical writing against reading into an existing course, Bleich would argue that autobiographical writing against reading should be the centerpiece of an entirely different kind of course. In *Readings and Feelings* (1975), Bleich suggests a sequence of four phases for such a course:

1. "Thoughts and Feelings," in which "time is spent exploring the nature of feelings, how they appear, why, and how to distinguish between a feeling and a thought;"

2. "Feelings about Literature," in which the class moves from the exploration of feelings in general to the exploration of emotional responses "in the particular context of a literary stimulus;"

3.  "Deciding on Literary Importance," in which the class studies the "relationship of intellectual judgment to emotional response;"

4.  "Interpretation as a Communal Act," which "deals with the interest of others in one's own responses and interpretation."

For each phase of instruction, Bleich gives examples of prompts that teachers can use to elicit the kinds of responses that will allow a class to explore the issues explained above. For instance, in the Thoughts and Feelings phase he suggests as one possibility asking students to tell their class of a recent dream. In the Feelings about Literature phase, he suggests writing three types of responses: restatements of literary works; affective responses, in which readers describe the actual affect they felt while reading a text; and associative responses, in which readers describe the personal associations they recollected while reading. In the Deciding on Literary Importance phase, he suggests asking students to respond to the most important word, passage, or aspect of a text. In the Interpretation as a Communal Act phase, he suggests analyzing all of the responses of a class in order to understand the feelings and values held in common by the class or perhaps some community within the group. For example, in *Readings and Feelings* Bleich analyzes responses of freshmen in college to *Vanity Fair* to point out a common preoccupation with sex and marriage, while in *The Double Perspective* (1988) he provides several instances of responses that are affected by the gender of the reader. Bleich makes a number of suggestions for opening up a discussion of the communal nature of interpretation, among them asking students to consider how their experience of a text is affected if they do not speak to anyone about it.

Although Bleich argues that classes should negotiate the format used to elicit these responses, his descriptions of his own pedagogy make it clear that when he teaches, he asks students to write a response to a prompt and that these responses in turn become the texts for subsequent class discussions. In these discussions, students and the teacher focus on helping each other understand what gives rise to a particular response, with the understanding that the discussion be limited to the analysis of the response as opposed to the analysis of the respondent. In *The Double Perspective* Bleich suggests that groups of three working together for the duration of a course are especially effective places for these kinds of discussions.

Talking freely about feelings and personal associations requires a great deal of trust, regardless of the format those discussions take. It is the teacher's role, therefore, to create a classroom environment in which students feel safe to respond freely. Bleich argues that this can only be accomplished when teachers are active participants in the response process, not only discussing the responses of others but, much more importantly, offering their own responses as the subjects for discussion. In addition, he notes that the pressure of grades will inevitably undercut the freedom students feel. He suggests a credit/no credit grading system as an ideal but also notes that his own institution did not allow him to make such an unconventional choice. Consequently, he gave all students who did all of the work B's and to those who did outstanding work A's. Of course, because there are no right or wrong subjective responses, outstanding work means evidencing an especially great engagement in producing or analyzing responses.

## *Underlying Assumptions*

Although autobiographical writing against reading quite obviously shares with the other two approaches a belief in the importance of readers' making connections between their lives and literature, Bleich's program is a radical challenge to the conceptions of literature upon which autobiographical writing before reading and autobiographical writing with reading are based. Both autobiographical writing before reading and autobiographical writing with reading have as a goal to help students make meaning within the framework provided by the text. Bleich, on the other hand, rejects the notion that any meaning inheres in a text. As he says in *Readings and Feelings*, "literature exists altogether on the basis of the subjective re-creation of the reader" (p. 96). Although Bleich's thinking has evolved to place increasing emphasis on intersubjective meanings, he still places primary attention on a reader's subjectivity, for as he explains:

> For experience to acquire meaning, for it to be known as private experience to begin with, an individual must have first performed "self-objectivication," and to have done this is to have internalized "the attitudes of others" toward oneself. Self-objectivication is the key to understanding subjective experience as intersubjectively grounded (1988, p. 70).

In all of his work Bleich maintains an outspoken rejection of the objective paradigm, the belief that a reality exists independent of the mind of the observer, a belief on which conventional notions of meaning are based.

Rosenblatt, whose work provides the theoretical underpinnings of autobiographical writing before reading and autobiographical writing with reading, speaks directly against Bleich's theories when she (1985) writes :

Like the Rorschach inkblot, a verbal text may be used to stimulate personal "free" associations and memories of childhood traumas. But this makes the text simply a passive tool in the psychological study of personality. The emphasis is then on free association, whereas — when the text is read aesthetically — emphasis is on selective attention, guided by the cues provided by the text. The whole matter cannot be dealt with here, but it should be recognized that an overemphasis on personality moves the discussion out of the realm of a primary concern for the *literary* transaction and the teaching of literature. (p. 36)

Although Bleich praises Rosenblatt's ground-breaking attention to the reader, he rejects the implied sense of objective correctness that appears in Rosenblatt's work, for example, in the notions of selective attention and cues in the above quote. (See *Subjective Criticism* pp. 108-110.) While autobiographical writing before reading and autobiographical writing with reading both emphasize the transaction between the reader and the text, both approaches presume that there is something "in" the text with which to have a transaction. Autobiographical writing against reading, on the other hand, presumes that everything of importance is instead "in" the reader.

A natural consequence of these conflicting beliefs is conflicting beliefs about the purposes for teaching literature. Both autobiographical writing before reading and autobiographical writing with reading see the teacher's role as helping students use their life experience to enrich their reading of a text. They are, therefore, rooted in a belief in the value of literary transactions, a belief that students may not share. On the other hand, autobiographical writing against reading has as its aim helping students understand what is in them, as the title of Bleich's course — "Studying One's Own Language" — would suggest. Rather than trying to help students do what they might not be able or want to do on their own, this goal is based on what Bleich understands as people's natural inclination to "think about themselves most of the time" (1975, p. 4) and their desire to understand themselves, what he calls everyone's "most urgent" motivation (1978, p. 297). Bleich, then, argues for the importance of responding to literature because it provides students an essential opportunity to meet their goal of self-awareness. He bases his argument on the fact that literature plays a special psychological role in readers' minds because it is associated with others, what Bleich calls the "not-me." He argues that as a consequence,

our orientation around the literature permits us to conceal from ourselves our actual sense of implication in both the literary language and its referential statements. The materials that we report as associations to the literature tend to be those that we would censor if we were trying to remember them as historical events. (1988, p. 185)

Unlike autobiographical writing before reading and autobiographical writing with reading, which are based, at least in part, on teachers' desire to improve the quality of their students' responses, Bleich's program rejects the belief in a hierarchical relation between teacher and student or in students' need for remediation (see especially 1988, p. 254).

Autobiographical writing against reading does, however, share an important belief about students with autobiographical writing with reading, although it is one that stands in contrast to the beliefs that inform autobiographical writing before reading. While autobiographical writing before reading is designed to break down barriers that may make students reluctant to respond to literature, autobiographical writing against reading presumes that literature will evoke affective and associative responses from all students. Although Bleich writes at length about how teachers can work to create an atmosphere in which students will feel free to share their feelings and associations, he does not believe that teachers need to do any work to help students experience them.

## The Effects of Autobiographical Writing against Reading

Of course, in rejecting the objective paradigm, Bleich also rejects research that would make any claims to having a predictive power. Instead, in all of his books he offers detailed accounts of students' doing the sort of writing he endorses. In my view, the most compelling of these accounts is the one he offers of Ms. K. in *The Double Perspective*, a student who, by the end of the course was able to articulate important understandings of herself and who noted in a final paper: "This is pretty neat finding out all this stuff just from the way I use language" (p. 239). And while Bleich does not argue that this student's experience predicts a similar experience for other students he does contend "that any student is potentially able to achieve the self-awareness that Ms. K. achieved . . . provided that the classroom structure is hospitable to such an inquiry" (1988, p. 251).

Petrosky (1982), who also worked with college students, also offers testimony to the approach Bleich advocates. When he used Bleich's response heuristic, he noted a number of effects:

First, everyone looked for and found consistent patterns in their readings that indicated how they were using their personal knowledge to create both the format and content of their responses. Second, the readers took varied theoretical stances to explain their readings, but regardless of their bent, they were able to explain them. And third, they recognized that they wrote considerably more sophisticated papers when they used the response heuristic. (p. 34)

Although Bleich (1985) dismisses reports from particular classes as "interesting, but generally not useful" because "such results pertain more to life in the local community at large — the school or university — rather than everyone teaching language" (p. 256), the persuasive power of his argument rests in large measure on these reports.

The belief that readers must relate their lives to literature in order to have meaningful transactions with texts and the belief that writing and reading are complementary acts have almost become commonplaces for researchers and theorists. Unfortunately, as Applebee (1989) discovered, current research and theory has had little effect on classroom practice. He calls for researchers and theorists to explore more fully the pedagogical implications of their work. Researchers and theorists exploring autobiographical writing in the study of literature have done just that. Autobiographical writing *before* reading, autobiographical *with* reading, and autobiographical writing *against* reading all offer teachers practical ways of translating theory and research into practice. However, teachers choosing among these approaches should not lose sight of the theoretical implications of their choice, for each approach derives from significant, and sometimes conflicting, beliefs about the nature of literature, the purpose of literary studies, and the abilities and attitudes of the students one is teaching.

## *REFERENCES*

Applebee, A.N. (1989). *The teaching of literature in programs with reputations for excellence in English*. (Tech. Rep. No. 1.1). Albany: University at Albany, State University of New York, Center for the Learning and Teaching of Literature.

Bartlett, F. (1932). *Remembering: A study in experimental and social psychology*. Cambridge, MA: Harvard University Press.

Beach, R. (1977). *Writing about ourselves and others*. Urbana, IL: ERIC and National Council of Teachers of English.

Beach, R. (1990) The creative development of meaning: Using autobiographical experiences to interpret literature. In D. Bogdan & S Straw (Eds.). *Beyond communication: Reading comprehension and criticism* (pp. 211–236). Portsmouth, NH: Boynton/Cook Publishers.

Beers, T. (1985). Commentary: Schema-theoretic models of reading: Humanizing the machine. *Reading Research Quarterly, 22*, 369–377.

Bleich, D. (1975). *Readings and feelings: An introduction to subjective criticism*. Urbana, IL: National Council of Teachers of English.

Bleich, D. (1978). *Subjective criticism*. Baltimore: The John Hopkins University Press.

Bleich, D. (1985). The identity of pedagogy and research in the study of response to literature. In C. Cooper (Ed.), *Researching response to literature and the teaching of literature: Points of departure* (pp. 253–272). Norwood, NJ: Ablex Publishing Corporation.

Bleich, D. (1988). *The double perspective: Language, literacy and social relations*. New York: Oxford University Press.

Booth, W. (1983). A new strategy for establishing a truly democratic criticism. *Daedalus*,112,193–214.

Bransford, J., & Johnson, M. (1972). Contextual prerequisites for understanding. *Journal of Verbal Learning and Verbal Behavior*,11,717–726.

Britton, J. (1984). Viewpoints: The distinction between participant and spectator role in language research and practice. *Research in the Teaching of English, 18*, 320–331.

Greene, S. (1992). Mining texts in reading to write. *Journal of Advanced Composition, 12,* 151–170.

Hamann. L., Schultz, L., Smith, M., & White, B. (1991). Making connections: The power of autobiographical writing before reading. *Journal of Reading, 35*, 24–29.

Hunt, R., & Vipond, D. (1986). Evaluations in literary reading. *Text, 6* (1), 53–71.

Hunt R., & Vipond, D. (1985). Crash testing a transactional model of literacy learning. *Reader, 14,* 23–39.

Hunt, R., & Vipond, D. (1987). Aesthetic reading: Some strategies for research. *English Quarterly, 20*,178–183.

Iser, W. (1978). *The act of reading*. Baltimore: The Johns Hopkins University Press.

Marshall, J. (1989 a). *Patterns of discourse in classroom discussions of literature*. (Tech. Rep. No. 2.9). Albany: University at Albany, State University of New York, Center for the Learning and Teaching of Literature.

Marshall, J. (1989 b). *Texts in contexts: Discussions of literature in suburban and inner-city schools*. Paper presented at the meeting of the National Council of Teachers of English, Baltimore, MD.

Nystrand, M. (1991). Making it hard: Curriculum and instruction as factors in the difficulty of literature. In A. Purves (Ed.), *The idea of difficulty in literature and literature learning: Joining theory and practice*. Albany: State University of New York at Albany Press.

Petrosky, A. (1982). From story to essay: Reading and writing. *College Composition and Communication, 33*, 19–36.

Rosenblatt, L. (1976). *Literature as exploration* (3rd ed.). New York: Noble and Noble Publishers, Inc.

Rosenblatt, L. (1978). *The reader, the text, the poem: The transactional theory of the literary work*. Carbondale, IL: Southern Illinois University Press.

Rosenblatt, L. (1985). The transactional theory of the literary work: Implications for research. In C. Cooper (Ed.), *Researching response to literature and the teaching of literature: Points of departure* (pp. 33–53). Norwood, NJ: Ablex Publishing Corporation

Scholes, R. (1985). *Textual power*. New Haven: Yale University Press.

Schultz, L. , Hamann, L., & Smith, M. (1990). Teachers as miners: Using the resources students bring to our classrooms. *Wisconsin English Journal, 33*(1), 11–22.

Smith, M. (1991). Constructing meaning from texts: An analysis of ninth-grade reader responses. *Journal of Educational Research, 84*, 263–272.

Smith, M. (1992). Submission versus control in literary transactions. In J. Many & C. Cox (Eds.). *Reader stance and literary understanding: Exploring the theories, research, and practice*. Norwood, NJ: Ablex Publishing Corporation

Smith, M., & White, B. (in press) "That reminds me of the time. . .": Using autobiographical writing before reading to enhance response. In D. Bogdan & S. Straw (Eds.). *Constructive reading: Teaching beyond communication*. Portsmouth, NH: Boynton/Cook Publishers.

Squire, J. (1964). *The responses of adolescents while reading four short stories*. Champaign, IL: National Council of Teachers of English.

Vipond, D., & Hunt, R. (1984). Point-driven understanding: Pragmatic and cognitive dimensions of literary reading. *Poetics, 13*, 261–277.

White, B. (1990). *Writing before reading: Its effects upon discussion and understanding of text*. Unpublished doctoral dissertation, University of Wisconsin.

Whitney, P. (1987). Psychological theories of elaborative inferences: Implications for schema-theoretic views of comprehension. *Reading Research Quarterly, 22*, 299–310.

# CHAPTER TWELVE

# Making the Foot Fit the Shoe

## Using Writing and Visual Response to Evaluate Literary Understanding and Appreciation.

♣ ♣ ♣

## Anna O. Soter

> When we think about designing curriculum, it does make a difference whether we assume that people learn because they are rewarded or because it is a natural part of life. It does make a difference whether we assume that what people think and feel are essential aspects of learning, or that the "right" responses are our only concern. (Wolfson, 1985, p.58)

Imagine, if you will, a group of 35 aspiring English teachers who have just been asked to write weekly informal written responses to the young adult novels selected for a quarter's perusal. They are told that the professor is interested in reading what they think and feel about the novels as they read them. They are also told that these responses will not be graded but that the professor will carry on a dialogue on paper with them, will share her own responses, and will enter into a readerly discussion but will not attempt to influence the students' subsequent responses. How will these responses be evaluated if no grade is to be assigned? The students are initially nervous, anxious, and definitely uncomfortable. How will the professor come up with the grades for the individuals in the course? What if one student (as their thinking goes) thinks harder than another? What if my response is off-center? Won't I be penalized if I like the book and the professor doesn't? And so on. Each student is provided with 50 points for responding to 10 novels —

five points for each response. The points are simply for handing in the response on time. A third of a page receives the same number of points as does a page and a half. What is the professor getting at? What's the hidden agenda?

These students initially do not believe that their personal, subjective, and unauthoritative responses will be genuinely valued. It takes approximately four responses before they understand that the pattern established with the first will be consistently maintained. The professor is indeed interested in hearing what they have to say about the books they are reading. The students loosen up, share more, and become more assertive, bolder, and honest. They also write more than they did in their first responses and reveal that they are truly engaged with what they are reading. They lose their discomfort in not being told (through quantified or letterized measurement) whether they are right or wrong in their thoughts and feelings and, interwoven with these, their understandings or interpretations of the novels and dramas enacted within their pages. They become more interested, and at times, compelled, to return to the novels, to explore more deeply what they had first thought they had read.

This form of recording students' interactions with the novels they read is not the only one used in the course. Nor does the overall evaluation of each student rest entirely upon what I would term individual students' perspectives on the literary texts selected. The teacher of literature seems at this time to be walking a narrow line between acknowledging as important that what an individual reader feels, thinks, and understands about what he or she is reading and answering the strong call for valuing community-set norms that determine what is central to the texts we read and what is not. We are at present in an uncomfortable no-man's land in terms of both instructional goals and assessment of literature. On the one hand, we know from ample reading/comprehension research that we can no longer discard the reader's background knowledge and experience as not having a significant impact on interpretation and understanding what is read. We also know from a growing body of scholarship in critical theory, particularly in the area of reader-response theories, that the subjective response of the reader exists, that the text alone is not the only agent in the literary transaction, and that the subjective response plays a significant role in the reader's interaction with text at the levels of interpretation and evaluation (Bleich, 1978; Holland, 1975; Iser, 1988; Rosenblatt, 1978). On the other hand, we are, in school contexts, still driven by the issue of societal accountability. What appears to be necessary as a strategy for negotiating that narrow line between current knowledge and traditional practices and values is to acknowledge the reader's background experiences, knowledge, values, and attitudes and to record it in such a way that we can be accountable to others who need to know what our students know.

## *ASSESSMENT AND GOALS IN LITERATURE TEACHING*

What are we really testing when we assess students' performance in literature? What are our goals in evaluating literature, and how do these goals reflect our goals for teaching it? Are the goals that we claim drive our teaching of literature (e.g., that students will learn to love and appreciate literature and find it relevant to them and to their lives) contradictory to the manner in which we assess literary performance? If we use alternative approaches to assessing literary performance, can we really devise forms of measurement (i.e., assessment) that can truly represent or reflect shifts in attitudes, changes in behaviors as readers, and engagement?

Other chapters in this book explore both the nature of response and the kinds of responses readers have when interacting with literary text. I will only discuss here what has direct bearing on how we might assess student growth from initial responses to more fully developed ones and how we might evaluate growth that reveals shifting links between reader and text rather than responses that remain purely subjective (e.g., the "I liked it" type).

In a literature curriculum, a teacher may become concerned if a student consistently approaches a reading of a literary text from a story-driven orientation or, conversely, in a response-centered classroom, from a point-driven orientation (Hunt & Vipond, 1984). On the other hand, shifts in orientation can become one focus in a teacher's assessment of what a student writes about a literary text or how a student visually depicts a response to a literary text. In their recent text on literature instruction, Beach and Marshall (1990) make distinctions between initial responses and fuller or more complete responses (p. 217). This distinction is critical in determining the manner in which we evaluate students' responses. Initial responses may be typically highly subjective with the students not required to justify their response or to evaluate its validity. A student should not be penalized for this level of subjectivity. The purpose of the initial response is to *begin the process of having the student engage with the literary text and sharing that engagement with the teacher and other readers*. A critical stance by the teacher or a numerical score reflecting a negative judgment will deter students from further revelations of what they think and feel about the text.

The critical judgment that evaluates not only the level of engagement with the text but also the kinds of strategies employed by students in developing their response to the text (e.g., analyzing vs. simply retelling or questioning vs. simply describing) should come after the student has had an opportunity to express initial responses to the text and after the student has received reactions and responses from the teacher and peers as well as heard other perspectives. Without the opportunity to express what Bleich (1988) describes as the "social, interpersonal" aspects of responding to literature, students will continue to see literary discussion as the "stiff, formal, presentational activity" that eliminates interpersonal involvement (Bleich, p. 33) rather than the rich exploration of the reader, the text, and the poem (Rosenblatt, 1978) that it potentially can become.

## *Guided Evaluation of Response*

When we recognize as valid and reward students for their initial, unmonitored responses to literature, we offer them a *form* for exploring what in the works they are moved to affirm as a result of the experience of reading them. Once such affirmation has been allowed expression, students are more able to stand back, not only from the text itself but also from their experiences of the text. If we assume that understanding and appreciation are two learning experiences that we desire as a consequence of reading literature, we must provide students with opportunities for developing reflective distance from the literary text. Initial experience is always spontaneous, subjective and reactive. Without it, and without its validity and its significance acknowledged, readers, as we have found to our cost in the past, do not feel confident in their understanding nor in their appreciation of what they read. They become, instead, dependent on another agent telling them what they should know about the text, what aspects of the text they should understand as having value and what aspects do not, and what thematic and aesthetic qualities of the text should be held in esteem by them.

In exploring how goals for literature teaching that focus on readers' responses can be linked with a variety of assessment practices that reflect those goals, I will provide illustrations of how various approaches to evaluation can be utilized as ongoing and cumulative records of students' growth of both literary knowledge and appreciation. Before discussing such approaches, however, a brief general discussion must be made to clarify what I mean by a response-centered curriculum and how this differs from the traditional literature curriculum.

## RESPONSE-CENTERED CURRICULA AND ASSESSMENT

Although many teachers are excited by increasing acceptance of reader-response theories as a new approach to literature instruction, few feel comfortable with assessing students' responses to literature or understand how such subjective response can be measured. Such concerns indicate that we are still, in fact, operating under the traditional instructional paradigm — that anything taught and learned must be measurable and quantifiable in some way. Or, put another way, that we must somehow be able to report objectively how students develop in their understanding and appreciation of literary text. More than a decade ago, Cooper and Purves (1973) provided researchers and teachers with quantifiable ways of recording response to literature, typically represented by various sets of scales. However, such scales, while used descriptively by Cooper and Purves, can be manipulated to reflect hierarchies that imply better and poorer responses. Perhaps we can argue, as educators, that we do have preferred responses. However, one of the major purposes of tapping students' responses is to ascertain what is actually occurring as students read and reread the literary text, which, in turn, will inform us of several facts: First, it will tell us whether students have really read the text as opposed to skimming it or relying on other sources of information; second, it will tell us how the students' own experiences, attitudes, and perspectives interact with the text; third, it will tell us how students comprehend and interpret what is happening in the text as they endeavor to explain their responses to us.

### Preferred Modes of Responding and Assessment

In our discussions of literature, we have traditionally focused on the verbal response (and within that response, the written verbal response rather than the oral). This is an outcome of what is valued in school settings; that is, the written mode is given higher value than any other in the area of English/language arts instruction (the problem of recording response in preferred mode). If we are going to honor the subjective content of response I will argue that we need also to go beyond that to acknowledging and honoring the subjectively preferred mode of response. In Purves, Rogers, and Soter (1990) we argued that the continuous selection of the written mode can in fact inhibit response and can also hinder the teacher in determining what a student actually feels and thinks with respect to a piece of literature. Not all students are equally effective communicators in the written medium. Nor are they all equally effective communicators in the oral medium. If our interest in literature instruction is in the content of response rather than in the form that it takes (e.g., written) then we will have to seek ways in which we can record students' responses over time in a variety of modes. I have frequently found in my teaching, that students who are hesitant and awkward as writers are able to tell me much more powerfully what they thought and felt about a piece of literature. A teacher can probe through informal writing and in speech what a student, for various reasons, cannot provide in a formal piece of written work.

In order to come to terms with the question of how to assess and report student performance in response-centered approaches to literature instruction, we must first, however, deal with our deeper goals of literature instruction. We must face to what extent we still believe that the text is the fact of the literary experience and to what extent we believe that responses to literature are highly individualistic and to what extent this is valid in the classroom setting. We must come to terms, in classroom settings, with the notion that response and interpretation, while closely related, are not one and the same phenomena. The subjectivity of response does not, yet, have the validity that the perceived objectivity of interpretation enjoys. Let me illustrate this challenge by providing an example of an initial, subjective response from a student as she wrote a first response to fiction. This response provided a springboard for discussion that moved from the initial response to hearing those of others and gradually shifted from what the student felt and thought about the text to the text itself.

*Example: (in response to Katherine Paterson's Jacob Have I Loved).*

I felt angry reading this book. And I guess that's just what Katherine Paterson wanted. Writing from the point of view of Sara Louise made us sympathize with her all the more. I didn't even want to try to discover what really was going on with her mother, or father, Caroline, or the Captain, or Call, or, especially, her grandmother. But didn't Sara Louise contribute to the way people treated her? Her parents treated her like a boy. She acted like a boy. Caroline was doted on because she needed it. Call even said he needed to take care of her, and in irony not lost on Sara Louise, said she was all alone out there. . . . My reaction to her finally having to come to terms with herself was strange in a way. It was just as hard for me to accept that she had put aside the hurt and anger and to do for herself, to do what she had to do.

Several students, just as this one had, felt that Paterson had not written a fitting conclusion; indeed, they felt that it was too neat. Sara Louise should not have accepted second best and accepted being a nurse instead of her long-desired aim of becoming a doctor. They also felt that having Sara Louise remain with the small village in the mountains simply returned her to as isolated a setting as the island had been for her. Hearing and reading others' responses, especially those for whom the ending had not been a problem but a logical outcome of the earlier events in the novel and of Sara Louise's increasing self-understanding, resulted in students returning to the text and reflecting on the extent to which their first response was text-based or reader-based. In some instances those who had felt the novel was initially disappointing in its conclusion revised their thinking and found themselves accepting what they had rejected. They had moved from a subjective, impressionistic level of response to an evaluative stance. In Adams' (1986) view, they had made a distinction between wish fulfillment, based on their own needs as readers who demand happy endings in which all dreams are realized, and an ending that was an outcome of what they perceived might be the author's purpose through closer reflection on the text itself.

In a subsequent response log entry the student wrote the following after the class discussion that had ensued concerning the ending:

> I think most young people want to go away to a place they feel is very different from home, naturally, and yet, after all the exploration, experimentation with locations, living, many people end up in places familiar to them because the past is so much a part of them. I guess it doesn't always happen and it may take a long time — but eventually it happens. And in Sara Louise's case it was necessary because it represented her place. One can only go back to a place so like your home if you have come to terms with yourself and your life. If one is still struggling to find an identity, I think a person would look everywhere but in their own backyard at first. But there comes a time when you realize you should no longer ignore your past but should embrace it as part of you — even if it is with modifications. Sara Louise has done this and this time she belongs. It also carries through the cycle of her mother and her choice to stay on Rass Island.

Elsewhere in this chapter I suggest that we could use a response checklist such as Probst's (1988) and adapt it to accommodate a scale (e.g., 0–5) so that we can evaluate and record changing behaviors of students as readers. In these two examples from the same student written three weeks apart, we can find several indications of changing reading behavior. In the first response, she responds from a personal, nontext-based perspective and even when there is reference to the text it is an acknowledgment rather than a point for further reflection. By the time she wrote a second response to the same novel her response reveals acceptance of the views of others that functioned as a catalyst for further consideration of how the conclusion might be textually consistent (completing a cycle begun by Sara Louise's mother).

Recording scores or grades or using any other sign system (e.g., checklists without scores, or "satisfactory/unsatisfactory") implies, of course, that certain desirable behaviors or strategies and/or products are among our goals as literature teachers. To deny this would bring into question the need for a literature curriculum at all. In my classroom I have made it clear from the beginning that I look for evidence of ways in which students bring the text into their discussion of their response to it. I also make it clear that I would like to see students consider the responses of others as springboards for further reflections about the text. As a way of recording these behaviors I have developed a system that includes the response logs, monitoring students during class and group discussions and an individual conference two thirds of the way through the quarter during which we discuss their thinking about the texts. In settings where classroom teachers would find it difficult, if not impossible, to conference with all their students (e.g., where teachers might have 120 or more students) the response checklist (p. 254–5) can serve as a convenient and effective indicator of student reading behavior by functioning cross-referentially with journals or logs and other writing students do throughout a course.

---

## *PROFILES FOR ASSESSING PROCESS*

In discussing how a teacher might assess students' responses to text through visual means or through writing, I have chosen to refer to young adult literature as the literary vehicle for one major reason. Traditionally used literary texts, classics, or lesser works already have a body of critical information written about them. Teachers will find themselves unable to stray easily from the path of correctness in terms of accepting students' responses and interpretations because so-called authorities have already determined plot, characters, themes and points of view. The great bulk of young adult literature has not been written about yet, although critical writing is already emerging about works such as S.E. Hinton's *The Outsiders*. Nevertheless, for many teachers, using young adult literature as a ve-

|  *Expressively* | *Transactively* | *Poetically* |
|---|---|---|
| for the self by the self as unrestrained | for others to give information facts, opinions to demonstrate knowledge | for others to give pleasure delight to play with language |

*Typical Forms*

| | | |
|---|---|---|
| journal | note-taking | creative stories |
| diaries | webbing | plays |
| letters | summary | poems to be read by |
| lists | dictation | others |
| mental notes | description | |
| jottings | persuasion | |
| personal peoms | argumentation | |
| | stories | |
| | reports | |

*Typical Processes*

| | | |
|---|---|---|
| rough drafts | expected to be finished | many drafts |
| free writing | conventions to be | deliberate control of |
| focussed drafts | observed | forms |
| writing resembles | should be revised and | crafting |
| speech of writer | edited | must meet aesthetic |
| conventions can be | is not expected to | criteria |
| ignored | resemble speech of | |
| can be unfinished | writer | |

**Figure 12-1: Functions for Writing About Literature and Related Assessment Approaches**

hicle for developing students' responses to literary text will represent a situation in which the guide (the teacher) as well as the travellers (the students) are exploring equally uncertain paths. The customary maps (the critical references) are nonexistent and the guide is as much at the mercy of the clues provided by the text and his or her own experience as a reader as are the novice travellers.

## Assessing Written Response

Since the acceptance and use of what is now commonly termed "the process approach" to writing instruction, we are able to offer students opportunities for extended writing that focus primarily on the content of students' knowledge and responses to that knowledge rather than on the forms and conventions that govern public writing. I will focus my discussion of assessing responses through writing on forms that reflect Britton et al's (1975) three primary functions of language: the expressive, the transactional, and the poetic (or aesthetic) functions (See Figure 12-1). In using this as a way of "classifying" the writing students may do in response to literature we create the opportunity to focus on the content of students' responses (e.g., expressive writing) as well as, at other times, requiring students to pay attention to conventions that affect writing with a more formal, public orientation.

By classifying the writing we have students do in response to literature in this way, we clearly distinguish between writing intended for personal exploration (expressive function) and for public demonstration of skills and communication of knowledge (transactional and poetic functions). This approach is useful for the teacher of literature who is interested in having students write extensively but who does not wish to be constrained always by conventions governing written language. If we use writing as a medium for response we must do so in a way that encourages students to explore their interaction with literature without fear of criticism or punitive judgement. This does not mean that we may never ask students to write a formal essay or that we totally ignore formal considerations in their written products (such as structure, usage, and mechanics). Rather, it means that we relate the purpose of their writing with the manner in which we ask them to deliver their responses and, consequently, with the manner in which we subsequently evaluate what they have written. A "grade" or number of points allocated for this kind of writing may simply reflect that the activity was carried out and the student has handed in a journal or log. Our evaluation, in this instance, takes the form of a written dialogue in which we respond to the student's response.

## Assessing Expressive Writing

The expressive function may be performed through modes of writing such as the journal, personal letters, rough drafts, or personal poems that can be described as fulfilling the expressive function (Britton, et al., 1975). These forms allow students to use writing as a medium for exploring what they know without being constrained by considerations such as structure, usage, and mechanics (See Figure 12-1). Students typically write for the self or a close and trusted audience and do so in language that may more closely resemble their daily speech than the formal language that rules the transactional function, where the purpose is to give information, facts, or opinions to others and to demonstrate knowledge acquired. Teachers typically respond to the writing done in the expressive forms through a kind of written dialogue, focussing on the content and the students' attitudes toward that content. It would be inappropriate, for example, to assign a grade to the following initial written response from a fifth grade student after a reading of Langston Hughes' "Jukebox Love Song":

> It makes me feel like I am put in a romantic position. When I hear this poem I think of two people dancing close together having a good time. The whole poem makes me feel like when you really love someone and it makes you feel really special. It was a great poem. The words are really nice.

As an example of personal engagement this piece is splendid. It clearly indicates, through the reader's images, that the student was receptive to the reading and became involved. As an example of considered, deliberated discussion linking the personal response to the text of the poem, the example is less effective. Yet, the purpose of the exercise was to discover to what extent the poem made an impact on each student in the class. If we want to use this as the springboard for further thinking by students, we might prod students to think more deeply about their content or to reconsider their perspective or to expand on what they wrote. Teachers can use this kind of writing to determine changes in students' attitudes toward reading literature, to evaluate the degree to which a student is ready to negotiate her perception of what has been read, and to help in evaluating to what extent a student engages with the literary text.

Even writing that ultimately has an analytic purpose (Purves, Rogers, and Soter, 1990) need not, in the early drafting forms, be subjected to a grade or numerical assessment if students understand that the writing will form the basis for subsequent elaboration or revision. In each of the three activities that follow, the early focus for students and the teacher should be on how form alters meaning, and this, in turn, would lead to discussions on how the style of a particular piece that may be read impacts on readers and causes them to respond the way they did. Should a product be required for formal records, teachers will need to give students the opportunity, as in any writing activity, to receive written and oral feedback (conferences) from the teacher and peers and to revise and edit the pieces until they meet agreed criteria for a final product.

### Example 1:

Read the attached poem, "Full Moon." Write your response to the poem, focussing on how you felt, what you saw, what it made you think, hear, taste, or touch.

Now look at the poem again. What interesting patterns can you see in the ways in which the poet has used the language through such things as: types of words (meanings, sounds, weights, lengths); line lengths; use of punctuation or not; use of title; word arrangements or any other feature which may have made an impression on you.

Try to link what you observed with how you felt and what you thought.

### Example 2:

Write the same poem in prose form, retaining where possible the same words. Describe what happens when you play around with the form (shape) to the effect of the original meaning the poem had for you.

### Example 3:

You may have been working, perhaps in a frustrated way, on a poem or story that just isn't working out. Try converting it, word for word, to an alternative form. If this looks promising, add or delete words, phrases, or clauses. You may decide to reconvert. Describe what happened to the way you felt about the piece as a result of these experiments. Have a peer or your teacher read the pieces and respond to them.

I am not arguing that we should never assign points or a grade to a rough draft or to a one-draft piece of writing. At times, however, teachers may simply view an assignment as valuable because it conveys information to them about what a student knows in relation to the text being read. For example, we may wish to discover if students were able to predict what was going to happen in a novel (e.g., Robin McKinley's *The Hero and The Crown*) and if they were aware of how their initial predictions were confirmed or unconfirmed. So, we might ask a question such as:

Go back to Chapter I in *The Hero and the Crown*. Write down what you thought would happen from this opening section of the novel. Write down what predictions you had to revise, if any, and where this happened in the rest of your reading and why.

We might devise a five or ten point scale for this kind of unrevised writing that will focus on the strategies the student appears to have used in predicting what will happen and that will reflect the degree to which the student is a careful reader rather than a skimmer. The degree to which a student can trace back the points at which confirmation or disconfirmation occurred would indicate a relatively more careful reading of the work. Assuming that we believe this kind of reading behavior is significant, we develop criteria that would reflect our orientations.

## Assessing Transactional Writing

The bulk of writing performed in schools is transactional in nature; that is, its purpose is to give information to others in order to demonstrate the knowledge acquired and the ability to convey that knowledge according to various conventions that govern different types of formal writing. We might argue that any writing that involves a distanced public audience and, therefore, conforms to conventions governing "public" writing, is transactional in function. Similarly, where teachers give some weighting in their assessment for structure, focus, wording, usage, and mechanics (i.e., weighting for form as well as content), we observe an orientation that moves away from the writer toward the unfamiliar reader (See Figure 1). Although not restricted to these, typical rhetorical forms include summary, description, persuasive writing, and argumentation, report writing, the ubiquitous essay.

Writing about literature from a response-perspective does not exclude writing for transactional purposes. Indeed, the fuller, more "complete" responses that teachers may prompt their students to pursue are transactional in intent. The teacher, here, adopts the role of a public, less familiar reader and requires the writer to move out of the original expressive mode by questioning the student in such a way that more information is provided and perhaps justifications or explanations are added. In doing so, the teacher is leading the student through the writing in a process-oriented way — providing constructive and positive feedback, allowing opportunities for revision and, possibly, correction.

**An Example.** A teacher might choose to have students explore in discussion their perceptions of the characters from a novel (e.g., Knowles' *A Separate Peace*) and from this to infer motives that may have prompted them to take actions as played out in the text. The students are given the opportunity to write a free response, in which they note their perceptions and how these relate to what they perceive to be thematic concerns in the text. The following example is drawn from a young adult literature class for English education majors.

In a class activity related to *A Separate Peace*, students identified the following thematic concerns: self in relation to others; social stratification and its impact on friendships; peer affiliation vs. individuality. Earlier discussion of their perceptions of the characters led to these thematic concerns through questions that explored the extent to which Gene was conscious of his actions when pushing Phineas from the tree; how Gene deals with feelings of guilt; the extent to which peer pressure influences the action of the main characters; the extent to which individuals are responsible for their actions. At this point no formal evaluation occurred. However, students were then given the opportunity for developing a paper based on a topic that emerged from their discussion. Drafts were requested and deadlines given in order to allow feedback from peer groups that had worked together.

The primary purpose for this writing activity was to have the students reconsider initial responses, reevaluate them after feedback from others, develop the initial response into a more fully fleshed interpretive stance, and present a product that illustrates how the reader interacted with the text and was able to use the text to confirm or disconfirm his or her interpretations. The form of the paper was, essentially, an argument and was evaluated from that perspective because the focus here is on the strategies the student can illustrate that reflect considered thinking, the ability to support personal perspectives with material from the text, and the ability to convince others. Consequently, the rubric focused on such aspects as adequacy of information, how the student showed relationships between his personal stance and the textual elements; accounting for alternative explanations or interpretations; framing of the argument itself; grouping of the information; and usage and mechanics.

Teachers may wish to develop scaled rubrics such as those already described in Purves, Rogers, and Soter (1990) and to which I have referred in the previous discussion, or they may wish to develop others focussing more directly on a combination of content and form in a finished product. In this case a primary trait scoring system is useful. The primary trait selected for focus could be a particular skill (e.g., analytic or synthesizing skill or evaluative skill) or focus on a particular form (e.g., the student's development of a story or a persuasive essay). Examples of these have already been developed by the National Assessment of Educational Progress (NAEP) and can be found in Fagan, Cooper, and Jensen's (1985) *Measures for Research and Evaluation in the English Language Arts*.

Whatever scale we choose to borrow or develop, its value as feedback for the student and its validity as a measuring instrument can only be evaluated in terms of how closely it captures our purpose in setting the assignment in the first place. The following example was written by an eleventh-grader in response to a request for a formal essay in the form of an argument. The essay was written in response to a quote from the play *Othello*, followed by the request to argue whether or not Shakespeare had used Iago as a symbol of evil that needs no motive.

**Another Example** Students were given the opportunity to revise drafts as often as they felt were needed, and feedback on each draft was provided by the teacher. Prior to writing on the assigned topic the teacher and the class extensively discussed the topic and brainstormed possible approaches that students might take. The example is a final draft.

> Shakespeare has written the play Othello as a tragedy, involving the themes of love, justice, and jealousy. Othello, so said by many, is the main character in the play,because he is the tragic figure. However in the sense of the themes of love, justice, and jealousy, Iago plays the main character in the play. Iago forces events to occur the way they do and is almost totally responsible for the evil in the play. In the opening scenes of the play the evil of Iago is revealed but is still a hidden factor of the character. The villain Iago expected the appointment of becoming Othello's lieutenant, but for certain reasons the position was given to Cassio. This made Iago angry and even more made him jealous of Cassio. Iago makes the decision that he should gain a friendly acquaintance with Roderigo, in order to "use" him.

It is not until well into the middle of the essay that the student addresses the central question of the topic — whether or not Iago represents evil without motive. How should we evaluate and assess this essay? I am going to suggest several approaches.

If we evaluate it from the perspective of the learner, we might ask what growth has occurred. We could consider where this student was as an analytic essay writer at the beginning of the year (the essay was written at the end of the year). We might also consider this essay in comparison with the first and second drafts that had been written. If we take the first view of growth, this essay is vastly superior to similar ones written at the beginning of the year. Having known the student well, I would say that she had written as well as she could at this time in this context. Does the essay, then, warrant an A? If we take the second view and consider this final draft in contrast to the first two, we would not find much variation. As with many other students, little substantive revision occurred despite feedback that focused on the content and form of the response. The student was not to be diverted from what she believed needed to be discussed and established early — that the play is supposed to be a tragedy and that, although Othello is supposed to be the tragic and central character, Iago certainly is the more interesting of the two. The other issue of whether or not Iago represents evil without motive is captured only in the conclusion, where she writes:

> I feel that Iago is a man of evil for he is forever lying for revenge, and loses friends for what he does. Iago in the sense of jealousy against the position gained by Cassio, and love as in everyone's life. Shakespeare has used him as the evil of the play and he played his part successfully.

The student really does not appear to know what to do with this aspect of the topic. She knows it must be addressed but does not wish to speculate further upon it because it does not fit her schema for what the play is "really" about — a tragedy about a tragic hero. In many respects, her essay is an example of an attempt to cover all her bases. From this perspective the essay might warrant a B if the teacher takes into account the degree of effort expended to produce it and the sincerity of the student in attempting to do what she thought was requested. However, if we take an external examiner's perspective we might have a different set of criteria. Firstly, all that the outside reader knows is embodied in the product itself. Nothing is definitely known (although it might be inferred) about the amount of thinking and work that went into the final product. Nothing is known about this final product relative to others that the student had produced. If the criteria for assessment are based on the view that the student should have developed a case by selecting relevant sections of the text throughout and that there is, in fact, an ideal essay in the mind of the examiner, this student's product might receive a C or perhaps even a D.

Thus the central issue is raised again: What *should* we be evaluating, and assessing, in literature teaching and learning? It would be absurd to argue that all final products merit the same score or grade given that quality is never identical, and especially not with developing students. What, indeed, does a grade actually represent? I would argue that its only useful meaning is always relative to other products produced by a student and, more significantly, always relative to the history of each performance. As the New Zealand Department of Education (in Taylor, 1990) argues, "In the assessment of learning, it is doubtful that numbers or grades can be thought of as anything more than rough estimates of the things they seem to measure" (p.67). I would also argue the need for a developmental perspective in terms of the age and experience of the students we have and in terms of where the students are at any point in the evaluation process. Finally, we also have to consider the specific purpose(s) in setting the assignment in the first place. A teacher may have several reasons for setting such an assignment. Firstly, he or she may intend it to serve the function of having the students synthesize what they think about the literary text. Secondly, the teacher may intend it to function as an exercise in developing literary arguments. Thirdly, the teacher may use it as a means of discovering how far the students have come in their understanding and interpretation of the text. In all three instances, the activity is seen as a culmination of a number of prior activities that may have included student and teacher generated discussion, response logs, or impressionistic writing. In other words, the student's performance is a history that, I will argue, needs to be taken into account in the context of classroom-based assessment. In that sense, this final performance, if it meets each of the purposes already stated, must be judged relative to what the student was able to do when first beginning the path of literature response-based discussion and analysis when he or she entered that class.

## *Assessing Poetic (Aesthetic) Writing*

Little has been written about assessing creative writing in the context of a response-centered curriculum. By "poetic" writing I mean writing that is designed for others to give pleasure, to delight the reader, to play with language and its forms for its own sake. The primary purpose of this form of communication is to capture the reader's affective and aesthetic responses. Or asking students to write a story or a poem in response to another piece of literature does not necessarily mean that we are asking them to write aesthetically if our primary purpose is to evaluate that creative response in terms of what it tells us of the students' attentiveness to the original that prompted the response. On the other hand, if we assign a grade that takes into account the aesthetic features of a story or a poem (for example, the structure of the story or poem, wording, arrangement, or the ability to capture and engage the reader), we are going beyond response to the creation of something new that will be evaluated for its own sake in terms of its merits as a creative, imaginative piece. Several considerations are critical. First, writing well, creatively, is an arduous task, requiring considerable motivation, orientation to do so, and serious crafting. If John Keats required 25 drafts to create his sonnet "On Chapman's Homer," before he was reasonably satisfied with it, similar possible crafting may occur for students who choose to write aesthetically in response to something read. Obviously, not every famous writer needs to take such pains. However, many have written about how demanding their craft is. Teachers will need to decide their primary focus in evaluating an imaginative piece prior to encouraging students to pursue this path. Consider how we could respond to an extract from a story presented in the form of a journal entry and written by a seventh-grader after having read Esther Forbes' novel, *Johnny Tremain*. What kind of grade or score could be assigned? Students were asked to create a character in a similar setting and, using the journal form, to write an imaginative entry that would recapture the period.

### NO WINNERS ONLY LOSERS

Dear diary,

My name is Erica White. I am 17 years old, and live in Concord, Massachusetts. I am average height, have brown hair and brown eyes. Overall, I'm a pretty average person. I have a brother, Sam, who is 19, and a sister, Kelly, who is 7. My father is a stubborn man, and although we rarely get along, I love him dearly. My mother is a sweet woman who always opens her arms to anyone who needs comfort. The British are coming to fight, and their is a committee meeting tonight in preparation. Everyone who is going to fight must sign the muster book. I want to fight and serve my country, but since I'm a girl, they won't let me. I have to find a way to get onto the commons tomorrow to fight. What should I do?

Sincerely,
Erica White
April 18, 1775.
8:00 pm.

If we adopt a stance that focuses on the student we could argue that this piece is an example of evocative writing that effectively recaptures a feel for the period in which it is set. It is arguably an A rather than a B example. The student strove successfully to recapture the more formal tone consistent with the style frequently conveyed in historical novels. She engages the reader with a concrete, vivid image of the main character and through economic depiction of the context in which the action is to take place.

If, on the other hand, we adopt a stance that is rhetorically based, impartially insisting upon adherence to absolute criteria, we may not be so impressed. We see some stylistic inconsistencies in the abbreviated forms "I'm", "won't," and usage-related errors "I am average height." It is also doubtful that a girl would be named Kelly in the period being written about. If this were a prefinal submission, we would require the student to address these concerns. If it were a final submission we may assign a B+.

The point of this discussion, however, is to consider on what basis we can assign grades to this kind of writing when it is done in response to a piece of literature that has been read and when the purpose of that activity has been to ascertain the links between students' reading and the resultant text they subsequently produce. What is achieved by comparing a creative piece written by a seventh grader with an absolute set of critical criteria for effective creative writing? More significantly, we should observe that the student made a genuine attempt to recapture the flavor of a particular period in history and, having been able to do so, revealed a careful reading of the stimulus text. In a response-centered curriculum we are not asking our students to become Newbery Medal winners. Rather, we are seeking to engage them with the literature being read, and we endeavor, through this engagement, to explore students' abilities to empathize with, to connect with, to explore and interpret, and to judge what they read (Beach & Marshall, 1990).

## *Assessing Visual Responses*

As stated earlier, the response-centered curriculum acknowledges and values the students' subjective thoughts and feelings about a literary text. Additionally, a "response-centered curriculum" and, therefore, "response-centered assessment" not only takes into account the subjective aspects of an individual's reading of literature but also acknowledges (though this has been less frequently discussed) the subjective aspects of how one responds (i.e., the natural, preferred, or spontaneously accessed mode in which one responds — i.e., verbally, visually, physically (kinesthetically).

In responding visually to a text, students may choose from a number of options that teachers feel they cannot adequately evaluate because they lack experience evaluating responses other than written ones or multiple-choice ones. These options include a range of activities from maps and diagrams to mime and dance to photography and illustration (Purves, Rogers & Soter, 1990). Teachers may draw upon visual response modes as avenues for early or initial responses by students so that they can begin the process of articulating their understanding as well as appreciation of the text. Therefore, measurement on a scale is not an essential component of such responses. If, on the other hand, a teacher wishes to develop a scale to evaluate the quality of a student's visual response the scheme adapted from Probst's (1988) questions (see Figure 12-3 in this chapter) offers categories that lend themselves to some form of quantification (e.g., a five-point scale). Alternatively, a teacher may wish to be more focused in evaluating a visual response. A teacher may ask students to present what they perceive to be the major relationships among characters in a novel and to depict this in such a way that the relationships are tied to what they perceive to be the point of the novel or the plot. In order to evaluate students in this kind of activity, the teacher may develop a set of scales that reflect the degree to which the student has visually depicted such relationships in a way that can be comprehended by others. Such an activity can help the teacher determine how the student perceives the characters' roles in the story in a relatively uncomplicated way and allow the student to revise those perceptions based on the responses of other students to the depiction in a sociogram (a diagrammatic representation of how characters relate to one another).

An example from the young adult novel, *My Brother Sam Is Dead* will help to illustrate the point. As a preliminary response-eliciting activity, students were asked to illustrate how they perceive relationships among the characters and to illustrate what each of the characters illustrates about thematic concerns of the novel as the students perceived them. Two of the sociograms are re-created below.

Nine groups were formed, and nine different sociograms emerged. The character, Tim, is central in most but in some groups shared that central place with his brother, Sam. In three other groups, the central space was shared among Tim, Sam, and their parents. In one sociogram, Tim is peripheral to Sam and his father. Each of the groups was able to relate characters to thematic concerns. The students had had several opportunities to discuss their depiction prior to presenting it to the whole class. All groups were provided with copies of other groups' sociograms. Each student in the groups was asked to provide a brief written description of how and what he or she contributed to the creation of the sociogram to enable the teacher to record involvement.

The first problem for the teacher's assessing procedures is that not one sociogram replicated another. Typical literature assignments, whether written or multiple-choice, enable teachers to assign a score or grade easily based on a student's response relative to some truth in the text or to a model answer in the teacher's head. Complicating the assessing process in this context is conformity, that is, should all students have the same so-called truths or facts in their answers? In a response-centered approach, however, the teacher creates a context that invites individuals to offer their own perceptions. Groups of students may negotiate agreement when individual per-

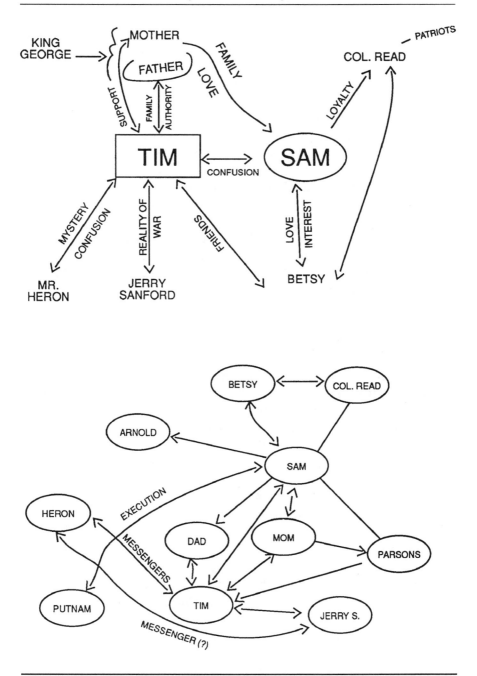

**Figure 12-2    Sociograms (a) and (b).**

spectives conflict. However, each group will not necessarily emerge with perceptions that are identical with those of another group. What can then be assessed?

In this case I chose not to assess product (that is, the sociogram itself) but process and performance (that is, the level of involvement, commitment to the activity, and taking of responsibility for one's share in the task required. This kind of approach requires the teacher to know each student, to become a keen observer of what is going on while groups work together, and to become a discerning recorder of student behavior. The task was made simpler by requiring each student to write a brief account of his or her contribution to the final product. Teachers may also ask individual students to create sociograms depicting character relationships and include the sociogram in a portfolio of student work on a particular novel. The sociogram may be a culminating activity accompanied by response logs and perhaps another written piece focusing on character relationships, thus providing a more comprehensive picture of how students perceive these relationships over a whole unit.

In my classes I use the group activity involving the creation of the sociogram as a prelude to further individual work related to the novel. In working through the relationships among characters and their links with student-perceived thematic material, students are required to articulate for themselves and others the major elements in the novel. A follow-up written activity is required of the students to respond to specific selections from the text and to develop the initial responses into what Beach and Marshall (1990) have termed "more complete responses" (p. 217). That is, students are asked to build on their initial interactions with the novel in order to interpret, to analyze and synthesize, and to evaluate character roles and their place in the thematic development of the novel. As students negotiate with each other in the initial sociogram activity, they are already required to justify and, in most instances, revise what they had first experienced as they read the text.

When we ask students to create a tableaux or mime, a poster or a collage in response to a reading of a literary text, a more productive and less inhibiting form of assessment centers not on the quality of the act itself but on the explanation students give for representing their response in the manner they chose. Additionally, we might also ask students to explain how their represented response relates to their understanding and interpretation of the events or characters in the story. A rating scheme that includes categories of the kinds of skills we have asked the students to demonstrate in their performance or creation might include the following:

| *Criteria* | *Scale* |
|---|---|
| Recreating | 1  2  3  4  5 |
| Interpreting | |
| Generalizing | |
| Analyzing | |
| Synthesizing | |
| Justifying | |
| Personalizing | |

(Adapted from Purves, A.C., Rogers, T. and Soter, A. (1990). *How Porcupines Make Love: Teaching a Response-centered Curriculum*. NY: Longman, pp. 172–3).

Creating a sociogram, justifying its components to the group, and explaining one's personal contribution to the whole involves skills reflected in the above scale. Other possible visual means of presenting responses include the following: collages, maps, charts or diagrams, cartoons, calligraphy, posters, scripted stories, filming or video, the creation of special effects for parts of a story or novel, mime, dance, or music. In each case, the assessment focus is more meaningful if it is linked with skills that indicate involvement with the text: empathizing, connecting, describing, interpreting, and judging or evaluating (Beach & Marshall, 1990).

In another class, I have asked students to respond first to the poem "Full Moon" in a brief paragraph. Then I asked them to think of an alternative form of response they might have chosen had I given them the option of doing so. Among the possible alternatives are dance, mime, photography, tableaux, drawing or painting, sculpture, a musical composition, a dramatic sketch, charting, graphing or diagramming, creating another poem, or writing a creative prose piece. Of the nineteen students in class, fourteen chose a mode other than writing. They felt that their chosen mode — whether it was photography, dance, or creating a visual image — allowed them to express what they felt and thought in relation to their reading far more accurately than the written mode, whether it was discursive, reflective, or creative.

In the reality of the elementary and secondary classroom setting, with limits of space and time, such alternatives may not be frequently possible. However, always restricting students' responses to the written mode can inhibit those students who are not comfortable as writers and for whom, therefore, writing limits their ability to express what it is they know and feel. Providing them with the opportunity to express their response in an alternative mode can help these students unlock their knowledge and enable them subsequently to develop more comprehensive written statements when required to write about their understanding of the text. Students are not judged on the quality of the form of the response, but, rather, the assessment related to the activity focuses on process.

What kinds of criteria might be involved in evaluating this process? For my own classrooms I have adapted an already existing scheme based on Probst's (1988) checklist of questions to identify progress and process in responding to literature. These can become part of a student's portfolio throughout the year or the teacher can select particular questions to create his or her own checklist to reflect progress and process in response to selected texts. Whether or not the teacher uses a four or five point scale or simple Yes/No categories depends on the purposes for which such a checklist is used.

Finally, in asking students to respond in a mode other than writing, we do not, as a rule, expect them all to perform in the same way, nor do we expect them all to perform equally well. We are not so certain, that is, of normative criteria for performance in domains other than in writing or in content-related multiple-choice types of questions. How, teachers may ask, is one group's or individual's tableaux response better than another's or equally as good as the one the teacher may have had in mind? Similarly, how is a sociogram a more effective illustration of the relationships a group of students, or an individual student, perceives as links among characters or as links between characters and thematic development? However, our purpose in choosing an approach to assessing literary understanding and appreciation is not response-centered to compare and/or contrast one student's response with an implicit perfect model of response. Nor is it to compare and/or contrast a student's response with that of another student's. Rather, the goal is to assess one student's response at any given time relative to earlier responses made by the student. How has the student grown? Is there more relating to the literary text or does the student still remain totally subjective in response? Has the student developed greater tolerance toward characters who are unlike himself or herself? Has the student developed greater acceptance of the validity of other ethical and moral issues as presented in the text or does he or she remain adamant that only one form of action or one set of values (personal) is valid? Has the student grown in his or her ability to show relationships between characters' motives and intentions and outcomes in the action of the plot? Of course, these questions are only valid if

(Using Probst's questions for identifying progress and process in Probst, R. (1984). Adolescent Literature:  Response and Analysis, pps. 218-219).

Teacher's Recording Key:  A = Always
S = Sometimes
R = Rarely
N = Never

**Desirable characteristics**                                    **Dates Observed**

1.  Seems willing to express responses rather than being cautious/constrained.

2.  Will change her mind rather than being intransigent.

3.  Participates in discussions, listens to others, presents own thoughts, considers those of others.

4.  Distinguishes between thoughts/feelings brought to the work vs those attributable to the text.

5.  Distinguishes between fact, inference, opinion when reading a literary work.

6.  Will relate, where relevant, literary works to other human experiences, especially own (can generalize, abstract).

7.  Accepts responsibility for making meaning out of lit.

8.  Perceives differences and similarities in visions offered by different literary works.

**Figure 12.3    A Checklist Approach for Identifying Progress and Process in Responses to Literature.**

we assume that the goals of a literature curriculum include not only becoming familiar with certain valued literary works and learning how to discuss literature using conventional literary terminology and reflecting desired critical stances (e.g., knowing kinds of plots) but also the development of certain reading behaviors and attitudes.

## CONCLUSION

For a long time in American schools, we have been accustomed to thinking about the teaching of literature as largely consisting of teaching content and, to a lesser extent, teaching about formal literary properties such as theme, plot, setting, characterization, point of view, and style (Brody, DeMilo & Purves, 1989). Furthermore, the traditionally held view that literature and literary study consists of a body of so-called facts to be learned has resulted in the adoption of a form of testing that has traditionally involved multiple choice or short-answer form — both forms that lend themselves to quantifiable results that are supposed to indicate that students have or have not learned such a body of learnable facts. However, the affective and aesthetic aspects of reading literature do not lend themselves easily, if at all, to quantifiable, definitively right, or wrong responses and have, therefore, been typically omitted in literature tests (Brody, DeMilo & Purves, 1989; Zancanella, 1991). Essentially, students have not been required to think and, therefore, reflect upon the literature they read but rather to memorize what teachers have told them are important facts about the literary texts they have selected to read.

Behind this approach lies the assumption that we teach literature largely to ensure that students become culturally literate (Purves, 1991); that is, that students know the most valued writers in a particular culture, the titles of their primary works, and what aspects of their texts are the most significant ones to know. As Purves argues, we have traditionally taught and evaluated literature in this way in order to ensure cultural hegonomy and cultural loyalty and to ensure the creation and maintenance of a community that reflects a system of particular values that, in turn, is reflected in the kinds of literary texts selected for school study and in the ways in which students are taught to approach such texts. Only when students have given evidence of the success of the induction process, Purves (1991) argues — that is, only "after one accepts the cultural "classics" — can one develop individual tastes and interests" (p. 5). For it is when students have proven, through their performance on objectively quantifiable test results, that they know the so-called facts of their culturally approved literary heritage that they have actually proven that the purpose of the larger school curriculum has been achieved; that is, "bringing young people into the local, regional, or national culture" (Purves, 1991, p.3). Unfortunately, among outcomes of such goals and assessment practices, students often lose their early love and appreciation of literature. They learn, instead, to figure out what the teacher wants and focus on how they can best deliver the expected goods.

They learn to memorize the facts of literature and the terminology used to discuss literature.

Evaluation from a response-centered perspective requires that teachers know their students well. A fuller image of students' as knowers of literary text emerges when we create an assessment system that includes a range of student writing and envisioning across the different functions described. Through such a record we are more able to identify what students know, how well they read, how well they write about what they read, how they think about what they read, and the nature of their aesthetic perceptions and judgments. A response-centered assessment perspective reflects the following assumptions:

- Becoming literate is a complex activity
- Learning to read literature involves the acquisition of knowledge.
- Learning to read literature implies a special set of preferred acts.
- Developing as a reader reflects individual preferences.
- Becoming literate as a reader of literature involves the development of aesthetic tastes.

If we choose to use writing or visual means as vehicles for evaluating students, we do so because these vehicles offer opportunities for the discovery of relationships within and across the texts students read; to discriminate between observations and inferences; to analyze lines of reasoning; to visualize outcomes in a line of thought and draw analogies. We use such activities, therefore, as means by which learning will occur. Our assessment should, therefore, reflect these criteria.

## REFERENCES

Adams, P. (1986). "Making Evaluative Responses to Literature Through Imaginative Writing. In Stephen N. Tchudi (Ed.), *English teachers at work: Ideas and strategies from five countries*. Upper Montclair, NJ: Boynton/Cook.

Beach, R., & Marshall, J. (1990). *Teaching literature in the secondary school*. NY: Harcourt Brace Jovanovich.

Bleich, D. (1988). "Reconceiving literacy: Language use and social relations. In C. Anson (Ed.), *Writing and response*. Urbana, IL: National Council of Teachers of English.

Bleich, D. (1978). *Subjective criticism*. Baltimore, MD:John Hopkins University Press.

Britton, J., et al. (1975). *The development of writing abilities 11–18*. London: Macmillan.

Brody, P., DeMilo, C., & Purves, A.C. (1989). *The current state of assessment in literature*. Albany, NY: Center for the Learning and Teaching of Literature.

Cooper, C., & Purves, A.C. (1973). *Responding: A guide to evaluation*. Lexington, MA: Ginn.

Fagan, W., Cooper, C., & Jensen, J. (Eds). (1985). *Measures for research and evaluation in the English language Arts, Vol.2* Urbana, IL: National Council of Teachers of English.

Holland, N. (1975). *Five readers reading*. New Haven: Yale University Press.

Hunt, R., & Vipond, D. (1984). "Point-driven understanding: Pragmatic and cognitive dimensions of literary reading." *Poetics*,13: 261–77.

Iser, W. (1988). "The reading process: A phenomenological approach." In C. Anson (Ed.). *Writing and response*. Urbana, IL: National Council of Teachers of English.

Probst, R. (1988). *Response and analysis: Teaching literature in junior and senior high school*. Portsmouth, NH: Heinemann.

Purves, A.C., Rogers, T. & Soter, A.O. (1990). *How porcupines make love II: Teaching a response-centered curriculum*. NY: Longman.

Purves, A.C. (1991). "Canons to right of them, canons to left of them: cultural concerns in the literature curriculum. Unpublished manuscript. Department of Education, SUNY, Albany.

Rosenblatt, L. (1978). *The reader, the text and the poem*. Carbondale, IL: Southern Illinois University Press.

Taylor, D. (1990). "Teaching without testing: Assessing the complexity of children's literary learning." *English Education* (Special Edition), Vol. 4.

Wolfson, B.J. (1985). "Psychological theory and curricular thinking." In Association for Supervision and Curriculum Development, *Current thought on curriculum*. Alexandria, Virginia: Association for Supervision and Curriculum Development.

Zancanella, D. (1991). "Teachers reading/readers teaching: Five teachers' personal approaches to literature and their teaching of literature. *Research in the Teaching of English*, 25 (1):5–32.

### PART FOUR

# Reader Response Theory and Practice: New Agenda for Instruction

♣ ♣ ♣

# CHAPTER THIRTEEN

# Reader Response Criticism and Classroom Literature Discussion

❧ ❧ ❧

## Steven Z. Athanases

> You shouldn't drag things out so much. It kind of seems like you want what you think for an answer and if anyone says something different you kind of say, "Yeah, but." And then you tell them what answer you think it is.

## INTRODUCTION

I recently unearthed the above critique from a dusty box labelled "Early Teaching Memorabilia." After skimming two or three hundred student evaluations I found in the box, I kept only the one on which this quote appears. Somehow this 10th grader wrote the painful but accurate critique I had hoped I would never earn. What, me too directive? Me tell them what to think? Certainly not. After all, I had entered the profession to counter the primarily didactic literature instruction I had received in high school. Student interpretations would lay the foundation in my class. Yet there it was, the quote to remind me how hard I had found the struggle to create a class in which this was possible.

After all, the demands in teaching literature are great. Which book should I teach? Can I find a class set when I need it? Can I hook the students on the reading so they'll stay with it? How do I help them process difficult passages and themes? What will the students' future teachers assume students know about the book? How do I balance that constraint with my desire to get them to respond personally to the work? Like so many other teachers, I found myself at times like the teacher pig in Sandra Boynton's cartoon in her "Animal Farm 1984 Doublespeak Calendar" (Boynton, 1983). In the reading circle sit the piglet students around their teacher, a book open on her lap. The teacher says to one of the piglets, "There is no such thing as a wrong answer. However, if there were such a thing, that certainly would have been it." The teacher pig pays lipservice to the notion of multiple interpretations but reveals through her doublespeak that she still firmly believes in a single right interpretation that she alone in this reading circle knows.

As the student evaluation from my box of early teaching memorabilia reveals, I was not unlike Boynton's teacher pig in my bewilderment with how to validate student interpretations out of the bounds of the meanings I found correct or at least plausible. I didn't gain a sense of how to manage all of this until six years into my teaching career when I began a three-part project: (1) I read rather extensively the work of literary critics who had explored ways that the reader shapes literary meaning, (2) I tried to adapt these theories into lesson designs appropriate for my 10th graders, and (3) I tested the lessons with my students. My efforts resulted in far more engaging classroom discussions and deeper student explorations of the literature.

Of the various recent schools of literary criticism I encountered in my course of study, reader-response criticism clearly held some of the richest possibilities for teachers of English and language arts precisely because it addresses these issues of personal response and multiple interpretations. While some reader-response writing has explored pedagogical practice, much of it features the reading process of individuals and has not been translated into practice for the teacher interested in using some of the principle tenets to guide instruction. In addition, one of the problems with trendy theory is that it gets tossed around at times in such a superficial manner as to lose its fundamental values. A teacher told me recently, for example, that he uses the "process approach" in writing: "I teach them the *process* of putting together the five-paragraph essay." Then he shared with me the outlining worksheets designed to help the students put the pieces in the right places. Somewhere the fundamental principles of the writing process had been lost in favor of highly formulaic practice focused almost strictly on written products.

Likewise, the term "response approach" in the teaching of literature gets bandied about in a number of ways, losing some of its potential. On the one hand, some teachers, including a professor of mine a few years ago, pay lipservice to "response" but, like Sandra Boynton's teacher pig, retreat ultimately to the practice of claiming the highest authority for literary meaning, stating things like, "But that's not what the story means." On the other hand, some teachers and researchers draw broad caricatures of reader-response classrooms as places where teacher and students engage in thoroughly nonacademic, touchy-feely exercises that certainly doom students to college failure. Some of the published critiques lift quotes from reader-response critics out of context or cite only secondary sources, never documenting that their authors have even read the work of reader-response.

This chapter explores issues of a response-centered class by drawing on some of the original and most influential work of reader-response criticism. The work of three of these critics, representing a range of foci, will be examined for its potential to shape classroom practice, particularly literature discussion. We begin with an overview of reader-response criticism.

## READER-RESPONSE CRITICISM

Literary theory in recent decades has ushered the reader into criticism. While acceptance of the reader into critical practice met with great resistance from the New Critics who feared that consideration of the reader would lead to interpretive anarchy (Tompkins, 1980a, 1980b), the reader now holds a firm place in literary criticism. Reader-oriented schools and subschools have burgeoned in an array of forms: transactional, subjective and psychoanalytic, hermeneutic, semiotic and structuralist, phenomenological.

Theorists of these various persuasions have argued against the New Critical notion that a literary work holds objective status and can be explicated in terms of its strictly formal properties. No longer viewing the text as the container of all possible meanings of a literary work, reader-oriented critics grant the reader a key position in their models of the act of reading literature. Louise Rosenblatt (1978) views the reading process, in fact, as an event involving three characters on a stage — author, text, and reader. She argues that while the reading experience depends on all three characters, the two most recent waves of criticism had spotlighted the author and the text and thus the reader now deserves the theater's spotlight so we can examine what part this leading actor plays in the performance.

The actual role the reader plays in literary study and criticism, however, remains a source of dispute. Reader-response critics do not agree, for example, on the relative centrality of the reader in the reading process. How much freedom does a reader hold in making meaning of a work? How constrained by the text is a reader's interpretation? Regarding this dilemma,

Rosenblatt (1985a) argues that "No metaphor or comparison does justice to this unique character of verbal art" (p. 36). Still, she and most reader-oriented critics explicitly or implicitly argue metaphors of reading, interpretation, and the balance of openness and constraint, metaphors that frequently coincide but also frequently collide.

While the New Critics tended to view the text through metaphors such as a container of meaning or a kind of specimen with formal properties to be examined under a laboratory microscope, reader-response critics tend to view the text more as a stimulus for meaning.

Table 13.1 shows a sampling of reader-response metaphors for the literary text. Texts for Rosenblatt are "merely scratches, marks on parchment or paper until some reader makes meaning out of them" (1981, p. 13). Her text is a musical score (1985a) or "merely inkspots on paper until a reader transforms them into a set of meaningful symbols" (1976, p. 25). Her reader "performs the poem or the novel, as the violinist performs the sonata. But the instrument on which the reader plays, and from which he evokes the work,

**Table 13.1   Reader-Response Metaphors of the Literary Text**

| Literary Critic | Metaphor for the Text | Focus |
|---|---|---|
| Louise Rosenblatt | inkspots on paper<br>scratches on the page<br>musical score<br>blueprint for meaning | reader-text transaction<br>reader in the spotlight |
| Walter Davis | mooring for interpretation | interpretation<br>    anchored in the text |
| David Bleich | mirror | subjective exploration<br>reader's self-discovery |
| Norman Holland | Rorschach | personal psychological<br>    identity themes |
| Stanley Fish | notations | meaning making<br>    process<br><br>how meaning is<br>    possible |
| Jonathan Culler | signs | pursuit of signs |

is — himself" (1976, p. 280). Her text is a blueprint for meaning (1978), guiding and constraining interpretation, not unlike the text that Walter Davis (1978) calls a mooring for interpretation. For Rosenblatt, a transaction between reader and text that evokes a poem occupies the focus of literary study and criticism. While the reader warrants the spotlight, examined textual cues always serve as guides and constraints for the transaction.

For David Bleich (1975, 1978), the text does not guide and constrain; it serves as a mirror held up to the self. Similarly, Norman Holland's text (1968, 1975) becomes a kind of Rorschach to explore personal psychological identity themes. For these critics, focus rests on the reader's self, with the text as prompt for self-examination. Still other critics examine the *process* of meaning-making above all, with the text serving as a kind of stimulus for such examination. For Stanley Fish (1980), there is no pre-existent text to which the reader responds; there are notations, but they do not hold objective status. How these notations are named and interpreted is itself a product of an interpretive strategy practiced by virtue of readers' memberships in various interpretive communities. And for Jonathan Culler (1981) the text is a collection of signs that make meaning possible; the reader must discover the conventions that make possible the emergent meanings.

While the metaphors suggest different notions of texts and different purposes for literary study and criticism, their sponsors share two underlying principles. First, these theorists have shifted attention away from the text as product to a focus on the reader-text interaction, or the *process* of reading. Wimsatt and Beardsley (1954) had argued that a move away from a focus on the text as object or product and the granting of permission for the reader to enter into criticism would lead to "the affective fallacy," a confusion of the text and its effects. But Fish (1980) has called this the "affective fallacy fallacy," arguing that "a poem *is* what it does" (1980, p. 349) and that the reading and interpretive processes, therefore, warrant critical focus. The second principle reader-response critics share is their view of the reader as not a passive receiver of meaning but an active meaning maker.

The evolution of these two principles of reader-oriented literary critics reflects parallel movements within philosophy, art, linguistics, and the social sciences. In an array of art forms (painting, sculpture, poetry, music, theater, dance) criticism has shifted focus from formal or aesthetic characteristics to what the art work does (Rothenberg, 1977). Social science fields have evolved to the point of self-reflexiveness, a questioning of the assumptions of a discipline, and a shift of focus from the observed to the interaction between observed and observer (Suleiman, 1980). Even in science, the discipline that developed the formalist practices the New Critics emulated, critics have come to accept that scientific truth is made and not found; seeing is through a paradigm, through a set of beliefs about the nature of reality, and thus the "truth" a scientist discovers is shaped by the view of the world to which the scientist subscribes (Kuhn, 1972).

The emphases of reader-response critics on an examination of the reading process and on the reader as meaning maker, then, are no mere trend in literary theory and critical practice. These principles underlie much recent writing on the teaching of literature as well.

Authors have recently worked to translate these rich, often dense critical theories into suggestions for practical classroom application. Rouse (1983), for example, has explored what the work of Holland, Bleich, and Rosenblatt suggests for teacher-student relationships. McCormick (1985) suggests classroom strategies that draw on Bleich, Holland, and others; Probst (1986, 1988a, 1988b) builds on Rosenblatt and Bleich. In addition, a number of teachers have reported applications of reader-response criticism that they have tested in their classrooms (c.f. Athanases, 1988; Carlson, 1988; Schears, 1988).

Much of this work takes on the whole of the teaching of literature and therefore at times in necessarily broad strokes. This chapter instead focuses on a particular and crucial area of literature instruction — that of classroom discussion. Marshall and Wilson (1990) have aptly stated that "the primacy of discussion as an instructional practice seems as central to our discipline as is laboratory practice to the teaching of biology or guided problem solving to the teaching of mathematics" (p. 1). Yet precious little literature for teachers specifically addresses the need so many teachers feel for developing principled literature discussion practice. Drawing on the work of three reader-response critics, this chapter will address ways that teachers can strengthen the reader-response component of their classes through discussion. Various questions will be considered. For example, what are some effective roles teacher and student might assume during talk about literature in a reader-response classroom? What kind of classroom talk might most effectively help students to construct and explore literary meaning? This review will examine the explicit and implicit claims the reader-response theorists have made about how literature discussion might effectively proceed.

## HOW READER RESPONSE CAN SHAPE LITERATURE DISCUSSION

Reader-response theory informs models of literature discussion that move beyond mere recitation. A number of theorists suggest ways teachers might effectively structure talk for classrooms. This chapter will first glean from the various theorists their fundamental notions of what purposes literature study ought to serve and how classroom talk can best serve those ends. Second, no longer a receiver and reciter of information, no longer in pursuit of the correct interpretation, the reader/student now assumes the role of meaning maker, with great interpretive freedom. How free can a reading be? What are the constraints on the reading process, according to the various theorists?

Just as the student takes on a new role in the reader-response mode, so the teacher must assume a new role. No longer the asker of known-information questions (Mehan, 1985) tied closely to details of the text, no longer merely the assessor of student knowledge and transmitter of information, what role should the teacher now play as discussion leader? What tone does the teacher set for literature talk? What does the teacher attempt to get students to do? Finally, does questioning still play a role in discussion? If questions are not used to elicit known information, how do they now function? What are their purposes? What forms should questioning take?

This review will cull the work of three reader-response theorists for their explicit and implicit suggestions for how to address these four areas of concern. While a great number of theorists offer provocative ideas that suggest ways to structure literature discussion, this review will be best served by an examination of three theorists who offer challenging and often disparate views of literary theory and study. The three reader-response theorists selected — Rosenblatt, Bleich, and Fish — are three of the most frequently cited in journals of research and pedagogy. This review will first attempt to illuminate some of the unique suggestions these theorists offer for literature discussion and, second, discuss ways in which pieces of the theories pose problems for classroom use that need to be addressed by thoughtful teachers, curriculum developers, and researchers.

## *Goals for Literature Study and Discussion*

All three theorists suggest for readers a two-step process that begins with individual work and moves outward to the group or community.

Table 13.2 shows this movement from private to public, or shared, response. While the second or public stage is served well by discussion, the first step, a process of self-inquiry, is, according to these theorists, better served by reflection and personal writing.

For Rosenblatt (cf. 1978, 1985b), the first essential step is engagement in a personal transaction with a text. While informational or technical ma-

**Table 13.2**    **Reader Activities: From Private to Public Response**

| | *Private Response* | *Public Response* |
|---|---|---|
| | *Read, React, Reflect* | *Share, Discuss, Reflect* |
| Rosenblatt | — literary transaction<br>— aesthetic experience<br>— stay alive to textual cues | — compare responses<br>— reflect on one's reading<br>— adjust interpretation |
| Bleich | — aim for self-enlightenment<br>— tap raw emotion<br>— write about affect<br>  & associations | — share feelings<br>— note common themes<br>— develop convictions |
| Fish | — focus on meaning-making<br>— predict | — dialogue<br>— persuasion<br>— debate |

terials such as science texts, handbooks, and manuals invite an *efferent* reading stance ("effere," from the Latin, meaning "to take away") so readers can absorb information to use *after* the reading process, literary works require *aesthetic* reading, a mode that focuses on what happens *during* the reading event. In the aesthetic reading stance, the reader undergoes a transaction between text and self. The text serves as blueprint, shaping the reading, but the reading is itself an active process, a lived-through experience. Because of the uniqueness of readers, in different transactions with the same text, different "poems" are born. Each transaction with the text evokes a new poem:

> Sensing, feeling, imagining, thinking under the stimulus of the words, the reader who adopts the aesthetic attitude feels no compulsion other than to apprehend what goes on during this process, to concentrate on the complex structure of experience that he is shaping and that becomes for him the poem, the story, the play symbolized by the text. (1978, p. 26)

Table 13.2 shows that Rosenblatt's reader must reflect on the transaction through public response as an essential next stage. Readers actively engage in discussion to determine how their evocations of the work compare. During discussion, the reader runs a check on the personal transaction: Why did I ignore that point? What made me sentimentalize the ending? Why did so many others find humor in what I perceived as a grim tale? Have I done justice to this text? The New Critical notion of a close reading extends now to a close reading of one's transaction. Such reflection and discussion often lead to adjustment of the reader's evocation of the literary work:

> For he can begin to achieve a sound approach to literature only when he reflects upon his response to it, when he attempts to understand what in the work and in himself produced that reaction, and when he thoughtfully goes on to modify, reject, or accept it. (1976, p. 76)

Thus, discussion serves as a forum for reflection on and adjustment of one's transaction with the literary work.

Table 13.2 shows that like Rosenblatt, Bleich would have his readers begin in a personal state of reading and reflection, but less for purposes of engaging in a literary transaction and more for purposes of self-enlightenment. The text serves as a stimulus for self-discovery, a process that begins with a student's emotional response to the reading experience. To achieve this response, readers must grow sensitive to affect, to raw emotion, to how they are feeling as they encounter texts. They also need to explore associative analogies, searching for the kinds of events in their lives that have provoked the same feelings (1975).

At the second, more public stage, Bleich's students report to their classmates the affect and associations they experienced while reading. They share, above all, their very personal feelings:

> Feelings — that part of us longest with us and most common in daily experience — are responsibly welcomed into public discussion. Our traditional sense of classroom or public reality is finally made to correspond with our subjective sense of private reality. (1975, p. 95)

Beyond this first purpose for discussion of freely expressing feelings from private readings, Bleich argues for the collection of response statements as a means of developing student awareness of common themes that emerge in readings, of what is shared and what is not. The goal here is to define a community of common interests, a process Bleich finds fundamental to authorizing any new knowledge (1978). The discussion emphasis rests on what is shared, with no suggestion that readers consider the kind of adjustment of personal readings that Rosenblatt's discussion required.

Finally, Bleich argues that discussion can enhance students' convictions about beliefs:

Each member of a group creates "the truth" through his response to other responses. What appears true to us is, above all, characterized by our inward conviction of belief in a proposition, a conviction subsequently validated by the assent of other authorities — group or individual. In the classroom, I believe the most important thing to be done is to nurture the ability to develop convictions responsibly based on our tastes. (1975, p. 95)

Bleich has argued, then, for the use of literature as a stimulus for self-reflection, group agreement, and growth in conviction. What he considers less is the use of literature as a prompt for change. If a reader, in examining her personal response to a text, for example, realizes she feels no empathy toward a character in a story because she has learned through relatives or from the media that members of that character's ethnic or cultural group are inferior or fundamentally bad, is it enough that she has reflected on this attitude and feels conviction about it? Shouldn't literary discussion examine the *disagreement* between this student and some peers in addition to examining the *shared* attitudes among class members? Can't literary discussion serve as a forum for change? Without consideration of this dimension, Bleich's model of literature study becomes incompatible with instructional contexts where change in values or attitudes is a key tenet.

While Rosenblatt's first stage emphasizes the living through of a literary transaction, and Bleich's features the raw emotion of affect and association for purposes of self-enlightenment, Table 13.2 shows that the first and personal stage of Fish's reading model would ask readers to focus during reading on how they make meaning as they move through texts, forming assumptions at the end of one line of a poem, for example, then revising those assumptions after subsequent lines. He would ask readers to examine how they form and change judgments, approvals, conclusions, and answers. Literature, Fish argues, is a kinetic art, and meaning is an act that develops as a reader interacts with a text. What the language of a text does and makes a reader do, by virtue of its ordering, its placement on the page, is what it means. The reader engages in "affective stylistics," a process not of determining what a word or line or pattern means, but

more exactly to specify what a reader, as he comes upon that word or pattern, is *doing*, what assumptions he is making, what conclusions he is reaching, what expectations he is forming, what attitudes he is entertaining, what acts he is being moved to perform. (1980, p. 92)

Fish's reader, then, concentrates on the experience being shaped during the reading process, but the focus lies more consciously on the meaning-making process than on the lived-through experience of Rosenblatt's reader, or the raw emotions of Bleich's.

For discussion, Fish pushes Bleich's notion of the development of conviction to the acquisition of persuasive power. While New Critical doctrine argued for the demonstration of interpretation, with facts from a text used for support, Fish argues that demonstration with facts is an impossible practice since there are no facts in texts, only notations named and interpreted by individual readers. Thus, readers discuss the texts they have "written" — prepared, after the careful examination of their meaning-making process, to argue that the meanings they have constructed are sound. In the community of the classroom, readers must harness their persuasive powers, altering the perceptions of others in whatever ways necessary, for the purpose of arguing that their texts are worthy.

## *Interpretive Constraints: How Free Can a Reading Be?*

Since under the tenets of reader-response criticism the text no longer holds the status of container of meanings and answers, students gain great interpretive freedom as they read, reflect, and discuss. Also, with the teacher no longer the assumed holder of correct interpretations, what constrains students' readings and interpretations? How free can a reading be?

Table 13.3 identifies the nature of interpretive constraints, according to the three reader-response critics under consideration. Rosenblatt provides some guidelines. Since the text is a blueprint for meaning, the reader must be alive to all of the textual cues, sensitive to all of the notations, like a musician with a musical score. The reader must adopt the aesthetic stance in order to fully participate in the transaction with the literary work. And such an aesthetic reading is not merely free association; it must be scrupulous, with the reader attending to "all the components of the work, the minor chords as well as the major" (1976, p. 116). Furthermore, readers must be flexible, must avoid stock responses, and must bring to texts all they can. And the process of reflection on and adjustment of the transaction afforded by discussion is essential. Her text is both stimulus and control; and the reader must return to this text to determine if the reading is sound and defensible. The two criteria of validity are that, first, a reader's interpretation not be contradicted by any element of the text and, second, nothing be projected for which there is no verbal basis.

Rosenblatt's constraints on interpretation might read as the following series of questions:

**Table 13.3    How Free Can a Reading Be?**

|  | *Interpretive Constraints* | *Problems/Challenges* |
|---|---|---|
| Rosenblatt | — Flexible reading but attentive to all cues<br>— No contradiction by any element of the text<br>— Nothing projected for which there is no verbal basis | — Who authorizes adequacy of interpretations? |
| Bleich | None | — Disagreements not negotiated<br>— Discussion not forum to change interpretations |
| Fish | — Community of interpreters<br>— Dialogue, persuasion, debate | — Students need persuasive skills<br>— Students need confidence in arguing<br>— Will class behave as active interpretive community? |

1. Has the reading been flexible but attentive to minor chords, free of stock responses and irrelevant associations?

2. Was the reader emotionally ready for this text and reading, able to avoid sentimentality and inhibition, political and social stances that might screen the text from him or her?

3. Has the reader brought all he or she can to the text, picking up contextual cues, examining various word meanings, avoiding meaning constructions that contradict what the text offers or that have no verbal basis in the text?

Rosenblatt's students have earned critical authority for construction of meaning, but she argues that their readings must be responsible to the blueprint and thoroughly examined for shortcomings. And during discussion,

> The readers point toward the set of symbols as they seek to compare what the words called forth for them. The adequacy or inadequacy of a reading

can be demonstrated by indicating the points of the text which have been ignored, or which have not been woven into the rest of the semantic structure built in the text. (1978, p. 129)

Rosenblatt's teacher, then, has guidelines and questions that constrain her students' interpretations, and her students have strategies for checking their own and each other's readings. A question arises, however, regarding the issue of an inadequate reading, which Rosenblatt would bring to light by drawing attention to "points of the text which have been ignored." While in some cases agreement might be simple regarding recognition of the failure to consider a piece of a text in a reading, other cases might arise in which such agreement is less possible since what is ignored is less tangible, more abstract, more open to interpretation. Who, in such cases, indicates the points ignored? Does the teacher still claim authority for adequacy of interpretation? If so, how does this affect discussion? How much power do students truly believe they have as meaning makers? Documented classroom testing of these problematic moments in discussion might shed light on such concerns.

Table 13.3 shows that Bleich provides no real constraints on students' interpretations. Whatever a text means to a reader is legitimate. The reader's responsibility is less to the text and more to a sensitive report of whatever the mind experiences during the process of reading (or shortly after reading) a text. He argues, "Under the subjective paradigm the epistemological role of these constraints is trivial: they function as any real object functions, since they can be changed by subjective action" (1978). Bleich grants the reader autonomy in the creation of meaning. He defends this radical move by attacking the notion of objectivity itself, arguing that even the sciences, which the New Critics imitated, have accepted the fallacy of objective reality and that literary criticism should follow suit. Readers create their own texts, according to their subjective perceptions.

Such a stand is consonant with Bleich's purposes for literature discussion. Bleich's teacher need not impose constraints on students' readings since discussion goals include these identified in Table 13.2: the sharing of personal feelings from readings; the development of awareness of common themes and common interests among classmates; and the enhancement of conviction about one's beliefs. Since readers need not adjust their readings during discussion, since literature discussion is not a forum for change of readings or beliefs, interpretive constraints become irrelevant.

While the issue of constraint is not irrelevant for Fish, he does not assign the text the authority for constraining interpretations as Rosenblatt does. No interpretation is inherently an impossible one. Yet some might be ruled out — not because the text cannot support them, but because other readers cannot accept them as possible. In fact, a seemingly outrageous interpretation, if convincingly argued to a number of other interpreters, becomes legitimate. Table 13.3 points out that, in Fish's model, interpretive constraints are handled through dialogue, persuasion, and debate. Fish suggests, for example, that a teacher need not fear handling an Eskimo reading of Faulkner's "A Rose for Emily" nor an analysis of Blake's "The Tyger" as an account of problems in the digestive tract. If the community of interpreters can accommodate such a seemingly outlandish interpretation, then outlandishness gets redefined. It is no threat to civilized literature discussion.

Fish offers little evidence, however anecdotal, that such a practice is workable in a classroom at the university level, much less at the high school or middle school level. Furthermore, little research in literature instruction has examined such alternative models of literature study and discussion. Fish's model assumes students will behave as responsible members of a community of interpreters. What if, however, students will not contribute to discussion? In many classroom settings, a small percentage of students actually participate in classroom discussion. What if one student develops a stunning reading of a work and the rest of the students stare into space, offering no assent? Does that interpretation fail since the class was not persuaded? Or what if a student offers some deliberately inane interpretation that some of his buddies decide to forcefully support? Has the interpretation succeeded? After all, under such a model of literary response, the teacher no longer stands in judgment of students' interpretations. Credit is not earned for right readings but for convincing ones. Such issues invite pedagogical extension and research.

In order to help a class develop into the responsible community of interpreters Fish describes, what kind of training program does a teacher need to implement? What kinds of incentives are needed? Should classroom talk be evaluated? And what kind of system does a teacher use to evaluate response in such a reader-response classroom? How much credit is due a daring interpretation, forcefully argued, that members of the community eventually rule out? How much credit is due the safer interpretation that the classroom community of interpreters easily accepts as sound? What are the effects of different kinds of evaluation incentives on students' participation in such a classroom community? In order to realize, particularly at the junior high and high school levels, the potential of the kind of community of interpreters Fish proposes, such questions deserve the attention of teachers, instructional leaders, and researchers.

## The Teacher's Role

No longer primarily an assessor of student knowledge of transmitted literary information, the teacher in a reader-response discussion carries new responsibilities. What role does this teacher play?

Table 13.4 identifies some of the teacher's roles in the private and public response stages, according to the three critics under examination. Rosenblatt's teacher must first examine her discussion prompts to be certain she is inviting an aesthetic reading stance for a literary work, and not an efferent stance. The raw data of discussion must be individual personal encounters with texts (1978). Second, since effective reading and reflection involve the transaction between a reader and a text, a lived-through experience, the clever teacher will train students to activate prior experiences:

> No matter how great the potentialities of the text, the reader can make a poem only by drawing on his or her own reservoir of past experiences with life and language. In bringing past experience to bear on the reading pro-

**Table 13.4    The Teacher's Role in Shaping Student Response to Literature**

|  | *Private Response* | *Public Response* |
|---|---|---|
| Rosenblatt | — invite aesthetic stance | — facilitate student to student talk |
|  | — train students to activate prior experience | — draw out timid students, keep aggressive in check |
|  | — help students connect sound and sense | — create tone: informal, friendly, spontaneous |
|  |  | — help students reflect on & refine interpretations |
| Bleich | 4 stage training process: | — training process: |
|  | (1) thoughts and feelings | — tone: trust & honesty |
|  | (2) feelings about literature | — model sharing process |
|  | (3) deciding on literary importance | — identify with students |
|  | (4) interpretation as a communal act |  |
| Fish | Nothing explicit | — create climate for persuasion and debate |

cess, we create, in the two-way relationship with a text, a new, more complex, experience. (1981, p. 18)

During the public response stage, as pieces of text are re-examined during discussion, the teacher must help students connect sound with sense, to savor the sound of the words in the inner ear (1985a), and to realize that for aesthetic reading experiences sound is intimately "involved with the full cognitive and affective 'sense' of words" (1981, p. 19). Rosenblatt's teacher participates as one of the group, with the conversational ball thrown student to student, rather than from teacher to student and back again (1976). The teacher must draw out the more timid students and keep the more aggressive from monopolizing discussion. The teacher develops a tone of informal, friendly exchange in which students need to show tolerance for one another's opinions. The setting must be spontaneous so students will share their personal evocations of texts without fear of being considered wrong:

> The classroom situation and the relationship with the teacher should create a feeling of security. (The student) should be made to feel that his own response to books, even though it may not resemble the standard critical comments, is worth expressing. Such a liberating atmosphere will make it possible for him to have an unselfconscious, spontaneous, and honest reaction. (1976, p. 66)

And Rosenblatt reminds us that discussion should not be a rehashing of the book. The teacher does not impart information but helps students "reflect on their experience, clarify its significance for themselves, become aware of alternative emphases, discover their own blind spots, or reinforce their own insights" (1985a, p. 49).

Much of what Rosenblatt recommends appears straightforward and fitting with her theory. And while she acknowledges that the aesthetic-efferent distinction is more a spectrum than a dichotomy, most of the writing and discussion prompts she offers for illustration tend toward the extremes: "What are the facts this poem teaches?" (efferent) versus "What kind of event have you lived through in transaction with this text?" (aesthetic). Still, in actual class operations, can discussion proceed strictly in the aesthetic domain? What about the questions that fall toward the center of this spectrum? How might we distinguish the efferent among these questions from the aesthetic? And what differences do these questions make on student learning?

Like Rosenblatt, Bleich would like for his discussions a tone of informality. However, because he holds the goal for his students of self-enlightenment, he wants students to report their personal feelings openly. Thus, he moves beyond the informal friendly exchange to an atmosphere of trust and honesty (1975). To encourage students to report the feelings inspired by their readings openly, Bleich believes that the most important thing teachers can do is to model the process by sharing their own personal responses. He further recommends that teachers do all they can to identify with students to elicit their responses. All of this is needed to break down the sense of teacher as interpretive authority, for "In the classroom, the teacher's authority is an effigy of the author's authority in the reading experience" (1975, p. 94). Teachers, then, who clarify that they are merely other readers and interpreters rather than the holders of the best or most correct readings will invite students to believe that *their* readings hold value and that they need not assume their job is to uncover an author's intention. The process of moving from the act of private writing to public reading of very personal responses would certainly require great sensitivity and care, particularly when we adapt Bleich's classroom model of nine university students in a literature seminar to the context of a middle school or high school English class of thirty 15- and 16-year-olds.

In order to help students with this process of sharing their personal feelings about readings, Bleich (1975) reports how he takes his students through an elaborate training process. In primarily written form, students respond to his prompts in four steps. In Step One, "Thoughts and Feelings," the teacher creates a forum for open expression of personal feelings before even moving to literary texts. In Step Two, "Feelings About Literature," the teacher trains students to report their perceptions, affect, and associative analogies in response first to symbolic objects such as photos and drawings and later to literature. Step Three, "Deciding on Literary Importance," takes students through the process of learning to decide on and discuss their personal choices of the most important word, passage, or aspect of a literary work. Students typically write about these elements in private and then perhaps share pieces of them in Step Four, "Interpretation as a Communal Act." Bleich finds this process essential in order to achieve his goals of the sharing of personal feelings, the development of an awareness of common interests, and the enhancement of convictions about personal beliefs.

Fish provides the fewest suggestions of the three theorists for how a teacher as leader of his style of discussion might perform. The tone Fish's teacher must establish, however, is clear: not perhaps the friendly exchange of Rosenblatt's discussion groups; not likewise the trust and honesty of Bleich's discussions. For Fish's discussions of literature, a climate of persuasion and debate becomes essential. The challenge for Fish's teacher is formidable and clear: how to transform a group of often reluctant speakers into a community of active and responsible interpreters willing to develop and argue competing texts. What kind of training process will work best to help students in a Fish model of discussion to gain confidence and skill in arguing their interpretations?

Perhaps Bleich's training process might serve as an effective model. Just as Bleich took his students through open sharing of feelings, then feelings about symbolic objects, then feelings about literature, a teacher adopting Fish's model of discussion might do well to start students off with practice in persuasion regarding everyday affairs, then persuasion involving meanings of symbolic objects such as cartoons, songs, and films, and finally persuasion regarding literary meaning. Such a process might train students in the very persuasive skills Fish's readers need.

Another problem arises, however. Rosenblatt has argued the need to avoid asking students before their reading of a literary work questions that might invite an efferent stance to reading. She argues for few prereading questions so that students will have the opportunity to adopt the aesthetic reading stance and comfortably engage in a transaction with the text, unconstrained by a teacher's questioning agenda. But what about the effects of a classroom climate of persuasion and debate on students' readings? If we are to accept Rosenblatt's warning that we avoid inviting students to adopt the efferent reading stance, might we not logically find the same problem if students know their post-reading task will be to engage in lively debate regarding their interpretations? Might we not first be robbing students of their opportunities for rich aesthetic readings, unencumbered by the need to develop provocative, forcefully argued interpretations of literary works? Second, if daring readings earn more credit or more peer approval than safe readings, might we not invite students to explore deliberately "fringe" interpretations that do not necessarily match their actual aesthetic, personal transactions with a text? Or worse, are we not perhaps inviting students to skip the aesthetic reading step altogether to adopt a stance of persuasion? And what does any of this mean for literary experiences and understanding?

Finally, in a Fish model of discussion, not only do students need to come to class prepared to argue that their interpretations are legitimate and perhaps the best possible readings, but classmates would need to be equally well prepared to determine if those interpretations work and to articulate why or why not. Listeners who neither support nor refute their peers' readings are not participating as responsible community members and would perhaps need to be evaluated accordingly. How willingly will high school students, sensitive to peer pressure, refute their peers' readings? What factors might encourage and inhibit such critical response to one another's ideas? These issues deserve attention.

## Questioning

While reader-response discussion departs from the practice of the teacher asking primarily known information questions in the recitation mode, what functions might questions serve for readers? What forms might they take? Rosenblatt warns that questions that focus student attention on things to be answered at the end of a reading might inspire a predominantly efferent reading. Instead, students need the freedom to experience whatever personal transactions they might have with a work. She likewise warns that questions following a reading should never concern an efferent reading of a work, should not treat a literary work as a body of facts; otherwise, analysis will be like algebra or an intellectual exercise (1981). Rosenblatt's key guide to questioning is that analysis or criticism must ask questions about the *experienced* work. Thus the following list represents sample questions gathered from Rosenblatt's various writings:

1. What kind of event have you lived through in transaction with the text?
2. What manner of world have you conjured up?
3. What, in the text or in the experiences, assumptions, preoccupations, that you brought to the text, contributed to the nature of the evocation and its impact on you?
4. What in the author's words and techniques led to or justifies your experience?
5. What do you know about the text? What did it mean to you? What did you think about, feel, as you read it?
6. Has your reading been attentive to all the minor chords of the text, all the cues available to you?

The basis of Rosenblatt's questions is always the transaction, the evoked work.

Once Bleich (1975) has trained his students in perception, affective responding and associative responding, he asks questions in sequence to first elicit personal responses to a piece of literature:

1. What did you feel while reading the poem? (affect)
2. What did the poem remind you of? (association)

Once these responses are reported, students respond to questions regarding the "subjectivity of critical judgment" (1975):

3.  What is the most important word in the work?
4.  What is the most important passage in the work?
5.  What is the most important feature in the work?

Finally, students move on to questions regarding interpretation as a communal act:

6.  What do the group's readings have in common?
7.  What does this say about the work or about us as a group of readers?

Thus, Bleich has taken his students, through a sequence of questioning, from personal responses to a work to a "collective subjectivity" (1975).

Again, Fish offers little explicit suggestion for how questioning might proceed with students, but implicit in his work are a few key principles. While Rosenblatt and Bleich explore primarily questions to ask students after they have read and experienced a literary work, Fish's work suggests that the questions must be asked *during* the reading: "A reader-response critic elaborates the structure of the reading experience, a structure which is not so much discovered by the interrogation but demanded by it" (1980, 345). Thus, the act of exploring a few key questions while one constructs meaning with a literary work helps bring to consciousness the meaning-making processes the reader engages in:

1.  What are you doing as you read this text?
2.  What is being done to you?
3.  For what purpose?

Fish claims that the act of asking oneself such questions helps readers become increasingly conscious of their reading processes.

Clearly, these questions only *begin* to tap the complexities of the process of constructing meaning when dealing with texts. And adapting such a process of questioning and examination of reading to a middle school or high school context becomes unthinkable if questioning procedures are not elaborated and made more explicit. Before implementation of Fish's ideas becomes a worthwhile venture for curriculum planners and teachers to endorse, teachers need to address a number of questions.

What kinds of questions beyond the three general ones Fish proposes might students ask themselves as they read? Which of these questions are most effective in helping students really examine how they construct meaning when working with literary texts? What should students do with the answers they find or develop? Record them in journals? Tape them? Remember them and report them the next day in small-group or full-class discussions? Analyze them in formal essays? Which of these methods best increases students' awareness of how they make meaning with texts?

Finally, Fish has claimed that no constraints need be imposed on readers' interpretations since the "community" itself serves as constraint, accepting only those interpretations currently possible and plausible, according to community norms. What portion of the community serves as check on interpretations? For a classroom community, are we talking about a majority? A consensus? In order for such a process to evolve into a workable plan, students certainly need to operate in the persuasive, perhaps argumentative manner Fish suggests. Will the act of examining one's reading and meaning making processes lead to greater conviction about one's interpretations and greater confidence and skill in persuading others to accept those readings? Which methods of examining one's reading process produce the greatest impact on a student's success in "literary persuasion"? And how might both the students' processes of examining their meaning construction and their developing skills of literary persuasion be effectively analyzed and assessed? Questions such as these invite classroom experimentation.

## *CONCLUSION*

Though reader-response critics vary significantly in how they explain the reading process, they share two important tenets: (1) They have shifted attention away from the text as product to a focus on the reader-text transaction, or the process of reading, and (2) they view the reader as not a passive receiver of meaning but an active meaning maker. These two principles make the work of reader-response critics especially pertinent to the concerns of middle school and high school teachers of literature because they feature the reader or learner. When we closely attend to the active process our students undergo as they make sense of literature, we move closer to ways to help these students learn to find meaning and value in literature.

The works of Louise Rosenblatt, David Bleich, and Stanley Fish — three of the most provocative and most frequently cited of these theorists — suggest in explicit and implicit ways some strategies for literature discussion that allow the student reader opportunities to engage in literary transactions, expression of personal responses to experienced works, the examination of personal meaning construction, and the practice of arguing competing tasks. As this chapter has made clear, however, the work of these critics, who have primarily focused on the reading processes of individual readers, poses countless questions and problems for teachers, all of which warrant classroom exploration. Still, these critics leave us with some helpful principles to guide literature discussion:

1.  *Private to public response*
    Class discussion moves well from private to public literary response, allowing students the chance for personal readings, feelings, and reflections, then a sharing of these responses with the larger group.

2.  *Integrated writing and speaking*
    Writing and speaking become mutually supportive learning tools in the study of literature: Students might begin with private written responses that they later share with the class; later, students can write critically about common themes in students' remarks and other patterns that emerge in class discussion.

3.  *Classroom climate*
    Attention must be paid to the creation of a classroom climate that best fosters the kind of discussion desired: If the goal is the open sharing of feelings, then the class needs a tone of trust and honesty; if the goal is persuasion and debate, then the class needs a tone that fosters argumentation.

4.  *Training and support*
    Students need training and support in engaging in the various kinds of response we might invite. This training includes the use of a range of writing and discussion prompts that invite a range of literary responses. Also, teachers can model the variety of kinds of response and the act of sharing these responses with the larger group.

5.  *Reflection*
    While the New Critics engaged in the act of close reading of a literary text, reader-response critics invite the close reading of the reading itself. Students need help in learning how to reflect on their interpretations and on how and why they responded similarly to and differently from other students.

6.  *The teacher as transfer of control*
    No longer the disseminator of a single correct interpretation of the literature, the teacher shifts role to a discussion facilitator. Most signifi-

cantly, the teacher clarifies to students that she or he is another (albeit bright and experienced) interpreter of the literature, thereby empowering students with the belief that their personal interpretations count.

These principles, supported by much of the thoughtful work of the three reader-response critics examined in this chapter, provide some guidance for the teacher interested in designing and orchestrating literature discussion founded on the private and public responses of their students.

## REFERENCES

Athanases, S. (1988), Developing a classroom of interpreters. *English Journal*, 77 (1), 45–48.

Bleich, D. (1975). *Readings and feelings: An introduction to subjective criticism*. Urbana, IL.: National Council of Teachers of English.

Bleich, D. (1978). *Subjective criticism*. Baltimore: Johns Hopkins University Press.

Boynton, S. (1983). Animal Farm 1984 doublespeak calendar. Urbana, IL.: National Council of Teachers of English.

Carlson, J. (1988). Readers responding to "Rappaccini's Daughter." *English Journal*, 77 (1), 49–53.

Culler, J. (1981). *The pursuit of signs: Semiotics, literature, deconstruction*. Ithaca, N.Y.: Cornell University Press.

Davis, W. A. (1978). *The act of interpretation*. Chicago: University of Chicago Press.

Fish, S. (1980). *Is there a text in this class? The authority of interpretive communities*. Cambridge, MA: Harvard University Press.

Holland, N. (1968). *The dynamics of literary response*. New York: Oxford University Press; rpt: Norton, 1975.

Holland, N. (1975). *5 readers reading*. New Haven, Conn.: Yale University Press.

Kuhn, T. S. (1972). *The structure of scientific revolutions*, 2d ed. Chicago: University of Chicago Press.

Marshall, J. D., & Wilson, D. (1990). Talking about texts: The role of the teacher in classroom discussions of literature. *Iowa English Bulletin*, 1–14.

McCormick, K. (1985). Theory in the reader: Bleich, Holland, and beyond. *College English, 47* (8), 836–850.

Mehan, H. (1985). The structure of classroom discourse. In Teun A. Van Dijk (Ed.), *Handbook of Discourse Analysis, Vol. 3*.

Probst, R. E. (1986). Three relationships in the teaching of literature. *English Journal*, 75 (1), 60–68.

Probst, R. E. (1988a). *Response and analysis: Teaching literature in junior and senior high school*. Portsmouth, NH: Boynton/Cook and Heinemann.

Probst, R.E. (1988b). Dialogue with a text, *English Journal*, 97, (1), 32–38.

Rosenblatt, L. M. (1976). *Literature as exploration*. Third Edition. New York: Noble and Noble.

Rosenblatt, L. M. (1978). *The reader, the text, the poem: The transactional theory of the literary work*. Carbondale: Southern Illinois University Press.

Rosenblatt, L. M. (1981). Act I, Scene 1: Enter the reader. *Literature in Performance, I* (2), 13–23.

Rosenblatt, L. M. (1985a). The transactional theory of the literary work: Implications for research. In C. Cooper (Ed.), *Researching response to literature and the teaching of literature: Points of departure*. (pp. 33–53). Norwood, N.J.: Ablex Press.

Rosenblatt, L. M. (1985b). Viewpoints: Transaction versus interaction — A terminological rescue operation. *Research in the Teaching of English, 19* (1), 96–107.

Rothenberg, J. (1977). New models, new visions: Some notes toward a poetics of performance. In M. Benamou & C. Caramello (Eds.), *Performance in postmodern culture* (pp. 11–17). Milwaukee: Coda Press.

Rouse, J. (1983). An erotics of teaching. *College English, 45* (6), 535–548.

Schaars, N.J. (1988). Teaching *My Antonia*, with guidance from Rosenblatt. *English Journal*, 77 (1), 54–58.

Suleiman, S. R. (1980). Introduction: Varieties of audience-oriented criticism. In S. R. Suleiman & I. Crosman (Eds.), *The reader in the text: Essays on audience and interpretation* (pp. 3–45). Princeton: Princeton University Press.

Tompkins, J. P. (1980a). The performance of literature and reader-response criticism. Unpublished paper. Speech Communication Association Convention.

Tompkins, J. P. (Ed.) (1980b). *Reader-response criticism: From formalism to poststructuralism*. Baltimore: Johns Hopkins University Press.

Wimsatt, W. K., Jr. & Beardsley, M. (1954). The affective fallacy. In *The verbal icon: Studies in the meaning of poetry*. Lexington: The University of Kentucky Press.

# CHAPTER FOURTEEN

# "Not Any, but Many" Responses to Literature

## Adapting Rosenblatt for the Classroom

❧ ❧ ❧

### Mary Beth Hines

Like most of us, I was trained in New Criticism, adamantly believing that the text — and only the text — was the appropriate sphere of discussion in my secondary literature classes. It was my duty to connect students' straggling asides back to plot, characters, and theme. Never mind that our discussions lagged, that the spark that flickered during writing classes never ignited in our discussions of literary works. After all, they needed to know literary terminology for college, didn't they?

Recently I have come to view those riddled memories not only as moments flagging the tensions in my own teaching but also as an index to the questions circulating in discussions about the teaching and learning of literature. Studies conducted by the Center for the Learning and Teaching of Literature, for instance, highlight the prevalence of teacher-centered New Critical approaches to literature that currently pervade secondary classrooms. Even in allegedly student-centered classrooms, students contributed short-answer responses shaped by teachers' request for summary, description or interpretation of the text (Applebee, 1989; Marshall, 1989). I understand now that my classroom discussions fell into those patterns the research has revealed — what Brause and Mayher (quoted. in Mayher, 1990, p. 65) call the "oral workbook" mode, in which students give one or two word-responses to fill-in-the-blank questions.

These research studies and my own classroom experiences have led me to wonder how we, as teachers, might develop more satisfying approaches to our literature classrooms, how we might cultivate modes of inquiry that enable students to nurture incipient responses — to explore and contest, refine and redefine positions — in their own terms, not ours or the literary critic's. In my search for a classroom model that might offer a counterpoint to those described in the research on secondary classrooms, I studied several college literature classes using frameworks forged from contemporary literary theories, approaches offering alternatives to an exclusive focus on the text. I wondered if extending the scope of classroom interpretive activity to include the reader as well as the text would change the dynamics of discussion. Would an approach that invited readers to acknowledge and incorporate their prior backgrounds enable students to explore texts and contexts in more meaningful ways? How would such reader-based discourse compare to those teacher-led and text-centered discussions described in the research on secondary classrooms?

I spent a semester researching these questions in a college literature class taught by my friend Michael, whose classroom practices were informed by the reader-response theory of Louise Rosenblatt. Michael was a mentor teacher, an experienced secondary and college literature instructor, considered one of the finest by the program director. Having taken a graduate course on reader response several years earlier, he was already a seasoned Rosenblatt practitioner when he agreed to participate in this study, welcoming my observations as an opportunity to understand how theory and practice conjoined in his classroom. He explained his theoretical framework, based on Rosenblatt's work, in an interview before the semester began. I then videotaped one half of the semester's sessions and analyzed the transcribed lessons, field notes, periodic interviews with students and teachers, handouts, and student written work in order to understand what benefits Rosenblatt's version of reader response might offer classroom teachers.

While this project was fueled by my interest in literary and educational theory, my own teaching experience always served as the backdrop. How might my students comprehend literature in terms of their lives? And how might class discussion and writing facilitate their understandings? In reconsidering these questions recently, I have turned back to Michael's classroom, prompted by the intensity of discussion, the rich and complicated student discourse. A glimpse into Michael's classroom might prove valuable not only in recasting my own approach to literature but also in refiguring the grim dynamics of classroom life pictured in the research reports. Because this is a story about a college classroom, we might also consider it an

effort to debunk the many myths surrounding college approaches to literature — enabling interested secondary teachers to reconsider their roles in
preparing students for college as they revitalize their literature classrooms.

## BACKGROUND ON THE STUDY

When I entered my friend Michael's undergraduate literature class, ready to
study his adaptation of reader response, I halted at the door, wondering
where the other half of the class was — surely some had gotten lost and
would soon enter. I anticipated the cacophony of laughter, gossip and sar-
donic remarks that had always marked the entrance of students in my own
secondary classroom; voices that challenged me to find ways to connect
with students, to engage them in learning, as the cliches go. But Michael
took roll and all seventeen of them were present, ready to take notes, texts
neatly stacked under their seats, each poised with pen in hand. I imagined a
sleepy semester as a researcher in this class, Michael and his students weaving a seamless web of theory and practice. Michael would, undoubtedly,
craft a textbook model of a reader-centered pedagogy.

As I positioned the camera in the back of Michael's first class, trying to be
an unobtrusive observer, I imagined reader response and student-centered
learning fitting like the encyclopedia overlays of the body, transparencies of
skeleton, joints and muscles, one supplementing the other, creating a full and
rich portrait of the human being. Response theory, with its emphasis on the
reader, would add depth and hue to our picture of teaching and learning in
literature classes; it would resonate without rippling those templates of student-centered learning, those that have created the so-called backbone of our
educational practices — or so I thought.

Michael based his classroom practices on Rosenblatt's transactional
theory, which suggests reading practices that encourage a range of meaning
rather than a single interpretation. By widening the scope of talk to include
both reader and text, the argument goes, students can bring relevant prior
experiences to the discussion. However, with Rosenblatt, that widened spectrum of response is held in check by the verbal symbols on the page and the
consensus of readers sharing the same interpretive values and cultural
background, a group Fish (1980a) calls the "interpretive community." A
transactional approach invites a variety of responses, then, but the range is
constrained. Readers must assess the validity of their responses in terms of
those limits as they explore the field of meaning. Let's now turn to the strategies Michael used to establish a reader-response framework in his college

literature classroom before we consider the implications of invoking Rosen-blatt in the secondary classroom.

## CREATING A FRAMEWORK FOR A RESPONSE-CENTERED CLASSROOM

During the first weeks of the term, Michael repeatedly emphasized several tenets he considered crucial to a reader-centered pedagogy. For instance, he insisted that students read differently because individuals brought different constellations of experiences, backgrounds, and cultures to the reading experience. He explained this notion to the class:

> I think what you bring to the text is really important. I cannot find the same meaning as you, no way. . . . And I wouldn't want you to find the same meaning I find. I hope you get a sense that a story has a multiplicity of meanings, depending on what you're looking for and what you want to focus on.

Michael's highlighting of "what you bring to the text" echoes the emphasis in much reader-response theory on the active role of the reader in the reading process. The reading experience is different for individuals because of their varied backgrounds.

Building on the assumptions regarding the centrality of the reader, Michael accentuated the power of each person's creative capacities to forge meaning. Claiming "imagination is at the center of the class," he encouraged students to activate their creative capabilities, similar to the arguments of Rosenblatt (1938, 1978). He then explained the reading process as Rosenblatt (1978) might, describing the incipient patterns that emerge as readers connect with texts.

While Michael underscored the differences among readers, he claimed repeatedly that this did not translate into unbridled interpretive freedom. Throughout the semester, Michael struggled to enable students to develop a sense of the configuration of meaning that arises when the reader's prior experience intersects with the marks on the page. Early on, and repeatedly, he emphasized that "many, but not any" responses might be considered appropriate. He explained that readers create "poems" when they weave personal experience and opinion with the surface features of the text into a coherent and consistent whole, as Rosenblatt (1978) argues.

However, following Rosenblatt, Michael emphasized that the reader's interpretation should not be contradicted by any feature of the text. Furthermore, the interpretive community determined the range of readings considered valid (Rosenblatt, 1938, 1978, 1985). In one of the first class meetings he said,

> Interpretation involves two things . . . seeing something . . . and being able to show someone what you see. It is possible to see all kinds of things, but it really isn't a valid interpretation unless you can get another person to see it. So the idea of saying, "This is how I see things," just isn't enough.

By focusing on how readers activate their imaginations to connect with the surface features on the page, Michael fostered a transactional approach to reading and writing. He encouraged multiplicity but insisted on a range of meaning issuing from — and constrained by — the text. Let us now examine how Michael's words affected the literary endeavors of his students.

## THE EMERGENCE OF CLASSROOM DISSONANCE

Michael typically began class by inviting students to brainstorm together on moments in their reading experience that proved troublesome. For instance, he began a short story discussion by asking, "What questions or problems did you have in reading? What parts didn't you understand?" This strategy usually elicited more questions than students could possibly discuss in a 75-minute period. Michael served as a facilitator, linking comments and questions for consideration. Typically we, as teachers, might consider this a positive strategy because it did generate discussion and encourage participation. However, Michael believed that the tactic might have proved troublesome to some students who equated his facilitative stance with a noncommittal anything goes approach.

This became evident to Michael when he read the first set of papers, he reported in an interview prior to returning them. Michael had asked students to respond to a short story in a transactional mode, describing the reading experience that resulted as the student's prior knowledge and experience intersected with the words on the page. He asked learners to describe the reading event by exploring the question, What does the text do to you as you read? Despite his careful directions and his explicit comments about the constraints on interpretation, many students failed to balance reader and text effectively. Michael speculated that perhaps some students had not perceived differences between his expectations for oral and written discourses. Because he wanted students to explore and rehearse ideas in discussion, he did not sanction comments that might be considered outside the sphere of possible interpretations. Consequently, Michael wondered if some students had assumed that the free play of ideas that characterized discussion would be appropriate in the formal papers as well, despite his written and oral directions regarding this assignment.

As he distributed the papers, disconsolate student voices confirmed his hypothesis. Michael explained to the class that many students talked exclusively about the text, failing to bring related personal experiences to bear on their interpretive activities. Others focused solely on their personal experiences, ignoring the work. In response, several students complained loudly and angrily about receiving low scores, arguing that because there was not a right answer to interpreting texts in this course all students should have received As on these papers. In actuality, one student received an A–, most received B's and C's, and a few earned D's. Obviously the students had not understood the integration of reader and text necessary in a transactional reading.

Expressing disappointment that she received a B instead of an A on that first formal writing assignment, one student, Kathy, gave her reading of the class in an interview following the return of the papers:

> At first we were always looking for one meaning, the right meaning, that all the rest were wrong. He said, "Wait, there's many meanings to this or to anything." That's when we went haywire with meanings, and now he has to round us back up again.

Kathy, echoing Michael's comments about the papers, aptly described the class as falling into two basic camps: those relying on one right answer and those endorsing an unrestrained pluralism of all right answers. And particularly problematic was the fact that neither embraced the constrained multiplicity characteristic of Michael's use of Rosenblatt's theory. However, it was not only a "new" approach to literature that proved unsettling to these students but also this teacher's new approach to learning. Let us turn now to several students who found the shift from teacher-centered to student-centered learning as disconcerting as the move from New Criticism to reader response.

## LEARNING TO SUCCEED IN LITERATURE CLASSES: "READING" TEXTS AND TEACHERS

Kathy argued that Michael's teaching strategies compounded the confusion and frustration she and her peers experienced as they responded to literature in Michael's class. Just as he refused to provide the one right answer in talking about texts, he also resisted supplying the one right answer for writing about their transactions with literary works. Kathy explained how she viewed Michael's priorities for writing about literature:

> He doesn't want to give us a formula. Each paper can be different. We can have our own styles and formats and our own formulas, but we have to be effective . . . so a lot of people are confused because they're used to having every teacher give a different formula and then just plugging in the components.

Michael's refusal to give students a structure for writing, such as the five-paragraph theme — which Kathy described as central to her prior high school and college writing experiences — and his resistance to supplying a formula for talking about their reading experiences meant that she had to consider new ways of talking and writing about literature. While she described Michael as a wonderful teacher and his class as her favorite, she admitted that her prior success in school hinged upon her prescient ability to read teachers and plug in the elements each instructor privileged. Because he didn't resort to such formulas, Michael's approach to texts and to learning proved unsettling for the very reasons she loved it.

Frustrated, another student, Jerry, also met with me to voice his concerns about the class:

> We're trying to figure out exactly what he wants, and it's not that he really wants anything. He wants us to do things for ourselves. That's what he wants, and I guess we just don't know how to go about doing that, or we want concrete things to do.

While Jerry appreciates the independence required in an inquiry approach, he also concedes that "we just don't know how" to discuss and write about literature using transactional strategies. Consequently, he and his peers seek "concrete things" that might enable them "to figure exactly what he [Michael] wants."

Furthermore, both enjoyed the freedom of responding to literature in new ways, but both described themselves as conscientious students who not only wanted to learn but also wanted good grades to reflect their commitments to learning. Because they didn't receive scores that satisfied them, both reported that the low marks added to their frustration. Kathy said, "It's just since the first grades came back that everyone is wondering where we should go and what we should do. I don't think there would be all this confusion if grades weren't a factor." Yet the confusion mounted because those concrete things used in prior writing and talking about literature tasks were not appropriate here.

## MICHAEL REVISES HIS GOALS

In an interview, Michael explained that reading the first papers and observing the rise of his students' anxiety levels had led him to rethink his objectives. He wanted to help students move away from using either text or reader exclusively to shape interpretation. He declared his new focus as guiding students away from the black and white readings — the poles of basing response on either text or reader — to constructing responses using both reader and text:

> It's the grey area that I finally want them to leave class with. I want them to see that there are certain moves we can make and some we can't, but you always say, "Can I do this?" We have to keep in mind that meaning is in flux.

Michael's focus on the ambiguities of meaning and his resistance to sanctioning singular responses seemed to stand in opposition to Kathy's prior experiences in literature classrooms. For example, while Kathy and Jerry clamored for fixed rules and formulas — to guide their procedures and to anchor their activities — Michael wanted students to acknowledge that meanings are in flux — not simply transmitted by the teacher but negotiated by teacher and students. As Michael encouraged students to consider both the text and their own experiences in developing responses, students wrestled with reading the attending variables surrounding the classroom context: the teacher's expectations, the so-called meaning as authorized by the teacher or the literary critics, and the grading scale.

Embracing the consternation of his students, Michael revised his syllabus, devising a midterm that would focus on the problems associated with multiplicity and constraint — the key terms of Rosenblatt's theory. As a student-centered instructor, he was determined to enable students to assess meaning and multiplicity themselves; he did not want to resort to what Barnes (1976) calls the "transmission mode," in which the teacher disseminates information and students passively receive it.

He composed a midterm project in which students would first discuss Frost's "Mending Wall" in small groups, then write individual papers about the poem. Following these activities, the class would convene in a large-group session to discuss and theorize the process of negotiating and defining meaning as the words on the page forged with their own experiences. Michael hoped that students might generate multiple responses to this poem and in the process come to understand how they arrived at those readings. In addition, he hoped that students could collaboratively theorize about making interpretive decisions using a transactional rubric. Before we examine how students negotiated the parameters of a transactional model using small group discussion and writing, let us look at Michael's construction of the project.

## THE MIDTERM: "WALLING IN OR WALLING OUT" MEANINGS

The handout explained that the midterm would be "an opportunity to explore two questions: (1) How do we interpret texts and (2) How do we decide between two interpretations?" In what proved to be a perfect metaphor for the activity, students focused on what responses to "Mending Wall" they were "walling in or walling out," as Frost (1969, p. 33) says. The questions that formed the basis for small-group discussion and for the written arguments were the following:

### Part I

1. Identify the speaker, audience, and situation.

2. How do speaker and neighbor differ in their attitudes toward the wall? Based on that difference, what inferences can we make about each of their personalities and beliefs? Use the poem to back up your points.

3. Show how lines 36–42 work. (What does "it's not elves exactly" mean? You may have other questions as well.)

4. "Something there is that doesn't love a wall." What is that "something"? Does the narrator tell us, give us any clues, or leave it completely up to us? If not, why doesn't he know?

### Part II.

Small group discussions: In discussing the poem, notice places where members of your group had different ideas about what the poem says or does. Pay attention to what happens when you disagree; notice which disagreements your group is willing to resolve and which ones you are willing to live with. *Look very closely at places where your group disagreed. Write about those disagreements with these questions in mind:*

When do you need to arrive at a consensus before moving on? When is it all right to disagree? How do you explain disagreements? Do they emerge from the reader, the text, or a combination of the two? How do you explain it when two readers see things differently yet neither is wrong? How do you decide between a wrong reading and a different reading?

As the directions indicated, the first part of the exam foregrounded what Iser (1978) calls the "gaps" of the text, those points where readers need to supply details imaginatively when none are explicitly stated. The second part, which students labeled the hardest, was designed to make students conscious of how they made decisions about their readings, individually and collectively. Michael's oral directions reinforced the integration of text and reader central to Rosenblatt's approach:

> I want you to say something about the wall and be able to defend it by looking at the text. Here's how I look at the text, and here's how I got that. . . . I could see how you need certain personal experiences to make sense of it and to help your reader make sense of it, and others seem peripheral or beside the point.

Notice that Michael stresses the confluence of reader and text: "Here's how I look at the text." Furthermore, he insists on prior background as integral to the formulation of response because "you need certain personal experiences" to create meaning.

Michael used this occasion to reinforce his resistance to providing formulas for interpretative activities. He said, "I would really rather that you have the tools to decide for yourself rather than I come in and tell you what you can and can't say." Michael reaffirmed his emphasis on student-centered learning, positioning the student in the role of meaning maker. By emphasizing student ability and responsibility, by focusing on the cultivation of meaning using the literary "tools" students possessed, he shifted the interpretive domain from teacher to students. Perhaps a closer look at the small group work that occurred during the project will reveal some of the issues students wrestled with as they negotiated the range of "appropriate" meanings.

## SMALL GROUP DISCUSSION: LITERAL VS. METAPHORICAL READINGS

Jerry was a participant in a group of four readers who decided to tackle the poem line by line (See Fish [1980b] for a discussion of this strategy.). As they worked, they discovered that most problematic was the recurrent issue of deciding if the poem should be read on a literal or metaphorical level or both. Consider the following excerpt:

*S1:* I don't think what I think about the poem is right. It's too simple.

*S2:* I know. I'm looking for underlying meanings.

*S3:* Yeah, I was looking for underlying meanings through the whole thing. I finally had my roommate read it, and he's telling me, "Oh, it's so easy. He's just talking about rebuilding a wall every spring." So I just took it for what it was worth on paper.

With the roommate's remarks in mind, the group explores the poem "for what it was worth on paper." In the midst of their attempts, students express their worries about not finding the "hidden" meanings of the poem:

*S:* Do you guys have any other ideas besides the straight meaning? When Michael said he's got all these ideas, I thought,"Wow, I've only got one."

*S:* There's got to be something else, do you think? Maybe not.

*S:* That's what I don't get. I think it's too easy.

To these students, the "straight" meaning is surely inadequate, for it is "too easy." Implicit here are assumptions about the reading of poetry — that it is replete with elusive "underlying" meanings, possibly springing from allusions or symbols which they have not yet located.

Traces of these beliefs became manifest when students sought to "uncover" the "deep" meanings that the poem must "contain." As one student said, "I put in my notebook that the mending wall is a symbol. It's mending their relationship. . . . It's just a symbol."

And when they confronted the line, "He moves in darkness as it seems to me," another student wondered, "Was he in the dark? Figuratively or literally?"

They faced the same question at another juncture in their discussion. Jerry said, "Is there any meaning when he says, 'My apple trees will never get across and eat his pine cones'? . . . Is there any symbol there?" In these excerpts we see students operating by implicit "rules" that seemed to have developed through their prior literary experiences. For example, certain words — such as "darkness" and "wall" — generated speculation about possible literal and figurative meanings. The quest for symbolic connotations figured as an integral part of that enterprise.

Because students aptly located the words that we might consider literary symbols, we can view these segments as evidence of the effective formalistic training these students received prior to Michael's class. However, undercutting that success were several comments that indicated that students felt otherwise. Consider, for instance, the following exchange:

S:    I think we understand it. I don't think it can be wrong, but I don't know.

S:    Obviously we're supposed to disagree about something, so maybe we don't understand it.

S:    I wish he [Michael] would come over here.

After students expressed these sentiments, they sat silently, waiting for Michael to confirm or to refute their responses. Stymied by their own desire for "the right answer(s)," these students had difficulty sustaining their roles as literary meaning makers.

While we might argue that students need to be familiar with the allusions and symbols that constitute our literary heritage, we might also argue that they need to engage in interpretive activities that enable them to explore other possible meanings as well — those that emanate from their partial and incipient understandings of texts. If students could play out the interpretive possibilities of multiple readings — if they were asked to respond to texts by garnering the appropriate received wisdom from our literary traditions as well as by developing their own initial, incipient responses — then the footholds they had in the interpretive community might seem less tenuous, their perches more secure. (See Beach and Marshall [1991] for a discussion of activities to elicit student responses to literature.) Let us see what happened when Michael's students took possession of their interpretive tools and created possible readings of Frost's "Mending Wall."

## SMALL GROUP COLLABORATION AND INTERPRETATION

Students did demonstrate a facility to engage in collaborative learning, "shaping at the point of utterance," as Britton (1982, p.139) says. In other words, they used discussion as a mode of learning, nurturing incipient ideas and rehearsing possible readings through talk. The following excerpt provided a glimpse of their interactions:

S:    I don't understand the part, "He moves in darkness." Does that mean something?

S:    It's really confusing.

S:    Maybe what he would lose in darkness. He'd lose like no reason, like darkness thinking of one thing. He's fixing the wall, but he doesn't — he just goes through the motions every year. So they say he moves in darkness.

S:    Like the shadow of something. The shadow of his father — could that be it?

S:    Yeah, because in the line after he talks about his father.

S:    That's a good point. What else?

S:    He's in the shadow of his father by feeling that "good fences make good neighbors."

S:    Right, and he says, "He will not go behind his father's saying."

In this exchange one student advances an hypothesis that the character is "going through the motions" of building a fence. The participants work collaboratively by tying that idea to the last four lines of the poem.

But what proved particularly interesting was how they developed their ideas. Students played both the literal and metaphorical ranges of meaning here, exploring possible significations for "darkness." Notice that each contribution complicated and extended the prior comment, that one student's hypothesis became a scaffold for another's growing understanding. Yet detail, question, and conjecture did not accumulate in a linear progression but evolved in a darting, zigzagging fashion — illustrating a horizontal, recursive, and nonlinear type of scaffolding that Dyson (1990) calls "weaving." Despite the students' self-deprecating remarks about determining the range of meaning and their heightened apprehension about symbols, they demonstrated a collective rehearsal of interpretive moves. Posing questions and exploring possibilities, they linked their opinions to the text as they tested the boundaries of "appropriate" response.

Participation in the small group conversation enhanced the individual's comprehension of the text in several ways. For instance, early in the discussion the students focused on the character traits of one of the main characters, and Jerry claimed that the character was foolish. When others failed to see his point, he had to clarify his thinking:

When I say he's foolish, I mean like in the 42nd line. I mean he lives in the darkness too. He's got the shelter and safety in his old ways. Like Jack in *Rain*

*Man*, how he gets in a habit of buying underwear at the same place. Both are
scared that if they try anything different it will mean the end to them.

Here Jerry weaves personal opinion and text, just as Michael had continually sought — despite this student's earlier claim that he didn't know
how. Tapping into prior knowledge, he comprehends the poem's persona by
linking him to a movie character he and his classmates know. Pressed to
explain how the character is foolish, Jerry has to defend his stance, and he
offers both textual evidence and an analogy to a movie character, Jack in
*Rain Man*. In arguing this point, Jerry takes advantage of an opportunity not
only to help others understand the character but also to rehearse a point of
view that he might develop more fully in his paper.

The group also provided an arena for students individually and collectively to brainstorm on difficult moments in their reading experiences. For
instance, students puzzled over their views of the wall, deliberating between
antithetical perceptions of the wall as "walling out or walling in":

S:      Yeah, walk the line together. It's like the wall is the thing that sepa-
        rates them, keeps them apart, but it brings them together. It
        doesn't really make sense. I can't understand.

S:      I've seen that on TV — farmers walking on their side of the fence,
        talking, walking down the fence, the breeze blowing.

S:      Yeah, they're just being neighbors.

S:      But they're walling out the cows.

S:      There you go. I'll buy that.

In this conversation, the group enables a student to understand how a
wall simultaneously encloses and excludes. One student filters the poem
through a media image she assumes will be familiar to all participants, that
of two farmers walking along a fence. Note that another student provides a
rationale for the fence, that it provides a necessary enclosure for the
farmer's cows. It is that cooperative scaffolding that finally enables the confused student to comprehend a scene. While the discussion leads to an understanding that the lone reader did not originally possess, it also
represents a level of interpretive activity that, as solo readers, they might
not have achieved.

Note that many dimensions of the inquiry demonstrated the dynamics
of student-centered learning (Lloyd-Jones and Lunsford, 1989). First, students worked collaboratively in small groups to fill the gaps in individual's
readings of the poem. They rehearsed arguments, collectively tapping into

prior knowledge and experience that might enrich their reading experiences. Michael's use of reader-centered exam questions that did not have "one right answer" enabled students to engage in what Barnes (1976) calls "exploratory" talk — characterized by questioning, hypothesizing, and improvising. Because students were able to work through these issues with others, they not only had a ready-made audience for testing and refining individual arguments but also had a variety of responses that, when consolidated, extended or refuted their initial positions. These discourse practices reveal the cognitive benefits of student interaction that Cazden (1988) describes: thinking enriched by "rough draft" exploratory talk, changed by encounters with those of different perspectives, extended by the joint efforts of partners working in tandem, and strengthened by peers reacting as various audience members might.

Such language practices required Michael to view students as capable and active producers of knowledge who already possessed the "tools" for inquiry. What Michael did then was to provide an occasion for students to use those tools and in so doing enabled students to sharpen their interpretive skills through collaborative activities. Perhaps a look at the papers students wrote will enable us to see how students used their interpretive tools in answering Michael's midterm questions on "Mending Wall."

## STUDENTS' WRITTEN WORK

Students' midterm papers displayed a range of responses to "Mending Wall" as well. For instance, Michael asked students to explore the first line of the poem, to explain what the "something" is which "doesn't love a wall." Here the responses diverged considerably. Several students claimed, for instance, that the "something" might have referred to two people who didn't want communication barriers in their relationship. Others catapulted the debate into the arena of international politics, figuring that the "something" was any impediment to diplomatic relations between countries. Others claimed it was a spiritual force while some suggested that it was a psychological trait, an essentially human desire to reduce barriers — personal, social, national — between people. Finally several argued that "something" simply signified a concrete wall literally separating two neighbors.

Michael also asked students to explain what "it's not elves exactly" means, to explain who the elves were in the last part of the poem. Here, too, students generated a wide array of responses. One wrote that the elves were angels, and another claimed that they represented the irrational thoughts of the neighbor. A student argued that it was the speaker's private joke, and another said it represented the speaker's regrets about the wall separating the neighbors. Finally, several argued that the elves were human beings with magical qualities.

While the poem's "gaps" elicited a wide range of responses from students, perhaps just as divergent — and more important — were the interpretive processes students reported using to arrive at those readings. In the second part of the exam, students were asked to describe their interpretive activities, identifying the issues stirring consensus and dissensus in the groups. Anna, for instance, described her initial reaction to the poem prior to the small-group discussion:

> My interpretation of the poem was completely different from all the others. When I began to read, I pictured the speaker as a woman and the neighbor as a man, and they had a struggling relationship. I gathered that the man did not want to expose his true self to the woman (speaker), and his mask — what he was hiding behind — was the fence.

Anna explained why she originally believed the poem was about a relationship between a man and a woman:

> When I think of relationships, I think of a man and a woman. Obviously things just clicked away when I started reading. Then when I went to line 24, I just thought of pine being male and apple orchard being female.

She described her classmates' reaction:

> My group had a difficult time seeing where I found the presence of the woman, and I didn't really have any evidence of the female within the poem, so my interpretation suffered.

The equating of male with pine and female with orchard pushed her reading outside of the group's interpretive range. Her response did not incorporate references to the text, as her group noted. In the subsequent large-group discussion, she confessed, "Now that I look back I wonder, 'What in the world was I thinking?'"

In her written analysis of the group's interpretive operations, she described how they determined so-called appropriate readings:

> It was the deep reading into the poem (like the man-woman relationship and the two countries at war) that didn't quite cut it with our group. We listened for the reasons for these deep thoughts and perceptions but could not find sufficient evidence to back up those interpretations, so we returned to the simplest one, that of two men with a fence between them.

Here, too, students used the text itself to check the range of meaning. In this case, the group came to a consensus view of the wall as a physical barrier.

This led Anna to reflect on the process of determining the range of interpretation. Despite her acknowledgment that her reading was not one she could defend with strong evidence, she did not believe her response was wrong. She wrote, "Readings are never wrong. Everyone's eyes will see different things, and these thoughts will trigger different feelings developed from the poem."

While she recognized the importance of social consensus, she insisted that response did not necessarily have to include textual evidence. She wrote, "If you see something one way, and you really believe that's what the poem means, then you shouldn't have to state why you think that. . . . A reading may be just a little different from one that bears evidence." To Anna, interpretations that allude to the linguistic markers are different from those that do not. For Anna the interpretive spectrum must be expanded to accommodate all reactions, even those not directly referring to the linguistic symbols. In her view the text is a stimulus that "triggers" ideas and associations, a starting ground for discussion — a view that response theorist Bleich (1975) might support because he advises readers to consider all responses valid but not one her teacher would probably endorse as a Rosenblatt practitioner. Tucking her original "male-female communication problem" reading of the poem into her journal, she took her group's advice and wrote her formal paper about the notion of a concrete and literal "Mending Wall." In this case the small group proved instrumental in Anna's efforts to develop and test literary hypotheses.

## USING DISCUSSION TO THEORIZE ABOUT INTERPRETATION

Fulfilling Michael's hope that students would ask, "Can I do this?," students in the large group directed that question to Anna when she posed those distinctions between the terms "wrong" and "different" to the class. Kathy opposed Anna's account of the range of meaning. She argued that there was a spectrum of response limited by the surface features on the page, and that, consequently, some responses must be considered wrong:

> If no one in the discussion group can understand one person's point of view after thorough explanations, then it is possible that this explanation is wrong. Clear explanation and support for your points can help show another person your point of view.

Kathy emphasized the social consensus and textual evidence needed to consider an interpretation plausible, closer to the transactionalist stance that Michael articulated. Noting that Kathy turned to the text to garner support for an argument and Anna used it to initiate conversation, the class considered the processes of negotiating meaning that students practiced, both as members of small groups and as individual writers. Students used this occasion to practice the reflective learning that Barnes (1976) endorses, asking, "How did we make meaning?" John advanced an hypothesis to explain how students produced varied readings:

It just seemed like the way that can happen is because the poem is so vague. . . . Anna could get women and men out of it, and Tom could get social values — that vagueness leaves it open for you to put your own opinions in as to what the function of the wall is.

John centers on the gaps of the text that readers filled in a variety of ways, those moments when "the poem is so vague."

This led other students to explore how they created that spectrum of readings constrained by the words on the page.

*S:*     If we go outside the poem and really go deep into it, you can't say it's wrong, can you?

*S:*     But if you're going outside, how are you going to go back in with the evidence inside?

*S:*     Why can't you do both? Why can't the outside reinforce what we saw inside?

*S:*     I think the only way you can reach outside the poem is to interpret Frost as saying he wants us to question certain things in our lives and think about them. Then you can go out to marriage or something like that. That's why we can all be everywhere, get so many different things.

*S:*     So if I were to say that the poem was about two countries, and the cows were mediators, can we say that's wrong? Or is it better to say that we can look at these differences and that *reminds* me of the United States and the Soviet Union. I think the second way is okay.

This discussion not only demonstrates students talking in the hypothetical mode but also reveals the power of collaborative enterprises in the classroom. Students explore the implications of responses gleaned from inside and outside the poem, discerning differences between right and wrong responses using transactional criteria.

Furthermore, they hypothesized about how they arrived at those readings, theorizing about their own interpretive activities — an important dimension of a transactional classroom, according to Rosenblatt (1938, p.26). She says, "Teaching becomes a matter of improving the individual's capacity to evoke meaning from the text by leading him [or her] to reflect self-critically on the process." As a student-centered instructor, Michael relied on collaborative learning strategies to promote the self-reflection Rosenblatt considers crucial to literary understanding.

## THE CONSTRAINTS ON A TRANSACTIONAL APPROACH IN THE CLASSROOM

The debate about correct readings led another student, Tracy, to locate one of the gaps of transactionalist theory:

> There may be points where you can be wrong if you can't really back it up. . . . Most of the time if you back up your opinion with the poem and ideas you can pretty much make anything sound like what you want it to be.

Tracy recognizes that evidence is required to persuade others of an idea. However, if one can effectively manipulate the text to make a point, then that reader "can pretty much make anything sound like what you want it to be." From Tracy's perspective, a transactionalist approach founders because the reader presenting the most persuasive rhetoric — and not necessarily the most substantial evidence — will often prevail in the interpretive community.

For other students, this concern became transmuted into a deliberation about grading. Because multiplicity was constrained, the possibility nevertheless existed for wrong answers; and students in Michael's class knew it. They wondered about the consequences of articulating responses that loomed outside the range of the plausible. For instance, Kathy openly expressed her ambition to receive an A in the course, admitting that she would write a paper relying on the interpretive authority of the teacher rather than her own opinions in order to be successful. For example, one day she announced in discussion:

> If you came in and told us what the poem was about, even if it were totally different, totally off the wall, I'd buy it. You're the authority — you're the one giving the grade, and that is that.

As demonstrated here, Kathy seemed resistant at times to assuming the role of an active respondent to literature — a stance that, ironically, Michael deemed integral to being successful, to getting good grades, in his class. To the consternation of this student and others, Michael did not provide his interpretation, the one right answer many yearned for.

As a result, Kathy seems to have had a different experience, one that not only shaped her understanding of literature but also led her to assume the active role of interpretive community member. She came to realize that she was capable of making literary decisions using transactional principles. In an interview several weeks after the midterm Kathy reflected on how that experience changed her role in the classroom and her relationship to the received wisdom of literary authority:

> I think maybe we had the tools; we just didn't realize it. Or we weren't confident enough to express them and feel as if we weren't off base. . . . I always needed someone to say, "Yeah, that's right, that's it." He never really says, "Yeah, that's it." So I'm standing behind some of my own readings, and I'm really looking for things. When I look at something, I am really trying to get something out of it. I'm looking at it closer because he's not going to say yes or no.

Because Michael refused to "say yes or no," students had to turn to themselves to decide interpretive matters. Through that process, they realized that perhaps they were capable of negotiating a range of appropriate readings, despite the lack of formulas and structures used in this setting. As Kathy said in a final interview, "I think the main thing here is that we're used to being like computers — you put the information in and we'll spit it out. With this we can put more of ourselves in it. We can decide some of the rights and wrongs."

## Reflections on Michael's Classroom

As a teacher attempting to transform a literary theory into a classroom enterprise, Michael was working in an arena where the pedagogical and the literary often overlapped and at times were mutually exclusive. While reader response seemed conducive to classroom activities, Michael often struggled with questions literary theorists don't ask but literature teachers do: How did grading practices compel and constrain interpretive practices? What were the relationships between talk and writing in the literature classroom? How did oral and written discursive practices enhance students' understanding of their texts and their lives? Without prior models, without a body of research literature to guide his forging of a literary theoretical pedagogy, Michael formulated his responses to these questions in light of student abilities, dynamically refiguring classroom strategies as needed.

Michael and his students demonstrated that Rosenblatt's theory offers teachers rich possibilities for multiple ways of knowing readers, texts, and cultures. In relying on student-centered learning techniques, Michael allowed students to create and assess divergent and overlapping responses. The variables of transactional theory — the dialectics of multiplicity and constraint — may complicate interpretive processes more than some teachers might consider necessary or worthwhile. However, it seemed to me that the original complaints about multiplicity and constraint dissolved once students realized, through the midterm, that they could participate in a community based on transactional theory, contingent upon student interpretive activity — despite its seeming unfamiliarity. Furthermore, it should be remembered that, although Kathy and Jerry regularly voiced their concerns about the class, their enthusiasm for Michael's class never wavered. His course remained their favorite throughout the semester.

Perhaps Jerry offered the most powerful endorsement of reader response when he described the inquiry and involvement that permeated class discussion: "Leaving that class is like leaving a good church sermon on Sunday. You always feel full of light and exhilaration."

For teachers hoping to avoid charges that all readings are equal and equally valid, Rosenblatt's theory seems most appropriate precisely because meaning is constrained. With a transactional approach, the possibility exists for debating questions of validity and value using the interpretive criteria and the group's norms. The teacher and students do not have to abandon standards to cultivate multiplicity; and such criteria might be used, as Michael did, in formulating the grading scale for formal written assignments. The widened spectrum of meaning enabled Michael to ask open-ended discussion questions that, by virtue of being elements of a reader response approach, *could not* have had "one right answer," in contrast to the patterns depicted in the center's technical reports.

## BEYOND THE MIDTERM: EPILOGUE

At the last class meeting, Michael announced that the final would follow the same format as the midterm, but students would respond to a short story rather than to a poem. When he asked students to raise questions about the final, no one did. Michael waited, expecting to be deluged with comments and queries. One student shouted, "No problem!" and students left the room smiling. Jerry slipped me a note as he left that day, explaining the change in perspective that had unfolded since the midterm project. Jerry wrote,

> I personally love the way Michael has taught this literature class. His style has forced us to make decisions, to present ideas, and to come to our own conclusions about what we read. This is the purpose of a class on interpretation, as I see it. The reason this class is so great is because we're challenged to do something we're not used to doing — thinking critically. Michael gets an A for this class.

For teachers who think critically not only about texts but also about the dynamics of their discussions, this window into Michael's classroom might reveal new ways to nurture literary understandings informed by student knowledge and experience effectively in secondary and college classes as preparation for post-secondary course work. In studying a small college class, we gained a view of a reader-centered pedagogy that was relatively unobstructed and provided an excellent opportunity for understanding the complexities of adapting Rosenblatt for the classroom. For secondary teachers seeking alternative approaches to literary studies, hoping to quicken the pulse of their literature classrooms, Michael's class offers a corollary to Rosenblatt's theory, an invitation to explore divergent ways of writing and talking about texts.

## *REFERENCES*

Applebee, A. (1989). *The teaching of literature in programs with reputations for excellence in English* (Report Series 1.1). Albany, NY: Center for the Learning and Teaching of Literature.

Barnes, D. (1976). *From communication to curriculum*. New York: Viking Penguin.

Beach, R. & Marshall, J. (1991). *Teaching literature in the secondary school*. New York: Harcourt Brace Jovanovich.

Bleich, D. (1975). *Readings and feelings: An introduction to subjective criticism*. Urbana, IL: National Council of Teachers of English.

Britton, J. (1982). Shaping at the point of utterance. In G. Pradl (Ed.), *Prospect and retrospect: Selected essays of James Britton* (pp. 139–145). Montclair, NJ: Boynton/Cook.

Cazden, C. (1988). *Classroom discourse: The language of teaching and learning*. Portsmouth, NH: Heinemann.

Dyson, A.H. (1990). Weaving possibilities: Rethinking metaphors for early literacy development. *The Reading Teacher*, 44, 202–213.

Fish, S. (1980a). *Is there a text in this class? The authority of interpretive communities*. Cambridge, MA: Harvard University Press.

Fish, S. (1980b). Literature in the reader: Affective stylistics. In J. Tompkins (Ed.), *Reader response criticism: From formalism to post-structuralism* (pp. 70–100). Baltimore: Johns Hopkins University Press.

Iser, W. (1978). *The act of reading: A theory of aesthetic response*. Baltimore: Johns Hopkins University Press.

Lloyd-Jones, R. and Lunsford, A. (Eds.) (1989). *The English coalition conference: Democracy through language*. Urbana, IL: National Council of Teachers of English.

Marshall, J. (1989). *Patterns of discourse in classroom discussions of literature* (Report Series 2.9). Albany, NY: Center for the Learning and Teaching of Literature.

Mayher, John. (1990). *Uncommon sense: Theoretical practice in language education*. Portsmouth, NH: Heinemann.

Rosenblatt, L. (1983). *Literature as exploration* (4th ed.). New York: Modern Language Association.

Rosenblatt, L. (1978). *The reader, the text, the poem: The transactional theory of the literary work*. Carbondale, IL: Southern Illinois University Press.

Rosenblatt, L. (1985). Viewpoints: Transaction versus interaction — A terminological rescue operation. *Research in the Teaching of English*, 19, 96–107.

# CHAPTER FIFTEEN

# Toward a Theory of Practice

### Readers, Texts, and The Teaching of Literature

❧ ❧ ❧

## James Marshall

In 1892, Professor Francis August March gave a paper at the annual meeting of the Modern Language Association (Graff & Warner, 1989). By the date of his talk, March had become an almost mythic figure in English studies. He had initiated the first college literature program in the country at Lafayette College in 1857, and he held the first professorship of its kind in either the United States or Britain — a chair in English Language and Comparative Philology. In 1892 — now that English studies was a more or less established discipline, with a professional organization (MLA), a journal (*PMLA*), and a growing number of graduate programs training new generations of scholars, March and his listeners could look back with pride at the distance they had travelled and could look forward with conviction to the work that remained to be done.

March's talk was entitled "Recollections of Language Teaching," and through most of it he detailed his early interest in the subject, the strategies he employed in teaching it, and the wide acceptance such strategies enjoyed. He was at great pains to show that the study of literature, when properly understood, was difficult, even recondite, and thus worthy of scholarly respect. In fact, he argued, current scholars and teachers had found ways to "make English as hard as Greek."

It was perhaps that theme of the difficulty of literary study that led

March, toward the end of his talk, to warn his listeners somewhat gravely that the discipline was threatened by those who saw the purpose of literature study differently than he. He argued that

> We are having an outcry just now against stopping to study particular passages in literature, urging rapid emotional reading, the seeking to produce love of reading rather than knowledge of books — love of reading all the new magazines, I suppose, and newspapers, and novels, and facts are stranger than fiction, instead of spending days and nights with the great authors. . . . Professors who aim at the highest usefulness and the most honored position must labor to give profound knowledge, and excite lasting love of great books and devotion to great thoughts. . . . Their literary studies must be mainly upon great authors. (p. 27)

There is a somewhat quaint, late-Victorian rhythm to his prose, but the issues March addresses here seem strikingly contemporary. Although written a century ago, his description of the tensions that beset the teaching of literature — tensions between the "knowledge of books" and the "love of reading," between the "great authors" and "the new magazines . . . and novels" — are precisely the ones that frame recent discussions of literary study and that inform many of the chapters in this volume. We use different terms in our current arguments — reader-response versus the New Criticism; the traditional canon versus alternative canons or no canon at all — but March, I think, would recognize in our debates the same basic issues that were at stake in the early years of the discipline: What literature should be studied? Why should it be studied? And, most practically for both March and ourselves, how should it be taught?

If the tensions that March described 100 years ago continue to shape our contemporary debates about literature teaching, then it may be that the tensions themselves need to be explored. If, in other words, we have been basically arguing about the same issues for the better part of a century, then perhaps an understanding of the argument itself, and not its resolution, is what we most need. In this chapter, I would like to examine some of the ways we have argued with each other about the teaching of literature and, in addition, explore how literature teachers have come to respond to those arguments in their classrooms. I will begin with a brief historical perspective and then move to a discussion of teachers, drawing on a series of case studies that I have conducted over the last several years (Marshall, 1989; Marshall, Klages, & Fehlman, 1990). I will close by exploring how the tensions that seem to define us might be turned to practical use in our teaching.

## READERS AND TEXTS

Francis March saw a basic conflict in literary study between the "love of reading" and the "knowledge of books." In a lecture entitled "The New Criticism," given at Columbia University about fifteen years later, Professor Joel Spingarn (1911) made a similar, albeit far more colorful argument.

> . . . it is the perpetual conflict of Criticism. In every age impressionism (or enjoyment) and dogmatism (or judgment) have grappled with one another. They are the two sexes of Criticism; and to say that they flourish in every age is to say that every age has its masculine as well as its feminine criticism — the masculine criticism that may or may not force its own standards on Literature, but that never at all events is dominated by the object of its studies; and the feminine criticism that responds to the lure of art with a kind of passive ecstasy. In the age of Boileau, it was the masculine type which gave the tone to Criticism; in our own, outside of the universities, it has certainly been the feminine. But they continue to exist side by side, ever falling short of their highest powers, unless mystically mated — judgment erecting its edicts into arbitrary standards and conventions, enjoyment lost in the mazes of its sensuous indecision. (p. 9–10)

The sexism here is so cartoon-like, of course, that our first thought might be to back away entirely from Spingarn and his metaphors. The characterization of judgment as masculine (forcing and erecting and refusing to be dominated) while enjoyment remains feminine (responding with "passive ecstasy" and "sensuous indecision") would be ludicrous if it did not so clearly reflect some invidious assumptions about gender.

Still, by choosing a sexual metaphor to describe the relationship between enjoyment and judgment, between impressionism and dogmatism, Spingarn signalled that both are necessary; that they complement one another; that they are, in fact, incomplete "unless mystically mated." The criticism that focuses on impressions of the text or enjoyment of the text would be, in Spingarn's view, criticism that centers largely on readers — on what happenens to them as they read, on what the reading makes them think or feel. The criticism that focuses on judgment or dogmatism would center largely on the text — on the way its parts succeed or fail to cohere, on how the complete text may be related to others of its time or in its form. As a kind of bride and groom, then, Spingarn has given us the reader and the text, intimate if not precisely equal marriage partners in the literary transaction. In 1892, March wanted to exclude from the academy what Spingarn would call a feminine love of reading, but by 1911 Spingarn seems willing to admit those with such womanly preoccupations into serious, intellectual debate — provided, we can only presume, that they remembered their place.

The "mystical mating" that Spingarn hoped for in 1911, however, in the long run became rather difficult to arrange. Those who studied and taught about literature could seldom agree on whether readers or texts, enjoyment or judgment, should be the center of interest in the development of literary understanding, and the debate concerning what the teaching of literature was for continued unabated. We can see a particularly compelling manifestation of the argument in two books published, ironically enough, in the very same year.

The first of these was *Understanding Poetry*, Cleanth Brooks' and Robert Penn Warren's compendium of poetry and critical commentary that appeared in 1938 and that is usually cited as one of the anchoring documents of the New Criticism (Spingarn's 'new criticism' turned out to be a bit premature). It was in *Understanding Poetry* that Brooks and Warren laid out a set of principles that, in their view, should guide the reading and analysis of literature. In the book's opening statement, a statement they frame as a "Letter to the Teacher," Brooks and Warren wrote some of the words and phrases that I think we still find ourselves using from time to time when we talk about literature. "This book has been conceived on the assumption," they argued

> that if poetry is worth teaching at all it is worth teaching as poetry. The poem in itself . . . remains finally the object for study. One must grasp the poem as a literary construct before it can offer any real illumination as a document. (In teaching literature) the treatment should be concrete and inductive (and) the poem should be treated as an organic system of relationships (p. iv–xv).

"Object," "construct," "concrete," "organic" — these words occurred often in the papers I wrote as an undergraduate English major in the late 1960s and early '70s. They came up frequently in the class discussions I remember from those years. What we would do in class is take a text — not just any text, but one recognized as important and canonical — and we would go after it. We would ask: What are its most important images? How does it hold together as a coherent object? How is this particular passage organically related to the whole? How do the opening lines of *Hamlet*, for instance, prefigure what is to happen in the play? Why does Faulkner begin *The Sound and the Fury* with the scattered, incoherent thoughts of Benjy? These were the questions about literature that I heard my teachers ask in college. And these were the questions that I learned to answer, clumsily, I'm sure, with an embarrassing combination of ignorance and high seriousness, but well enough to keep me an English major and make me decide that I could go out and ask comparable questions of students.

I never questioned the questions. I never asked whether it was appropriate to treat literary texts as objects. And I never committed those fallacies that my professors had warned me about — I never really considered my own reactions to literature as important. I never wrote papers about why a text reminded me of something in my own life. The text was what we called back then an "artifact." It was *out there*, objective, other — a "well-wrought urn," as Brooks later called poetry — a construct made and thus a construct made to be studied. It was unto itself nearly perfect; that was why it was worthy of study.

What was it about the New Criticism that made it such a powerful force in our field? Why is it that more than fifty years later the arguments of Brooks and Warren still seem so authoritative? Part of the reason, of course, is the very apparent reasonableness of those arguments. Brooks and Warren were attempting to construct an intellectually coherent and systematically objective method for reading texts — a method that would produce accurate, sound, and defensible interpretations. Drawing heavily from the positivistic assumptions of the natural sciences, they were trying to make the study of texts like the study of other phenomena. If texts are defined as objective, organic constructs, then close reading can be defined as the detached, objective analysis of those constructs. Studying literature, in other words, is a bit like studying biology or physics. The object of study is different, of course, but the method — the close, inductive investigation of parts and wholes — is comparable. Poetry, Brooks and Warren insisted, is not at all like scientific writing, but criticism of poetry should probably aim for the same kind of clear-headed intelligence we find in the best scientific inquiry.

It was a powerful argument. Given the enormous prestige enjoyed by the natural sciences in 1938 — and the hegemony of scientific method in almost every discipline, the principles of criticism suggested by Brooks and Warren swiftly became a framework that effectively governed the production and consumption of knowledge in literary studies. What made the New Criticism so successful, however, was not simply its implicit identification with scientific objectivity. Its case was helped enormously by the fact that it worked in classrooms (Ohmann, 1976; Eagleton, 1983). Students could be trained to do close readings, as I was, and they didn't have to know a great deal about the author of the text or the period of the text to do so. What was important about literature, the New Critics told us, was *in* the text. It was there for anyone to read, and even high school students could be taught to look for it. The New Criticism, then, was not just scientific; it was, in a cryptic way, democratic. Close reading was a skill that could be learned, and, just as important, it was a skill that could be evaluated. Readings could be judged as good, bad, or indifferent by a clear criterion of accuracy — by how adequately those readings accounted for the objective reality of the text itself. The enterprise of literary study, as outlined by the New Critics, mapped so neatly onto the enterprise of schooling that it almost seemed as if the two were made for each other. And the New Criticism continues to exert such a powerful influence in our classrooms, I think, precisely because it seems so eminently teachable.

But *Understanding Poetry* was only the first of two important books about the teaching of literature that appeared in 1938. The other was and is no less a classic statement: Louise Rosenblatt's *Literature as Exploration*. A disciple of John Dewey, Rosenblatt was writing at a time when progressive thought about education was rich and lively, and she opened her book, as her title suggests, with a different agenda than the authors of *Understanding Poetry*. "In a turbulent age," she wrote

> our schools and colleges must prepare the student to meet unprecedented and unpredictable problems. He needs to understand himself; he needs to work out harmonious relationships with other people. He must achieve a philosophy, an inner center from which to view in perspective the shifting society about him; he will influence for good or ill its future development. Any knowledge about man and society that schools can give him should be assimilated into the stream of his actual life. (p.3)

Whereas Brooks and Warren open their volume with a discussion of what poetry is, Rosenblatt opens hers with a discussion of what students need. Whereas Brooks and Warren are at pains to say what a text is so that we might bring ourselves into a proper relationship with it, Rosenblatt is at pains to say who students are so that texts may be brought into proper relationships with them. Her language, of course, reflects many of the assumptions of the progressive tradition in education — its concern for the future, its emphasis on harmonious social relationships, its insistence that learning begins and ends with learners themselves. For Rosenblatt, reading literature is not objective analysis but an exploration, a process, an experience in which readers draw upon their own personal history, their own emotions, their own knowledge in order to *make sense*, quite literally, of the text. Meaning for Rosenblatt is not found in the text; it is made by the reader in transaction with the text. Because it is always a transaction, always an event, it is never quite the same for any two readers. It is never quite the same for the same reader twice. Readers cannot, in Rosenblatt's view, say what the text says. They can only says what the text says to them, and what it says to them will always be the result of what they were ready to hear.

It is a very different perspective, clearly, from that offered by Brooks and Warren, so different that we may be surprised that the two perspectives were articulated in the very same year. More surprising still, however, is that fact that today, more than 50 years later, we are still trying to work out the implications of what Brooks and Warren on the one hand and Rosenblatt on the other were trying to teach us. We're still trying, in other words, to figure out what we're supposed to *do* when we teach literature. We will turn now to a discussion of that teaching.

## TEACHERS AND STUDENTS

How do teachers articulate the tensions that we have been exploring — the tensions between readers and texts, enjoyment and judgment, "love of reading" and "knowledge of books." Here is an excerpt from an interview with Jeff, an 8th grade teacher of literature.

> In a classroom discussion, ideally I'm just a facilitator. I just set the scene and get the ball rolling and get kids talking about stuff and when the discussion lags throw in a question that maybe puts a new twist on things — help them think about things from a new angle. But I hold on to the traditional idea that maybe there are some universal correct things to get out of literature. I think it's very important for kids to bring their own experience to literature and talk about what it means to them, and they're not right or wrong. But when the author was writing this, *this* is what he had in mind. {For example}, Hemingway in *The Old Man and the Sea* definitely had an idea that he wanted to convey to his readers. If nobody picks up on it in discussion, then I become maybe not a facilitator but maybe another participant in the discussion and say, "well, this is what I think." But then you get wrapped up in the whole way I was trained in literature — those values that there were universal right answers. . . . We're cheating ourselves and our students if we don't make sure that they at least walk away with an understanding that the author did have something that he or she wanted readers to get from the piece. . . . There's a road in my mind that the kids can't see that I want to a certain extent lead them down.

It is in that last sentence that Jeff most succinctly captures the ambivalence he feels about his role, but the excerpt as a whole speaks clearly to his divided responsibilities as a teacher of literature. On the one hand, he feels that he would be "cheating" his students if he does not make them aware of an author's probable intention in a work, at least as that intention has been constructed in the critical tradition. In the case of *The Old Man and the Sea*, he might want to point out, among other things, that the novella is about nobility, about grace under pressure, about the dignity that can be achieved even in failure. His use of the word "cheating" suggests that he feels an implicit obligation to make sure that his students know these things about the text and that he would be failing in that obligation if they were to leave his class not knowing them.

But Jeff feels a responsibility not only to the text but also to his students as readers. Thus, though he wants his students to *have* specified kinds of knowledge, he feels uncomfortable about *giving* them that knowledge, about simply telling them what the story means. Ideally, he says, he wants to be a "facilitator . . . [helping] kids bring their own experience to literature and talk about what it means to them." He seems distinctly uneasy with "the whole way [he] was trained in literature — those values that there were universal right answers," but he seems unable to articulate an alternative. Thus, it is only to a "certain extent" that Jeff wants to lead his students down the road in his mind, and the road is hidden in any case. In a sense, it seems, Jeff has internalized in his teaching the tensions we have been exploring, and the multiplication of "buts" and qualifications in his remarks suggest that those tensions are far from resolved.

The divisions of purpose that Jeff experiences as an 8th grade teacher may become even more critical for teachers working with older students preparing for college. For these teachers, and for their students, college can exert an enormous gravitational pull on the curriculum, and the demand for "universal right answers" with which Jeff struggled may be even more in evidence. Sarah, for instance, a 12th grade teacher of college-bound students, had this to say:

> When I first started teaching, I probably lectured twice a week and I'd feel dizzy at the end of the day from talking so long and hard and practically standing on my head as I saw them fade. It really is true: You work way too hard doing that. And I worked awfully hard as I fed every question to them. You don't have to do that very long before your realize that you can only formulate so many manipulative questions in order to get them to say what you think they ought to say — what you want them to say — before you realize that you just have to admit to the kids "See, I was trying to get you to say something and you didn't say it." So I'm trying to relinquish my control as a teacher. I'm trying to turn it over. But it's a hard thing to do because sometimes you don't feel like they're under your control.

It seems interesting, though not particularly surprising, that Sarah's efforts to lecture and to "get students to say what she wanted them to say" occurred when she first started teaching, fresh from her own college courses. It was then, perhaps, that she felt the strongest pressure to provide students with the kinds of knowledge about literature that she had come to possess. In practice, that meant a good deal of teacher talk and a good many "manipulative questions" — questions meant to lead students down the same kind of road, unseen by students, to which Jeff referred. But Sarah has become frustrated by that approach. Not only does it put inordinate pressure on the teacher to perform, but it pays, she has found, only moderate dividends. The students "fade." Uninvolved themselves in the work of literary interpretation, they can wait for the teacher to tell them whatever they need to know about a particular text. Sarah has attempted to "relinquish [her] control as a teacher," but even as she does so she is confronted with the expectation that her students will have been exposed to a certain body of material before they leave her classroom. In discussing the kinds of texts she asks students to read, for instance, Sarah said:

> I guess I like to select materials that the college board thinks are significant. It would be nice for my students to have some background in that sort of material. With my college-bound kids, I feel strongly that somebody is dictating to me what I should do with the literature. And I think it's too easy to say, "Well, the heck with that, we'll just do what we want to do." I don't want to shortchange my kids. They are going to have certain demands made of them — expectations. I don't want to think that I did them wrong just because I have another set of ideas about what should be done with literature.

Like Jeff, Sarah seems torn between two conflicting views of her role as a teacher of literature. On the one hand, she wants to be a facilitator, to foster her students' tentative responses to texts, to relinquish some of her authority over literary meaning; but on the other hand, she does not want to "shortchange" her kids (just as Jeff did not want to "cheat" them). The institutional expectations surrounding the study of literature, especially for those students going on to college, fit uneasily with the progressive, reader-response approaches to teaching with which Sarah feels most comfortable.

It is, of course, that "on the one hand . . . but on the other hand" formulation that I am attempting to explore here, that sense of trying to balance two legitimate sets of responsibilities — one to the text and one to the student readers of that text. Neither Jeff nor Sarah could find a way of choosing between these without feeling a kind of cognitive dissonance, and neither could articulate a way of attending to both at the same time.

And yet it is possible to trace in our actual teaching, I think, the effort to attend to both at the same time. If we look closely at one of the the the most characteristic features of our work in classrooms — the discussion of literature — we can perhaps see how the tensions between readers and texts are managed in practice. Consider, for instance, this excerpt from an 11th–12th grade classroom discussion of *Antigone*.

| | |
|---|---|
| *Teacher:* | What happened to Jocaste? |
| *Students:* | (in unison) She killed herself. |
| *Teacher:* | All she does is exit, goes to her room, and commits suicide. No focus on the woman. The focus is on the man throughout the myth. For awhile, the throne is passed on to Creon, but our obvious questions would revolve around what characters? |
| *Student:* | The kids. |
| *Teacher:* | Exactly what happened to Polyneices, Eteocles, Ismene, and Antigone? After all, they are the royal family that has encountered this bizarre situation that their father is also their brother and they are suddenly bereft of their mother. . . . Creon steps in to take over for a while, but his sons would inherit the throne. We must be talking about what kind of society? |
| *Students:* | (in unison) Patriarchal. |
| *Teacher:* | Sure, patriarchal. The sons automatically inherit from the father. |

Perhaps the most obvious reading of this excerpt would suggest its text-centered concerns and its teacher-centered form. The focus throughout is on the play itself, with little effort to elicit from students their developing responses to that play. And the one who controls that focus is the teacher: He provides the direction of discussion by asking all the questions, and he absorbs most of the conversational space by expanding upon the students' slender answers. If we wished to make an argument against text-centered/ teacher-centered instruction, we could hardly find a better instance of what we didn't want.

But if the excerpt is an especially egregious example of a certain kind of traditional teaching, then it is also an example of how that teaching has been shaped by the tensions we have been examining. If the teacher's concerns here were solely with the text, after all, and if he were only interested in transmitting information to the students, why would he bother with even the pretense of a discussion? Why would he ask questions and then so energetically expand upon his students' answers ("All she does is exit, goes to her room, and commits suicide")? In doing so, he not only validates what they have said ("She killed herself"), he dramatizes it for them — allowing them to see more fully and more colorfully what they have already seen, reflecting their own responses back to them in a more developed form. He is, in other words, through the discussion attempting to deal with his students as readers. We might argue that he is unsuccessful, but we could not argue that he is unconcerned with his students' responses to *Antigone*.

We can see the problem even more fully, perhaps, in a final example, this one from a 9th grade discussion of Dickens' *Great Expecations*. The class here has been working on the novel for three days, and, sensing that things are not going all that well, the teacher asks the students for their perspective on the text and their approach to it.

| | |
|---|---|
| *Teacher:* | So, how's it going? |
| *Abby:* | I don't know how anybody else feels, but I do not like picking apart a book. We could spend an entire period on just one page. It just makes the book a lot less enjoyable. |
| *Jenny:* | Yea, this isn't a lab or something. |
| *Teacher:* | Putting it under the microscope . . . |
| *Brian:* | Yeah, that's true because it gets sort of boring after a while. I read it and I understand it, but why do we have to go over it? |
| *Teacher:* | All right. Some of you understand and want to get on with it and others find the discussion helps in understanding. Tony, something you want to add? |
| *Tony:* | I just don't care for the book. I think it's boring. |
| *Teacher:* | You're not pleased with the book. |
| *Tony:* | And doing it over and over and over again doesn't help. |
| *Teacher:* | That's enough. All right. I hear you, and we'll see what we can do about it. But for today, let's go on precisely the way we were. |

As with the discussion of *Antigone*, of course, we could use this excerpt to mount a critique of traditional, text-centered teaching. The practice of "picking apart the book," as Abby puts it, is clearly not working with this group, and the fact that the book in question is old and canonical ("I think it's boring") renders the case against this teacher's teaching all the easier to make.

But notice: it is the teacher herself who has made that case, or rather, it is the teacher herself who has provided the opportunity for such a case to be made. Sensing her students' frustration, she asks the opening question ("So, how's it going?"). She then nurtures the students' criticisms by repeating and even elaborating upon them ("Putting it under the microscope . . . "; "You're not pleased with the book") as they are made. She does put a stop to the onslaught ("That's enough. All right"), but what I find telling about this episode is that she allowed it, even encouraged it, to begin. Whatever uneasiness we might feel about this teacher's teaching, then, would have to take account of the fact that the teacher herself seems to share it. And she shares it because she is at least as concerned with her students' "love of reading," as Francis March would put it, as she is with their "knowledge of books." She decides at the end that the class will go on "precisely the way [they] were," but I think it's clear that she does so with a frustration that is comparable to her students'. The question she doesn't ask but could is simple: What alternatives are available?

## THEORY AND PRACTICE

In attempting to address that question of alternatives, I think it is important that we avoid two dangers. The first is to ignore the theoretical implications of what we suggest; that is, to offer what Stephen North (1986) has called teaching "lore" — purely practical, recipe-like strategies ("Have them keep a double-entry journal" or "Nothing scares them like a pop quiz") that, when taken together, can make for a scattered and finally incoherent approach to literature in our classrooms. As Knoblauch and Brannon (1984) have argued, teaching "methods derive from philosophical perpspectives whether teachers wish to become philosophical about them or not" and these perspectives may be "opposed rather than complementary" (p. 2). It is not enough that our teaching strategies somehow "work;" they must work together, finally as a meaningful whole.

But the other danger, and one just as serious, is to offer theoretically coherent but practically improbable suggestions — suggestions that ignore the realities of schools, grades, tests, textbooks, and institutional inertia. Tracy Kidder's (1989) widely read observations of teaching are sobering in this regard. "Decades of research and reform," he writes

> have not altered the fundamental facts of teaching. The task of universal, public, elementary education is still usually being conducted by a woman alone in a little room, presiding over a youthful distillate of a town or city. If she is willing she tries to cultivate the minds of children both in good

and desperate shape. Some of them have problems that she hasn't been trained even to identify. She feels her way. She has no choice. (p. 53).

We might quibble that, at the secondary level at least, it is sometimes a man who is "alone in a little room," but about these "fundamental facts of teaching" Kidder seems inarguably right, and any suggestions we would make about the teaching of literature, I think, no matter how theoretically systematic, would have to take account of those fundamental facts.

What might help here is not a new theory of reading or interpreting literature; these we have in abundance. Rather, what we need is a theory of our practice in the teaching of literature, a statement that would account for some of the tensions we have been exploring and, at the same time, would help shape our discussions about the teaching we will do on Monday. Gerald Graff (1990) has simply and usefully defined theory as "the kind of reflective discourse about practices that is generated when a consensus that was once taken for granted in a community breaks down" (p. 32). It seems clear that we are currently at a point of consensus breakdown; what seems less clear is what kind of "reflective discourse about practices" will prove most productive.

I'd like to suggest five issues that such reflective discourse about practices might address; that is, five issues that a theory of practice in the teaching of literature would have to account for. The list is clearly not exhaustive but is meant only to suggest the nature of the task before us.

A theory of practice, then, would need to address the following issues.

## A THEORY OF PRACTICE

### The Institutional Structures of Schooling

As Kidder's observations about the "facts of teaching" suggest, schools, like most institutions, are stubbornly resistant to change. Larry Cuban (1984) has established that the basic architectural features of classrooms — teacher's desk fronting a blackboard, students' desks in rows — have remained largely the same for the better part of a century in spite of repeated calls for a restructuring of classroom life. Hoetker and Ahlbrand (1969) have demonstrated the "persistence of the recitation," again, in spite of repeated calls for reform. And Arthur Applebee (1974) summarizes his history of the teaching of literature by arguing that "Teachers of literature have never successfully resisted the pressure to formulate their subject as a body of knowledge to be imparted." (p. 245) I think it is clear that the way schools organize students (in rows) and talk (in recitations) does a great deal to abet the formulation of our subject as a body of knowledge to be imparted. To formulate the subject in any other way — including (and especially) those proposed by reader-response theorists — would require a resistance, not only to old ways of reading but to old ways of schooling as well. A theory of practice, then, would have to begin by acknowledging that we teach in schools and that schools have their own structures, conventions, and forms of discourse that may be fundamentally opposed to those we would suggest for the teaching of literature. Those structures and conventions cannot be ignored, nor can they be easily changed.

## The History of Teaching Literature

A basic truism of the social sciences is that the best predictor of future behavior is past behavior. If, as I've tried to demonstrate here, we have been arguing about readers and texts, about the love of reading and the knowledge of books, from the very beginning of our history as a discipline, then it seems likely that the argument is not going to end, that we are not going to resolve the issue once and for all. Instead, I think we might use the argument itself as a way of organizing our instruction. That is, I think we might ourselves consider what text-oriented and reader-oriented approaches to literature can offer students and then help them use the lenses provided by these approaches in their own reading. The fact that the tension between reader and text has been framed as a debate can trick us into believing that we must somehow choose sides, that we must stand with Brooks and Warren on the one hand or with Rosenblatt on the other. A theory of our practice in the teaching of literature, though, would have to make room for both of these perspectives, demonstrating that each is necessary but finally insufficient in providing students with an understanding of literature. A theory of our practice, in other words, would find ways to bring our most central argument directly into our classrooms as a means of framing our instruction.

## New Developments in Literary Theory

While a productive theory would need to look back to our origins as a profession, it would at the same time need to look forward to what that profession is becoming. The post-modern rush of literary theories is dizzying in its multiplicity, but a central feature of most of these, I think, is the relatively simple observation that texts are written and read within communities. These communities have their own conventions about what counts as literature and their own rules for how that literature is to be read and discussed. This may seem so obvious that it deserves little elaboration, but what follows from it has opened a lively and at times confusing debate about how we should proceed in the literature classroom. For once we recognize that some group following some set of conventions has decided that *The Scarlet Letter*, say, is great literature while the latest Harlequin romance is not, then we must ask what group made the decision and what set of conventions they were following. We can no longer assume, in other words, that great literature is great because it's great and anyone can see that it's great. Rather, we *say* it's great because we believe certain things about literature — things our communities, through schools, have taught us to believe. Those same communities, through schools, might just as easily have taught us about *Black Elk Speaks* or *Native Son* or *The Awakening* or *Their Eyes Were Watching God*. New developments in literary theory, in other words, have at the very least alerted us to the fact that any decisions we make about literary quality and literary understanding rest upon assumptions that might well vary across cultures and across time. Our theory of practice will have to take account of these new developments.

## The Other Subjects We Teach in the English Classroom

We can, of course, for the purposes of argument, clarity, or curriculum guides separate the teaching of literature from the teaching of writing. These things, however, are experienced by our students, taught by us, and named on report cards as "English," and it would seem necessary that any theory of practice in the teaching of literature would need to take account of our practice in the teaching of writing as well. If we are attempting a workshop approach in our writing instruction — process, revision, conferences, cooperative learning — then it seems likely that we will need an approach in our literature instruction that is consonant, not only in its form but also in the assumptions that inform it. That is, if we assume that students are makers of meaning when they write, that they often need to find their own way into a topic, and that our job as teachers is to support rather than direct their efforts, then those same assumptions should probably guide us when we teach literary texts. As Janet Emig (1990) has suggested, undergirding all the teaching we do — literature, writing, language — should be a coherent theory of *learning* that recognizes the interrelatedness of what we teach and exploits that interrelatedness to the advantage of our students. A theory of practice in the teaching of literature, then, would proceed from a larger theory of learning in the English classroom and, in fact, would be only a part of that larger theory.

## *Our Own Situation*

A theory of practice, though, would finally need to account for the differences among us. I mean not only the differences in the students that we teach or the communities that we serve but also the different ways in which we have come to the reading of literature and to the teaching of literature. Our theory must take account, in other words, not only of our history as a discipline but also of our individual history and experience. As James Britton (1988) has put it

> . . . what matters most is that teachers should intuitively behave in ways that facilitate learning. But their intuitive responses to what happens in the classroom are strengthened when by reflection they cumulatively build their own rationale for what they are doing. That is to say, they need to theorise from their own experience — not in the narrowly pragmatic sense, consolidating what has been found to succeed, but finding reasons, ways to explain both their failures and their successes. And once they have begun theorising in this way, they can selectively make use of other people's thinking, other people's theories, the evidence of research. (p. 16).

In 1892, Francis March was attempting in his MLA paper to theorize from his own experience, finding "ways to explain both [his] failures and [his] successes." When we ask students to think about their response to a text, we are similarly asking them to theorize, if only tentatively. Britton's observation, I think, suggests that teachers must themselves make that move into theory — must through reflection "cumulatively build their own rationale for what they are doing." The most productive theory of practice, in other words, will be developed only when those who practice are given the scope and the time to reflect upon what they currently do and the encouragement to imagine a new range of alternatives.

## REFERENCES

Applebee, A.N. (1974). *Tradition and reform in the teaching of ENglish*. Urbana, IL: National Council of Teachers of English.

Britton, J. (1988). Writing, learning, and teacher education. In Davis, J.S., & Marshall, J.D. (Eds.). *Ways of knowing: Reasearch and practice in the teaching of writing*. Urbana, IL: National Council of Teachers of English, 15–44.

Brooks, C., & Warren, R.P. (1938). *Understanding poetry*. New York: Henry Holt & Co.

Cuban, L. (1984). How teachers taught. New York: Longman.

Eagleton, T. (1983). *Literary theory: An introduction*. Minneapolis: U. of Minnesota Press.

Emig, J. (1990). Our missing throry. In Moran, C., & Penfield, E. (Eds.) *Conversations: Contemporary critical theory and the teaching of literature*. Urbana, IL: National Council of Teachers of English, 87–96.

Graff, G. (1990). Debate in the canon class. *Harper's Magazine*, April, 31–35.

Graff, G., & Warner, J. (1989). *The origins of literary study in America: A documentary anthology*. New York: Routledge.

Hoetker, J. & Ahlbrand, W.P. (1969). The persistance of the recitation. *American Educational Resedarch Journal, 6*, 145–167.

Kidder, T. (1989). *Among school children*. Boston: Houghton Mifflin.

Knoblauch, C.H., & Brannon, L. (1984). *Rhetorical traditions and the teaching of writing*. Upper Montclair, NJ: Boynton-Cook.

Marshall, J.D. (1989). Patterns of discourse in classroom discussions of literature. Technical report No. 2.9. Center for the Learning and Teaching of Literature. SUNY Albany.

Marshall, J.D., Klages, M.B., & Fehlman, R. (1990) Discussions of literature in lower-track classrooms. Technical report No. 2.10. Center for the Learning and Teaching of Literature.

North, S. (1986). *The making of knowledge in composition*. Portsmouth, NH: Boynton-Cook.

Ohmann, R. (1976). *English in America*. New York: Oxford U. Press.

Rosenblatt, L. (1983) *Literature as exploration*. New York: Noble & Noble.

Spingarn, J. (1911). *The new criticism*. New York: Columbia U. Press.

# Bibliography
# of Literary Works Cited

❧ ❧ ❧

## Book-Length Works

Angelou, M. *I Know Why the Caged Bird Sings*

Alcott, L. M. (1983). *Little Women*, Toronto; New York: Bantam Books.

Allen, W. *Side Effects*

Baldwin, J., *The Fire Next Time*

Borland, *When the Legends Die*

Brown, C. (1965). *Manchild in the Promised Land*, New York: Macmillan.

Cather, W. (1913). *O Pioneers*. Boston: Houghton Mifflin Company.

de Cervantes, M (1956). *Don Quixote* Middlesex, England: Penguin Books.

Dickens, C. (1961). *Hard Times*. Penguin Books.

Faulkner, W. (1936). *Absalom, Absalom*. New York: Random House.

Fitzgerald, F.S. *The Great Gatsby*

Guest, J. *Ordinary People*

Hawthorne, N. (1927). *The Scarlet Letter*. New York: The Macmillan Co.

Hemingway, *The Old Man and the Sea*

Hesse, H. (1951). *Narcissus and Goldmund*. New York: Bantam Books.

Homer, *The Illiad*

Homer, *The Odyssey*

Knowles, J. *A Separate Peace*

Lee, H. *To Kill a Mockingbird*

Miller, A. (1953). *The Crucible*. New York: Viking Press.

Milton, J. *Paradise Lost*

Oates, J. C. (1985). *Solstice*. New York: Dutton.

Orwell, G. (1951). *Burmese Days* London: Secber and Warburg.

Sophocles, *Antigone*

Steinbeck, J. (1938). *Of Mice and Men*. New York Triangle Books.

Thurston, Z.N. *Roll of Thunder, Hear My Cry*

Walker, A. *The Color Purple*

## Short Stories

Achebe, C. (1972) A Man of the People. *Girls at War and Other Stories*. New York: Doubleday.

Baldwin, J. (1961). The Man Child. *Nobody Knows My Name*. New York: Dial Press.

Benét, S. V. (1937). By the Waters of Babylon. *The Selected Works of Stephen Vincent Benét*. Holt, Rinehart, & Winston Inc.

Deal. B. (1961). Antaeus. In D.A. Sohn (Ed.). *Ten Modern American Short Stories*. New York: Bantam Books.

Buck, P. (1955). The Frill. *Great American Short Stories*. New York: Viking Press.

Callaghan, M. (1940). All the years of her life. In *Short Stories from the New Yorker*. New York: Simon & Schuster.

du Maurier, D. (1953). The Birds. *Kiss Me Again Stranger: A Collection of Short Stories*. Garden City, New York: Doubleday.

Galsworthy, J. (1969). The Apple Tree. *The Apple Tree and Other Stories*. New York: Scribner.

Hemingway, E. (1987). The Short Happy Life of Francis Macomber. *The Complete Stories of Ernest Hemingway*. New York: Scribners.

Jackson, S. (1980). The Lottery. In S. Jackson *The Lottery*. New York: Farrar, Strauss, & Giroux, Inc.

London, J. (1990). To Build A Fire. *The Call of the Wild, White Fang and Other Stories*. New York: Oxford University Press.

Maugham, W. S. (1952). The Letter. *The Complete Short Stories*. Garden City, New York: Doubleday.

Minturn, S. (1973). The house on the hill. In K. Kleiman (Ed.), *Double Action* (pp. 64-71). New York: Scholastic.

Nicol, A. (1965). The Devil at Yolahun Bridge. *The Truly Married Woman*. Oxford: Oxford University Press.

Taylor, J. (1981). Only clowns passing through. In O. S. Niles, J. Walker, & J.J. Tuinman. (Eds.). *Nova*. Glenview, IL: Scott and Co.

Thurber, J. (1970). The Secret Life of Walter Mitty. *My World and Welcome to It*. New York: Harcourt Brace Jovanovich.

Updike, J. (1959). Tomorrow and Tomorrow and So Forth. In *The Same Door*. New York: Knopf.

Updike, J. (1980). A&P. In *Pigeon Feathers and Other Stories*. New York: Knopf.

## *Poetry*

Frost, R. "Mending Wall"

Frost, R. "Stoping by Woods on a Snowy Evening"

# Author Index

# Subject Index

❧ ❧ ❧

*The Teaching of Literature in Programs with Reputations of Excellence in English*, 5
Teacher-guided and teacher-presented approaches, 54–58
Teacher's role, 4, 13–14, 273–277
  as literary expert, 122
  as facilitator, 122–123
  as fellow-reader, 123–126
  as dialogic partner, 126–127
  in developing a community, 56–57, 72
  as professional, 8
Technology, 18, 175–190
  and integrated curriculum, 176–182
  CD ROM, 179
  hypercard, 181–182
  multimedia, 187–188
  virtual reality, 189
Text
  as authorized creation, 115–117
  as aesthetic object, 117–118

  as purveyor of information, 118–120
  as cultural artifact, 120–121
  and intertext, 121
Theory of practice, 12, 20, 141–144
*To Kill a Mockingbird*, 77
Transactional theory, 265–267
  and teaching literature, 285, 301–303

"Tularecito," 34–38

*Understanding Poetry*, 310

*When the Legends Die*, 70,77
Writing and literature
  effective prompts for, 213
  and personal experience, 165–168
  and reasoning processes, 59–64
  and literary understanding, 6, 19, 85
Writing instruction
  process approach to, 3, 23, 65–66

# *Contributors*

❧ ❧ ❧

**George E. Newell** is an Associate Professor of Education at The Ohio State University, where he is program coordinator of English education and teaches undergraduate and graduate courses in literature, writing, and literacy. His research interests include teaching and learning in English and the content areas. He received his Ph.D. from Stanford University.

**Russel K. Durst** is Associate Professor of English at the University of Cincinnati. He received his Ph.D. from Stanford University. He is interested in the development of analytical writing abilities. He has published numerous articles and book chapters.

**Christopher M. Anson** received his Ph.D. from Indiana University. He is an Associate Professor of English at the University of Minnesota. He is author and coauthor of numerous articles, book chapters, and books, including *A Field Guide to Writing* and *Writing in Context*, both with L.E. Wilcox.

**Deborah Appleman** is Assistant Professor of educational studies and director of the Summer Writing Program at Carleton College, Minnesota. Before receiving her Ph.D. from the University of Minnesota, she taught high school for nine years. Her primary research interests include adolescent response to literature, teaching literary theory to secondary students, and adolescent response to poetry.

**Steven Z. Athanases** is currently a Postdoctoral Research Fellow at Stanford University, where he expects to receive his Ph.D. in Fall 1992. His research features the study of how thoughtful urban high school teachers lead literature discussions that both support student understanding and sensitize students to diversity.

**Laura E. Desai** has taught in Duluth, Georgia and is currently working on her Ph.D. at The Ohio State University, where she is a Research Assistant with the Apple Classroom of Tomorrow program. She is a coauthor of *Portfolio Assessment in the Reading-Writing Classroom.*

**Adam Gamoran** is Professor of Sociology and Educational Policy Studies at the University of Wisconsin and Faculty Associate at the Wisconsin Center for Education Research at the University of Wisconsin-Madison. He received his Ph.D. from The university of Chicago. His research concerns on the effects of ability grouping and instruction on student achievement.

**Mary Beth Hines** is Assistant Professor at the University of Houston. She received her Ph.D. from the University of Iowa. Her interests include literary and critical theory as well as composition theory and research.

**Susan Hynds** is an Associate Professor and Director of the English Education program at Syracuse University. She received her Ph.D. from George Peabody College at Vanderbilt University. Her work focuses on the areas of writing, response to literature, and language across the curriculum.

**Judy Johnson** is an English teacher at Lafayette High School in Lexington Kentucky. She in on the (KY) State Writing Advisory Committee developing implementation of writing assessment (12th grade) and she also works with the Secondary Language Program Committee at the University of Kentucky. She has recently been named one of seven Kentucky Distinguished Educators.

**Ronald D. Kieffer** Ron Kieffer is an Assistant Professor in the Department of Language Education, at the University of Georgia. He is currently teaching courses in early childhood language arts and children's literature. His research interests are in oval and written language development, emergent literacy, and assessment. He is particularly interested in ways that literature can be used in classroom settings to advance the learning of reading and writing.

**Judith A. Langer** is Professor of Education at the University at Albany, State University of New York and co-director of the National Research Center on the Learning and Teaching of Literature. Her major works examine the nature of literature thought—the knowledge students use when they make sense and the ways in which their thinking is affected by activities and interactions in the classroom. She has published extensively. Dr. Langer received her Ph.D. from the University of Iowa.

**James Marshall** is an Associate Professor of English and Education at the University of Iowa. He received his Ph.D. from Stanford University after teaching high school English for a number of years. He has authored numerous articles and book chapters on the teaching of literature and the teaching of writing. His books include *Teaching Literature in the Secondary School* (with Richard Beach), and *Ways of Knowing: Research and Practice in the Teaching of Writing*, which he co-authored with James Davis.

**Martin Nystrand** received his Ph.D. from Northwestern University. He is currently Professor of English and Faculty Associate at the Wisconsin Center for Education Research at the University of Wisconsin-Madison, as well as Editor off *Written Communication*. His current research, with sociologist Adam Gamoran, concerns the effects of instructional discourse, including writing, reading, and talk, on achievement in high school English and social studies.

**Cecily O'Neill** is an Associate Professor at The Ohio State University. She holds a Ph.D. in Theatre from Exeter University, England. She has written numerous articles and book chapters, and is coauthor of two influential books on drama, *Drama Structures* and *Drama Guidelines*.

**Marjorie Roemer**, Assistant Professor and Director of Freshman English at the University of Cincinnati, received her Ph.D. from Brandeis University. Her research interests include critical pedagogy, literary theory, postmodernism, and institutional change.

**Theresa Rogers** received her Ph.D. from the University of Illinois at Urbana-Champaign. She is an Assistant Professor at The Ohio State University. Her research interests include response to literature and urban literacy issues. Her publications include numerous articles and *How Porcupines Make Love II: Notes Toward a Response-centered Curriculum*, which she coauthored with Alan C. Purves and Anna O. Soter.

**Peter Smagorinsky** is an Assistant Professor at the University of Oklahoma. He received his Ph.D. from the University of Chicago. He has coauthored a number of books, including *Explorations: Introductory Activities for Literature and Composition* and *Expressions: Multiple Intelligences in the English Class.*

**Michael W. Smith**, Assistant Professor of English Education at Rutgers University, received his Ph.D. from the University of Chicago. He is interested in exploring how to increase students' ability and inclination to make meaning in their reading and writing, and working to understand what knowledge, strategies, and attitudes students must have to be successful readers and writers.

**Anna O. Soter** is an Assistant Professor at The Ohio State University. She earned her Ph.D. from the University of Illinois at Urbana-Champaign. Her specific interests include writing as a tool for learning, the learning and teaching of literature, cross-cultural aspects of literacy development, and teacher learning and development in the English/Language Arts. She is a coauthor with Alan C. Purves and Theresa Rogers, of *How Porcupines Make Love II: Notes Toward a Response-centered Curriculum.*

**Robert J. Tierney** is a professor in the Department of Educational Theory and Practice at The Ohio State University. His specialties are critical thinking, reading comprehension, and reading and writing. The co-author of several successful books, including *Portfolio Assessment in the Reading-Writing Classroom*, he received his Ph.D. from the University of Georgia.

**Richard Beach**, Professor of English Education at the University of Minnesota, received his Ph.D. from the University of Illinois. Best known for his research on composition and literary response, he is co-editor of *New Directions in Composition Research*, *Developing Discourse Practices in Adolescence and Adulthood*; and co-author of *Teaching Literature in the Secondary School* and *Literature and the Reader*.